WOMEN SPEAKING

GARLAND REFERENCE LIBRARY
OF SOCIAL SCIENCE
Vol. 108

WOMEN SPEAKING
*An Annotated Bibliography of
Verbal and Nonverbal Communication
1970–1980*

Mary E.W. Jarrard
Phyllis R. Randall

GARLAND PUBLISHING, INC. • NEW YORK & LONDON
1982

© 1982 Mary E.W. Jarrard and Phyllis R. Randall
All rights reserved

Library of Congress Cataloging in Publication Data
Jarrard, Mary Elizabeth W.
  Women speaking.

  (Garland reference library of social science ; v. 108)
  Includes index.
    1. Women—United States—Language—Abstracts.
  2. Communications—Social aspects—United States—
  Abstracts.   3. Nonverbal communication—United States—
  Abstracts.   4. Women—United States—Psychology—
  Abstracts.   I. Randall, Phyllis R.   II. Title.
  III. Series.
  HQ1426.J37   1982   016.3054'0973   82-15737
  ISBN 0-8240-9281-3

Printed on acid-free, 250-year-life paper
Manufactured in the United States of America

CONTENTS

Preface   vii

PART ONE: SETTINGS FOR COMMUNICATION
- WITHIN THE SELF   3
  - Concept of Self   3
  - Concepts of Other Women   31
- WITH ANOTHER   37
- IN SMALL GROUPS   82
- IN THE FAMILY   131
- IN PUBLIC   154
- IN ORGANIZATIONS   169
  - Business   169
  - Political   181
    - Feminist Movement   181
    - Political Parties   187
  - Professions   191
    - Academic   191
    - Counseling   202
    - Law   211
    - Medical   213
  - General References   221

PART TWO: CHARACTERISTICS OF COMMUNICATION
- LEADERSHIP   227
- LISTENING AND FEEDBACK   244
- PERSUASION AND PERSUASIBILITY   257
- SELF DISCLOSURE   272
- MISCELLANEOUS CHARACTERISTICS   293

PART THREE: MEANS OF COMMUNICATION
- VERBAL   305

Language Used by Women	305
Language Used about Women	340
Generic Noun and Pronoun	352
General References	359
NONVERBAL	367
Body Movement	367
Eye Contact/Gaze	370
Facial Expression	382
Physical Attractiveness	388
Space/Distance	402
Touch	425
Vocal Characteristics	430
General References	440
PART FOUR: COMPREHENSIVE REFERENCES	465
Subject Index	469

PREFACE

The 1970s were the first full decade of scholarly interest in the communication of women. As the decade wore on, interest in research on women's communication spread into many different disciplines—psychology, linguistics, anthropology, sociology, women's studies, speech communication, education, speech and hearing sciences, business management, and political science, to name the most prominent ones. The goal of this bibliography is to provide a guide to the decade's published empirical and scholarly research conducted in these many disciplines. The scope, therefore, is wider than any one discipline might entail.

Because of the wide scope, particular care has been taken to organize the material. For those in the field of speech communication (the discipline of one of the compilers), the Contents will suggest a traditional approach to the material based on the settings in which communication occurs and on the verbal and nonverbal aspects of communication. Besides those more traditional divisions, it has a section on the characteristics of communication that cut across settings (for example, leadership and self disclosure). We retained in the Contents multiple terms for the same concept (e.g., Eye Contact/Gaze), since different disciplines use different terms.

For those researching some particular facet of women's communication, the Subject Index may be more helpful than the Contents. The Index lists the entries by specific topics, ranging from articulation to topic of conversation. The extensive section in the Index on sex differences will become, we trust, the most referred-to pages of the volume. The Index also includes references to bibliographies, reviews of literature, and to instructional programs in women's communication.

Because of the length of the bibliography, it has been impossible to include mass communication, an area broad enough to deserve a bibliography of its own. (See Leslie J. Friedman, *Sex Role Stereotyping in the Mass Media: An Annotated Bibliography.* New York: Garland Publishing, 1977.) Neither the development of speech communication skills in women nor the literary skills of women are included for the same reason, although both would reveal a good deal about women's communication. Since we are interested only in empirical or scholarly articles, material appearing in the popular press is not included. Originally we had hoped to include papers read at meetings, but the problems of collecting references to such meetings, the addresses of the readers, and ultimately the papers themselves proved too time-consuming. Seven months or so into the year-long process of collecting and annotating the entries, we decided to include papers read at meetings only if they had been published. Unpublished theses and dissertations are not included.

Our method of collecting entries included computer searches, searches of bibliographies on various aspects of women's communication, and searches by topic in the card catalogues of major university libraries, including one with an extensive women's studies collection. The chief method of collection, however, was a year-by-year search for the decade of more than sixty journals in a wide variety of fields. From these journals we collected not only the pertinent articles but also all citations. From the citations, in turn, new references were gathered.

Almost all of the research that we have surveyed has been conducted in the United States on white college undergraduates. For the purposes of this bibliography, we consider "women" to be post-high school females; research using younger females is not included unless older females are used as well. All research done in other countries or done with other ethnic groups or with a non-college population is clearly identified within our annotations.

All of the sources that have been annotated have been read by one or the other of the compilers. If a reference could be verified only by correspondence or by telephone, it is included but is not annotated. A few entries with self-explanatory titles are likewise not annotated.

Within the wide boundaries of the present bibliography, the entries are selective. All articles using women's actual spoken communication are included as are those which investigate

Preface ix

women's verbal or nonverbal communication indirectly, often via tests or questionnaires. Furthermore, any research which used only women as subjects and which fits within the scope of the bibliography is included. Despite what seemed like clear-cut goals, there were controversial decisions which, needless to say, were ultimately subjective.

Decisions concerning placement of entries also presented difficult choices. We could frequently make an argument for two equally valid placements for an article. To resolve this dilemma, we put such an entry in the area of the focus of the research and cross-referred the article to its other appropriate location. All such cross-references are asterisked; they carry full citations and the entry number for the annotation. If a reference could be placed in more than two sections within a single heading of the Contents, it was placed in the General References category at the end of that section. For example, in the Verbal portion of the bibliography, books and articles that deal with Language Used by Women, Language Used about Women, and the Generic Noun and Pronoun controversy are in the General References section.

The compilers of this bibliography could not have undertaken such a project without the help of many others. We would like to thank our universities, the University of North Carolina at Chapel Hill and North Carolina Central University, for released time from teaching in order to complete this project. In addition, the University of North Carolina at Chapel Hill provided Mary E.W. Jarrard a generous R. J. Reynolds Faculty Development Grant. The library staffs of the University of North Carolina at Greensboro and Duke University extended services beyond the ordinary. Others, mostly graduate students, have helped to check references, proofread, collate, and find elusive books or journals. They were Emilie Sandin, Gloria Locklear, Stacey Cox, Jan Ceropski, Tara McKenzie, and Cassandra Thorpe. To them all, many thanks for keeping us from making more errors than have passed, still unnoticed, into the completed bibliography. For all such errors, we alone, of course, accept responsibility.

We appreciate the help of Professor Linda Pratt of North Carolina Central University's Research and Development Office, who gave generously of her time to lead us, relatively unscathed, through the perils of using a computer program. Professor Kimball King's encouragement and aid at the right moment pushed this project from "hold" to "go," and we are grateful to him. To our typists, Patty Herring, Muriel Dyer, Sharon Pigott, and especially to Elizabeth Hunt, who bore the major burden of deciphering our handwritten note cards, we owe special thanks.

Last, our gratitude to those of our families who have suffered through the eighteen months of this project to the moment when this Preface is being written.

Phyllis R. Randall
Mary E.W. Jarrard
20 March 1982

PART ONE
SETTINGS FOR COMMUNICATIONS

WITHIN THE SELF

CONCEPT OF SELF

1. Aldag, Ramon J., and Arthur P. Brief. "Some Correlates of Women's Self-Image and Stereotypes of Femininity." *Sex Roles*, 5 (1979), 319-328.

   A total of 362 female nursing personnel completed a version of the Gordon Self-Image and the Stereotypes of Femininity scales. Relationships of their perceptions of doctor's image of them, male's image of them, and their own image of a feminine woman were uniformly weak. Self-perceptions of potency and spontaneity were consistently related to self-assurance, initiative, decisiveness, and need for self-actualization. Authors suggest that female self-image may play a pervasive role in work adjustment.

2. Antill, John K., and John D. Cunningham. "Self-Esteem as a Function of Masculinity in Both Sexes." *Journal of Consulting and Clinical Psychology*, 47 (1979), 783-785.

   In this brief report of a correlation study of two self-esteem measures and three sex-role measures of 104 males and 133 females, age range 17 to 45, all undergraduates, significant positive correlations were found in all cases between masculinity and self-esteem in both sexes, while nil or slightly negative correlations were found between femininity and self-esteem.

3. Archibald, W. Peter, and Ronald L. Cohen. "Self-Presentation, Embarrassment, and Facework as a Function of Self-Evaluation, Conditions of Self-Presentation, and Feedback from Others." *Journal of Personality and Social Psychology*, 20 (1971), 287-297.

   Ninety-six female undergraduates with either high or

low levels of self evaluation described themselves to another under either public or private conditions (expecting to meet the other or not, identity known or not). Each received either negative or positive feedback from the other. No significant differences between conditions relating to self-presentation occurred. Low self-evaluation females decreased their involvement in the interaction, perhaps to prevent embarrassment. They were most embarrassed in the public failure, negative feedback condition. Self-presentation, whether positive or negative, did not relate to subsequent embarrassment. Facework generally varied with level of embarrassment, and, in the public conditions, subjects discredited those who evaluated them in a way inconsistent with their own self esteem.

* Athanassiades, John C. "An Investigation of Some Communication Patterns of Female Subordinates in Hierarchical Organizations." *Human Relations*, 27 (1974), 195-209. See item 423.

4. Bannon, Jill A., and Mara L. Southern. "Father-Absent Women: Self-Concept and Modes of Relating to Men." *Sex Roles*, 6 (1980), 75-84.

   Four groups of female undergraduates were used to determine the relationship between absence of father in childhood and adult self-concept and interpersonal relationships with men. Groups consisted of 15 father-present subjects who came from intact homes, 15 father-absent subjects with no older brothers who experienced the death of their father early in life, 15 father-absent subjects with no older brothers who experienced father loss due to divorce, and 12 father-absent subjects with one or more older brothers whose parents were divorced. The Tennessee Self-Concept Scale and a self-report questionnaire of modes of relating to men were the dependent variable measures. Results revealed no significant differences among groups in most areas of self-concept or interpersonal relationships with either older or age-peer men. Only in social self-concept and "nurturance behavior" with age-peer men were significant differences observed.

5. Bedeian, Arthur G., and John Touliatos. "Work-Related Motives and Self-Esteem in American Women." *Journal of Psychology*, 99 (1978), 63-70.

   A study of 85 female business majors to determine the

relationship between their self-esteem and their needs for autonomy, aggression, power, deference, affiliation, and achievement (subscales of the Adjective Check List) found that those with high self-esteem scored high in need for achievement and for power, as predicted, and for affiliation, not predicted. The hypothesis that low self-esteem females would score high was not supported.

* Bernard, Jessie. "Where Are We Now? Some Thoughts on the Current Scene." *Psychology of Women Quarterly*, 1 (1976), 21-37. See item 771.

* Blakar, Rolv M., and Tove B. Pederson. "Control and Self-confidence as Reflected in Sex-Bound Patterns in Communication: An Experimental Approach." *Acta Sociologica*, 23 (1980), 33-53. See item 99.

6. Bonner, Florence B. "Black Women and White Women: A Comparative Analysis of Perceptions of Sex Roles for Self, Ideal-Self and the Ideal Man." *The Journal of Afro-American Issues*, 2, No. 3 (1974), 237-247.

    Data from a questionnaire on perceptions of self, ideal self, and ideal male from 29 black females and 49 white females did-not support the hypothesis that the perceptions of white females would be markedly different from those of black females.

7. Broverman, Inge K., Susan R. Vogel, Donald M. Broverman, Frank E. Clarkson, and Paul S. Rosenkranz. "Sex-Role Stereotypes: A Current Appraisal." *Journal of Social Issues*, 28, No. 2 (1972), 59-78.

    This survey of 45 studies of sex-role stereotypes reveals that women are perceived as relatively less competent, less independent, less objective, and less logical than men, while men are perceived as lacking interpersonal sensitivity, warmth, and expressiveness. Generally, though, stereotypically masculine traits are more often perceived desirable. Both men and women incorporate both the positive and negative traits of the appropriate sex stereotype into their self-concepts. Since more feminine traits are negatively valued than masculine traits, women tend to have more negative self-concepts than men. Individual differences in sex-related self-concepts are related to sex-role relevant behaviors and society's perceptions.

8. Carlson, Rae. "Sex Differences in Ego Functioning." *Journal of Consulting and Clinical Psychology*, 37 (1971), 267-277.

   Using theoretical formulations of D. Gutman and D. Bakan, Carlson hypothesized various sex differences in personality. The first study, using 213 college students and community adults, showed males significantly more likely to represent own experiences, others, space and time in individualistic, objective, and distant ways. Females represented these experiences and concepts in interpersonal, subjective, immediate ways. In the second study, with 18 male and 23 female college students, reports of significant emotional experiences were "communal" for females (individual as part of a larger whole) and "agentic" for males (individual alone--both terms from Bakan). In a third study, predictions from the agency-communion concept were tested against 200 published abstracts of sex differences research, with the concept found relevant in over 80% of the studies.

9. Chandler, Theodore A., Bettyanne Cook, and David A. Dugovics. "Sex Differences in Self-Reported Assertiveness." *Psychological Reports*, 43 (1978), 395-402.

   Seventy-four male and 137 female undergraduates completed a self-report assertiveness measure. A t-test showed that the males were more assertive. Multiple regression analysis, however, showed that on four of the five items accounting for the largest block of variance, females scored higher. On 24 of the 30 items, there were no significant differences by sex.

10. Chartier, Jan, and Myron R. Chartier. "Perceived Parental Communication and Self-Esteem: An Exploratory Study." *Western Speech*, 39 (1975), 26-31.

    The relationship between the self-esteem of 51 male and 36 female undergraduates and their perceptions of their parents' communication as constructive was examined using measures of self-esteem and a relationship inventory. Females' self-esteem correlated positively with father's regard, empathy, and congruence, but male's self-esteem was not correlated to either parent for those variables. There was a significant negative correlation between female's self-esteem and mothers' empathy, and a positive one for mothers' unconditionality.

11. Cohen, David B. "Sex Role Orientation and Dream Recall." *Journal of Abnormal Psychology*, 82 (1973), 246-252.

    An analysis of the dreams of 27 male and 32 female undergraduates, chosen from a pool of 338 to represent high masculine or feminine orientation, revealed that sex-role orientation was stronger than gender in influencing dream content. Masculine subjects of either gender had dreams with significantly higher agency (assertiveness, mastery, libido) than feminine subjects, but male subjects did not have significantly higher agency than female subjects. Feminine subjects of either gender had dreams with significantly higher communion content (social cooperation, passive social connection, warmth) than masculine subjects, but, again, no gender effect the same way. Masculine subjects, especially males, had more aggression in their dreams, and subjects, especially males, whose sex-role orientation was contrary to gender reported more unpleasant dreams.

12. Cole, C. W., E. R. Oetting, and N. G. Dinges. "Effects of Verbal Interaction Conditions on Self-Concept Discrimination and Anxiety." *Journal of Counseling Psychology*, 20 (1973), 431-436.

    Eighty undergraduates, an equal number of each sex, were divided into those talking about self-positive or self-negative topics to an interviewer who either responded or not, and were pre- and post-tested on various measures. No differences by sex emerged. Talking negatively about self in no-feedback condition resulted in an increase in anxiety, while talking positively in that condition decreased anxiety. With feedback, anxiety ratings showed no difference by negative-positive topic. A fuller, more "meaningful" concept of self occurred in interviews with feedback; a less "meaningful" concept in those without feedback. Thus, interaction itself can affect both affective and denotative aspects of the dyad.

* Coplin, Jane W., and John E. Williams. "Women Law Students' Descriptions of Self and the Ideal Lawyer." *Psychology of Women Quarterly*, 2 (1978), 323-333. See item 558.

* Deaux, Kay. "Self-Evaluations of Male and Female Managers." *Sex Roles*, 5 (1979), 571-580. See item 428.

13. De Fronzo, James, and Frances Bourdeau. "Further Research into Antecedents and Correlates of Androgyny." *Psychological Reports*, 44 (1979), 23-29.

    The Bem Sex-Role Inventory was given to 243 male and 367 female college students, who also completed various measures about home life, self-concept, and attitudes. For males, level of identification with their mothers was positively related to their femininity; for females, mothers working had a positive effect on their masculinity. For both males and females, masculinity had a strong positive effect on self-esteem. By and large, sex-role identification had a stronger role for females on forming a family and for males on social and political attitudes.

* Dellacava, Frances A., and Madeline H. Engel. "Resistance to Sisterhood: The Case of the Professional Woman." *International Journal of Women's Studies*, 2 (1979), 505-512. See item 560.

14. Deutsch, Connie J., and Lucia A. Gilbert. "Sex Role Stereotypes: Effect on Perceptions of Self and Others and on Personal Adjustment." *Journal of Counseling Psychology*, 23 (1976), 373-379.

    Sixty-four female and 64 male undergraduates completed the Bem Sex-Role Inventory for real self, ideal self, ideal other sex, and perception of other sex's ideal other and completed as well the Revised Bell Adjustment Inventory. Results indicated that for females, real self, ideal self, and perception of men's ideal women were highly dissimilar, whereas for males they were not. Good adjustment and androgyny were related for women but not for men, for whom masculinity and adjustment were related.

* DiMarco, Nicholas, and Susan E. Whitsitt. "A Comparison of Female Supervisors in Business and Government Organizations." *Journal of Vocational Behavior*, 6 (1975), 185-196. See item 429.

* Eagly, Alice H., and George I. Whitehead, III. "Effect of Choice on Receptivity to Favorable and Unfavorable Evaluations of Oneself." *Journal of Personality and Social Psychology*, 22 (1972), 223-230. See item 634.

15. Ellis, Linda J., and P.M. Bentler. "Traditional Sex-Determined Role Standards and Sex Stereotypes." *Journal*

of *Personality and Social Psychology,* 25 (1973), 28-34.

In this questionnaire survey, 152 college students rated others and themselves on masculine/feminine traits and other variables. For females, opposition to traditional sex-role standards related to seeing similarity between males and females, perceiving similarity of self to males, and to intelligence. For both sexes, disapproval of stereotyped sex roles was related to liberalism, extralegality, and nonreligiousness.

16. Elman, Judith, Allan Press, and Paul Rosenkrantz. "Sex Roles and Self-Concepts: Real and Ideal." *Proceedings of the 78th Annual Convention of the American Psychological Association* (1970), 455-456.

    To discover the relationships between sex roles and both real and ideal self-concepts, 52 male and 52 female undergraduates responded on a bipolar questionnaire to real and ideal self-concepts and real and ideal sex roles. Results supported the hypothesis that sex-role stereotypes are stronger influences on actual self-concept than on ideal self-concept, and that sex-role ideals are stronger influences on ideal self-concept than stereotyped self-concepts are.

17. Feldman, Gail. "The Only Child as a Separate Entity: Differences Between Only Females and Other Firstborn Females." *Psychological Reports,* 42 (1978), 107-110.

    Measures of self-image, sexual identity, perception preferences and perceptions attributed to parents were given to 25 only-child women, 25 firstborn with younger brother, and 25 firstborn with younger sister. A factor analysis yielded 16 factors, which in turn were used in a discriminant analysis. Only-child women were confident, resourceful, and assertive, the most independent and the least anxious and conventional. Firstborns with brothers were most responsible, logical, and thoughtful, and were most interested in the opposite sex. Firstborn women with sisters were the most conventional and the most dependent, expressing self-doubts, appearing at times enthusiastic and insightful, but also at times impatient and withdrawn.

* Fish, Sandra L. "A Phenomenological Examination of Femininity." *Journal of Applied Communications Research,* 4 (1976), 43-53. See item 226.

* Follingstad, Diane R., Elizabeth A. Robinson, and Martha Pugh. "Effects of Consciousness-Raising Groups on Measures of Feminism, Self-Esteem, and Social Desirability." *Journal of Counseling Psychology*, 24 (1977), 223-230. See item 229.

18. Fowler, Marguerite G., and Hani K. Van de Riet. "Women, Today and Yesterday: An Examination of the Feminist Personality." *Journal of Psychology*, 82 (1972), 269-276.

    The Adjective Checklist was administered to eighteen feminist women, sixteen undergraduate women (both groups with average age under 25) and twelve elderly noninstitutionalized women and seventeen elderly institutionalized women (both groups with average age of 67). The younger women's groups did not differ significantly, but both differed significantly from the older groups. Feminist women manifested most autonomy and aggression, with university women, noninstitutionalized and institutionalized following. Feminist women were significantly more autonomous, aggressive, dominant, self-confident, and less deferent and affiliative than females in a standardizing normative group. Feminists' ideal self significantly exceeded real self in nurturance, endurance, self-confidence, self-control, and personal adjustment.

19. Freeman, Harvey R. "Sex-Role Stereotypes, Self-Concepts, and Measured Personality Characteristics in College Women and Men." *Sex Roles*, 5 (1979), 99-103.

    This study involved 150 undergraduates who ranked 15 descriptions of the average female and the average male, the ideal female and the ideal male, or themselves. Extensive similarity was found between the responses of female and male subjects. Subjects perceived numerous differences between the average female and the average male, but very few differences between the ideal female and ideal male. The self-concepts of female and male subjects were highly similar.

* Friedman, Howard S. "Effects of Self-Esteem and Expected Duration of Interaction on Liking for a Highly Rewarding Partner." *Journal of Personality and Social Psychology*, 33 (1976), 686-690. See item 115.

20. Gilbert, Lucia A., Connie J. Deutsch, and Robert F. Strahan. "Feminine and Masculine Dimensions of the Typical, Desirable, and Ideal Woman and Man." *Sex Roles*,

4 (1978), 767-778.

To investigate differences between the masculine and feminine components of typical and ideal perceptions, items of the Bem Sex-Role Inventory were given to 432 male and female undergraduates to describe a typical, desirable, or ideal man or woman. Both sexes agreed that it is typical and desirable for a man to be more masculine than a woman, and for a woman to be more feminine than a man. Although males and females agreed in their masculinity ratings of the ideal man, females described the ideal woman to be as masculine as their ideal man, whereas males described her as significantly less masculine than their ideal man.

21. Gordon, Francine E., and Douglas T. Hall. "Self-Image and Stereotypes of Femininity: Their Relationship to Women's Role Conflicts and Coping." *Journal of Applied Psychology,* 59 (1974), 241-243.

    A questionnaire survey of over 200 college graduates on interrelationships between self-image, own and perceived male images of femininity, role conflict, and coping revealed the most common conflict was the home/not home one. Significantly correlated with it was the perceived male's image of a feminine woman. Coping behavior was best predicted by self-image; if a female perceived herself as supportive, she coped. Self-image also was the best predictor of both satisfaction and happiness.

22. Graham, Martin, and Cannie Stark Adamec. "The Complexity of Attitudes toward Women: I. Personal Attitudes and Their Sources." *International Journal of Women's Studies,* 1 (1978), 482-502.

    Seventy male and 108 female undergraduates completed a personality inventory and an attitudes-toward-women questionnaire. Personal attitudes were found to differ by sex, by present religious affiliation and by self-perception. Female attitudes were best predicted by self-perception and personality variables, while male attitudes were more frequently predicted by background variables.

23. Gump, Janice P. "Comparative Analysis of Black Women's and White Women's Sex-Role Attitudes." *Journal of Consulting and Clinical Psychology,* 43 (1975), 858-863.

    Using the Revised FAND Inventory to measure sex-role attitudes of 77 black female undergraduates and 40 white ones, Gump found that black women were more likely to define their identity with wife/mother roles and were more home-centered and submissive than white women were.

24. Hansen, James C., and Barbara A. Putnam. "Feminine Role Concepts of Young Women." *Sex Roles,* 4 (1978), 127-130.

    Using 250 white high school senior women, the authors hypothesized a significant difference between perceptions of the feminine role concept of self, of an ideal woman, and of man's ideal woman, and a significant difference in these three feminine role concepts between the college-bound and the not college-bound. The college-bound females not only viewed their ideal role as traditional but also believed that men wished them to be even more traditional. Their own role concept was nearly a balance between self- and other-orientation. The noncollege-bound females tended to have a self-role concept closer to their ideal and to perceived man's ideal.

 * Heilman, Madeline, and Kathy E. Kram. "Self-Derogating Behavior in Women--Fixed or Flexible: "The Effects of Co-Worker's Sex." *Organizational Behavior and Human Performance,* 22 (1978), 497-507. See item 583.

25. Hensley, Wayne E. "Differences Between Males and Females on Rosenburg Scale of Self-Esteem." *Psychological Reports,* 41 (1977), 829-830.

    Scores on the Rosenburg Self-Esteem measure for 487 male and 707 female college students did not significantly differ, and a factor analysis of responses suggested that the structure of self-esteem is the same for both sexes.

26. Hogan, H. Wayne. "German and American Responses to the Bem Sex Role Inventory." *Journal of Social Psychology,* 109 (1979), 141-142.

    Correlation analysis of the responses to the Bem Sex-Role Inventory of male and female German university students (N=160), American university students (N=234), and American high school students (N=187) revealed a greater within-sex and within-culture agreement to self-attributions of the Inventory traits and greater agreement on the "female" than on the "male" items. Females both within and across the cultures tended to be less positive in their self-perceptions and to make finer distinctions between their masculine and feminine attributes.

27. Hollender, John. "Sex Differences in Sources of Social Self-Esteem." *Journal of Consulting and Clinical Psychology,* 38 ((1972), 343-347.

   This correlation study of scores on a questionnaire and scores on tests on social self-esteem of 40 female and 38 male undergraduates revealed sex differences. Those high in social self-esteem were males with high need for approval and females with low need; males with A or B grades, females with C grade; and, for males only, firstborn with younger sister.

28. Houston, Lawrence N., and Susan I. Springer. "Self-Esteem and Conservatism among Female College Students." *Psychological Reports,* 47 (1980), 543-546.

   Since authoritarianism is negatively related to self-esteem and since authoritarianism is part of the broader concept of conservatism, this study investigated the relationship of conservatism to self-esteem of 93 college women using the Janis and Field Self-Esteem Inventory and the Conservatism Scale. No significant relationship was found.

* Jandt, Fred E., and Delmer M. Hilyard. "An Experimental Study of Self-Concept and Satisfactions." *Today's Speech,* 23, No. 4 (1975), 39-44. See item 249.

29. Judd, Larry R., and Carolyn B. Smith. "The Relationship of Age, Educational Classification, Sex, and Grade to Self Concept and Ideal Self Concept in a Basic Speech Course." *Communication Education,* 26 (1977), 289-297.

   Stepwise multiple regression analysis of pre- and post-course scores on self-concept and ideal self-concept as speakers revealed that the age and education level of 227 male and female college students were not significant variables accounting for self-concept and ideal self-concept scores at the end of the course, but that sex and grade in course were. Of the factors of self-concept investigated, females changed on self-concept and on ideal self-concept more than males did.

30. Kincaid, Marylou B. "Changes in Sex-Role Attitudes and Self-Actualization of Adult Women Following a Consciousness Raising Group." *Sex Roles,* 3 (1977), 329-336.

After participation in a consciousness-raising group, 48 married community college females completed an inventory of female values. They perceived their own role and that of their ideal woman as more extrafamilial, more inner-directed, and maintained a consistently more positive attitude toward other women than before participation.

31. King, Marc, and Guy J. Manaster. "Body Image, Self-esteem, Expectation, Self-assessment, and Actual Success in a Simulated Job Interview." *Journal of Applied Psychology,* 62 (1977), 589-594.

    Measures of body satisfaction, self-esteem, and performance expectation were obtained from 98 female undergraduates, who then had a simulated interview, after which they rated themselves and were rated by two judges. Their expectation of job interview success was significantly related to both body satisfaction and self-esteem. Self-esteem was also related significantly to post-interview self-rating and to the tendency to over- or underrate oneself. Judges' rating of the interviewees was unrelated to either body satisfaction or self-esteem.

* Kramer, Cheris. "Women's and Men's Ratings of Their Own and Ideal Speech." *Communication Quarterly,* 26, No. 2 (Spring 1978), 2-11. See item 410.

32. Krauss, Herbert H., and Leslee L. Critchfield. "Contrasting Self-Esteem Theory and Consistency Theory in Predicting Interpersonal Attraction." *Sociometry,* 38 (1975), 247-260.

    Eighty female undergraduates participated in an experiment in which the independent variables were high and low levels of performance, high and low levels of reward, and direct involvement or not with the reward contingencies. The dependent variable was attraction rating of the experimenter. The experimenter was rated more favorable when his behavior was consistent (high performance, high reward) by subjects in the "cold" condition (unaffected by the experimenter or his cohorts). Subjects in the "warm" condition, however, rated the experimenter more favorably when he gave a high reward, regardless of the performance level. Self-esteem theory is used to account for the findings.

33. Kravetz, Diane F. "Sex Role Concepts of Women." *Journal of Consulting and Clinical Psychology*, 44 (1976), 437-443.

    One hundred and fifty women completed sex-role questionnaires, equal numbers for a healthy adult woman, a healthy adult man, and for self. In each group half were active in the women's liberation movement and half were not. No sex-role stereotypes appeared for a healthy adult, with social desirability determining the traits used to describe both sexes. Differences on specific items indicated a trend for women's liberation subjects to be closer to the masculine pole than other subjects and healthy adult woman images to be more masculine than either healthy adult man or self-images.

* Lehmann, Stanley. "Personality and Compliance: A Study of Anxiety and Self-Esteem in Opinion and Behavior Change." *Journal of Personality and Social Psychology*, 15 (1970), 76-86. See item 685.

34. Lenney, Ellen. "Women's Self-Confidence in Achievement Settings." *Psychological Bulletin*, 84 (1977), 1-13.

    Reviewing over 40 articles on male-female achievement from childhood on, Lenney concludes that women are not lower in self-confidence than men in all situations; mitigating variables include specific ability area (if sex-related, appropriate sex is more confident), feedback (if it is provided, women are not different from men in self-confidence), and certain social factors (if to be supervised or judged by another, women's self-confidence declines; working alone, it does not).

35. Lerner, Richard M., and Barbara E. Brackney. "The Importance of Inner and Outer Body Parts Attitudes in the Self-Concept of Late Adolescents." *Sex Roles*, 4 (1978), 225-238.

    To investigate sex differences in the importance of inner and outer body "space" for personality, 107 female and 72 male undergraduates drew and labeled their internal body parts and responded to a short self-concept scale. Females demonstrated greater knowledge of their inner body and attached generally higher levels of importance to their internal and external body parts. Inner body parts attitudes predicted self-concepts for males, but not for females. More external than internal body parts were significant predictors of females' self-concepts, and they accounted for more variance in self-concept as well.

36. Lerner, Richard M., Stuart A. Karabenick, and Joyce L. Stuart. "Relations Among Physical Attractiveness, Body Attitudes, and Self-Concept in Male and Female College Students." *Journal of Psychology*, 85 (1973), 119-129.

    One hundred ninety female and 118 male college students rated 24 body characteristics for own satisfaction, importance in own physical attractiveness, and importance in opposite-sex physical attractiveness, and completed a self-concept measure. Importance of body characteristics for attractiveness for own sex and for opposite sex were rated alike by males and females. Self-concept and body satisfaction were positively correlated for both sexes, though specific body parts correlating with satisfaction and self-concept differed somewhat by sexes. Physique type was not related to self-concept.

37. Lieberman, Cheryl A. "Reflections and Legacies," *Journal of Sociology and Social Welfare*, 4 (1977), 908-914.

    Interviews with 25 women aged sixty-seven to eighty-eight revealed their perceptions of themselves, their family life, and their social role as they aged, and the treatment others, family, and doctors accorded them. Problems of communication and lack of understanding were mentioned.

38. Loeffler, Dorothy, and Lois Fiedler. "Woman: A Sense of Identity: A Counseling Intervention to Facilitate Personal Growth in Women." *Journal of Counseling Psychology*, 26 (1979), 51-57.

    A ten-week program consisting of development in awareness, power, and goal setting was devised and evaluated in three studies of college women. Pre- and post-test and follow-up results indicated significant increases in important areas such as self-esteem, confidence, autonomy, freedom from distortion of reality, and environmental mastery.

39. Mahoney, E.R. "Subjective Physical Attractiveness and Self-Other Orientations." *Psychological Reports*, 43 (1978), 277-278.

    A questionnaire survey of 98 male and 120 female college students containing self-esteem, self-rating of attractiveness, acceptance of others, and machiavellianism measures revealed that for both sexes self-esteem and perceived physical attractiveness were correlated significantly. For neither sex, however, was there a correlation between perceived attractiveness and either acceptance of others or machiavellianism.

40. Mahoney, E.R., and M.D. Finch. "Body-Cathexis and Self-Esteem: A Reanalysis of the Differential Contribution of Specific Body Aspects." *The Journal of Social Psychology*, 99 (1976), 251-258.

    A stepwise regression analysis of the responses of 98 male and 129 female undergraduates to a self-esteem test and to a body-satisfaction questionnaire revealed that for males the body aspects contributing most to explain variance in self-esteem were voice, chest, and facial features. For females, the aspect was overall physical attractiveness, with voice, calves, height, and hips contributing minimally.

41. Mahoney, John, and Donna M.L. Heretick. "Factor-Specific Dimensions in Person Perception for Same- and Opposite-Sex Friendship Dyads." *The Journal of Social Psychology*, 107 (1979), 219-225.

    This study of 43 male and 45 female undergraduates' perceptions of themselves, their same-sex best friends, and their opposite-sex best friends found males' self- and same-sex descriptions emphasized rivalry while females' self- and same-sex descriptions emphasized social competency. Females assessed males on leadership and achievement; males assessed females on fun-loving companionship.

* Maslin, Audrey, and Jerry L. Davis. "Sex-Role Stereotyping as a Factor in Mental Health Standards Among Counselors-in-Training." *Journal of Counseling Psychology*, 22 (1975), 87-91. See item 549.

* Merluzzi, Thomas V., Paul G. Banikiotes, and Joseph W. Missbach. "Perceptions of Counselor Characteristics: Sex, Experience, and Disclosure Level." *Journal of Counseling Psychology*, 15 (1978), 479-482. See item 550.

* Meyer, John P. and Susan Pepper. "Need Compatibility and Marital Adjustment in Young Married Couples." *Journal of Personality and Social Psychology*, 35 (1977), 331-342. See item 358.

* Millar, Frank E., L. Edna Rogers-Millar, and John A. Courtright. "Relational Control and Dyadic Understanding: An Exploratory Predictive Regression Model." *Communication Yearbook 3*. Ed. Dan Nimmo. New Brunswick, N.J.: Transaction Books, 1979. Pp. 213-224. See item 359.

42. Moffett, Louis A. "Sex Differences in Self-Concept." *Psychological Reports,* 37 (1975), 74.

    Using a semantic-differential scale, 50 male and 50 female undergraduates described their actual and their ideal selves. Males described themselves as slightly active, tough, rational, and dominating, and their ideal selves as relaxed, active, outgoing, tough, slightly dominating, calm, rational, and humorous. Females described themselves as slightly tender, active, conventional, and tense, and their ideal selves as quite relaxed, active, outgoing, slightly tender, humorous, calm, rational, and imaginative. Data lend support to the suggestion that men are more agentic and women are more communal, but neither sex exclusively so. Women were less committed to "feminine" actual and ideal descriptions than men were to "masculine" ones.

43. Nevill, Dorothy, and Sandra Damico. "Development of a Role Conflict Questionnaire for Women: Some Preliminary Findings." *Journal of Consulting and Clinical Psychology,* 42 (1974), 743.

    This brief report of the development of a role-conflict questionnaire and its try-out with 276 women from service, educational, and church organizations noted that the greatest levels of role conflict focused on the area of self-image.

44. Ober, Nelson, and Fred E. Jandt. "Students' Self Concepts and Evaluations of Discussion Instruction." *Speech Teacher,* 22 (1973), 64-66.

    Forty females and 37 males in an undergraduate discussion course completed self-concept measures at the beginning of the course and a course evaluation at the end. Correlation analysis showed that high self-concept males perceived high value in self-grading and rated the course as good, while low self-concept males indicated opposite perceptions and females had no such significant correlations. Females who expressed high acceptance of others perceived the student-instructor relationship as closed and rated the course as poor, while low-acceptance-of-others females rated just the opposite and males had no such significant correlations.

45. O'Connor, Kevin, David W. Mann, and Judith M. Bardwick. "Androgyny and Self-Esteem in the Upper-Middle Class: A Replication of Spence." *Journal of Consulting and Clinical Psychology,* 46 (1978), 1168-69.

    This brief report of a replication of the 1975 Spence, Helmreich, and Stapp study (see item 63), using 43 upper-middle class males and 48 females between 40 and 50 years old, supports the earlier finding that androgynous males and females have highest mean self-esteem, followed, within each sex, by masculine, feminine, and undifferentiated groups.

46. O'Leary, Virginia E., and Charlene E. Depner. "College Males' Ideal Female: Changes in Sex-Role Stereotypes." *The Journal of Social Psychology,* 95 (1975), 139-140.

    A questionnaire survey of 47 male and 47 female undergraduates on self- and ideal-other perceptions revealed that males rated themselves significantly more aggressive, independent, dominant, stronger, and tougher. Females rated themselves brighter and more responsible. Both sexes used sex-role stereotypes, but males' ideal female was a veritable wonder woman. She was significantly more competent, adventuresome, and independent than females' self-ratings, than males' self-ratings, and than females' ratings of the ideal male.

47. Orlofsky, Jacob L. "Sex-Role Orientation, Identity Formation, and Self-Esteem in College Men and Women." *Sex Roles,* 3 (1977), 561-575.

    To determine the relationship between sex-role orientation and identity formation and self-esteem, 111 college males and females completed measures of sex-role orientation, identity formation, and self-esteem. Androgyny was conducive to identity achievement and high self-esteem in both sexes. Feminine females had low self-esteem in all areas except physical attractiveness. Cross-sex typing appeared to have positive consequences for females leading to high self-esteem and identity achievement, but less positive consequences for males. Low levels of both masculine and feminine characteristics were associated with low self-esteem and identity diffusion.

48. Orlofsky, Jacob L., and Michael T. Windle. "Sex-Role Orientation, Behavioral Adaptability and Personal Adjustment." *Sex Roles*, 4 (1978), 801-811.

 One hundred and eleven undergraduates, classified by the Bem Sex-Role Inventory as masculine, feminine, androgynous, or undifferentiated, were tested for emotional expressivity, assertiveness, and personal integration. An androgynous sex-role orientation led to greater behavioral flexibility than a sex-typed or cross-sex typed orientation and was associated with high levels of self-esteem and personal adjustment. Undifferentiated orientation subjects had no flexibility and tended to be associated with low self-esteem and personal integration. While sex typing permitted a subjective sense of well-being, in women it was generally associated with lower self-esteem and in both sexes with a lowered effectiveness in cross-sex tasks. Cross-sex typing was associated with high self-esteem in women (but low self-esteem in men), a lowered ability to engage in sex-appropriate tasks, and subjective feelings of discomfort and alienation in both sexes.

49. Priest, Robert F., and Paul G. Wilhelm, "Sex, Marital Status, and Self/Actualization as Factors in the Appreciation of Sexist Jokes." *The Journal of Social Psychology*, 92 (1974), 245-249.

 A survey of 287 undergraduates, male and female, married and unmarried, rating 40 jokes (20 moderately hostile sexist ones and 20 others), found no sex differences in total appreciation. Married subjects preferred nonsexist jokes. Females rated antimale jokes higher than antifemale jokes; males did just the opposite. High self-actualizers, both male and female, did not enjoy antifemale jokes as much as low self-actualizing males.

50. Rappaport, Alan, David Payne, and Anne Steinmann. "Perceptual Differences Between Married and Single College Women for the Concepts of Self, Ideal Woman, and Man's Ideal Woman." *Journal of Marriage and the Family*, 32 (1970), 441-442.

 Forty-five married and 45 single female students were compared for their perceptions of self, ideal woman, and man's ideal woman using the Inventory of Female Values. The single group was significantly more family oriented than the married group in perceiving self and ideal woman; both groups perceived the man's ideal woman as family oriented. The results are explained in terms of cultural stereotypes of female sex roles.

* Reardon, Robert C. "Individual Differences and the Meanings of Vocal Emotional Expressions." *Journal of Communication,* 21 (March 1971), 72-82. See item 1244.

51. Reich, Stephen, and Andrew Geller. "Self-Image of Nurses." *Phychological Reports,* 39 (1976), 401-402.

    Scores on the Adjective Check List of 163 female graduate nurses revealed they perceived themselves higher on dominance, self-control, achievement, order, self-confidence, counseling, readiness, and nurturance than female norms would indicate. The nurses scored lower than the female norm on succorance, change, abasement, liability, and number of undesirable items checked.

52. Reich, Stephen, and Andrew Geller. "Self-Image of Social Workers." *Psychological Reports,* 39 (1976), 657-658.

    Scores on the Adjective Check List of 105 female social workers indicated that, compared to the norms for females, they saw themselves as higher on achievement, endurance, dominance, self-control, order, self-confidence, defensiveness, personal adjustment, and aggression. They scored lower than the norm on the number of unfavorable items checked and on affiliation and succorance.

53. Richmond, Bert O., Robert L. Mason, Jr., and Harry G. Padgett. "Self-Concept and Perception of Others." *Journal of Humanistic Psychology,* 12, No. 2 (1972), 103-111.

    To investigate the relationship between self-concept and perception of others, 98 female and 52 male undergraduates responded to two inventories. Females viewed others as more unselfish, sympathetic, and concerned about themselves than males did. Females also held a higher concept of themselves as integral, worthwhile members of the family group. Males exhibited more variability and uncertainty in self-concept and revealed less integration in self-concept, viewing themselves as quite high in some aspects and quite low in others.

* Rosenbluh, Edward S. "Interaction of Subject and Experimenter Sex with the Body Percept in Verbal Concept Identification." *Journal of Abnormal Psychology,* 80 (1972), 149-156. See item 160.

54. Ryckman, Richard M., and Martin F. Sherman. "Relationship Between Self-Esteem and Internal-External Control for Men and Women." *Psychological Reports,* 32 (1973), 1106.

    Using 178 male and 204 female undergraduates, the authors determined that both males and females with high self-esteem tended to have internal locus of control, a finding previously verified only with males.

55. Sappenfield, Bert R., and Cynthia L. Harris. "Self-Reported Masculinity-Femininity as Related to Self-Esteem." *Psychological Reports,* 37 (1975), 669-670.

    Thirty-three male and 45 female undergraduates completed measures for self-esteem and for masculinity-femininity. Correlations of high and low masculinity scorers and self-esteem revealed a significant difference, with high-masculine males having significantly higher self-esteem. No significant differences were found for females.

* Schein, Virginia E. "Relationships Between Sex Role Stereotypes and Requisite Management Characteristics Among Female Managers." *Journal of Applied Psychology,* 60 (1975), 340-344. See item 451.

56. Schiff, Ellen, and Elizabeth J. Koopman. "The Relationship of Women's Sex-Role Identity to Self-Esteem and Ego Development." *Journal of Psychology,* 98 (1978), 299-305.

    From a pool of 153 female undergraduates, four groups of 25 were selected--androgynous, feminine, masculine, and undifferentiated--to complete various sex role, self-esteem, and ego development measures. Androgynous women had significantly higher self-esteem than feminine and undifferentiated ones, but not than masculine women. Ego development in androgynous women did not differ significantly from that of feminine and undifferentiated women, but was significantly greater than for masculine subjects.

* Schlenker, Barry R. "Self-Presentation: Managing the Impression of Consistency when Reality Interferes with Self-Enhancement." *Journal of Personality and Social Psychology,* 32 (1975), 1030-37. See item 289.

57. Shrauger, J. Sidney. "Self-Esteem and Reactions to Being Observed by Others." *Journal of Personality and Social Psychology*, 23 (1972), 192-200.

    Sixty-four female undergraduates of high or low self esteem estimated their performance on a task (specific self-esteem) and then performed a concept-attainment task either with or without an audience. General esteem was not related to performance, though high-esteem subjects estimated they had done better than low-esteem subjects. High specific-self-esteem subjects performed better than low specific, who also performed more poorly in front of an audience. The audience variable had no significant effect on high specific-self-esteem subjects.

* Sigall, Harold, and John Michela. "I'll Bet You Say That to All The Girls: Physical Attractiveness and Reactions to Praise." *Journal of Personality*, 44 (1976), 611-626. See item 1124.

58. Silverman, Alan F., Mark E. Pressman, and Helmut W. Bartel. "Self-Esteem and Tactile Communication." *Journal of Humanistic Psychology*, 13, No. 2 (1973), 73-77.

    To investigate the relationship between self-esteem and tactile communication, dyads varying both in the sex of the subject and the sex of confederate, 80 female and male undergraduates altogether, were asked to communicate an emotion to their partner without words, sounds, or eye contact. The higher the subject's self-esteem, the more intimate the subject was in communicating through touch, especially when communicating with a female. High self-esteem subjects found the task easier and perceived the communication as being transmitted more clearly than did the low self-esteem subjects. Males found the task significantly easier than females did. Both male and female subjects tended to be more intimate with female confederates than male confederates.

59. Smith, Carolyn B., and Larry R. Judd. "A Study of Variables Influencing Self-Concept and Ideal Self-Concept among Students in the Basic Speech Course." *Speech Teacher*, 23 (1974), 215-221.

    This study was designed to reveal differences between ideal and reported self-concepts of 226 male and female students at the beginning and the end of a basic college speech course and whether differences, if any, were related to sex of student or to discrepancy between reported and ideal self-concepts or both. In a moderate discrepancy group, males and females had different self-concepts (males--strong, bold, successful; females--gracious, safe, pleasant) and different ideal self-concepts, but both groups increased in self-concept, though females more. No sex differences appeared in the extreme discrepancy groups, either high or low.

60. Spence, Janet T., and Robert L. Helmreich. *Masculinity and Femininity: Their Psychological Dimensions, Correlates, & Antecedents*. Austin: University of Texas Press, 1979.

    This report of the extensive research of the authors, who developed the Personal Attributes Questionnaire, a two-scale masculinity-femininity measure, covers the results of their testing and the relationship between sex-role orientation and attributes, attitudes, self-esteem, motivation, and parental attributes, attitudes, and self-esteem. A 15-page list of references is included.

61. Spence, Janet T., Robert L. Helmreich, and Carole K. Holahan. "Negative and Positive Components of Psychological Masculinity and Femininity and Their Relationship to Self-Reports of Neurotic and Acting Out Behaviors." *Journal of Personality and Social Psychology*, 37 (1979), 1673-82.

    Negatively valued sex-role personality traits were collected, with negative masculinity judged as those traits more typical of males, undesirable, and instrumental, while negative femininity was judged as more typical of females, undesirable, and communion-like or verbal passive-aggressive. Tested on 583 male and female undergraduates, sex differences occurred in the predicted direction. Self-esteem correlated positively with positive sex-role scores, but negatively with negative femininity only. Neuroticism was most highly correlated, negatively, with positive masculinity for both sexes, and acting-out behavior was positively correlated with negative masculinity.

62. Spence. Janet T., Robert Helmreich, and Joy Stapp. "Likeability, Sex-Role Congruence of Interest, and Competence: It All Depends on How You Ask." *Journal of Applied Social Psychology*, 5 (1975), 93-109.

Four videotapes of a male or female being interviewed, portrayed as competent or not and as having masculine or feminine interests, were rated by over 900 liberal or conservative male and female students, some immediately and some later. In immediate-rating condition, subjects liked competent interviewees better than incompetent ones and masculine ones better than feminine. In the delayed rating, conservative males and females and liberal males liked the feminine competent female interviewee better than her masculine counterpart.

63. Spence, Janet T., Robert L. Helmreich, and Joy Stapp. "Ratings of Self and Peers on Sex Role Attributes and Their Relation to Self-Esteem and Conceptions of Masculinity and Femininity." *Journal of Personality and Social Psychology*, 32 (1975), 29-39.

    Two hundred forty-eight male and 282 female undergraduates completed the Personal Attributes Questionnaire, the Attidudes Toward Women Scale, and a measure of social self-esteem. They also rated themselves and then compared directly the typical male and female college student on personal attributes. Self-ratings were divided into male-valued, female-valued, and sex-specific items, all stereotype scores. Correlations of the self-ratings with stereotype scores and the Attitudes Toward Women Scale were low in magnitude, suggesting that sex-role expectations do not distort self-concepts. For both men and women, "femininity" on the female-valued items and "masculinity" on the male-valued items were positively correlated and both were significantly related to self-esteem.

64. Stake, Jayne E., and Joan Pearlman. "Assertiveness Training as an Intervention Technique for Low Performance Self-Esteem Women." *Journal of Counseling Psychology*, 27 (1980), 276-281.

    Pre- and post-tests measuring performance self-esteem and self-ratings of job performance were given to 121 women in assertiveness training groups. Follow-up measures were obtained from 9 to 12 months later from 79% of the sample. All in the training sample increased their scores on the performance self-concept measure from pretest to follow-up, and the change scores were negatively related to the initial self-esteem scores. Findings suggest assertiveness training is a viable method to improve low performance self-esteem.

* Stake, Jayne E., and Michael N. Stake. "Performance-Self-Esteem and Dominance Behavior in Mixed-Sex Dyads." *Journal of Personality,* 47 (1979), 71-84. See item 163.

65. Steinmann, Anne, and David J. Fox. "Attitudes Toward Women's Family Role Among Black and White Undergraduates." *The Family Coordinator,* 19 (1970), 363-368.

    An Inventory of Female Values was administered to 100 black and 126 while female undergraduates and to 100 black and 82 white college men. The self-perceptions and ideal woman of black and white women did not differ; both were slightly self-achieving. However, black and white women differed in their perceptions of man's ideal woman: white women perceived men as preferring a home-oriented woman, while black women felt men wanted a woman who balanced home and career. Both white and black men perceived the ideal woman as balancing home and career.

66. Stericker, Anne B., and James E. Johnson. "Sex-Role Identification and Self-Esteem in College Students: Do Men and Women Differ?" *Sex Roles,* 3 (1977), 19-26.

    To explore the relationship between sex-role identification, achievement motivation, and self-esteem, 312 male and female college students responded to a stereotype questionnaire, an achievement motivation test, and a self-concept scale. Self-esteem scores of males and females did not differ significantly. Achievement motivation was a significant correlate of self-esteem for both sexes, but the relationship was significantly stronger for females than for males. A significant direct relationship was found for both sexes between a more masculine orientation and self-esteem.

67. Stewart, Abigail J. "A Longitudinal Study of Coping Styles in Self-Defining and Socially Defined Women." *Journal of Consulting and Clinical Psychology,* 46 (1978), 1079-84.

    Selecting 51 female college graduates previously classified as self-defining or socially defining (accepting of sex role norm) through the Thematic Apperception Test for follow-up interviews 10-14 years later, Stewart found the self-defining women different in their coping and problem-solving behavior. They interpreted personal problems as existing outside themselves while the solutions were inside, they articulated their problems and solutions better, and they initiated action to solve the problems. By contrast, socially defining women saw problems as within the self and the solution as more external, they articulated these problems less clearly, and they either took no action or action discursive to the problem.

* Stratton, Lois O., Dennis J. Tekippe, and Grad L. Flick. "Personal Space and Self-Concept." *Sociometry,* 36 (1973), 424-429. See item 1192.

68. Tesser, Abraham. "Self-Esteem Maintenance in Family Dynamics." *Journal of Personality and Social Psychology,* 39 (1980), 77-91.

To support predictions made from a self-esteem maintenance model, Tesser analyzed questionnaire data previously collected from 255 male and 258 female first-year college students with one sibling. General findings included a decrease in identification and an increase in friction with closeness in age when the sibling performed better on important dimensions. Differences by sex of respondent in sibling identification are noted and discussed since results for females did not support the hypotheses predicted from the model the way that results for males did.

69. Tessler, Richard C., and Shalom H. Schwartz. "Help Seeking, Self-Esteem, and Achievement Motivation: An Attributional Analysis." *Journal of Personality and Social Psychology,* 21 (1972), 318-326.

This study used 48 female undergraduates in a task for which they could seek help but in doing so they threatened their self-esteem. Independent variables were level of self-esteem, attribution for failure on self or external factor, and levels of centrality (perceived intelligence and mental health). Help was sought significantly more often by low, not high, achievement-motivation subjects; by external, not self, attribution subjects; by low, not high, self-esteem subjects; and, for high self-esteem subjects only, by peripheral, not central, attribution subjects.

* Tognoli, Jerome, and Robert Keisner. "Gain and Loss of Esteem as Determinants of Interpersonal Attraction: A Replication and Extension." *Journal of Personality and Social Psychology,* 23 (1972), 201-204. See item 658.

70. Tolor, Alexander, Bryan R. Kelly, and Charles A. Stebbins. "Assertiveness, Sex-Role Stereotyping, and Self-Concept." *Journal of Psychology*, 93 (1976), 157-164.

> Sixty-one male and 73 female undergraduates completed assertiveness, self-expression, and self-concept scales as well as a sex-stereotyped list measure. Though no significant differences in assertiveness were found between high and low sex-role stereotyped females or males, as hypothesized, investigators did find a positive relationship between assertiveness and favorable self-concept for both sexes. Females low in sex-role stereotyping were significantly more assertive than males were, and they had significantly more positive self-concepts as well.

71. Voss, Jacqueline H., and Denise A. Skinner. "Concepts of Self and Ideal Woman Held by College Women: A Replication." *Journal of College Student Personnel*, 16 (1975), 210-213.

> Twenty-five single and 25 married female undergraduates were compared in their perceptions of self, ideal woman, and man's ideal woman using the Inventory of Female Values. Perceptions of female sex-role held by college women in 1969 and 1973 were also compared. No significant differences were noted between the married and single groups; both groups indicated orientation toward self-achievement and appeared less influenced by traditional stereotypes regarding femininity and more concerned with their personal growth and development outside the family context. The 1973 group differed from the 1969 group in having greater extrafamilial orientation.

* Waetjen, Walter B., James M. Schuerger, and Eleanor B. Schwartz. "Male and Female Managers: Self-Concept, Success, and Failure." *Journal of Psychology*, 103 (1979), 87-94. See item 456.

72. Whitehurst, Carol A. "An Empirical Investigation of Women's Self-Evaluation." *International Journal of Women's Studies*, 2 (1979), 76-86.

> The idea that women have poorer self-evaluations than men is discussed and tested with 117 female and 69 male undergraduates who responded to attitude and self-evaluation scales. Results showed no measurable differences in self-evaluations by sex.

73. Wiggins, Jerry S. "A Psychological Taxonomy of Trait-Descriptive Terms: The Interpersonal Domain." *Journal of Personality and Social Psychology,* 37 (1979), 395-412.

This theoretical article is designed to lead to a taxonomy of trait terms, but traditional sex differences are noted on the Interpersonal Adjective Scale. Males label themselves more ambitious-dominant, arrogant-calculating, cold-quarrelsome, and aloof-introverted, while females see themselves as more lazy-submissive, unassuming-ingenuous, warm-agreeable, and gregarious-extroverted.

74. Wilson, John P. "Coping-Defense Employment in Problematic Interpersonal Situations." *Small Group Behavior,* 9 (1978), 135-148.

This study posited the idea that if ego-identity were found to affect coping and defense mechanisms in certain ways, then the means of interpersonal conflict resolution in group operation would be more definitive. Subjects were 85 undergraduate nursing students, who used self-rating questionnaires. The hypothesis was upheld: positive-oriented individuals reported greater amounts of coping mechanisms than negative-oriented individuals, who reported greater amounts of defense mechanisms. Positive-oriented individuals were more flexible in their use of defenses, while negative-oriented individuals were more rigid.

75. Wilson, John P., and Stephen B. Wilson. "Sources of Self-Esteem and the Person x Situation Controversy." *Psychological Reports,* 38 (1976), 355-358.

A content analysis of a measure of self-esteem given to 79 male and 56 female community college students revealed that male self-esteem came from success experiences in vocations, positions of power, and competition. Female self-esteem came from achievement of personal goals, self- and body-image, existential concerns, and family relationships.

76. Wilson, Stephen R., and Larry A. Benner. "The Effects of Self-Esteem and Situation Upon Comparison Choices during Ability Evaluation." *Sociometry,* 34 (1971), 381-397.

In this study using 291 male and female undergraduates, the predictions that an average-in-ability person would choose a top person to compare himself with in a private situation but would moderate his choice defensively in a public situation and that a high-esteem person would choose the person highest in ability for comparison were verified for male but not for female subjects. Female deviation from predictions was theorized to stem from sex-role differences perpetuated in the culture.

* Wittig, Michele A., and Paul Skolnick. "Status Versus Warmth and Determinants of Sex Differences in Personal Space." *Sex Roles,* 4 (1978), 493-503. See item 1204.

77. Yockey, Jamie M. "Role Theory and the Female Sex Role." *Sex Roles,* 4 (1978), 917-927.

    This study investigated the hypothesis that contemporary women vary both their perception of the female role and their enactment of it according to the situation. Yockey expected that expressive (feminine) behaviors would characterize social situations and instrumental (masculine) behaviors work situations. One hundred sixty unmarried female undergraduates completed a questionnaire which examined sex-role perceptions and perceived outcome for masculine and feminine behaviors. Seven to ten days later they interacted with a male confederate in a social interaction and in a group discussion. Analysis of videotaped interactions upheld the hypothesis. The subjects varied their behavior with the situation, combining masculine and feminine behaviors within both the social and work situations.

78. Zanna, Mark P., and Susan J. Pack. "On the Self-Fulfilling Nature of Apparent Sex Differences in Behavior." *Journal of Experimental Social Psychology,* 11 (1975), 583-591.

    Eighty undergraduate women characterized themselves to a desirable or undesirable male partner, whose stereotype of the ideal woman either conformed to the traditional female stereotype or not. When the male partners were attractive, the females conformed to the male partner's ideal, conventionally if he had a conventional stereotype in his description and unconventionally if he had an unconventional stereotype.

CONCEPTS OF OTHER WOMEN

79. Beere, Carole A., and Lynda A. King. "Sexism: Abstracts of Studies Using Disguised or Unobstrusive Measures." *JSAS: Catalog of Selected Documents in Psychology,* 10 (1980), 39. (Ms. No. 2043)

    Abstracts of 157 studies which compared responses between males and females or between females who differed on some sex-related or sex-typed variable are organized into ten sections, including one on communication.

80. Burns, Robert B. "Male and Female Perceptions of Their Own and the Other Sex." *The British Journal of Social and Clinical Psychology,* 16 (1977), 213-220.

    An investigation of 154 female and 219 male university students' perceptions of their own and the opposite sex, using a semantic differential, showed that both sexes held conventional stereotypes of masculinity and femininity. The female's perception of the male differed significantly from his perception of how the female viewed him. Males thought females perceived them as more dominant, more aggressive, less warm, and more able to see things objectively than the females actually did. Females saw themselves as less submissive, peaceful, kind, dependent, weak, warm, and neurotic, and more likely to express anger verbally than males actually perceived them.

81. Deaux, Kay, and Janet Taynor. "Evaluation of Male and Female Ability: Bias Works Two Ways." *Psychological Reports,* 32 (1973), 261-262.

    Fifty female and 47 male college students rated one of four stimulus persons, male and female, on the basis of a taped interview on academic background and on an oral examination, the interviewee manipulated to have one of two levels of intelligence and one of two levels of competence for each sex. Highly competent males were rated more positively than highly competent females, but low competent males were rated lower than low competent females. Sex of raters was not significant.

82. Hall, James R., and J. Diane Black. "Assertiveness, Agressiveness [sic], and Attitudes toward Feminism." *The Journal of Social Psychology,* 107 (1979), 57-62.

    Two forms of an attitude-toward-women test were given

to 36 male and 36 female undergraduates, either with a
planted interruption between the two in which an assertive or an aggressive female interrupted or with no interruption. The interruptions made no significant difference on scores from males, but with females those
exposed to the aggressive condition significantly
changed to a less positive view of feminism. Those in
the assertive condition did not.

* Harris, Mary B. "The Effects of Sex, Sex-Stereotyped Descriptions, and Institution on Evaluations of Teachers."
  Sex Roles, 2 (1976), 15-21. See item 512.

* Harris, Mary B. "Sex Role Stereotypes and Teacher Evaluations." *Journal of Educational Psychology,* 67 (1975),
  751-756. See item 513.

* Jablin, Frederic M. "Subordinate's Sex and Superior-Subordinate Status Differentiation as Moderators of the
  Pelz Effect." In *Communication Yearbook 4.* Ed. Dan
  Nimmo. New Brunswick, N.J.: Transaction Books, 1980,
  pp. 349-366. See item 438.

83. Kristal, Jane, Deborah Sanders, Janet T. Spence, and
    Robert Helmreich. "Inferences about the Femininity of
    Competent Women and Their Implications for Likability."
    Sex Roles, 1 (1975), 33-40.

    Sixty female and 59 male undergraduates were given a
    written description of a competent, achievement-oriented
    female stimulus person with either a masculine or feminine pattern of vocational and avocational interests.
    They were then asked to rate the female on likability
    in work and social settings, femininity, and a number
    of personal attributes. Two groups given the masculine-pattern information were also supplied with the female's
    responses to items from a personality test answered in
    a predominantly feminine (masculine-feminine) or masculine (masculine-masculine) direction. The remaining
    groups were given no additional information (neutral).
    The masculine-neutral female was liked more in social
    settings than was the feminine-neutral one and was perceived as similar to the masculine-feminine female in
    femininity and likability, which were judged higher for
    these stimulus females than for the masculine-masculine
    ones. Complex results were obtained from the ratings
    of other attributes, but, overall, they indicated that
    the masculine-feminine female, in whom femininity was

explicitly suggested, received the weakest ratings on a series of achievement-related attributes and the masculine-neutral female the strongest.

84. Locksley, Anne, Eugene Borgida, Nancy Brekke, and Christine Hepburn. "Sex Stereotypes and Social Judgment." *Journal of Personality and Social Psychology*, 39 (1980), 821-831.

    A total of 195 undergraduates (97 F, 98 M) read a transcript of a male, female, or unidentified person behaving assertively or passively and, after a delay, predicted that individual's behavior in four new situations and rated the person's personality. Contrary to expectation of stereotypic beliefs influencing judgment, no effects of target persons' sex were found on inferences about their personality traits. Results are interpreted in light of the normative use of prior probabilities in judgment tasks. A second experiment with 130 undergraduates (75 F, 55 M) supported the hypothesis that a minimal amount of subjective information that individuates the unidentified person would be sufficient to eradicate stereotyping. Discussion of the seeming paradox of persistent stereotypic beliefs with these results is included.

* Massengill, Douglas, and Nicholas DiMarco. "Sex-Role Stereotypes and Requisite Management Characteristics: A Current Replication." *Sex Roles,* 5 (1979), 561-570. See item 443.

* Matteson, Michael T. "Attitudes toward Women as Managers: Sex or Role Differences?" *Psychological Reports,* 39 (1976), 166. See item 444.

85. Mezydlo, Linda S., and Nancy E. Betz. "Perceptions of Ideal Sex Roles as a Function of Sex and Feminist Orientation." *Journal of Counseling Psychology,* 27 (1980), 282-285.

    Eighty-six female and 83 male undergraduates picked characteristics from the Bem Sex-Role Inventory to describe the ideal man or woman. In addition, all completed the Attitudes Toward Women measure, with median splits of the scores used to determine feminists from non-feminists. Non-feminist males and females described the ideal man and woman in traditional sex-role stereotyping terms. Feminists, however, whether male or female, rated the ideal woman as similar to the ideal man, that is, having characteristics typical of masculine sex typing.

86. Nielsen, Joyce M., and Peggy T. Doyle. "Sex-Role Stereotypes of Feminists and Nonfeminists." *Sex Roles,* 1 (1975), 93-95.

    This study used a semantic differential questionnaire to compare the perceptions and sex-role stereotypes of 137 female undergraduates, identified as feminists or nonfeminists. The feminists had a higher regard for women in general and a slightly more positive self-concept; the nonfeminists held a negative view of women in the feminist movement. The feminists had a negative evaluation of men in general and a positive one of movement women. Both groups stressed positive feminine traits in describing their ideal woman as well as women in general but the feminists wanted to see more dominance in women.

87. Parelius, Ann P. "Emerging Sex-Role Attitudes, Expectations, and Strains Among College Women." *Journal of Marriage and the Family,* 37 (1975), 146-153.

    A comparison of the responses of 147 college women to a questionnaire on perceived sex roles and attitudes of men toward women's roles taken in 1969 with the responses of 200 more taken in 1973 revealed a marked shift toward feminism in attitudes toward work, division of home labor, and financial responsibilities. Their perceptions of men's attitudes toward women's roles did not shift correspondingly, with women seeing men as even more conservative on marital and maternal roles in 1973 than they saw them in 1969.

88. Pines, Ayala. "The Influence of Goals on People's Perceptions of a Competent Woman." *Sex Roles,* 5 (1979), 71-76.

    The perceptions of males and females toward a competent woman who chose either to pursue a career or to stay at home were compared. Male and female undergraduates (no number given) responded to an attitudes-toward-women questionnaire and rated a competent woman seen on a taped interview presented as either pursuing a career or staying at home. The woman was perceived as more competent when she planned to pursue her career. Females' perceptions were more positive in the career condition and males in the at-home condition. Females' perceptions were consistent with their attitudes toward women, while males' perceptions were not.

89. Potts, Cheryl, Walter T. Plant, and Mara L. Southern. "Conventional Sex Differences in Personality: Does Sex or Verbal Ability Level Account for More Variance?" *Psychological Reports,* 43 (1978), 931-936.

    A total of 106 male and female college students representing high and low levels of verbal ability completed a personality inventory and the Attitudes Toward Women Scale. Various statistical tests supported the hypotheses that the personality and attitudes toward women of high verbal ability subjects would not differ from each other, that the same would hold true for low verbal ability subjects, and that verbal ability would account for a greater proportion of the variance in both personality and Attitude Toward Women scores than sex would.

90. Pursell, Sandra A., and Paul G. Banikiotes. "Androgyny; and Initial Interpersonal Attraction." *Personality and Social Psychology Bulletin,* 4 (1978), 235-239.

    Fifty-six male and 49 female undergraduates, previously tested on the Bem Sex-Role Inventory, rated on the Interpersonal Judgment Scale bogus male and female stereotyped persons and male and female androgyns. Four-way analysis of variance revealed that stereotyped persons of either sex rated the stereotyped protocols higher in attraction, and androgynous subjects rated the androgynous protocols higher. Female subjects found androgynous persons significantly more attractive than stereotyped ones, while male subjects found just the opposite. Females were rated more attractive than males by male subjects.

* Rappaport, Alan F., David Payne, and Anne Steinmann. "Marriage as a Factor in the Dyadic Perception of the Female Sex Role." *Psychological Reports,* 27 (1970), 283-284. See item 365.

* Renwick, Patricia A. "The Effects of Sex Differences on the Perception and Management of Superior-Subordinate Conflict: An Exploratory Study." *Organizational Behavior and Human Performance,* 19 (1977), 403-415. See item 448.

91. Richmond, Virginia P., and James C. McCroskey. "Whose Opinion Do You Trust?" *Journal of Communication,* 25 (Summer 1975), 42-50.

Though earlier studies found a strong negative bias by women against females as opinion leaders on a wide variety of topics, this study of three populations, undergraduate students (61 M, 125 F), female graduate students (38 single, 28 married), and community adults (126 M, 146 F), aged 22 to 65, did not. Female adults, whether married or unmarried, preferred to turn to other females for opinions on school information and on fashion, although they still turned to males for opinions on politics.

92. Seyfried, B.A., and Clyde Hendrick. "When Do Opposites Attract? When They Are Opposite in Sex and Sex Role Attitudes." *Journal of Personality and Social Psychology,* 25 (1973), 15-20.

In this study using 48 male and 49 female undergraduates evaluating the attractiveness of a male or a female stranger manipulated to have masculine or feminine attitudes (sex roles), the authors found that when the subject and stranger were of the same sex, similarity of sex role attitudes increased attraction. When of opposite sexes, females preferred masculine males to feminine males, but males showed no significant preference between masculine or feminine females.

93. Shaffer, David R., and Carol Wegley. "Success Orientation and Sex-role Congruence as Determinants of the Attractiveness of Competent Women." *Journal of Personality,* 42 (1974), 586-600.

Forty-eight male and 48 female undergraduates responded on the Interpersonal Rating Form and an Adjective Checklist to one of four stimulus females manipulated to be of high or low success orientation and of masculine or feminine sex-role preference. Both sexes preferred feminine-competent females to masculine-competent ones, including as work partners. Both sexes, however, would rather hire the masculine-competent woman than the feminine-competent one. Success-oriented stimulus females were not judged any less attractive socially than non-success oriented ones.

* Sherman, Julia, Corinne Koufacos, and Joy A. Kenworthy. "Therapists: Their Attitudes and Information About

Women." *Psychology of Women Quarterly*, 2 (1978), 299-313. See item 555.

* Simas, Kathleen, and Michael McCarrey. "Impact of Recruiter Authoritarianism and Applicant Sex on Evaluation and Selection Decisions in a Recruitment Interview Analogue Study." *Journal of Applied Psychology*, 64 (1979), 483-491. See item 453.

* Simons, Janet A., and Janet E. Helms. "Influence of Counselors' Marital Status, Sex, and Age on College and Non-College Women's Counselor Preferences." *Journal of Counseling Psychology*, 23 (1976), 380-386. See item 556.

94. Spence, Janet T., and Robert Helmreich. "Who Likes Competent Women? Competence, Sex-Role Congruence of Interests, and Subjects' Attitudes Toward Women as Determinants of Interpersonal Attraction." *Journal of Applied Social Psychology*, 2 (1972), 197-213.

    Undergraduates (343 F, 264 M) viewed four videotapes of an interview of a woman portrayed as competent or not and as masculine (physics major) or feminine (fine arts major) in interest. Females significantly preferred the competent, masculine woman, as did males, but females found her more likeable. Both males and females rated the competent interviewees more social, sincere, and intelligent than the incompetent ones.

* Stead, Bette A., ed. *Women In Management*. Englewood Cliffs, N.J.: Prentice-Hall, 1978. See item 454.

* Taylor, Shelley E., Susan T. Fiske, Nancy L. Etcoff and Audrey J. Ruderman. "Categorical and Contextual Bases of Person Memory and Stereotyping." *Journal of Personality and Social Psychology*, 36 (1978), 778-793. See item 301.

WITH ANOTHER

95. Adams, Kathrynn A., and Audrey D. Landers. "Sex Differences in Dominance Behavior." *Sex Roles*, 4 (1978), 215-223.

    In this study designed to investigate sex differences in dominance as a function of sex and sex-role orientation, 28 female and 28 male undergraduates who completed the Attitudes Toward Women Scale recorded individual preferences and then joint decisions with a confederate for the most attractive of 20 pairs of pictures. The number of challenges subjects sustained each time a disagreement occurred about their preferences was recorded. Males withstood significantly more challenges against their preferences than females did. No differences were found as a function of the sex of confederate. Scores on the Attitudes Toward Women Scale were not good predictors of dominance.

* Ahmed, S.M.S. "Reactions to Crowding in Different Settings." *Psychological Reports,* 46 (1980), 1279-84. See item 1133.

* Aiello, John R. "A Further Look at Equilibrium Theory: Visual Interaction as a Function of Interpersonal Distance." *Environmental Psychology and Nonverbal Behavior,* 1, No. 1 (1977), 122-140. See item 1038.

* Aiello, John R. "A Test of Equilibrium Theory: Visual Interaction in Relation to Orientation, Distance and Sex of Interactants." *Psychonomic Science,* 27 (1972), 335-336. See item 1039.

* Albrecht, Terrance L., and Ralph E. Cooley. "Androgyny and Communication Strategies for Relational Dominance: An Empirical Analysis." In *Communication Yearbook 4.* Ed. Dan Nimmo. New Brunswick, N.J.: Transaction Books, 1980, pp. 699-719. See item 316.

* Archer, Richard L., and John H. Berg. "Disclosure Reciprocity and Its Limits: A Reactance Analysis." *Journal of Experimental Social Psychology,* 14 (1978), 527-540. See item 704.

* Argyle, Michael, and Roger Ingham. "Gaze, Mutual Gaze, and Proximity." *Semiotica,* 6 (1972), 32-49. See item 1041.

* Argyle, Michael, Luc Lefebvre, and Mark Cook. "The Meaning of Five Patterns of Gaze." *European Journal of Social Psychology,* 4 (1974), 125-136. See item 1042.

* Arlett, Christine, J. Allan Best, and Brian R. Little. "The Influence of Interviewer Self-Disclosure and Verbal Reinforcement on Personality Tests." *Journal of Clinical Psychology,* 32 (1976), 770-775. See item 706.

96. Ayres, Joe. "Uncertainty and Social Penetration Theory Expectations About Relationship Communication: A Comparative Test." *Western Journal of Speech Communication,* 43 (1979), 192-200.

   To determine the number and use of questions in relationships, 24 female undergraduates engaged in half-hour conversations with six strangers and with six friends. The videotapes of the interactions were coded and rated by trained observers. No difference was found in the number of questions, but friends asked more evaluative questions than strangers did, partially supporting predictions made from a social penetration theory.

* Bailey, Kent G., John J. Hartnett, and Frank W. Gibson, Jr. "Implied Threat and the Territorial Factor in Personal Space." *Psychological Reports,* 30 (1972), 263-270. See item 1135

* Bath, Kent E., and Daniel L. Daly. "Self-Disclosure: Relationships to Self-Described Personality and Sex Differences." *Psychology Reports,* 31 (1972), 623-628. See item 707.

* Bauer, Ernest A. "Personal Space: A Study of Blacks and Whites." *Sociometry,* 36 (1973), 402-408. See item 1137.

* Baxter, James C. "Interpersonal Spacing in Natural Settings." *Sociometry,* 33 (1970), 444-456. See item 1139.

97. Baxter, Leslie A., and Tara L. Shepherd. "Sex-Role Identity, Sex of Other, and Affective Relationship as Determinants of Interpersonal Conflict-Management Styles." *Sex Roles,* 4 (1978), 813-825.

   To assess behavioral differences in interpersonal conflict-management style, 55 undergraduates, classified as masculine, feminine, androgynous, or undifferentiated (based on the Bem Sex-Role Inventory) completed a questionnaire on five conflict-management styles in hypothetical situations which varied by sex and interpersonal liking. Feminine subjects disapproved of competition more than masculine and androgynous ones. Masculine subjects differentiated less between liked and disliked others in their competitive behavior than feminine and androgynous persons did. Conflicts with liked, as opposed to disliked, others were managed with less competition and more accommodation, collaboration, and compromise for all sex-role identity groups.

* Bellack, Alan S., Michel Hersen, and Danuta Lamparski. "Role-Play Tests for Assessing Social Skills: Are They Valid? Are They Useful?" *Journal of Consulting and Clinical Psychology,* 47 (1979), 335-342. See item 770.

* Benjamin, Gail R., and Chet A. Creider. "Social Distinctions in Non-Verbal Behavior." *Semiotica,* 14, No. 1 (1975), 52-60. See item 1259.

* Berger, Stephen E., Jim Millham, Leonard I. Jacobson, and Kenneth N. Anchor. "Prior Self-Disclosure, Sex Differences, and Actual Confiding in an Interpersonal Encounter." *Small Group Behavior,* 9 (1978), 555-562. See item 710.

98. Berkowitz, Leonard. "Aggressive Humor as a Stimulus to Aggressive Response." *Journal of Personality and Social Psychology,* 16 (1970), 710-717.

    This study used 80 female undergraduates exposed to a job applicant's remarks about university women (either neutral or negative) and then to four minutes of humor (either neutral or hostile). In a subsequent evaluation of the job applicant, those who had heard hostile humor were more aggressive toward the applicant than others.

* Billings, Andrew. "Conflict Resolution in Distressed and Nondistressed Married Couples." *Journal of Consulting and Clinical Psychology,* 47 (1979), 368-376. See item 319.

* Birchler, Gary R., Robert L. Weiss, and John L. Vincent. "Multimethod Analysis of Social Reinforcement Exchange Between Maritally Distressed and Nondistressed Spouse and Stranger Dyads." *Journal of Personality and Social Psychology,* 31 (1975), 349-360. See item 320.

99. Blakar, Rolv M., and Tove B. Pederson. "Control and Self-confidence as Reflected in Sex-Bound Patterns in Communication: An Experimental Approach." *Acta Sociologica,* 23 (1980), 33-53.

    Twenty-four same- and mixed-sex dyads of University of Oslo undergraduates in explainer-follower problem-solving situations (one simple, the other complicated by conflicting information given each participant), revealed different patterns of control and self-confidence. The most efficient (in time) problem solvers for the simple task were the male explainer-female follower dyads; the opposite pattern was the most inefficient, and same-sex dyads ranged between. In the complicated task, however, same-sex dyads were more efficient, with male-male dyads the fastest and the male-female dyads the slowest in solving the task. The results are interpreted relevant to women's lower self-esteem and self confidence and to the communication situation. Written in English.

* Blass, Thomas, and Aron W. Siegman. "A Psycholinguistic Comparison of Speech, Dictation and Writing." *Language and Speech,* 18 (1975), 20-34. See item 1223.

* Boderman, Alvin, Douglas W. Freed, and Mark T. Kinnucan. "'Touch Me Like Me': Testing an Encounter Group Assumption." *Journal of Applied Behavioral Science,* 8 (1972), 527-533. See item 1205.

100. Bonoma, Thomas V., James T. Tedeschi, and Bob Helem. "Some Effects of Target Cooperation and Reciprocated Promises on Conflicted Resolution." *Sociometry,* 37 (1974), 251-261.

    Forty female undergraduates played a modified Prisoner's Dilemma Game with a robot who was either cooperative or competitive. Subjects sent more promises to cooperative partner than to competitive one, irrespective of robot's actual response. If robot reciprocated promises, subjects followed through on theirs, again irrespective of robot's subsequent action.

* Borden, Richard J., and Gorden M. Homleid. "Handedness and Lateral Positioning in Heterosexual Couples: Are Men Still Strong-Arming Women?" *Sex Roles,* 4 (1978), 67-73. See item 1261.

* Brady, Adele T., and Michael B. Walker. "Interpersonal Distance as a Function of Situationally Induced Anxiety." *British Journal of Social and Clinical Psychology,* 17 (1978), 127-133. See item 1141.

101. Brickman, Philip, Lawrence J. Becker, and Sidney Castle. "Making Trust Easier and Harder Through Two Forms of Sequential Interaction." *Journal of Personality and*

Social Psychology, 37 (1979), 515-521.

This study tested the hypotheses that cooperation in 84 same-sex dyads would be harder to achieve in continuing interaction (one player's move always follows the other's) than in alternating interaction (each player alternates between being first and second in choosing moves) and that males would benefit more from alternating interaction than females. Data supported both hypotheses. Failure to achieve trust appeared different for males and females. Testing and communicating cooperative intentions were critical for males in resolving trust dilemmas, but not for females, a puzzling finding since in other situations females have been found to be more cooperative than males.

* Brockner, Joel, and Walter C. Swap. "Effects of Repeated Exposure and Attitudinal Similarity on Self-Disclosure and Interpersonal Attraction." *Journal of Personality and Social Psychology,* 33 (1976), 531-540. See item 712.

* Brouwer, Dédé, Marinel Gerritsen, and Dorian De Hann. "Speech Differences Between Men and Women: On the Wrong Track?" *Language in Society,* 8 (1979), 33-50. See item 806.

102. Brown, Robert C., Jr., Bob Helm, and James T. Tedeschi. "Attraction and Verbal Conditioning." *The Journal of Social Psychology,* 91 (1973), 81-85.

    In a verbal conditioning experiment, 40 females were reinforced positively by either a liked or a disliked female. Subjects with a liked reinforcer responded more and increased responses at a more rapid rate than those with a disliked reinforcer, for whom response increased slowly, as did their movement toward liking the reinforcer.

103. Buck, Ross, Robert E. Miller, and William F. Caul. "Sex, Personality, and Physiological Variables in the Communication of Affect via Facial Expression." *Journal of Personality and Social Psychology,* 30 (1974), 587-596.

    Using 32 same-sex and opposite-sex dyads communicating responses to 25 emotionally loaded color slides while their facial expressions were recorded, authors found females sent more accurate communication than males. More accurate senders had smaller skin conductance and slower heart rate and gave a more personal report of their emotions. Females tended to be externalizers (above median on communication accuracy, below on skin conductance), while males were internalizers (opposite pattern).

* Burke, Ronald J., and Tamara Weir. "Patterns in Husbands' and Wives' Coping Behaviors." *Psychological Reports,* 44 (1979), 951-956. See item 323.

* Cary, Mark S. "The Role of Gaze in the Intiation of Conversation." *Social Psychology,* 41 (1978), 269-271. See item 1046.

* Cary, Mark S., and Dave Rudick-Davis. "Judging the Sex of an Unseen Person from Nonverbal Cues." *Sex Roles,* 5 (1979), 355-361. See item 1265.

* Casciani, Joseph M. "Influence of Model's Race and Sex on Interviewee's Self-Disclosure." *Journal of Counseling Psychology,* 25 (1978), 435-440. See item 713.

* Cash, Thomas F. "Self-Disclosure in Initial Acquaintanceship: Effects of Sex, Approval Motivation, and Physical Attractiveness." *JSAS: Catalog of Selected Documents in Psychology,* 8 (1978), 11. (Ms. No. 1642). See item 714.

* Cash, Thomas F., and Jo Anne Kehr. "Influence of Nonprofessional Counselors' Physical Attractiveness and Sex on Perceptions of Counselor Behavior." *Journal of Counseling Psychology,* 25 (1978), 336-342. See item 532.

* Cegala, Donald J., Sydel Sokuvitz, and Alison F. Alexander. "An Investigation of Eye Gaze and Its Relation to Selected Verbal Behavior." *Human Communication Research,* 5 (1979), 99-108. See item 1047.

* Centers, Richard, and Bertram H. Raven. "Conjugal Power Structure: A Re-Examination." *American Sociological Review,* 36 (1971), 264-278. See item 324.

104. Cherry, Louise. "Teacher-Child Verbal Interaction: An Approach to the Study of Sex Differences." In *Language and Sex: Difference and Dominance* (item 1326), pp. 172-183.

    To determine how the sex of a child affected the verbal interaction between four female teachers and 38 boys and girls in nursery school (age range from two years four months to four years five months), spontaneous classroom interactions were recorded and analyzed. Based on previous findings, it was hypothesized that teacher-girl dyads would be more fluent and would be teacher-initiated, while teacher-boy dyads would be boy-initiated, teacher-boy question-answer interactions would more likely be acknowledged, and teacher's speech to boys would be more controlling and attention-getting. The first two hypotheses were not substantiated, the third was significant for teacher-girl dyads, not teacher-boy dyads. The fourth hypothesis was supported for attention-getting but was not for controlling, though the trend was in the predicted direction.

* Chelune, Gordon J. "A Multidimensional Look at Sex and Target Differences in Disclosure." *Psychological Reports,* 39 (1976), 259-263. See item 716.

* Chelune, Gordon J. "Sex Differences, Repression-Sensitization, and Self-Disclosure: A Behavioral Look." *Psychological Reports,* 40 (1977), 667-670. See item 719.

* Chelune, Gordon J., Faye E. Sultan, and Carolyn L. Williams. "Loneliness, Self-Disclosure, and Interpersonal Effectiveness." *Journal of Counseling Psychology,* 27 (1980), 462-468. See item 721.

105. Cherulnik, Paul D., William T. Neely, Martha Flanagan, and Max Zachau. "Social Skill and Visual Interaction." *The Journal of Social Psychology,* 104 (1978), 263-270.

    Twenty-three dyads of unacquainted male and female undergraduates, representing high- or low-dating frequency and high- or low-social skills, were observed in unstructured conversation. High-skill subjects had more eye contact, including when speaking, and shared conversation time more equally. No significant differences by sex were found.

* Cheyne, James A., and Michael G. Efran. "The Effect of Spatial and Interpersonal Variables on the Invasion of Group Controlled Territories." *Sociometry,* 35 (1972), 477-489. See item 1148.

* Clore, Gerald L., Nancy H. Wiggins, and Stuart Itkin. "Gain and Loss in Attraction: Attributions from Nonverbal Behavior." *Journal of Personality and Social Psychology,* 31 (1975), 706-712. See item 1267.

* Cole, C.W., E.R. Oetting, and N.G. Dinges. "Effects of Verbal Interaction Conditions on Self-Concept Discrimination and Anxiety." *Journal of Counseling Psychology,* 20 (1973), 431-436. See item 12.

* Courtright, John A., Frank E. Millar, and L. Edna-Rogers-Millar. "Domineeringness and Dominance: Replication and Expansion." *Communication Monographs,* 46 (1979), 179-192. See item 325.

* Coutts, Larry M., and Maribeth Ledden. "Nonverbal Compensatory Reactions to Changes in Interpersonal Proximity." *The Journal of Social Psychology,* 102 (1977), 283-290. See item 1149.

* Coutts, Larry M., and Frank W. Schneider. "Affiliative Conflict Theory: An Investigation of the Intimacy, Equilibrium and Compensation Hypothesis." *Journal of Personality and Social Psychology,* 34 (1976), 1135-42. See item 1049.

* Coutts, Larry M., and Frank W. Schneider. "Visual Behavior in an Unfocused Interaction as a Function of Sex and Distance." *Journal of Experimental Social Psychology,* 11 (1975), 64-77. See item 1050.

* Cozby, Paul C. "Self-disclosure, Reciprocity and Liking." *Sociometry,* 35 (1972), 151-160. See item 723.

106. Cunningham, John D. "Boy Meets Girl: Patterns of Interaction and Attribution in Heterosexual Attraction." *Journal of Personality and Social Psychology,* 34 (1976), 334-343.

    Fifty male and female undergraduates evaluated the pairing possibility of two males and two females in a conversation reflecting five potential patterns of interaction. Subjects rated high-interaction couples more likely to pair up than the others, and popularity-based couples, contrary to prediction, more likely to have a future close relationship than pairing-based couples (conversation specific to each other). High correlations between friendliness and popularity and between judgments of who spoke more often and was spoken to more often accounted for the deviation from prediction. Correlations were higher for males than for females, suggesting sex-role stereotyping that females should be passive partner, not talking one, in heterosexual relationships.

107. Davis, Deborah, and Harry J. Martin. "When Pleasure Begets Pleasure: Recipient Responsiveness as a Determinant of Physical Pleasuring Between Heterosexual Dating Couples and Strangers." *Journal of Personality and Social Psychology,* 36 (1978), 767-777.

Using 160 couples, known or unknown to each other, giving and receiving varying amounts of pleasure through a Niagara wave generator chair and with or without verbal feedback from receiver, researchers found females gave significantly less pleasure than males and felt significantly less comfortable doing so. Both findings were attributable to responses of females to male strangers who verbally responded. Generally, however, verbal responsiveness increased liking for recipient and enjoyment from giving pleasure, whether couple or stranger pairs.

108. Davis, Deborah, and William T. Perkowitz. "Consequences of Responsiveness in Dyadic Interaction: Effects of Probability of Response and Proportion of Content-Related Responses on Interpersonal Attraction." *Journal of Personality and Social Psychology,* 37 (1979), 534-550.

In dyads formed with 176 male and female undergraduates and a same-sex confederate, in which the confederate's responses were manipulated for frequency and probability (Experiment 1) or for proportion of content-related responses (Experiment 2), authors found that both probability of response and proportion of content-related responses were positively related to attraction, subject's perception of confederate's attraction to them, and degree of perceived acquaintanceship. No sex differences were found.

109. Davis, Deborah, Hal G. Rainey, and Timothy C. Brock. "Interpersonal Physical Pleasuring: Effects of Sex Combinations, Recipient Attributes, and Anticipated Future Interaction." *Journal of Personality and Social Psychology,* 33 (1976), 89-106.

In a series of four experiments using between 89 and 439 undergraduate subjects delivering via mechanical means physical pleasure to a partner under varying conditions, researchers found more pleasuring given to opposite-sex than same-sex partner, and responsive and attractive recipients in same-sex pairs elicited more pleasuring than nonresponsive and unattractive. Oral responsiveness led to lower giving of pleasure in opposite-sex pairs except males to unattractive females. Expectation of future interaction increased pleasuring; interaction with a dissimilar, hostile recipient before experiment reduced pleasuring.

110. Davis, John D. "When Boy Meets Girl: Sex Roles and the Negotiation of Intimacy in an Acquaintance Exercise." *Journal of Personality and Social Psychology,* 36 (1978), 684-692.

    Using 74 female and 38 male undergraduates in mixed-sex dyads discussing topics selected from intimacy-scaled list, Davis found that males controlled topic choice and the pace of disclosure as well, proceeding independently of female partner. Females matched the pace, but selected less intimate topics and reported less enjoyment of the encounters. Data were interpreted as consistent with sex-role stereotyped behavior in interpersonal encounters.

111. Davis, John D., and Adrian E.G. Skinner. "Reciprocity of Self-Disclosure in Interviews: Modeling or Social Exchange?" *Journal of Personality and Social Psychology,* 29 (1974), 779-784.

    A male interviewed 18 male and 18 female undergraduates on ten high-intimacy topics under varying degrees of disclosure by the interviewer or by a male-audiotape model. In-person disclosure facilitated disclosure of subjects more than the audiotape model did. For males, interviewer disclosure enhanced content modeling as well.

* Deaux, Kay, and Janet Taynor. "Evaluation of Male and Female Ability: Bias Works Two Ways." *Psychological Reports,* 32 (1973), 261-262. See item 81.

* Derlega, Valerian, and Alan L. Chaikin. "Norms Affecting Self-Disclosure in Men and Women." *Journal of Consulting and Clinical Psychology,* 44 (1976), 376-380. See item 725.

* Derlega, Valerian J., Midge Wilson, and Alan L. Chaikin. "Friendship and Disclosure Reciprocity." *Journal of Personality and Social Psychology,* 34 (1976), 578-582. See item 728.

* Doster, Joseph A. "Sex Role Learning and Interview Communication." *Journal of Counseling Psychology,* 23 (1976), 482-485. See item 730.

* Duckworth, Douglas H. "Personality, Emotional State, and Perception of Nonverbal Communication." *Perceptual and Motor Skills*, 40 (1975), 325-326. See item 1271.

112. Dumas, Bethany K. "Male-Female Conversational Interaction Cues: Using Data From Dialect Surveys." In *The Sociology of the Languages of American Women* (item 1003), pp. 41-52.

    A preliminary examination of the use of dialect data for sex differences in conversational interaction, using as examples two interviews with married couples in Newton County, Arkansas, leads Dumas to conclude that before full examination can be made three factors must be accounted for: the roles, primary or secondary, played by the interviewees; the "rules" of interaction for this kind of interview; and the relationship between the couple being interviewed.

* Ellsworth, Phoebe C., Howard S. Friedman, Deborah Perlick, and Michael E. Hoyt. "Some Effects of Gaze on Subjects Motivated to Seek or to Avoid Social Comparison." *Journal of Experimental and Social Psychology*, 14 (1978), 69-87, See item 1052.

* Ellsworth, Phoebe, and Lee Ross. "Intimacy in Response to Direct Gaze." *Journal of Experimental Social Psychology*, 11 (1975), 592-613. See item 1054.

* Ellyson, Steve L., John F. Dovidio, Randi L. Corson, and Debbie L. Vinicur. "Visual Dominance Behavior in Female Dyads: Situational and Personality Factors." *Social Psychology Quarterly*, 43 (1980), 328-336. See item 1055.

* Eubanks, Sheryle B. "Sex-Based Language Differences: A Cultural Reflection." In *Views on Language*. Eds. Reza Orboubadian and Walburga von Raffler-Engel. Murfreesboro, Tenn.: Inter-University Publishing, 1975, pp. 109-120. See item 776.

* Feldman, Robert S., and Lawrence F. Donohoe. "Nonverbal Communication of Affect in Interracial Dyads." *Journal of Educational Psychology*, 70 (1978), 979-987. See item 508.

* Ferguson, Nicola. "Simultaneous Speech, Interruptions and Dominance." *British Journal of Social and Clinical Psychology*, 16 (1977), 295-302. See item 821.

* Fishman, Pamela. "Interaction: The Work Woman Do." *Social Problems*, 25 (1978), 397-406. See item 332.

* Fishman, Pamela. "What Do Couples Talk About When They're Alone?" In *Women's Language and Style*. Eds. Douglas Butturff and Edmund Epstein. Akron, Ohio: University of Akron Press, 1978, pp. 11-22. See item 333.

* Fitzpatrick, Mary A., and Patricia Best. "Dyadic Adjustment in Relational Types: Consensus, Cohesion, Affectional Expression, and Satisfaction in Enduring Relationships." *Communication Monographs*, 46 (1979), 167-178. See item 334.

113. Fitzpatrick, Mary A., and Jeff Winke. "You Always Hurt the One You Love: Strategies and Tactics in Interpersonal Conflict." *Communication Quarterly*, 27, No. 1 (1979), 3-11.

    The conflict and control tactics of 183 female and 86 male undergraduates revealed that the five broad strategies used in interpersonal conflict were manipulation, nonnegotiation, emotional appeal, personal rejection, and empathic understanding. Same- and opposite-sex friends indicated that they utilized significantly different strategies: males and females reported that they employed different strategies with their same but not with opposite-sex friends. No significant differences were found in the conflict strategies employed in satisfied versus dissatisfied same-sex friendships.

114. Ford, W. Randolph, Gerald D. Weeks, and Alphonse Chapanis. "The Effect of Self-Imposed Brevity on the Structure of Dyadic Communication." *The Journal of Psychology*, 104 (1980), 87-103.

    Sixteen male pairs and 16 female pairs of undergraduates communicated to solve a problem either by voice or by teletypewriter. Half of each sex group was given no restrictions; the other half was given a monetary incentive to use as few words as possible. Analysis of the messages revealed that subjects trying to be brief made more information statements and fewer conversation control, judgmental, and feedback statements. These subjects used a higher percentage of nouns and adjectives and a lower one of pronouns, verbs, prepositions, interjections, and articles than unrestricted subjects. No differences by sex were found and few by mode of communication.

* Fox, Greer L., and Judith K. Inazu. "Patterns and Outcomes of Mother-Daughter Communication About Sexuality." *Journal of Social Issues,* 36, No. 1 (1980), 7-29. See item 335.

* Frances, Susan J. "Sex Differences in Nonverbal Behavior." *Sex Roles,* 5 (1979), 519-535. See item 1272.

* Fraser, Colin, and Naomi Roberts. "Mothers' Speech to Children of Four Different Ages." *Journal of Psycholinguistic Research,* 4 (1975), 9-16. See item 336.

* Freedman, Norbert, James O'Hanlon, Philip Oltman, and Herman A. Witkin. "The Imprint of Psychological Differentiation on Kinetic Behavior in Varying Communicative Contexts." *Journal of Abnormal Psychology,* 79 (1972), 239-258. See item 1033.

115. Friedman, Howard S. "Effects of Self-Esteem and Expected Duration of Interaction on Liking for a Highly Rewarding Partner." *Journal of Personality and Social Psychology,* 33 (1976), 686-690.

    Forty female undergraduates, in either induced high- or low-self-esteem conditions, either expecting or not to continue interacting with a confederate, received high rewards for an anagram task from that confederate. Those with low self-esteem reacted favorably to high rewards and those with high self-esteem unfavorably under the expectation of continuing interaction condition.

* Garnica, Olga K. "The Boys Have the Muscles and the Girls Have the Sexy Legs: Adult-Child Speech and the Use of Generic Person Labels." In *Language, Children and Society: The Effect of Social Factors on Children Learning to Communicate.* Eds. Olga K. Garnica and Martha L. King. Oxford: Pergamon, 1979, pp. 135-148. See item 933.

* Gilbert, Shirley J., and David Horenstein. "The Communication of Self-Disclosure: Level Versus Valence." *Human Communication Research,* 1 (1975), 316-322. See item 733.

* Givens, David B. "Contrasting Nonverbal Styles in Mother-Child Interaction: Examples from a Study of Child Abuse." *Semiotica,* 24, No. 1/2 (1978), 33-47. See item 338.

* Goffman, Erving. "Footing." *Semiotica,* 25, 1/2 (1979), 1-29. See item 935.

* Goldman, William, and Philip Lewis. "Beautiful Is Good: Evidence that the Physically Attractive Are More Socially Skillful." *Journal of Experimental Social Psychology,* 13 (1977), 125-130. See item 1105.

116. Golin, Sanford, and Michael A. Romanowski. "Verbal Aggression as a Function of Sex of Subject and Sex of Target." *Journal of Psychology,* 97 (1977), 141-149.

    Eighty students, equal numbers of each sex, were assigned randomly to a provocation or to a no-provocation condition in a situation in which they were to give a message varied in hostile content to a male or female confederate. No difference by sex in delivering the verbally aggressive message appeared, but sex of target/confederate did make a difference in the unprovoked condition, with verbal aggression inhibited for a female recipient. In the provoked condition, no sex differences appeared.

* Good, Thomas L., and Jere E. Brophy. "Behavioral Expression of Teacher Attitudes." *Journal of Educational Psychology,* 63 (1972), 617-624. See item 510.

* Good, Thomas L., J. Neville Sikes, and Jere E. Brophy. "Effects of Teacher Sex and Student Sex on Classroom Interaction." *Journal of Educational Psychology,* 65 (1973), 74-87. See item 511.

* Grantham, Robert J. "Effects of Counselor Sex, Race, and Language Style on Black Students in Initial Interviews." *Journal of Counseling Psychology,* 20 (1973), 553-559. See item 535.

* Greenberg, Roger P. "Sexual Bias in Rorschach Administration." *Journal of Personality Assessment,* 36 (1972), 336-339. See item 536.

* Greene, Les R. "Effects of Field Dependence on Affective Reactions and Compliance in Dyadic Interactions." *Journal of Personality and Social Psychology,* 34 (1976), 569-577. See item 1156.

* Greene, Les R. "Effects of Verbal Evaluative Feedback and Interpersonal Distance on Behavioral Compliance." *Journal of Counseling Psychology,* 24 (1977), 10-14. See item 1157.

* Greif, Esther B. "Sex Differences in Parent-Child Conversations." *Women's Studies International Quarterly*, 3 (1980), 253-258. See item 341.

* Haase, Richard F. "The Relationship of Sex and Instructional Set to the Regulation of Interpersonal Interaction Distance in a Counseling Analogue." *Journal of Counseling Psychology*, 17 (1970), 233-236. See item 1159.

* Hackney, Harold. "Facial Gestures and Subject Expression of Feelings." *Journal of Counseling Psychology*, 21 (1974), 173-178. See item 1084.

117. Hammen, Constance L., and Letitia A. Peplau. "Brief Encounters: Impact of Gender, Sex-Role Attitudes, and Partner's Gender on Interaction and Cognition." *Sex Roles*, 4 (1978), 75-90.

    The authors investigated the impact of gender and sex-role attitudes in interaction, information gathering, and liking, using 74 male and female undergraduates. They hypothesized that sex-role attitudes of the participant, his/her gender, and the partner's gender would affect responses. Sex-role-traditional subjects displayed behaviors consistent with previous research, while sex-role-liberal subjects exhibited different patterns, sitting closer, looking more, and talking more. Recall and description of the partner were also affected in complex fashion by participant gender and sex role and by partner gender. Liberal women were less accurate and detailed in describing other women than more traditional women were.

* Harris, Sandra, and Joseph Masling. "Examiner Sex, Subject Sex, and Rorschach Productivity." *Journal of Consulting and Clinical Psychology*, 34 (1970), 60-63. See item 538.

* Hawkins, James L., Carol Weisberg, and Dixie L. Ray. "Marital Communication Style and Social Class." *Journal of Marriage and the Family*, 39 (1977), 479-490. See item 345.

* Hedge, B.J., B.S. Everitt, and C.D. Frith. "The Role of Gaze in Dialogue." *Acta Psychologica*, 42 (1978), 453-475. See item 1058.

* Heilman, Madeline, and Kathy E. Kram. "Self-Derogating Behavior in Women--Fixed or Flexible: The Effects of

Co-Worker's Sex." *Organizational Behavior and Human Performance*, 22 (1978), 497-507. See item 583.

* Hershey, Sibilla, and Emmy Werner. "Dominance in Marital Decision Making in Women's Liberation and Non-Women's Liberation Families." *Family Process*, 14 (1975), 223-233. See item 348.

* Heshka, Stanley, and Yona Nelson. "Interpersonal Speaking Distance as a Function of Age, Sex, and Relationship." *Sociometry*, 35 (1972), 491-498. See item 1164.

* Highlen, Pamela S., and Sheila F. Gillis. "Effects of Situational Factors, Sex, and Attitude on Affective Self-disclosure and Anxiety." *Journal of Counseling Psychology*, 25 (1978), 270-276. See item 738.

* Hillman, Stephen B., and G. Gregory Davenport. "Teacher-Student Interactions in Desegregated Schools." *Journal of Educational Psychology*, 70 (1978), 545-553. See item 514.

118. Hilpert, Fred P., Cheris Kramer, and Ruth A. Clark. "Participants' Perceptions of Self and Partner in Mixed-Sex Dyads." *The Central States Speech Journal*, 26 (1975), 52-56.

   Fifty-seven undergraduate mixed-sex dyads discussed a specific problem for ten minutes, and then each participant completed a questionnaire indicating who contributed more to feelings of trust and friendship, who contributed more to the decision, and who talked more. Both males and females selected their partners slightly more frequently than themselves as the ones who contributed more to feelings of trust and friendship. In decision making, males selected themselves and their partners with almost equal frequency, whereas females selected their male partners twice as often as themselves. Females selected male partners as the one who talked more (estimated as 72% of the time), males selected themselves (estimated as 58% of the time); analysis of the actual time talked revealed that males spoke more (59% of the time).

* Holstein, Carolyn M., Joel W. Goldstein, and Daryl J. Bem. "The Importance of Expressive Behavior, Involvement, Sex, and Need-Approval in Induced Liking." *Journal of Experimental Social Psychology*, 7 (1971), 534-544. See item 1281.

* Horenstein, David, and Shirley J. Gilbert. "Anxiety, Likeability, and Avoidance as Responses to Self-Disclosing Communication." *Small Group Behavior,* 7 (1976), 423-432. See item 739.

* Horowitz, Leonard M., David Weckler, Amanda Saxon, Julie D. Livaudais, and Lana I. Boutacoff. "Discomforting Talk and Speech Disruptions." *Journal of Consulting and Clinical Psychology,* 45 (1977), 1036-42. See item 1233.

119. Höweler, Marijke, and Arie Vrolijk. "Verbal Communication Length as an Index of Interpersonal Interaction." *Acta Psychologica,* 34 (1970), 511-515.

    Forty male and 40 female undergraduates of the Free University in the Netherlands "spoke" two letters to a male or female, either liked or not, living in the United States to test the hypotheses that liked persons would evoke more words than unliked ones and that males would evoke more words than females regardless of sex of the "sender." Both hypotheses were supported.

120. Ickes, William, and Richard D. Barnes. "Boys and Girls Together--And Alienated: On Enacting Stereotyped Sex Roles in Mixed-Sex Dyads." *Journal of Personality and Psychology,* 36 (1978), 669-683.

    Forty-three dyads were formed of varied sex-role stereotyped and androgynous female and male college students for an unstructured five-minute discussion. Dyads in which both subjects were stereotypical had significantly less interaction and interpersonal attraction than the other dyads (talked, looked, gestured, etc., less frequently).

121. Ickes, William, and Richard D. Barnes. "The Role of Sex and Self-Monitoring in Unstructured Dyadic Interactions." *Journal of Personality and Social Psychology,* 35 (1977), 315-330.

    Thirty male and 30 female dyads, all selected on the basis of scores on a self-monitoring test, were covertly videotaped as they participated in an interview and then gave impressions of their own and partner's behavior. Female dyads had greater involvement and affiliation than male dyads. High self-monitoring subjects were more likely to initiate conversation and to perceive own and partner's behavior consistent with self-monitoring concepts. Dyads of a low and a high self-monitoring subject had most difficulty interacting.

122. Ickes, William, Brian Schermer, and Jeff Steeno. "Sex and Sex-Role Influences in Same-Sex Dyads." *Social Psychology Quarterly,* 42 (1979), 373-385.

   In this study, 126 males and females, previously tested for sex-role affiliation, intereacted in single-sex dyads and were evaluated for instrumental (masculine) and expressive (feminine) behaviors and interactional involvement (talking, looking, gesturing, etc.) Interactional involvement was high in dyads in which both instrumental and expressive capacities were used (androgynous males or females) and low in dyads in which only one set of capacities was used. In dyads with one stereotypically sex-typed individual and the other androgynous, the level of interaction appeared to depend on whether the androgyn used both sets of capabilities.

* Janofsky, A. Irene. "Affective Self-Disclosure Telephone Versus Face to Face Interviews." *Journal of Humanistic Psychology,* 11 (1971), 93-103. See item 740.

123. Johnson, David W. "The Distribution and Exchange of Information in Problem-Solving Dyads." *Communication Research,* 4 (1977), 283-298.

   Twenty female and twelve male college seniors were used as subjects in this study of the effects on problem-solving of information distributed equally in the dyad (homogeneously) or partially to each (heterogeneously) and the use of perspective-taking or egocentric styles of information exchange. Perspective-taking improved the quality of the problem solving, interpersonal trust, attitudes toward each other and the problem-solving experience, and perceptions of the value of the other's information. Heterogeneity of information did not affect problem-solving outcome when perspective-taking was used, but had a negative effect when egocentric style was used. No sex differences were found.

* Jourard, Sidney, and Robert Friedman. "Experimenter-Subject 'Distance' and Self-Disclosure." *Journal of Personality and Social Psychology,* 15 (1970), 278-282. See item 742.

124. Jourard, Sidney M., and Peggy E. Jaffe. "Influence of an Interviewer's Disclosure on the Self-Disclosing Behavior of Interviewees." *Journal of Counseling Psychology,* 17 (1970), 252-257.

   Forty female undergraduates, assigned to four groups based on levels of past disclosure, were interviewed by a female who varied the length of her remarks by group. A significant matching relationship was found; if the experimenter spoke briefly, the subjects did too; if she spoke at length, so did the subjects. Likewise, when the experimenter switched length of utterance, subjects matched the switch. Intimacy of topic did not significantly affect disclosure time.

* Jourard, Sidney M., and Jaquelyn L. Resnick. "Some Effects of Self-Disclosure Among College Women." *Journal of Humanistic Psychology,* 10 (1970), 84-93. See item 743.

* Jurich, Anthony P., and Julie A. Jurich. "Correlations Among Nonverbal Expressions of Anxiety." *Psychological Reports,* 34 (1974), 199-204. See item 1284.

125. Kelley, Harold H., John D. Cunningham, Jill A. Grisham, Luc M. Lefebvre, Cathy R. Sink, and Gilbert Yablon. "Sex Differences in Comments Made During Conflict Within Close Heterosexual Pairs." *Sex Roles,* 4 (1978), 473-492.

    Two studies, using 108 undergraduates and 56 student couples, tested the hypothesis that men would be both expected and reported to behave in an independent and rationalistic way, and women would be both expected and reported to show dependency and emotionality. Questionnaires from the undergraduates provided data on the stereotypes of what each sex would do and say during conflict, and reports from the couples provided data on what each one would likely do or say. Both sets of data revealed that the female was expected and reported to cry and sulk and to criticize the male for lack of consideration of her feelings and for insensitivity to his effect on her. The male was expected and reported to show anger, to reject the female's tears, to call for a logical and less emotional approach to the problem, and to give reasons for delaying the discussion. The results are interpreted in terms of the interaction between a conflict-avoidant person (the male) and his partner (the female), who is frustrated by the avoidance and asks that the problem and the feelings associated with it be confronted.

* Kelser, George J., and Irwin Altman. "Relationship of Nonverbal Behavior to the Social Penetration Process." *Human Communication Research,* 2 (1976), 147-167. See item 1285.

* Kendon, Adam. "Some Functions of the Face in a Kissing Round." *Semiotica*, 15, No. 4 (1975), 299-334. See item 1086.

126. Kerr, Barbara A., and Don M. Dell. "Perceived Interviewer Expertness and Attractiveness: Effects of Interviewer Behavior and Attire and Interview Setting." *Journal of Counseling Psychology*, 23 (1976), 553-556.

    Eighty undergraduates (34 males, 46 females), after a brief interview with a female interviewer playing an expert or an attractive (making positive similar self-disclosures) role, dressed professionally or casually, and interviewing in a professional or casual setting, rated the interviewer. Interviewer attractiveness was affected by interviewer behavior, while interviewer expertness was affected by both behavior and attire.

* King, Marc, and Guy J. Manaster. "Body Image, Self-esteem, Expectation, Self-assessment, and Actual Success in a Simulated Job Interview." *Journal of Applied Psychology*, 62 (1977), 589-594. See item 31.

127. Kleck, Robert E., and Angelo Strenta. "Perceptions of the Impact of Negatively Valued Physical Characteristics on Social Interaction." *Journal of Personality and Social Psychology*, 39 (1980), 861-873.

    In a series of four experiments, three with female undergraduates (N=25, 30, and 32) and one with 50 male and female undergraduates, subjects who thought they possessed a negatively valued physical characteristic (scar) found strong reactivity to the deviance from their partner in a dyadic interaction; those with more neutral characteristics (allergy) did not. An expectancy/perceptual bias mechanism was suggested, and established in subsequent experiments, as the explanation for the results.

128. Kleinke, Chris L. "Effects of False Feedback About Response Lengths on Subjects' Perception of an Interview." *The Journal of Social Psychology*, 95 (1975), 99-104.

    Sixty-four female college students were interviewed in four conditions: three had interruptions with feedback on her responses taking longer than average, about average, or shorter than average, and one had no interruption. Subjects in the feedback of longer-than-average response significantly increased their response length in the rest of the interview and rated interviewer's questions more favorably than the other groups of subjects.

* Kleinke, Chris L., Armando A. Bustos, Frederick B. Meeker, and Richard A. Staneski. "Effects of Self-Attributed and Other-Attributed Gaze on Interpersonal Evaluations Between Males and Females." *Journal of Experimental Social Psychology,* 9 (1973), 154-163. See item 1060.

* Kohen, Janet. "Liking and Self-Disclosure in Opposite Sex Dyads." *Psychological Reports,* 36 (1975), 695-698. See item 745.

* Kohen, Janet A.S. "The Development of Reciprocal Self-Disclosure in Opposite-Sex Interaction." *Journal of Counseling Psychology,* 22 (1975), 404-410. See item 746.

* Krail, Kristina, and Gloria Leventhal. "The Sex Variable in the Intrusion of Personal Space." *Sociometry,* 39 (1976), 170-173. See item 1167.

* Krivonos, Paul D. "The Effects of Attitude Similarity, Spatial Relationship, and Task Difficulty on Interpersonal Attraction." *Southern Speech Communication Journal,* 45 (1980), 240-248. See item 1168.

* Lalljee, Mansur, and Mark Cook. "Uncertainty in First Encounters." *Journal of Personality and Social Psychology,* 26 (1973), 137-141. See item 1235.

* Larwood, Laurie, and John Blackmore. "Sex Discrimination in Managerial Selection: Testing Predictions of the Vertical Dyad Linkage Model." *Sex Roles,* 4 (1978), 359-367. See item 608.

* Lesko, Wayne A. "Psychological Distance, Mutual Gaze, and the Affiliative-Conflict Theory." *The Journal of Social Psychology,* 103 (1977), 311-312. See item 1171.

* Levine, Marion H., and Brian Sutton-Smith. "Effects of Age, Sex, and Task on Visual Behavior during Dyadic Interaction." *Developmental Psychology,* 9 (1973), 400-405. See item 1064.

* Libby, William L., Jr., and Donna Yaklevich. "Personality Determinants of Eye Contact and Direction of Gaze

Aversion." *Journal of Personality and Social Psychology,* 27 (1973), 197-206. See item 1065.

129. Lindskold. Svenn, Robert A. Forte, Charles S. Haake, and Edward K. Schmidt. "The Effects of Directness of Face-to-Face Requests and Sex of Solicitor on Streetcorner Donations." *The Journal of Social Psychology,* 101 (1977), 45-51.

    Three male and three female undergraduates solicited contributions from about 3000 people in either a direct or indirect manner and in either sparse or thick pedestrian traffic conditions. The direct appeal was found more effective than the indirect, the amount contributed was greater in the sparse traffic conditions, and the female solicitors were more effective than the males in the interpersonal situation.

* Lombardo, John P., and Michael D. Berzonsky. "Sex Differences in Self-Disclosure During an Interview." *The Journal of Social Psychology,* 107 (1979), 281-282. See item 747.

130. Lowe, Roland, and James Murphy. "Communication Patterns in Engaged Couples." *Psychological Reports,* 31 (1972), 655-658.

    The communication of seven engaged couples was compared to that of seven stranger couples on various measures. Engaged couples interrupted more, changed topics more, disagreed more, and were more committed in their communication than strangers. Strangers asked more questions. No sex differences were reported.

131. Lowery, Carol R., C.R. Snyder, and Nancy W. Denney. "Perceived Aggression and Predicted Counteraggression as a Function of Sex of Dyad Participants: When Males and Females Exchange Verbal Blows." *Sex Roles,* 2 (1976), 339-346.

    Thirty male and 35 female undergraduates evaluated participants in written, hypothetical dyadic interactions. Female aggressors were not perceived as more aggressive than male aggressors. No difference in aggresiveness between a male insulting another male and a male insulting a female was perceived. A female who insulted another female was perceived as more aggressive, however, than a female who insulted a male. Subjects predicted that a female would elicit less counteraggression than a male only when interacting with a male.

* Lynn, Steven J. "Three Theories of Self-Disclosure Exchange." *Journal of Experimental Social Psychology*, 14 (1978), 466-479. See item 749.

132. McClintock, Charles C., and Raymond G. Hunt. "Nonverbal Indicators of Affect and Deception in an Interview Setting." *Journal of Applied Social Psychology*, 5 (1975), 54-67.

    Ten male and 10 female college students were interviewed on topics manipulated for pleasantness to interviewer and for deception. Unpleasant topics resulted in more smiling, postural shifts, and self-touching, and deception responses in less smiling and more postural shifts and self-touching. No significant sex differences were found, although females smiled more than males.

133. McCormick, Naomi B. "Come-ons and Put-offs: Unmarried Students' Strategies for Having and Avoiding Sexual Intercourse." *Psychology of Women Quarterly*, 4 (1979), 194-211.

    To test the hypothesis that both sexes view males as using strategies to have sex while females use strategies to avoid sex, 120 male and 109 female unmarried undergraduates responded on a dating attitudes questionnaire about their use of strategies such as reward, coercion, logic, manipulation, body language, etc. Men and women were unexpectedly similar in their personal strategies for influencing a sexual encounter. Both reported using more indirect strategies to have sex and more direct strategies to avoid sex.

* McCroskey, James C., Virginia P. Richmond, John A. Daly, and Barbara G. Cox. "The Effects of Communication Apprehension on Interpersonal Attraction." *Human Communication Research*, 2 (1975), 51-65. See item 787.

134. McNeel, Steven P., Charles G. McClintock, and Jozef M. Nuttin, Jr. "Effects of Sex Role in a Two-Person Mixed Motive Game." *Journal of Personality and Social Psychology*, 24 (1972), 372-380.

    Using 72 males and 72 females in same-sex and mixed-sex dyads playing the Prisoner's Dilemma game, authors found that female dyads were less competitive but not significantly so; mixed-sex dyads were significantly less competitive than same-sex ones, due primarily to reduction in male competitiveness; and females were less willing to lose to males than males to females.

* Mahoney, John, and Donna M.L. Heretick. "Factor-Specific Dimensions in Person Perception for Same- and Opposite-Sex Friendship Dyads." *The Journal of Social Psychology,* 107 (1979), 219-225. See item 41.

* Mandelcorn, Berenice S., and R.O. Pihl. "Maternal Expectation and the Mother-Child Interaction." *Psychological Reports,* 47 (1980), 307-317. See item 356.

135. Manis, Melvin, S. Douglas Cornell, and Jeffrey C. Moore. "Transmission of Attitude-Relevant Information Through a Communication Chain." *Journal of Personality and Social Psychology,* 30 (1974), 81-94.

    Ninety-six female undergraduates, all in favor of legalizing marijuana, summarized the main points of a speech on the topic to a bogus other who was either for or against legalization. Raters of summaries judged those summaries to pro-legalization others as from speeches more favorable than summaries to anti-legalization others. In a subsequent study, raters judged as better those summaries that supported the listener's viewpoint, regardless of the viewpoint of the summarizer.

136. Markel, Norman N., Joseph F. Long, and Thomas J. Saine. "Sex Effects in Conversational Interaction: Another Look at Male Dominance." *Human Communication Research,* 2 (1976), 356-364.

    To assess the independent and interactive effects of communicator sex, listener sex, and interpersonal distance on temporal measures of conversational interaction, 30 male and 30 female undergraduates in same- and mixed-sex dyads conversed in near (three feet) or far (12 feet) conditions. The average duration of speech acts was significantly longer for females than for males. Communicators, regardless of sex, spoke for a greater proportion of the total conversation when the listener was female. Within same-sex male dyads, far interpersonal distance was associated with significantly greater simultaneous speech compared to the near condition. The results are interpreted to refute traditional notions of male dominance.

* Markel, Norman N., Layne D. Prebor, and John F. Brandt. "Biosocial Factors in Dyadic Communication: Sex and Speaking Intensity." *Journal of Personality and Social Psychology,* 23 (1972), 11-13. See item 1239.

137. Marlatt, C. Alan. "A Comparison of Vicarious and Direct Reinforcement Control of Verbal Behavior in an Interview Setting." *Journal of Personality and Social Psychology,* 16 (1970), 695-703.

In a study to compare the effects of various kinds of reinforcement on discussion of personal problems by 96 male and female undergraduates in interviews, vicarious reinforcement had the greatest effect. Female interviewers received more information than male interviewers, and female subjects gave most information, regardless of reinforcement, to a female interviewer, and least to a male interviewer. Male subjects, however, talked significantly more.

138. Marquis, Kent H. "Effects of Social Reinforcement on Health Reporting in the Household Interview." *Sociomtry,* 33 (1970), 203-215.

In this field study, the responses of 429 adult females to questions about family health from specially trained females using various interview methods were analyzed in light of the interview method. The reinforcement method of interviewing resulted in an increase in the number of reported items, including embarrassing ones.

139. Mazanec, Nancy, and George J. McCall. "Sex Factors and Allocation of Attention in Observing Persons." *Journal of Psychology,* 93 (1976), 175-180.

Thirty-three male and 39 female undergraduates viewed standard videotapes of two males and two females in interview situations and then responded in an unstructured, free-recall test. Female subjects were relatively more attentive to gestures and verbal style, while male subjects were more attentive to appearance and verbal content. For male interviewees, subjects focused attention on verbal stimuli, while for female interviewees, attention was focused on visual stimuli. Females had a significantly greater number of responses than males.

140. Mazen, Ragaa, and Howard Leventhal. "The Influence of Communicator-Recipient Similarity Upon the Beliefs and Behavior of Pregnant Women." *Journal of Experimental Social Psychology,* 8 (1972), 289-302.

In this field experiment, the effects of communicator-recipient similarity (race, pregnant or not) and verbal communication (informative only, or informative with personal endorsement, or no information) on breast feeding and rooming-in on the attitudes and behaviors of 140 pregnant women at a medical clinic were studied. Communication conditions did not significantly affect either attitude change or behavior. Similarity of race and pregnancy did not affect attitude either, but both affected behavior. Generally, attitude change was unrelated to behavioral compliance.

141. Meeker, Barbara F., and Carlton A. Hornung. "Strategies of Interaction." *Social Science Research,* 5 (1976), 153-172.

    This study investigated status, reciprocity, and sex roles as bases for the strategies or rules that individuals in task-oriented groups use in deciding how to organize their interactions. One hundred undergraduates (38 mixed-sex dyads, 40 same-sex dyads, and 22 married pairs) participated in a two-person, Prisoner's Dilemma-type game in which information to participants was systematically controlled. Higher status persons contributed more to the task solution than lower status persons when they were rewarded as a dyad and less when they were rewarded as individuals. Females were less likely to contribute to solutions under both cooperative and competitive conditions. Females cooperated less; both sexes cooperated less with females than with males.

142. Mehrabian, Albert. "Verbal and Nonverbal Interaction of Strangers in a Waiting Situation." *Journal of Experimental Research in Personality,* 5 (1971), 127-138.

    One hundred twenty-six female and 128 male undergraduates were observed as they interacted with a same-sex confederate behaving either slightly negatively or slightly positively toward the subject in both verbal and nonverbal ways. Positive affect cues correlated positively with the number of statements made, and in general subjects reciprocated the behavior of the confederates. Females were more affiliative and more intimate; males showed greater distress when the confederate was negative.

143. Messé, Lawrence A., et al. "Interpersonal Consequences of Person Perception Processes in Two Social Contexts." *Journal of Personality and Social Psychology,* 37 (1979), 369-379.

    Over 1100 undergraduates viewed on videotape and then

interacted with a male or female child; a subset of these subjects discussed issues with a male or female confederate. Several sex differences were found: male adults were more dominant, females more cooperative; children were more dominant toward female adults and were more cooperative with and submissive to male adults. In the discussion study with a female confederate, coders rated subjects more intelligent and comfortable, while discussants themselves rated each other as more negative, less likable, and persuasive.

144. Miller, Larry D. "Dyadic Perception of Communicator Style: Replication and Confirmation." *Communication Research,* 4 (1977), 87-112.

This replication of an earlier study which found that the style of a communicator was related to the perception of communicator behavior in a dyad used 327 undergraduates, pretested for communicator style, in same- and mixed-sex dyads completing a joint task. Analysis of dominance and control of outcome by trained raters confirmed that low-scoring pretest subjects did not perceive a difference between their style and that of high-scoring subjects, who did perceive the difference. Sex of subject had no effect on these findings.

145. Morton, Teru L. "Intimacy and Reciprocity of Exchange: A Comparison of Spouses and Strangers." *Journal of Personality and Social Psychology,* 36 (1978), 72-81.

Non-structured conversation of 24 married couples and 24 opposite-sex strangers on topics selected from a list containing intimate and nonintimate topics were analyzed. Married couples communicated more descriptive intimacy (private facts), but not more evaluative intimacy (personal feelings), and reciprocated intimacy less. Females had greater evaluative intimacy than males. A tendency was noted for strangers to trivialize intimate topics and for spouses to personalize nonintimate ones.

146. Murray, Robert P., and Hugh McGinley. "Looking as a Measure of Attraction." *Journal of Applied Social Psychology,* 2 (1972), 267-274.

One hundred and sixty-six female undergraduates either read a female stranger's bogus questionnaire or viewed a tape of a stranger reading her responses, the responses controlled for varying levels of agreement with subject's own attitudes. Later, time in looking at photographs of the bogus stranger or another stranger was measured. The degree of attitude similarity was significantly related to looking time toward the bogus stranger's photograph, both for those who were aware of similarity-attraction interaction and those who were not.

* Murstein, Bernard I., and Patricia Choisty. "Physical Attractiveness and Marriage Adjustment in Middle-Aged Couples." *Journal of Personality and Social Psychology,* 34 (1976), 537-542. See item 1119.

147. Natale, Michael. "Effects of Induced Elation-Depression on Speech in the Initial Interview." *Journal of Consulting and Clinical Psychology,* 45 (1977), 45-52.

    Three groups of 45 female college students participated in a telephone interview interrupted mid-way by a manipulated emotional state (elation, depression, neutral). Elation resulted in shorter response latencies, faster speech and articulation rates, and a lower silence quotient. Depression produced a greater silence quotient than either elation or neutral conditions.

148. Natale, Michael, Elliot Entin, and Joseph Jaffe. "Vocal Interruptions in Dyadic Communication as a Function of Speech and Social Anxiety." *Journal of Personality and Social Psychology,* 37 (1979), 865-878.

    Using 36 dyads (12 of each sex, 12 mixed sex) in 30-minute unstructured conversations, authors analyzed interruptions and personality measures. Interruptive behavior was inversely related to speech anxiety, positively related to speaker confidence, and inversely related to social anxiety (avoidance, fear of negative evaluation). Males engaged in more vocal interruptions than females.

* Noller, Patricia. "Misunderstandings in Marital Communication: A Study of Couples' Nonverbal Communication." *Journal of Personality and Social Psychology,* 39 (1980), 1135-48. See item 360.

149. Octigan, Mary, and Sharon Niederman. "Male Dominance in Conversations." *Frontiers,* 4, No. 1 (1979), 50-54.

    The taped interactions of 30 single- or mixed-sex dyads whose members had varying attitudes toward sex stereotyping were examined for dominance behavior. Halfway through the 20-minute conversations dyads were informed that males were more likely to interrupt conversations than females. Thereafter, interruptions for all dyads dropped significantly, but overall males produced almost all of the dominant behavior, including interruptions. Attitude toward sex stereotyping made no difference.

150. Olesker, Wendy, and Lawrence Balter. "Sex and Empathy." *Journal of Counseling Psychology,* 19 (1972), 559-562.

    Ninety-six students (48 M, 48 F) judged the feelings of eight male and female clients seen in videotapes. No sex difference in empathetic ability emerged, but each sex showed more empathy when judging same-sex clients than opposite-sex clients.

* O'Neill, Michael S., and James F. Alexander. "Family Interaction Patterns as a Function of Task Characteristics." *Journal of Applied Social Psychology,* 1 (1971), 163-172. See item 361.

* Pakizegi, Behnaz. "The Interaction of Mothers and Fathers with Their Sons." *Child Development,* 49 (1978), 479-482. See item 362.

* Pasternack, Thomas L., and Martha Van Landingham. "A Comparison of the Self-Disclosure Behavior of Female Undergraduates and Married Women." *Journal of Psychology,* 82 (1972), 233-240. See item 752.

151. Patterson, Miles L., and Lee B. Sechrest. "Interpersonal Distance and Impression Formation." *Journal of Personality,* 38 (1970), 161-166.

    To examine impression formation as a function of interpersonal distance in an interview, 24 male and 24 female undergraduates were approached by three male and three female undergraduate confederates who took seats for an interview at varying distances from the subjects. Subjects rated the confederates less friendly, aggressive, extroverted, and dominant as the distance increased. Male confederates were rated more dominant than female confederates, while females were rated more extroverted than males. No differences were found in aggressiveness or friendliness between male and female confederates.

* Pearce, W. Barnett, Paul H. Wright, Stewart M. Sharp, and Katherine M. Slama. "Affection and Reciprocity in Self-Disclosing Communication." *Human Communication Research,* 1 (1974), 5-14. See item 753.

* Pedersen, Darhl M., and Anne B. Heaston. "The Effects of Sex of Subject, Sex of Approaching Person, and Angle of Approach Upon Personal Space." *Journal of Psychology,* 82 (1972), 277-286. See item 1183.

* Pellegrini, Robert J., Robert A. Hicks, and Susan Myers-Winton. "Effects of Simulated Approval-Seeking and Avoiding on Self-Disclosure, Self-Presentation, and Interpersonal Attraction." *Journal of Psychology,* 98 (1978), 231-240. See item 755.

* Pellegrini, Robert J., Robert A. Hicks, Susan Meyers-Winton, and Bruce G. Antal. "Physical Attractiveness and Self-Disclosure in Mixed-Sex Dyads." *The Psychological Record,* 28 (1978), 509-516. See item 756.

152. Peplau, Letitia A. "Impact of Fear of Success and Sex-Role Attitudes on Women's Competitive Achievement." *Journal of Personality and Social Psychology,* 34 (1976), 561-568.

    This experimental and correlational study of 91 college couples performing a verbal task alone or together and various measures of ability, sex-role attitudes, etc., revealed that females with traditional attitudes performed better in pairs than individually; nontraditional females did just the opposite. Fear of success was found not to correlate with own sex-role attitudes, career aspirations, college grades, SAT scores, or self-ratings on intelligence, but sex-role traditionalism was associated with lower measures on all of these but college grades.

* Poling, Tommy H. "Sex Differences, Dominance, and Physical Attractiveness in the Use of Nonverbal Emblems." *Psychological Reports,* 43 (1978), 1087-92. See item 1122.

* Polit, Denise, and Marianne La France. "Sex Differences in Reaction to Spatial Invasion." *The Journal of Social Psychology,* 102 (1977), 59-60. See item 1184.

153. Pope, Benjamin, Aron W. Seigman, and Thomas Blass. "Anxiety and Speech in the Initial Interview." *Journal of*

Consulting and Clinical Psychology, 35 (1970), 233-238.

Thirty-two nursing students were interviewed twice, 16 in low-anxious and then high-anxious situations, and 16 in two low-anxious situations. The first group had a significantly increased amount of talking as well as an increase in speech disturbances.

154. Powell, J.C., D.V. Belcher, J.T. Kitchens, and L.C. Emerson. "The Influence of Selected Variables on the Employment Interview Situation." *Journal of Applied Communications Research,* 3 (1975), 33-51.

    The interviews of 45 males and 16 females by one male and one female interviewer with the City of Gainesville, Florida, were analyzed for communication willingness, effectiveness, and personal impression related to sex, educational level, work experience, and status level of job applied for. The sex difference findings were that females received higher ratings, and the female interviewer gave higher ratings than the male interviewer.

155. Powell, James L., and James T. Kitchens. "Elements of Participant Satisfaction in Dyads." *Southern Speech Communication Journal,* 41 (1975), 59-68.

    Twenty-one male-female dyads conversed on any topic, and then each member completed a satisfaction scale and wrote an essay on his or her orientation toward self and the other in the dyad. An individual's perception of the other's contributions to the conversation was significant in determining satisfaction with that dialogue. Females expressed their reactions in more self-oriented terms, while males had more mutual-oriented statements.

156. Powers, William G., and Robert B. Glenn. "Perceptions of Friendly Insult Greetings in Interpersonal Relationships." *Southern Speech Communication Journal,* 44 (1979), 264-274.

    Ninety-two male and 92 female undergraduates evaluated the acceptability and use of friendly insult greetings to a stranger, an acquaintance, a friend, and an intimate friend. Under same-sex conditions, acceptability and use increased from stranger to acquaintance to friend levels; under opposite-sex conditions, they increased between acquaintance and friend levels, but not between friend and intimate friend levels.

* Powers, William G., and Delana Guess. "Research Note on 'Invasion of Males' Personal Space by Feminists and Non-Feminists.'" *Psychological Reports,* 38 (1976), 1300. See item 1186.

* Putnam, Linda L., and Linda McCallister. "Situational Effects of Task and Gender on Nonverbal Display." In *Communication Yearbook 4.* Ed. Dan Nimmo. New Brunswick, N.J.: Transaction Books, 1980, pp. 679-697. See item 1295.

157. Rivera, Alba N., and James T. Tedeschi. "Public Versus Private Reactions to Positive Inquiry." *Journal of Personality and Social Psychology,* 34 (1976), 895-900.

    Sixty female undergraduates in a worker-with-supervisor/confederate situation received two levels of rewards or an equal reward for a task in which all subject input was identical, and then rated their supervisor and their feelings. Those reporting via a paper-and-pencil test reported feeling guilty and less happy and liking supervisor less the greater the reward they received. Those reporting via a bogus pipeline reported happier feelings and liking supervisor more the greater the reward.

* Robert, M. Evans, Paul D. Cherulnik, et al. "Sex Composition and Intimacy in Dyads: A Field Study." *Journal of Social Psychology,* 110 (1980), 139-140. See item 1297.

158. Rogers, William T., and Stanley E. Jones. "Effects of Dominance Tendencies on Floor Holding and Interruption Behavior in Dyadic Interaction." *Human Communication Research,* 1 (1975), 113-122.

    Eighteen dyads (10 F, 8 M), each with one high and one low dominance person, completed a cooperative problem-solving discussion task. Analysis of their interaction revealed that high dominance persons held the floor more and attempted more interruptions in proportion to their partners' total speaking time than did those with less dominant personalities. The results appeared to be consistently stronger among males, but there were no significant sex differences.

* Rogers-Millar, L. Edna, and Frank E. Millar, III. "Domineeringness and Dominance: A Transactional View." *Human Communication Research,* 5 (1979), 238-246. See item 368.

* Rosegrant, Teresa J., and James C. McCroskey. "The Effect of Race and Sex on Proxemic Behavior in an Interview Setting." *Southern Speech Communication Journal*, 40 (1975), 408-420. See item 1187.

159. Rosen, Sidney, Robert D. Johnson, Martha J. Johnson, and Abraham Tesser. "Interactive Effects of News Valence and Attraction on Communicator Behavior." *Journal of Personality and Social Psychology*, 28 (1973), 298-300.

    Fifty-five female undergraduates were asked to transmit good or bad news to an attractive or unattractive recipient. Good news was more likely to be communicated than bad news, and bad news more likely to attractive than to unattractive recipients. Subjects perceived unattractive recipients as less deserving of good news.

160. Rosenbluh, Edward S. "Interaction of Subject and Experimenter Sex with the Body Percept in Verbal Concept Identification." *Journal of Abnormal Psychology*, 80 (1972), 149-156.

    Sixty-four male and 64 female undergraduates divided into high- and low-body percept scorers were tested by making sentences from body part cue words and by problem-solving with either a male or female experimenter. With same-sex experimenter, high-percept subjects talked more and solved the problem more quickly. Low-percept subjects did better with opposite-sex experimenters. Overall, high percept subjects solved problems faster than low-percept subjects.

161. Rosenthal, Saul F. "The Relationship of Attraction and Sex Composition to Performance and Nonperformance Experimental Outcomes in Dyads." *Sex Roles*, 4 (1978), 887-898.

    This study of 90 same- and mixed-sex dyads, either intra- or interracial, investigated the relationship of interpersonal attraction and sex composition to performance on a verbal and on a quantitative problem-solving task. Rosenthal found no relationship between interpersonal attraction and dyadic performance. Nearing significance, high levels of attraction appeared to facilitate performance for mixed-sex and all-female dyads, but not for all-male dyads. Among the all-female dyads, racial composition of the dyad was significantly related to satisfaction: interracial dyads had higher levels of satisfaction than intraracial dyads. No significant association between attraction and performance was evident, but attraction and satisfaction appeared to be related.

* Roth, Marvin, and Don Kuiken. "Communication Immediacy, Cognitive Compatibility, and Immediacy of Self-Disclosure." *Journal of Counseling Psychology,* 22 (1975), 102-107. See item 760.

* Rubin, Zick, Charles T. Hill, Letitia A. Peplau, and Christine Dunkel-Schetter. "Self-Disclosure in Dating Couples: Sex Roles and the Ethic of Openness." *Journal of Marriage and the Family,* 42 (1980), 305-317. See item 761.

* Saine, Thomas J., Madlyn A. Levine, and Gaylynn E. McHose. "Assessing the Structure of Nonverbal Interaction." *Southern Speech Communication Journal,* 40 (1975), 275-287. See item 1303.

* Sanders, Jeffrey L. "Relation of Personal Space to the Human Menstrual Cycle." *Journal of Psychology,* 100 (1978), 275-278. See item 1188.

* Schneider, Frank W., and Christine L. Hansvick. "Gaze and Distance as a Function of Change in Interpersonal Gaze." *Social Behavior and Personality,* 5 (1977), 49-53. See item 1069.

* Schwarzwald, Joseph, Naomi Kavish, Monica Shoham, and Mark Waysman. "Fear and Sex-Similarity as Determinants of Personal Space." *Journal of Psychology,* 96 (1977), 55-61. See item 1189.

* Sermat, Vello, and Michael Smith. "Content Analysis of Verbal Communication in the Development of a Relationship." *Journal of Personality and Social Psychology,* 26 (1973), 332-346. See item 762.

* Shuter, Robert. "A Field Study of Nonverbal Communication in Germany, Italy, and the United States." *Communication Monographs,* 44 (1977), 298-305. See item 1305.

* Skotko, Vincent P., and Daniel Langmeyer. The Effects of Interaction Distance and Gender on Self-Disclosure in the Dyad." *Sociometry,* 40 (1977), 178-182. See item 763.

* Smith, Robert J., and Patrick E. Cook. "Leadership in Dyadic Groups as a Function of Dominance and Incentives." *Sociometry*, 36 (1973), 561-568. See item 620.

162. Spence, Janet T., Robert Helmreich, and Joy Stapp. "Likeability, Sex-Role Congruence of Interest, and Competence: It All Depends on How You Ask." *Journal of Applied Social Psychology*, 5 (1975), 93-109.

    Four videotapes of a male or female being interviewed, portrayed as competent or not and as having masculine or feminine interests, were rated by 385 male and 552 female students, some immediately, and some after completing an open-ended question measure. In immediate-rating condition, subjects liked competent interviewees better than incompetent ones and masculine better than feminine ones. However, in the delayed rating of female interviewees, conservative male and female subjects liked the feminine competent interviewee better than the masculine competent, and liberal males shifted likewise but even more strongly both in increased liking for feminine competent and dramatically decreased liking for the masculine competent. For male interviewee in delayed condition, females and conservative males ranked generally like those in the immediate condition, but liberal males liked masculine interviewees better than feminine ones, regardless of competence level in each category.

163. Stake, Jayne E., and Michael N. Stake. "Performance-Self-Esteem and Dominance Behavior in Mixed-Sex Dyads." *Journal of Personality*, 47 (1979), 71-84.

    Forty-four mixed-sex dyads of college undergraduates, either matched or opposites on a Performance-Self-Esteem-Scale, rated individually and then discussed and rated together solutions to a campus crime problem. When performance self-esteem was held constant, no sex differences in dominance appeared. High performance self-esteem females were more dominant in their dyads than low performance self-esteem females were in theirs. High females indicated more satisfaction in the decision-making process when they participated more; low females indicated more satisfaction when they participated less.

* Steingart, Irving, Norbert Freedman, Stanley Grand, and Charles Buchwald. "Personality Organization and Language Behavior: The Imprint of Psychological Differen-

tiation on Language Behavior in Varying Communication Conditions." *Journal of Psycholinguistic Research,* 4 (1975), 241-255. See item 900.

* Sternberg, Daniel P., and Ernst G. Beier. "Changing Patterns of Conflict." *Journal of Communication,* 27 (Summer 1977), 97-100. See item 375.

* Sterrett, John H. "The Job Interview: Body Language and Perceptions of Potential Effectiveness." *Journal of Applied Psychology,* 63 (1978), 388-390. See item 1308.

164. Stewart, Abigail J., and Zick Rubin. "The Power Motive in the Dating Couple." *Journal of Personality and Social Psychology,* 34 (1976), 305-309.

    Testing 63 dating couples on the Thematic Apperception Test, obtaining questionnaire data on their relationship, and determining two years later the disposition of the couples, the experimenters found a "hope of power" in men associated with dissatisfaction and anticipation of problems. Couples in which the male had "hope of power" were more likely to break up. Women's "hope of power" was unrelated to dissatisfaction or to stability of relationship.

165. Sussman, Lyle, Terry A. Pickett, Irene A. Berzinski, and Frederick W. Pearce. "Sex and Sycophancy: Communication Strategies for Ascendance in Same-Sex and Mixed-Sex Superior-Subordinate Dyads." *Sex Roles,* 6 (1980), 113-127.

    To examine communication strategies, derived from Bales' Interaction Process Analysis categories, for ascendance in same-sex and mixed-sex superior-subordinate dyads, 24 male and 24 female business graduate students participated in a role-playing case study exercise. Analysis of their interaction indicated that the perceived importance of the task and the social facilitative strategies varied both within and across the four types of dyads, and that female subordinates expected to be more satisfied working under female supervision than male subordinates did.

* Sussman, Nan M., and Howard M. Rosenfeld. "Touch, Justification, and Sex: Influences on the Aversiveness of Spatial Violations." *The Journal of Social Psychology,* 106 (1978), 215-225. See item 1193.

166. Swanson, Marcia A., and Dean Tjosvold. "The Effects of Unequal Competence and Sex on Achievement and Self-Presentation." *Sex Roles,* 5 (1979), 279-285.

This study of 316 undergraduates explored how the self-presentation efforts of highly competent and less competent males and females affected their achievement on problem-solving cooperative tasks. The achievements of less competent males and females were lower when their partner was a highly competent female rather than a highly competent male, which suggests that self-presentation concerns aroused by sex of partner and relative ability can inhibit achievement.

* Talley, Mary A., and Virginia P. Richmond. "The Relationship between Psychological Gender Orientation and Communicator Style." *Human Communication Research,* 6 (1980), 326-339. See item 793.

* Taylor, Marylee C. "Race, Sex, and the Expression of Self-Fulfilling Prophecies in a Laboratory Teaching Situation." *Journal of Personality and Social Psychology,* 37 (1979), 897-912. See item 525.

* Tennis, Gay H., and James M. Dabbs, Jr. "Sex, Setting and Personal Space: First Grade Through College." *Sociometry,* 38 (1975), 385-394. See item 1194.

* Tesch, Frederick E. "Interpersonal Proximity and Impression Formation: A Partial Examination of Hall's Proxemic Model." *The Journal of Social Psychology,* 107 (1979), 43-55. See item 1195.

167. Tesch, Frederick E., Ted L. Huston, and Eugene A. Indenbaum. "Attitude Similarity, Attraction, and Physical Proximity in a Dynamic Space." *Journal of Applied Social Psychology,* 3 (1973), 63-72.

Using 116 female undergraduates in a condition manipulated for attraction for a female confederate, followed by interaction with the confederate during which use of space was observed, authors found subjects' attraction to confederate, their accuracy of perception of agreement, and their liking for confederate after meeting were all related to the manipulation of attitude similarity, but use of space was not.

168. Tesser, Abraham, Sidney Rosen, and Thomas Batchelor. "Some Message Variables and the MUM Effect." *Journal*

of Communication, 22 (Sept. 1972), 239-256.

This report of five studies (N ranged from 53-56) shows the relationship of felt desire to transmit message, felt obligation to transmit it, and the quality of the news, good or bad, with actual transmission of the message. Correlations between male and female responses to each of the 55 items for felt desire, felt obligation, message pleasantness, and probability of transmission were high (.88-.99). Actual transmission was a function of felt desire and obligation for all levels of message pleasantness, but the determinants of the desire and obligation were different for good versus bad news.

169. Tesser, Abraham, Sidney Rosen, and Ellen Waranch. "Communicator Mood and the Reluctance to Transmit Undesirable Messages (The Mum Effect)." *Journal of Communication,* 23 (Sept. 1973), 266-283.

To determine the effects of mood on the transmission of good or bad news, 48 female undergraduates "overheard" a message intended for another and then were put into a pleasant or unpleasant mood. When confronted with the person for whom the message was intended, subjects significantly shifted mood in the direction of the pleasantness of the message and transmitted good news more fully. Those in induced unpleasant mood communicated more spontaneously than those in pleasant mood, especially when news was good.

170. Teyber, Edward C., Lawrence A. Messé, and Gary E. Stollak. "Adult Responses to Child Communications." *Child Development,* 48 (1977), 1577-82.

To study adult responses to emotion-laden male child communication, the authors factor analyzed the oral responses of 180 undergraduates (90 M, 90 F) to taped scenarios with positive-loving, neutral-informative, and negative-rejecting content. The factors of modes of responding were directing-control, power assertion, expression of child's influence on adult, empathy, ridicule-interrogation, and instrumental control. Females were more accepting and displayed less power assertion and ridicule-interrogation in response to an angry child than males did.

* Tipton, Robert M., Kent G. Bailey, and Janet P. Obenchain. "Invasion of Males' Personal Space by Feminists and

Non-Feminists." *Psychological Reports*, 37 (1975), 99-102. See item 1196.

* Toler, Sue A. and Nicholas W. Bankson. "Utilization of an Interrogative Model to Evaluate Mothers' Use and Children's Comprehension of Question Forms." *Journal of Speech and Hearing Disorders*, 41 (1976), 301-314. See item 377.

171. Tubbs, Stewart L. "Two Person Game Behavior, Conformity-Inducing Messages and Interpersonal Trust." *Journal of Communication*, 21 (Dec. 1971), 326-341.

    To investigate the influence of cooperation or competition combined with conformity-inducing message on trust, 60 female undergraduates played the Prisoner's Dilemma game under those conditions in a systematically varied design. The competitive player was rated higher in expertness but lower in character, while dynamism, the third factor in trust, was unaffected. Previous public speaking research had found that all three factors tended to rise together. Game behavior from one set of games influenced subsequent behavior, with competitive behavior inducing competition and cooperative behavior inducing cooperation in the partner.

* Tulkin, Steven R., and Jerome Kagan. "Mother-Child Interaction in the First Year of Life." *Child Development*, 43 (1972), 31-41. See item 378.

172. Turnbull, Allen A., Lloyd Strickland, and Kelly G. Shaver. "Medium of Communication, Differential Power, and Phasing of Concessions: Negotiating Success and Attributions to the Opponent." *Human Communication Research*, 2 (1976), 262-270.

    This study of the negotiation outcomes and negotiator attributions used three different communication modes (audio, audio-video, face-to-face), and three levels of power (high, equal, low), and three concession-phasing strategies (alternating, increasingly cooperative, decreasingly cooperative). Subjects were 136 male and female undergraduates who participated in same-sex dyads in simulated disarmament negotiations. The data indicated no differences for either concession phasing or sex of the negotiating pair. Communication mode and power variables were potent, with the face-to-face communication mode producing the best joint outcomes, followed by the audio-video, and the audio-only modes.

Males perceived their own nation and their opponent's as more powerful than females did.

* Tyler, Ann I., Wayne L. Waag, and Clay E. George. "Determinants of the Ecology of the Dyad: The Effects of Age and Sex." *Journal of Psychology,* 81 (1972), 117-120. See item 1198.

173. Tyler, Tom R., and David O. Sears. "Coming to Like Obnoxious People When We Must Live with Them." *Journal of Personality and Social Psychology,* 35 (1977), 200-211.

    Two studies using female undergraduates (N=134, 90) both supported the balance theory of increased liking toward ambivalent or negative other if interaction was expected with that other. In the first study, information about the other was in written form; in the second, subjects actually interacted with the other.

* Valentine, Mary E., and Howard Ehrlichman. "Interpersonal Gaze and Helping Behavior." *The Journal of Social Psychology,* 107 (1979), 193-198. See item 1074.

174. Wahrman, Ralph, and Meredith D. Pugh. "Sex, Nonconformity and Influence." *Sociometry,* 37 (1974), 137-147.

    Seventy-five male subjects were put in a problem-solving game with a female confederate who violated rules early, late, or in the middle of 15 trials, either with or without success. The earlier the female violated the rules, the more she was disliked, the less influential and less desirable as a co-worker she became (unlike male confederates in a previous study whose early nonconformity led to increased influence and increased desirability as co-worker). Competent (successful), nonconforming females were rated less influential than the incompetent, nonconforming male.

* Walker, David N. "A Dyadic Interaction Model for Nonverbal Touching Behavior in Encounter Groups." *Small Group Behavior,* 6 (1975), 308-324. See item 1218.

175. Walsh, Nancy A., Lynn A. Meister, and Chris L. Kleinke. "Interpersonal Attraction and Visual Behavior as a Function of Perceived Arousal and Evaluation by an Opposite Sex Person." *The Journal of Social Psychology,* 103 (1977), 65-74.

    Four males interviewed 40 female undergraduates who

were given bogus evaluations and bogus heart rates. High perceived arousal (heart rate) subjects with favorable evaluations expressed more willingness to return and gazed more than those with low evaluations. For unaroused subjects (heart rate normal), evaluations had no effect on willingness to return. Interviewers' evaluations, but not heart-rate information, influenced subjects' ratings of liking for the interviewer.

176. Waters, Thomas J. "Further Comparison of Video Tape and Face-to-Face Interviewing." *Perceptual and Motor Skills,* 41 (1975), 743-746.

    Twenty-four male and 24 female college students were interviewed either face-to-face or via the Standardized Video Tape Interview by either a male or a female interviewer. Pre- and post-interview State Anxiety Inventory measures were also taken. No significant differences by mode of interview were found, but several interviewer sex differences were. Subjects responded with greater subjective anxiety when interviewed by a male than by a female, but spoke longer to the male. Subjects had higher physiological anxiety (galvanic skin response) when interviewed by the female.

* Watson, Wilbur H. "The Meanings of Touch: Geriatric Nursing." *Journal of Communication,* 25 (Summer 1975), 104-112. See item 1219.

* Weitz, Shirley. "Sex Differences in Nonverbal Communication." *Sex Roles,* 2 (1976), 175-184. See item 1312.

* Wellens, A. Rodney, and Martin V. Faletti. "Interrelationships of Six Measures of Interpersonal Attraction." *Psychological Reports,* 42 (1978), 1022. See item 1313.

* Wellens, A. Rodney, and Myron L. Goldberg. "The Effects of Interpersonal Distance and Orientation upon the Perception of Social Relationships." *Journal of Psychology,* 99 (1978), 39-47. See item 1201.

* West, Candace. "Against Our Will: Male Interruptions of Females in Cross-Sex Conversations." In *Language, Sex, and Gender.* Eds. Judith Orasanu, Mariam K. Slater, and Lenore L. Adler. New York: New York Academy of Sciences, 1979, pp. 81-97. See item 911.

* West, Candace, and Don H. Zimmerman. "Women's Place in Everyday Talk: Reflections on Parent-Child Interaction." *Social Problems,* 24 (1977), 521-529. See item 379.

177. Whalen, Carol K., and John V. Flowers. "Effects of Role and Gender Mix on Verbal Communication Modes." *Journal of Counseling Psychology,* 24 (1977), 281-287.

    Twelve male and 29 female undergraduates viewed role-played problem vignettes and responded as though interacting with the speakers either as counselor or as friend. Analysis of written responses indicated those serving as friends made fewer reflections and gave more advice than those serving as counselors. More advice and information-seeking questions were directed to female than to male stimulus persons, and the latter received more positive feedback. Females used more interrogative interpretations. Same-sex pairings had more interpretation than opposite-sex pairings, and more negative feedback was given to same-sex stimulus person in friend condition and opposite-sex stimulus person in counselor condition.

178. Wheaton, Blair. "Interpersonal Conflict and Cohesiveness in Dyadic Relationships." *Sociometry,* 37 (1974), 328-348.

    A questionnaire survey of 204 female college roommates on their conflicts, principled or communal, and on their cohesiveness found that principled conflict had a negative effect on cohesiveness and communal conflict had a positive effect, creating more cohesiveness than if no conflict at all.

* White, Michael J. "Interpersonal Distance as Affected by Room Size, Status, and Sex." *The Journal of Social Psychology,* 95 (1975), 241-249. See item 1202.

179. Wichman, Harvey. "Effects of Isolation and Communication on Cooperation in a Two-Person Game." *Journal of Personality and Social Psychology,* 16 (1970), 114-120.

    Using 88 female undergraduates playing a Prisoner's Dilemma game under four conditions of communication--neither seeing nor hearing each other, seeing only, hearing only, and both seeing and hearing--Wichman found increasing cooperation in the order of conditions given. He concluded that the competitiveness usually found in this game is a function of the isolated condition of playing it.

180. Wiley, Mary G. "Sex Roles in Games." *Sociometry,* 36 (1973), 526-541.

   Forty-eight male and 48 female undergraduates played the Prisoner's Dilemma game in single- or mixed-sex dyads, with verbal only, nonverbal only, or no communication. No differences between the sexes occurred in the no-communication situation or in same-sex verbal communication. In mixed-sex verbal communication, however, there was greater cooperation and less competition, theorized as attributable to traditional sex roles, a chivalrous attitude on part of the males, and deference to male authority on the part of the females.

181. Wiley, Mary G., and Arlene Eskilson. "Sex Differences in Attractiveness of Women as a Function of Sex Role Attributes and Age of Actor." *Pacific Sociological Review,* 2 (1978), 141-158.

   In three studies the attractiveness of women having traits associated either with the traditional female role or a modern role was evaluated by college students. In the first study (46 F, 43 M), traits that distinguished the two roles were established. In the second (26 F, 26 M), evaluations were made of a college-age woman displaying in an interview either the traditional or the modern set of traits, and in the third study (48 F, 48 M), the same was done for a middle-aged woman. In both cases, the modern as opposed to the traditional role woman was judged more attractive by both males and females.

* Wilson, David W. "Helping Behavior and Physical Attractiveness." *The Journal of Social Psychology,* 104 (1978), 313-314. See item 1131.

* Wilton, Keri, and Ann Barbour. "Mother-Child Interaction in High Risk and Contrast Preschoolers of Low Socioeconomic Status." *Child Development,* 49 (1978), 1136-45. See item 381.

* Winter, William D., Antonio J. Ferreira, and Norman Bowers. "Decision-Making in Married and Unrelated Couples." *Family Process,* 12 (1973), 83-94. See item 382.

* Wittig, Michele A., and Paul Skolnick. "Status Versus Warmth as Determinants of Sex Differences in Personal Space." *Sex Roles,* 4 (1978), 493-503. See item 1204.

* Yockey, Jamie M. "Role Theory and the Female Sex Role." *Sex Roles,* 4 (1978), 917-927. See item 77.

* Young, Jerald W. "The Subordinate's Exposure of Organizational Vulnerability to the Superior: Sex and Organizational Effects." *Academy of Management Journal,* 21 (1978), 113-122. See item 767.

182. Zanna, Mark P., and Susan J. Pack. "On the Self-Fulfilling Nature of Apparent Sex Differences in Behavior." *Journal of Experimental Social Psychology,* 11 (1975), 583-591.

    Eighty undergraduate women characterized themselves to a desirable or undesirable male partner, whose stereotype of the ideal woman either conformed to the traditional female stereotype or not. When the male partners were attractive, the females conformed to the male partner's ideal, conventionally if he had a conventional stereotype in his description and unconventionally if he had an unconventional stereotype.

183. Zeichner, Amos, John C. Wright, and Sheryl Herman. "Effects of Situation on Dating and Assertive Behavior." *Psychological Reports,* 40 (1977), 375-381.

    Twelve male and 12 female undergraduates, selected from high scores on an assertiveness test, interacted with role-players in simulated situations designed to elicit either assertiveness or dating behavior. Role-players were either of same sex or not, stranger or not, responsive, neutral, or negative to subject's request. Subjects used more verbalizations in assertiveness situations and were more direct. In dating condition, subjects verbalized more before making the request and had longer eye contact as well, especially with a "friend" rather than a "stranger." Subjects talked more to positive feedback role-players, whether in dating or assertiveness situation, and gave more justifications for their demand in friend-dating condition than in stranger-dating condition no matter what type of feedback. No differences by sex of subject emerged.

184. Zimmerman, Don H., and Candace West. "Sex Roles, Interruptions and Silences in Conversation." In *Language and Sex: Difference and Dominance* (item 1326), pp. 105-129.

    Using the developments in the study of turn-taking in

ordinary conversation (studies cited at end of article), the authors analyzed the overlaps, interruptions, silences, and minimal responses of 31 tape recorded naturally occurring conversations. Subjects, all white adults, some university students, were recorded unobtrusively in coffee shops, drug stores, etc. The frequency of interruptions and overlaps was greater in male-female dyads than in same-sex dyads; most interruptions and all the overlaps were done by males to females. Males also revealed more delayed minimum response (mmm, yea), and these plus the interruptions and overlaps were related to longer silence before next speaker's turn. Women, therefore, had longer silences before speaking than men, especially in cross-sex dyads. Explanations of the asymmetrical pattern of conversational modes of communication relating to dominance are included, as is an appendix showing the transcription codes used.

* Zimmerman, Mary. "Alignment Strategies in Verbal Accounts of Problematic Conduct: The Case of Abortion." In *The Sociology of the Languages of American Women*. Eds. Betty L. Dubois and Isabel Crouch. San Antonio, Texas: Trinity University, 1976, pp. 171-183. See item 912.

IN SMALL GROUPS

* Alderton, Steven M., and William E. Jurma. "Genderless/Gender-Related Task Leader Communication and Group Satisfaction: A Test of Two Hypotheses." *Southern Speech Communication Journal*, 46 (1980), 48-60. See item 588.

185. Alfgren, Scott H., Elizabeth J. Aries, and Rose R. Olver. "Sex Differences in the Interaction of Adults and Preschool Children." *Psychological Reports*, 44 (1979), 115-118.

    Two male and two female counselors at a summer camp program were observed for individual interactions with 16 male and 16 female children ranging in age from three to five with whom they worked in groups. Using the number of times the counselors responded to satisfactory behavior at a task as a measure, researchers found boys received more attention from adults than girls did, female adults gave more attention to boys than male adults, and the attention received by the child was not correlated with either attention-seeking or eliciting behavior on the part of the child.

186. Altemeyer, Robert A., and Keith Jones. "Sexual Identity, Physical Attractiveness and Seating Position as Determinants of Influence in Discussion Groups." *Canadian Journal of Behavioural Science*, 6 (1974), 357-375.

   In two experiments using mixed-sex groups of five including either a male or female confederate (total of 120 in first experiment, 108 in second), problem-solving discussions were held on a male-oriented topic or (second experiment) a neutral one. Male subjects were more active and exerted more influence than female subjects. The male confederate was more likely than the female confederate to get an elegant solution to both kinds of problems. Physical attractiveness of the confederate had no influence, but sitting at the head of the table had some effect on making that person influential.

187. Anderson, Alonzo B. "Combined Effects of Interpersonal Attraction and Goal-Path Clarity on the Cohesiveness of Task Oriented Groups." *Journal of Personality and Social Psychology,* 31 (1975), 68-75.

   One hundred and twenty female college students, placed in triads in which all members were either high or low in similarity of values, completed a get-acquainted session and a task session which was manipulated for clarity of the goal. In the first session, results showed that interpersonal attraction was a function of value similarity, and in the second, only clarity, not value similarity or interpersonal attraction level, affected cohesion.

188. Annis, Lawrence V., and Donald F. Perry. "Self-disclosure Modeling in Same-sex and Mixed-sex Unsupervised Groups." *Journal of Counseling Psychology,* 24 (1977), 370-372.

   Six groups of four college students, all male, all female, or mixed, were videotaped in unsupervised discussion groups, half the groups after seeing a videotape model, the other not. Level of self-disclosure was greater in the modeling groups and females disclosed more than males. Sex composition of group had no significant effect.

189. Aries, Elizabeth. "Interaction Patterns and Themes of Male, Female, and Mixed Groups." *Small Group Behavior,* 7 (1976), 7-18.

   Aries examined the content and structure of interaction patterns of same-sex and opposite-sex groups. Two all-male, two all-female, and two mixed groups of five to seven undergraduates were studied over five one-and-one-half hour sessions. An analysis of the transcripts of five-minute reactions taken every half hour, an analysis using the computer-aided content analysis system General Inquirer, revealed many differences. All-male groups established a dominance pattern over the sessions, all-female groups had greater flexibility, and males dominated in the mixed-sex groups. Female groups spoke frequently and directly about themselves and their feelings; male groups talked little about themselves and had more references to competition, self-aggrandizement, and aggression. In mixed groups males spoke infrequently of competition and aggression and more about their feelings; women spoke less. Both sexes used more qualifiers in the mixed groups, more exaggerated words, and more doubtful, uncertain words, indicating a more defensive style of speech in mixed-sex groups.

* Arnett, Matthew D., Richard B. Higgins, and Andre P. Priem. "Sex and Least Preferred Co-Worker Score Effects in Leadership Behavior." *Sex Roles*, 6 (1980), 139-152. See item 589.

190. Babinec, Carol S. "Sex, Communication Structures and Role Specification." *Sociological Focus*, 11 (1978), 199-210.

    Ten four-member groups of two male and two female undergraduates solved human relation problems with an appointed coordinator, either a male or female. Analysis indicated differences by sex of coordinator in number of turns taken in discussion and a near-significant difference in providing certain types of feedback, with males providing more. Both sexes of coordinators had more task behavior than other members, but male coordinators engaged in more social-emotional activity, and female coordinators in less than others. Attributions of leadership were made to males primarily on their task contributions and to females primarily on their directiveness.

191. Baird, John E., Jr. "Sex Differences in Group Communication: A Review of Relevant Research." *Quarterly Journal of Speech*, 62 (1976), 179-192.

    Reviewing research from 1950 to 1974 on women's communication in groups, Baird concludes that women are more willing to disclose and to express emotion, are better able to perceive others' emotions, to interpret nonverbal cues, and to cooperate in bargaining, but are less able at problem-solving, less willing to take risks, less able to withstand social pressure, and less likely to assume leadership. All references are in footnotes.

192. Ballou, Mary, Jeanette Reuter, and Thomas Dinero. "An Audio-Taped Consciousness-Raising Group for Women: Evaluation of the Process Dimension." *Psychology of Women Quarterly,* 4 (1979), 185-193.

    A consciousness-raising program involving 28 women compared those in communications skills training and in explorations of women's issues or in just one or the other. The group receiving only the communications skills component made significant progress (determined by trained observer/raters and structured descriptive narratives) toward the four goals of development of effective communication, an awareness of the issues facing women, the discovery of new options for behavior, and the establishment of a supportive environment. The group that received both the communication training and women's issues components made significant progress toward two goals, and the group that received only the women's issues component made no apparent progress toward any of the goals.

193. Bander, Ricki S., Richard K. Russell, and Gerald N. Weiskott. "Effects of Varying Amounts of Assertiveness Training on Level of Assertiveness and Anxiety Reduction in Women." *Psychological Reports,* 43 (1978), 144-146.

    Two groups of women in assertiveness training sessions of two and eight hours and two control groups (total N = 36) completed post treatment and two-week follow-up self-report indices of assertiveness. Only the 8-hour treatment group had significant increases on both measures. No group showed significant reduction in trait or state anxiety levels.

194. Baron, Robert S., Gard Roper, and Penny H. Baron. "Group Discussion and the Stingy Shift." *Journal of Personality and Social Psychology,* 30 (1974), 538-545.

    Using 28 groups of three or four, all females, making decisions about contributions to worthwhile causes, individually and then in groups, authors found group decisions less generous than individual ones despite the fact that individuals perceived generosity as socially desirable. Generous individuals appeared reluctant to use coercive power on less-generous ones in the group situation.

195. Barrett, Carol J. "Effectiveness of Widows' Groups in Facilitating Changes." *Journal of Consulting and Clinical Psychology,* 46 (1978), 20-31

Seventy widows ranging in age from 32 to 74 were assigned to one of three discussion groups: self-help, confident (stress on establishing close pair relationship), and consciousness raising, or to a control, no-discussion group. Personality, attitude, and behaviorial measures were obtained before and after the sessions, and at a 14-week follow up. At posttest, subjects in all conditions had significantly higher self-esteem, greater grief, and more negative attitudes toward remarriage than the control group. At follow-up, treatment gains were maintained and the consciousness-raising group made significantly more positive life changes.

196. Barrios, Billy, and Martin Giesen. "Getting What You Expect: Effects of Expectation on Intragroup Attraction and Interpersonal Distance." *Personality and Social Psychology Bulletin,* 3 (1977), 87-90.

Twenty-two female and 22 male undergraduates participated in same-sex groups of two or three with a male moderator to discuss a topic after they had had their expectations aroused to be friendly or hostile. Measures of pre- and post-discussion ratings of attraction to others and to moderator, discussion evaluation, and seating distance were obtained. Results were that friendliness increased in the friendly expectation condition, which also led to increased attraction for others, but not for moderator. Females sat closer to each other than to males, and, under friendly expectation, sat closer to each other than to the moderator.

* Bartol, Kathryn M. "The Effect of Male versus Female Leaders on Follower Satisfaction and Performance." *Journal of Business Research,* 3 (1975), 33-42. See item 590.

* Bartol, Kathryn M. "Male Versus Female Leaders: The Effect of Leader Need for Dominance on Follower Satisfaction." *Academy of Management Journal,* 17 (1974), 225-233. See item 591.

* Bath, Kent E., and Daniel L. Daly. "Self-Disclosure: Relationships to Self-Described Personality and Sex Differences." *Psychology Reports,* 31 (1972), 623-628. See item 707.

197. Bauer, Richard H., and James H. Turner. "Betting Behavior in Sexually Homogeneous and Heterogeneous Groups." *Psychological Reports,* 34 (1974), 251-258.

   Forty-eight male and 48 female undergraduates made bets individually, and then half continued that way and the other half bet in groups of four males, four females, three males-one female, or three females-one male when others' bets were known. Males were more risky than females in individual conditions and became more risky in all-male or three-male groups. Females in all-female groups were cautious, became slightly more risky with one male in group, and much more with three males in group. Results suggest shifts toward risk or caution are influenced by conformity to group pressure.

* Baum, Andrew, and Stuart Koman. "Differential Response to Anticipated Crowding: Psychological Effects of Social and Spatial Density." *Journal of Personality and Social Psychology,* 34 (1976), 526-536. See item 1138.

198. Bednarek, Frank, Louis Benson, and Husain Mustafa. "Identifying Peer Leadership in Small Work Groups." *Small Group Behavior,* 7 (1976), 307-316.

   A trait approach and a situational approach were combined to assess the structure of a small, informal work group consisting of 21 female employees in clerical positions in a payroll division. Analysis revealed a single strong leader who had significant task leadership traits and maturity and who showed social influence and flexibility.

199. Beinstein, Judith. "Friends, the Media, and Opinion Formation." *Journal of Communication,* 27 (Autumn 1977), 30-39.

   An exploratory study of the source of opinion formation of 30 women from each of three towns with widely varying population densities found that both network density (number of friends) and population density influenced the primary source used to form opinions. Women with close-knit interpersonal networks tended to rely on others as source, while those with loose-knit networks used mass media. Overall, however, the mass media was a source of identifying and of influencing opinion on national problems for all three groups.

200. Bell, Mae A. "The Effects of Substantive and Affective Verbal Conflict on the Quality of Decisions of Small Problem Solving Groups." *The Central States Speech Journal*, 30 (1979), 75-82.

This study tested the assumption that good solutions in group discussion emerge from systematic, rational discourse which allows for flexibility. Using 154 undergraduates (83 M and 71 F) in a discussion of a horse-trading problem while controlling for levels of both substantive and emotional conflict and for sex, Bell found no differences in overall quality of solutions. Males' flexibility increased in high substantive conflict. Females were as likely to change their minds when no substantive reasons were offered as when good reasons were offered.

201. Bennett, Charles, Svenn Lindskold, and Russell Bennett. "The Effects of Group Size and Discussion Time on the Risky Shift." *The Journal of Social Psychology*, 91 (1973), 137-147.

Ninety-six females met in groups of four or eight with discussion time varied in a problem-solving task for which they had previously indicated individual answers. Subjects in the four-person group showed significantly more risky shifts. Time was significant only with interaction of four-person group in three-minute situation. A second experiment with all four-person groups revealed a significant shift at three-, five-, and unlimited-minute situations, but not in the nine-minute situation.

202. Bird, Anne M. "Team Structure and Success as Related to Cohesiveness and Leadership." *The Journal of Social Psychology*, 103 (1977), 217-223.

A statistical analysis of the responses of 71 players and eight coaches (sex of coaches not given) of winning and losing teams of a women's volleyball league to tests on cohesion and leadership style revealed that winning players and coaches perceived greater cohesion than losing ones. Coaches saw themselves as task-oriented while players saw coaches as socio-emotional in leadership style. When leadership style was factored with team success, winning coaches were seen as socio-emotional and losing ones seen as task-oriented.

203. Bleda, Paul R. "Conditioning and Discrimination of Affect and Attracting." *Journal of Personality and Social Psychology,* 34 (1976), 1106-13.

Forty-five male and 57 female undergraduates, randomly paired with same sex, were then separated into three teams for a competitive manual task. All groups gave and received their reactions to the other teams. Teams giving unfavorable feedback caused more depression, anxiety, and hostility. Opposing teams generated more anxiety and hostility in males than in females. The control team (no feedback) evoked more hostility in males and greater anxiety and less attraction in both sexes after subjects had been given unfavorable feedback from another group.

204. Bocher, Arthur P., and Janet Yerby. "Factors Affecting Instruction in Interpersonal Competence." *Communication Education,* 26 (1977), 91-103, 120.

Over 690 male and female college students, meeting in discussion groups of 8 to 13, rated their peer facilitators' interpersonal skills and in turn were rated by them. Besides other factors, demographic variables, including sex, had an impact on the performance measures. Females received higher ratings than males, possibly because the interpersonal skills emphasized focused on self-disclosure, empathy, and owning thoughts and feelings, all more closely associated with females' socialization patterns than with males'.

205. Bohart, Arthur C. "Role Playing and Interpersonal-Conflict Reduction." *Journal of Counseling Psychology,* 24 (1977), 15-24.

Eighty undergraduate females, to resolve personal anger conflicts, participated in one of three treatment counseling groups--role playing, intellectual analysis, or discharge--or were in a control group. On various measures, role playing was more effective than the other methods in modifying anger, hostile attitudes, and behavioral aggression.

206. Bonacich, Phillip. "Norms and Cohesion as Adaptive Responses to Potential Conflict: An Experimental Study."

Sociometry, 35 (1972), 357-375.

Groups of five played the Prisoner's Dilemma game (players win at expense of others but cooperation brings gains for all) to test hypotheses unrelated to sex differences. Bonacich found, however, that the 67 males were less cooperative than the 53 females and more likely to initiate noncooperative behavior.

* Bormann, Ernest G., Jerie Pratt, and Linda Putnam. "Power, Authority, and Sex: Male Response to Female Leadership." *Communication Monographs,* 45 (1978), 119-155. See item 594.

207. Bouchard, Thomas, Jr., Jean Barsaloux, and Gail Drauden. "Brainstorming Procedure, Group Size, and Sex as Determinants of the Problem-Solving Effectiveness of Groups and Individuals." *Journal of Applied Psychology,* 59 (1974), 135-138.

Male or female groups of four or seven (total number unspecified), in lit or in dark conditions, discussed what it would be like to be blind under free brainstorming conditions or modified conditions (taking turns). The female groups performed better than the male groups in the lights-on condition but worse in the dark condition. Those in the free brainstorming conditions generated more ideas than those who took turns, but the increase in size of group helped generate more ideas for the taking turns groups than for the free groups.

208. Bradley, Patricia H. "Sex, Competence and Opinion Deviation: An Expectation States Approach." *Communication Monographs,* 47 (1980), 101-110.

A male or female confederate, presented as either a high or low competent person, took a position contrary to that of five males in a group (24 groups all told) in order to assess the effects of sex and competence on discussion. An analysis of the videotaped sessions on a seven-point bipolar scale revealed that sex and competence interacted with dominance, with significantly more dominant statements directed to a low-competent female than to a high-competent female or to a low-competent male. Although male confederates were treated reasonably no matter what competence level they displayed, high-competent females were treated significantly more reasonably than low. Low-competent confederates, regardless of sex, were treated with significantly more hostility, but low-competent females with significantly more hostility than low-competent males. High-competent males were significantly more persuasive than low-competent ones, and low-competent females significantly less influential than either high-competent females or low-competent males. As for liking, male deviates were better liked than female deviates, regardless of competence level. Discussion of both theoretical and practical implications of the results is included.

209. Bray, Robert M., Norbert L. Kerr, and Robert S. Atkin. "Effects of Group Size, Problem Difficulty, and Sex on Group Performance and Member Reactions." *Journal of Personality and Social Psychology*, 36 (1978), 1224-40.

Using 349 undergraduates in all-male or all-female groups of five different sizes ranging from two to ten, all groups solving problems on three levels of difficulty, the authors found size and difficulty of problem affected performance more than sex, with groups falling below potential as size and difficulty level increased. Sex differences found were that males solved moderately difficult problems better than females and that the group size variable was more potent for male than for female groups (none of which differed significantly from each other) for the moderately difficult problem.

210. Bray, Robert M., Cindy Struckman-Johnson, Marshall D. Osborne, James B. McFarlane, and Joanne Scott. "The Effects of Defendant Status on the Decisions of Student and Community Juries." *Social Psychology*, 41 (1978), 256-260.

In this simulated trial study, six-person mixed-sex groups, either from student (194) or town (143) populations, determined the guilt and punishment of a high- or low-status indicted male murderer. The higher status murderer received a longer sentence, although guilty verdicts were unaffected by status. No significant differences were found between student and town juries, but a sex difference noted was that males made harsher judgments before deliberation, but after deliberation converged with females' judgments.

211. Brown, Jane D. "Adolescent Peer Group Communication, Sex-Role Norms and Decisions about Occupations." In *Communication Yearbook 4*. Ed. Dan Nimmo. New Brunswick,

N.J.: Transaction Books, 1980, pp. 659-678.

To determine the influence of interpersonal communication and sex roles on career decision-making, 597 male and female undergraduates were interviewed and completed various measures on occupation decision-making, interpersonal communication, and the Bem Sex-Role Inventory. Results of correlation and multivariate multiple regression analyses indicated that gender does have a direct effect on decision-making, but that both sex-role norms and interpersonal communication norms independently account for some of the influence. Masculine subjects of either sex reported higher levels of information-seeking about careers, while feminine subjects reported greater flexibility of choice.

212. Burroughs, W., W. Schultz, and S. Autrey. "Quality of Argument, Leadership Votes, and Eye Contact in Three-Person Leaderless Groups." *The Journal of Social Psychology,* 90 (1973), 89-93.

Thirty undergraduate females participated in discussions in triads which included a confederate while eye contact, quality of argument, and perceived leadership measures were taken. Members giving high-quality arguments received more eye contact, and perceived leaders in post-group questionnaires were those receiving most in-group eye contact.

213. Caldwell, Michael D. "Communication and Sex Effects in a Five-Person Prisoner's Dilemma Game." *Journal of Personality and Social Psychology,* 33 (1976), 273-280.

Thirteen five-member groups of each sex of undergraduates played the Prisoner's Dilemma game under three conditions of communication and one for sanctions as well. No significant sex differences were found but strong communication differences, with groups in talk-sanction condition being more cooperative than others.

* Calsyn, Robert J. "Group Responses to Territorial Intrusion." *The Journal of Social Psychology,* 100 (1976), 51-58. See item 1146.

214. Cannavale, F.J., H.A. Scarr, and A. Pepitone. "Deindividuation in the Small Group: Further Evidence." *Journal of Personality and Social Psychology,* 16 (1970), 141-147.

Graduates and undergraduates in nine all-male, two all-female, and three mixed-sex groups of from four to seven discussed feelings toward parents, and then were tested for recall of content and of individual making a comment. Results confirmed the previously found association between deindividuation and reduction in restraint, which is essentially a group phenomenon. Mixed groups showed apprehension associated with deindividuation while all-male groups did not.

* Caproni, Valerie, Douglas Levine, Edgar O'Neal, Peter McDonald, and Gray Garwood. "Seating Position, Instructor's Eye Contact Availability, and Student Participation in a Small Seminar." *The Journal of Social Psychology,* 103 (1977), 315-316. See item 1043.

* Certner, Barry C. "Exchange of Self-Disclosures in Same-Sexed Groups of Strangers." *Journal of Consulting and Clinical Psychology,* 40 (1973), 292-297. See item 715.

215. Coet, Larry J., and Patrick J. McDermott. "Sex, Instructional Set, and Group Make-Up: Organismic and Situational Factors Influencing Risk-Taking. *Psychological Reports,* 44 (1979), 1283-94.

    Two hundred male and female students, undergraduate and graduate, completed some items of the Choice Dilemma Questionnaire individually under either risk-oriented instructions or neutral instructions, and then in same-sex or mixed-sex groups discussed the items and reached a group decision. Risk-oriented instructions produced significantly greater risk for both individuals and groups. Males had more risk-taking behavior than females, and all-male groups took more risks than any other group.

216. Crosbie, Paul V. "The Effects of Sex and Size on Status Ranking." *Social Psychology Quarterly,* 42 (1979), 340-354.

    This theoretical study included an experiment with 159 male and female undergraduates in a game-playing situation. The mixed-sex small groups were measured for sex, size, status rank, and other sociocultural variables. The intervening sociocultural variables explained some but not all of the relations between sex, size, and status. Noting that the research model accounts for the class variable but not the sex and size variables, Crosbie controlled for each and found that size alone but not sex alone was a major contributor to status.

217. Crosbie, Paul V., and Vicki K. Kullberg. "Minimum Resources or Balance in Coalition Formation." *Sociometry*, 36 (1973), 476-493.

To test the viability of the minimum resource theory or the balance theory in coalition formation, 348 undergraduates (116 triads of same or mixed sex) took part in a card-playing game for points in which two could join their cards for a greater chance to win but at the cost of splitting evenly the winnings. All six critical conditions of the game manipulations could be predicted by the minimum resource theory. There were few sex differences in player strategy, although female-oriented triads had fewer or even no coalitions under one of the critical conditions.

218. Daly, John A., James C. McCroskey, and Virginia P. Richmond. "Judgments of Quality, Listening, and Understanding Based Upon Vocal Activity." *Southern Speech Communication Journal*, 41 (1976), 189-197.

One hundred thirty undergraduates (65 F, 65 M) evaluated a hypothetical man or woman who talked for varying amounts of time in a small-group discussion for the quality of the contribution and perceptions of participants' listening and understanding. Results indicated that the more the person talked, the more subjects attributed quality to that person's contributions. Those who talked more than average were perceived as poorer listeners; those who talked less were perceived as better listeners. The data revealed no significant effects for sex of the subject or of the hypothetical discussant.

219. D'Augelli, Anthony R. "Group Composition Using Interpersonal Skills: An Analogue Study on the Effects of Members' Interpersonal Skills on Peer Ratings and Group Cohesiveness." *Journal of Counseling Psychology*, 20 (1973), 531-534.

Seventy female and 68 male undergraduates, previously measured for interpersonal skills, were placed in same-sex triads of high or low (median split) level of skills for a two-hour leaderless discussion. Post-discussion measures revealed that high skills group members were seen as more empathetically understanding, honest, open, and accepting. High-skill groups were rated as discussing more personally meaningful topics and as being more cohesive.

220. Dion, Kenneth L., Norman Miller, and Mary A. Magnan. "Cohesiveness and Social Responsibility as Determinants of Group Risk Taking." *Journal of Personality and Social Psychology,* 20 (1971), 400-406.

   Though authors hypothesized that emotional bonds among group members would increase group risk taking, the 112 female undergraduates when placed in groups of four manipulated for group cohesiveness and social responsibility shifted conservatively under high-cohesiveness conditions.

* Downs, Cal W., and Terry Pickett. "An Analysis of the Effects of Nine Leadership-Group Compatibility Contingencies upon Productivity and Member Satisfaction." *Communication Monographs,* 44 (1977), 220-230. See item 599.

221. Durham, Thomas W. "Changing One's Mind Following Group Discussion: Sex Differences as a Function of the Diversity of Opinion." *Psychological Reports,* 47 (1980), 838.

   To determine whether the degree of variability of individual decisions affects group decision, 75 male and 120 female college students made individual decisions and then a group decision on the amount of noise to be tolerated while studying. All groups were same sex, varying from 2 to 4 members. Males selected higher noise levels, both individually and as groups. No sex differences in amount of change between the average of individuals' levels and group levels were found. For males, however, greater individual variance was related to greater polarization of group level; no such effect was found for females.

* Eagly, Alice H. "Leadership Style and Role Differentiation as Determinants of Group Effectiveness." *Journal of Personality,* 38 (1970), 509-524. See item 600.

* Eakins, Barbara, and Gene Eakins. "Verbal Turn-Taking and Exchanges in Faculty Dialogue." In *The Sociology of the Languages of American Women.* Eds. Betty L. Dubois and Isabel Crouch. San Antonio, Texas: Trinity University, 1976, pp. 53-62. See item 506.

* Edney, Julian J. and Nancy L. Jordan-Edney. "Territorial Spacing on a Beach." *Sociometry,* 37 (1974), 92-104. See item 1151.

* Efran, Michael G. "The Effect of Physical Appearance on the Judgment of Guilt, Interpersonal Attraction, and Severity of Recommended Punishment in a Simulated Jury Task." *Journal of Research in Personality,* 8 (1974), 45-54. See item 1103.

222. Ellis, Donald G. "Relational Control in Two Group Systems." *Communication Monographs,* 46 (1979), 153-166.

    Four groups, two decision-making ones (N not given) and two women's consciousness-raising ones (N = 16) were examined, and their relational control interactions patterns were explained. The groups differed in their relationship to the external environment, with the decision-making groups organizing information from the environment and the consciousness-raising groups turning away from the external environment. Decision-making groups required a free exchange, an open system with the environment, while the consciousness-raising ones served the individual, a closed system. Consciousness-raising groups established behavior patterns early in their history and rarely departed from them, while decision-making groups went through various stages of relational interaction.

223. Ellis, Donald G., and Linda McCallister. "Relational Control Sequences in Sex-Typed and Androgynous Groups." *Western Journal of Speech Communication,* 44 (1980), 35-49.

    The purpose of this investigation was to establish whether or not groups composed of sex role-typed individuals used different modes of relational control, and, if they did, what sequential structure would emerge from each group. Forty-five undergraduates completed the Bem Sex-Role Inventory and participated in a group decision-making discussion. Masculine sex-typed groups employed significant amounts of dominance in relationships resulting in sequences of competitive symmetry (members competing for dominance). The feminine sex-typed groups used more relational submissiveness than any other group but did not organize the relational maneuver into predictable patterns. Androgynous groups fell between and avoided overuse of a single relational definition, although they developed predictable sequences.

* Epstein, Norman, and Elizabeth Jackson. "An Outcome Study of Short-Term Communication Training with Married

Couples." *Journal of Consulting and Clinical Psychology,* 46 (1978), 207-212. See item 331.

* Eskilson, Arlene, and Mary G. Wiley. "Sex Composition and Leadership in Small Groups." *Sociometry,* 39 (1976), 183-194. See item 601.

224. Falbo, Toni. "Relationships Between Sex, Sex Role, and Social Influence." *Psychology of Women Quarterly,* 2 (1977), 62-72.

    Sixty subjects, 30 of each sex, pretested to represent equal numbers of masculine, feminine, and androgynous persons on the Bem Sex-Role Inventory, completed various measures of social influence and were rated by peers for their influence in a social group discussion. Regardless of sex, masculine and androgynous persons were rated more positively by peers than feminine subjects. Feminine persons, regardless of sex, reported using tears, emotional alteration, and subtlety significantly more often to influence others. Females reported using reasoning to get their own way more than males did.

225. Fenigstein, Allan. "Self-Consciousness, Self-Attention, and Social Interaction." *Journal of Personality and Social Psychology,* 37 (1979), 75-86.

    In two studies the effects of attention to oneself on social interactions were tested. In the first, 80 female undergraduates, high or low in self-consciousness, were placed in a triad in which two confederates engaged in conversation, ignoring the subject. Those high in self-consciousness reacted more negatively to the situation than those low in self-consciousness. In the second, 48 female undergraduates were interviewed under conditions manipulated for positive or negative feedback and with a mirror facing the subject or not. Seeing oneself in a mirror increased negative response to negative feedback and tended to increase positive response to positive feedback.

226. Fish, Sandra L. "A Phenomenological Examination of Femininity." *Journal of Applied Communications Research,* 4 (1976), 43-53.

    In this exploratory study to determine the meaning of femininity phenomenologically, Fish analyzed the transcripts of nine women's consciousness-raising meetings at which she was a participant. Four major categories of topics discussed were feelings about other women, self-perception, feelings about men, and feelings about motherhood and children. The overriding discussion theme was the desire to overcome their passive social role.

227. Flowers, Matie L. "A Laboratory Test of Some Implications of Janis's Groupthink Hypothesis." *Journal of Personality and Social Psychology,* 35 (1977), 888-896.

   Forty teams of three male and female undergraduates with established high or low cohesiveness, plus either a directive or non-directive male or female leader, solved a crisis problem. Non-directive leadership produced significantly more suggestions for solutions and used available facts more than directive leadership did. Cohesiveness level was immaterial to solution. Sex differences either for leader or for group were not found.

228. Follingstad, Diane R. "Effects of Sex of Pressuring Group, Perception of Ability, and Sex of Communicator Influencing Perceived Ability on Conformity of Males and Females." *Psychological Reports,* 44 (1979), 719-726.

   Sixty-four male and 64 female undergraduates were presented an article ascribed to a male or a female stating that males or females were more accurate on visual perception tasks, and then were placed in a group-task situation with a male or a female confederate responding first. Overall, females did not conform more than males. Males conformed more with male confederates, and females more when led to believe males were more accurate at the task. Females conformed significantly less in the condition of a male source stating that females were more accurate on a visual task.

229. Follingstad, Diane R., Elizabeth A. Robinson, and Martha Pugh. "Effects of Consciousness-Raising Groups on Measures of Feminism, Self-Esteem, and Social Desirability." *Journal of Counseling Psychology,* 24 (1977), 223-230.

   Twenty-two female undergraduates were assigned to a marathon group or a time-spaced group format for consciousness-raising and their measures of personality and self-esteem compared with each other and with a no-treatment group (12 females). No lasting changes on self-esteem or social desirability were revealed, and both treatment groups shifted toward more pro-feminist attitudes and behaviors than the control group.

* Fowler, Gene D., and Lawrence B. Rosenfeld. "Sex Differences and Democratic Leadership Behavior." *Southern Speech Communication Journal*, 45 (1979), 69-78. See item 603.

230. Frank, Frederic, and Lynn R. Anderson. "Effects of Task and Group Size Upon Group Productivity and Member Satisfaction." *Sociometry*, 34 (1971), 135-149.

    In four different sizes of single-sex groups, 144 male and 144 female undergraduates completed tasks in which either all members (conjunctive) or only one member (disjunctive) of the group was to finish a task before going on to a new one. The larger size groups increased performance on disjunctive tasks but decreased it on the conjunctive tasks. Pleasantness and task enjoyment revealed the same kind of interaction. Females were significantly more satisfied with their own performance regardless of group size or type of task than males were.

231. Freeman, Jo. "The Tyranny of Structurelessness." *Berkeley Journal of Sociology*, 17 (1972-73), 151-164.

    In this discussion of organization and consciousness-raising groups, Freeman declares that true structurelessness is impossible, that often such groups really have an informal structure, usually a small group with a network of communication outside any regular channels. That kind of organization presents many decision-making problems. Structuring principles are proposed to overcome this problem.

232. Freese, Lee. "Conditions for Status Equality in Informal Task Groups." *Sociometry*, 37 (1974), 174-188.

    One hundred and fifty-one female undergraduates in a problem-solving task with a bogus television cohort, young for high-status subjects and middle-aged for low-status ones, were given predetermined scores on the pretests, low scores for high-status subjects (while her partner and three bogus others were given high scores), and high scores for low-status subjects (with low scores for her partner and three bogus others). High-status subjects were less influenced by others than low-status ones until two "comparison actors" were introduced, when influence rates began to invert.

233. Fry, P.S. "Effects of Male and Female Endorsement of Beliefs on the Problem Solving Choices of High and Low Dogmatic Women." *The Journal of Social Psychology*, 96 (1975), 65-77.

Forty-four high- and 45 low-dogmatic female undergraduates completed a problem-solving task either with expert advice from a male or female or no advice. Expert male advice facilitated high dogmatics in their task, but expert female advice inhibited high-dogmatics while facilitating low-dogmatics in their task. Fry concluded that the study gave support for a sex bias for male authority in problem solving.

234. Galassi, John, Marion P. Kostka, and Merna D. Galassi. "Assertive Training: A One-Year Follow-Up." *Journal of Counseling Psychology*, 22 (1975), 451-452.

In a one-year follow-up study of 52 male and female students who had been in a group assertive training program compared to a control group, the assertive group scored significantly higher on two self-report measures and on two of the four behavioral measures. No differences by sex were found.

235. Genovese, Rosalie G. "A Woman's Self-Help Network as a Response to Service Needs in the Suburbs." *Signs: Journal of Women in Culture and Society*, 5, Supplement (1980), 248-256.

The informal interpersonal processes in the formation of a network are examined through the case study of a group of suburban women who formed a self-help network.

236. Gibbard, Graham S., and John J. Hartman. "The Oedipal Paradigm in Group Development: A Clinical and Empirical Study." *Small Group Behavior*, 4 (1973), 305-354.

The developmental change of two self-analytic groups using 50 male and female undergraduates was examined as the development reflected an oedipal paradigm. Looking at member-member and member-leader interactions using clinical and statistical methods, the authors found that in one group the sex differences were consistent with traditional sex-role expectations and the oedipal paradigm: male leader dominant; females ambivalent, forcing men to woo them, leading to an attack on the leader. The second group showed a different interaction since it was a female-dominant group.

237. Giesen, Martin, and Clyde Hendrick. "Physical Distance and Sex in Moderated Groups: Neglected Factors in Small Group Interaction." *Memory and Cognition,* 5 (1977), 79-83.

Groups of three students and a moderator (total N=120 males, 120 females) discussed women's liberation issues while seated at various distances. Subjects then made various ratings (mood, discussion evaluation, personal attitudes, peer evaluations of intelligence, morality, and knowledge of topics). Sex of moderator interacted strongly with distance and attitudes; all subjects were more comfortable and had more positive attitudes when close to a female moderator and far from a male moderator. Authors conclude that the ranking person, the moderator, defines spacing norms for the group and that there are sex differences in "personal space."

238. Giesen, Martin, and Harry A. McClaren. "Discussion, Distance and Sex: Changes in Impressions and Attraction During Small Group Interaction." *Sociometry,* 39 (1976), 60-70.

Single-sex triads (48 M, 48 F undergraduates) with a male or female moderator met in discussion groups and then completed rating measures. Discussion lessened negative feelings and heightened attraction and positive feelings. Females sat closer together, and both male and female subjects sat closer to a female moderator than to a male moderator.

* Ginter, Gary, and Svenn Lindskold. "Rate of Participation and Expertise as Factors Influencing Leader Choice." *Journal of Personality and Social Psychology,* 32 (1975), 1085-89. See item 604.

239. Gouran, Dennis S. "Correlates of Member Satisfaction in Group Decision-Making Discussion." *The Central States Speech Journal,* 24 (1973), 91-96.

To determine if the perception of the quality of one's own contributions, the others' contributions, frequency of participation, sex, decisional outcome, and group history were related to member satisfaction in decision-making groups, 52 male and 119 female undergraduates participated in two decision-making discussions and completed a rating form. Perception of the quality of the other members' contributions had the strongest relationship to level of satisfaction with the discussion. Perception of the quality of own performance did not contribute substantially, and frequency of participation, group history, and sex had no apparent relationship to satisfaction.

240. Gray, Louis N., Bruce H. Mayhew, Jr., and Richard Campbell. "Communication and Three Dimensions of Power: An Experiment and a Simulation." *Small Group Behavior,* 5 (1974), 289-320.

    To examine the effects of the experimental situation on experiments, the authors devised simulation procedures to determine the results of an experimental situation. The experiment itself used 21 three-person groups (10 M, 11 F) participating in a word game in which three dimensions of power, proactivity (initiating an interaction sequence), and reinforcement of proactivity were the variables observed. Male groups differed from simulation to experiment, but female groups did not; explanations based on the relationships between and among the variables are given. For females, some degree of contingency for the proactivity compliance relation (but not other power dimensions) may be operating. For males, the effect of proactivity on the other variables was greater in the experiment than in the simulation, and stronger interrelations among the three power dimensions developed.

241. Gulanick, Nancy A., George S. Howard, and John Moreland. "Evaluation of a Group Program Designed to Increase Androgyny in Feminine Women." *Sex Roles,* 5 (1979), 811-827.

    This study investigated the effectiveness of a group treatment program using consciousness-raising and assertiveness training to promote androgyny. Subjects were 51 female undergraduates; facilitators were four advanced graduate students. At the posttest, the full-treatment group was more assertive than the consciousness-raising group and wait-list control group. No posttest differences were found among the groups on sex-role orientation. At the two-month follow-up, the full-treatment group was more androgynous and more masculine than the wait-list group, while the differences between groups in assertiveness and consciousness-raising had dissipated. The one-year follow-up revealed the full-treatment group to be superior to the wait-list group in androgyny, masculinity, and assertiveness.

242. Hagen, Randi L., and Arnold Kahn. "Discrimination Against Competent Women." *Journal of Applied Social Psychology,* 5 (1975), 362-376.

Sixty male and 60 female undergraduates either competed with or cooperated with or only observed two males or two females, one of whom was reported as highly competent and the other as incompetent, to determine discrimination patterns. Males liked competent women only when in observer condition and not in either of the two interaction conditions. Both males and females were more willing to exclude a competent woman from their group than a competent man, but to include an incompetent woman more than an incompetent man. On the leadership measure, no discrimination appeared, with competent persons of either sex preferred to incompetent ones.

243. Hall, Jay, and Martha S. Williams. "Personality and Group Encounter Style: A Multivariant Analysis of Traits and Preferences." *Journal of Personality and Social Psychology,* 18 (1971), 163-172.

This study used both multivariate and canonical analyses of the scores of 43 male and 40 female undergraduates on seven personality measures and on the authors' Group Encounter Survey, designed to assess a preference for one of five styles in group decision-making situations. For females, one vector in the canonical analysis was significant, reflecting an underlying system of social competence and interpresonal sensitivity, and adaptability in interpersonal encounters. For males the significant vectors reflected negative systems, one of general maladjustment and social incompetence and the other of hostility and social-presence variables. These differences were reflected in the preferences for styles of decision making as well.

244. Hamby, Russell. "Effects of Gender and Sex-Role on Tension and Satisfaction in Small Groups." *Psychological Reports,* 42 (1978), 403-410.

One hundred and eight undergraduates, divided into 20 mixed-sex groups of five or six, participated in task-oriented discussions which were tape recorded and coded for tension indices and for behavior. Participants, all of whom had participated in earlier matrix games and taken the Bem Sex-Role Inventory, also completed a satisfaction questionnaire after the discussion. Gender had no effect on competition in the matrix games or on tension and satisfaction in the discussion groups. Androgynous subjects were lowest in all but one of the measures of tension and highest in satisfaction. A follow-up study with all females revealed masculine females high in tension and dissatisfaction. Masculine subjects of both genders were more antagonistic and showed less solidarity than feminine subjects; males and females did not differ significantly on those measures.

* Higbee, Kenneth L. "Group Influence on Self-Disclosure." *Psychological Reports,* 32 (1973), 903-909. See item 737.

245. Holmes, David P., and John J. Horan. "Anger Induction in Assertion Training." *Journal of Counseling Psychology,* 23 (1976), 108-111.

    Forty-five female university students were assigned randomly to a standard assertion training program, to a program incorporating anger induction, or to placebo counseling. On an assertiveness measure, the standard training group showed most improvement, but on one post-treatment behavioral measure, the subjects in the anger-induction group scored better.

246. Hrycenko, Igor, and Henry L. Minton. "Internal-External Control, Power Position, and Satisfaction in Task-Oriented Groups." *Journal of Personality and Social Psychology,* 30 (1974), 871-878.

    Fifty-two female and male undergraduates selected from internal or external locus of control populations were placed in task-performing triads and were led to believe they had either high or low power in the communication network. The hypotheses were that internals would prefer high power to low; externals would prefer low power; in high-power position, internals would be more satisfied; in low-power position, externals would be more satisfied. All hypotheses were supported, but for males only. Authors speculate sex-role stereotyping might account for sex differences.

247. Insko, Chester A., and Midge Wilson. "Interpersonal Attraction as a Function of Social Interaction." *Journal of Personality and Social Psychology,* 35 (1977), 903-911.

    Same-sex triads comprised of 54 male and female undergraduates, previously unknown to each other, evaluated each other after discussions in which one possible pair did not interact. Explicit interaction significantly increased liking as well as other assessments.

248. Jacobs, Alfred, Marion Jacobs, Norman Cavior, and John Burke. "Anonymous Feedback: Credibility and Desirability of Structured Emotional and Behavioral Feedback Delivered in Groups." *Journal of Counseling Psychology,* 21 (1974), 106-111.

    The credibility of personal information selected by members of small groups to describe each other's characteristics and delivered to the members by the group leader without naming the source was investigated. Twenty-four male and 24 female undergraduates engaged in consensus and self-disclosure exercises and then selected feedback from lists of positive or negative and behavioral (referring to the behaviors of the recipient) or emotional (referring to feelings of the deliverer about the recipient) descriptions. Positive feedback was rated by recipients as more credible, desirable, and as having more impact than negative feedback. Group cohesion was higher after the delivery of positive emotional feedback, not negative. Those receiving behavioral feedback reported the most gain from the experience. Males rated their feedback as more credible and desirable than females. There was no significant sex difference on the impact variable.

* Jacobson, Marsha B., and Joan Effertz. "Sex Roles and Leadership: Perceptions of the Leaders and the Led." *Organizational Behavior and Human Performance,* 12 (1974), 383-396. See item 607.

249. Jandt, Fred E., and Delmer M. Hilyard. "An Experimental Study of Self-Concept and Satisfactions." *Today's Speech,* 23, No. 4 (1975), 39-44.

    One hundred and seventeen male and female college students participated in unstructured group discussions to test the hypotheses that subjects expressing high acceptance of others would have greater satisfaction in the group than low-acceptance subjects, would make more sociometric choices, would have more communication directed to them, and that sex would not make a difference. The first three hypotheses were accepted for males only, invalidating the fourth hypothesis.

* Javornisky, Gregory. "Task Content and Sex Differences in Conformity." *The Journal of Social Psychology*, 108 (1979), 213-220. See item 680.

250. Jenkins, Lee, and Cheris Kramer. "Small Group Process: Learning From Women." *Women's Studies International Quarterly*, 1 (1978), 67-84.

    This review of sources ranging from personal accounts to empirical studies focuses on interactions in the early feminist groups, difficulties in organizing large campaign groups, research on sex differences in small group communication, and a theoretical model for understanding the origins of the differences in female and male interaction patterns.

251. Johnson, Daniel J., and I. Robert Andrews. "Risky-Shift Phenomenon Tested With Consumer Products as Stimuli." *Journal of Personality and Social Psychology*, 20 (1971), 382-385.

    Forty female undergraduates decided individually and then in a group discussion their willingness to try new consumer products already pre-judged as low-, medium-, and high-risks. Risky shifts occurred in groups for low-risk products, but no shift occurred with medium-risk products, and a conservative shift occurred with high-risk products.

* Johnson, David L., and Larry R. Ridener. "Self-Disclosure, Participation, and Perceived Cohesiveness in Small Group Interaction." *Psychological Reports*, 35 (1974), 361-362. See item 741.

252. Johnson, Norris R., James G. Steinler, and Deborah Hunter. "Crowd Behavior as 'Risky Shift': A Laboratory Experiment." *Sociometry*, 40 (1977), 183-187.

    Individually 76 males and 76 females responded on paper about the most radical action he/she would be willing to engage in to protest four hypothetical situations. In groups of eight of same sex, group decisions were made. For both males and females, the group decision was riskier for all situations than the individual decisions.

* Jourard, Sidney, and Robert Friedman. "Experimenter-Subject 'Distance' and Self-Disclosure." *Journal of Personality and Social Psychology*, 15 (1970), 278-282. See item 742.

253. Kahan, James P. "A Subjective Probability Interpretation of the Risky Shift." *Journal of Personality and Social Psychology*, 31 (1975), 977-982.

To test the theory that the risky-shift phenomenon is not a shift in advocated risk but a result of a rational process of attitudinal change, 36 undergraduate females made decisions where the odds of successful outcome were given, first individually, then in groups, and last, as they thought the person in the dilemma would actually make a decision. In the last, the odds stated for the dilemma were manipulated to match either the individual's or the group's odds. The usual risky shift occurred between the individual and the group decisions, but the shifts in the third choice were associated with the level of objective probability, supporting the theory.

* Kanter, Rosabeth M. "Some Effects of Proportions on Group Life: Skewed Sex Ratios and Responses to Token Women." *American Journal of Sociology*, 82 (1977), 965-990. See item 439.

* Kincaid, Marylou B. "Changes in Sex-Role Attitudes and Self-Actualization of Adult Women Following a Consciousness-Raising Group." *Sex Roles*, 3 (1977), 329-336. See item 30.

* Kirshner, Barry J., Robert R. Dies, and Robert A. Brown. "Effects of Experimental Manipulation of Self-Disclosure on Group Cohesiveness." *Journal of Consulting and Clinical Psychology*, 46 (1978), 1171-77. See item 744.

254. Klein, Helen M., and Lee Willerman. "Psychological Masculinity and Femininity and Typical and Maximal Dominance Expression in Women." *Journal of Personality and Social Psychology*, 37 (1979), 2059-70.

Four groups of 112 undergraduate females differing in masculinity/femininity ratings were evaluated for dominance (quality of remarks as well as quantity) in two laboratory problem-solving triad discussions, one designed to measure typical dominance and the other maximal dominance. Two in the discussion were confederates, either male or female. Undifferentiated and feminine sex-role females were significantly less dominant than masculine and androgynous females. Females were significantly less dominant with male confederates in the typical condition, not in the maximal one. This result was interpreted to mean that women inhibit a dominance trait before men when it is socially desirable to do so, but when salience for dominance is high, do not.

255. Klopfer, Frederick J., and Thomas Moran. "Influences of Sex Composition, Decision Rule, and Decision Consequences in Small Group Policy Making." *Sex Roles,* 4 (1978), 907-915.

    This study investigated the relationship of decision rule (consensus vs. majority rule), decision consequence (high vs. low consequences), adherence to group decision, and sex composition of the group. On a previously rated topic, 128 undergraduates in four-person groups of males and females deliberated an academic policy decision. Males made more emotional decisions based on need, while females used the objective criterion, grade point average. The effects of consensus versus majority rule or high versus low consequence on decision making were not significant.

* Knowles, Eric S., and Rodney L. Bassett. "Groups and Crowds as Social Entities: Effects of Activity, Size, and Member Similarity on Nonmembers." *Journal of Personality and Social Psychology,* 34 (1976), 837-845. See item 1166.

* Krebs, Dennis, and Allen A. Adinolfi. "Physical Attractiveness, Social Relations, and Personality Style." *Journal of Personality and Social Psychology,* 31 (1975), 245-253. See item 1113.

256. Lao, Rosina, Wilhelmina H. Upchurch, Betty J. Corwin, and William F. Grossnickle. "Biased Attitudes Toward Females as Indicated by Ratings of Intelligence and Likeability." *Psychological Reports,* 37 (1975), 1315-20.

    Using 643 undergraduates rating videotapes of two males and two females in high, medium, or low assertive roles in group situations on their likeability and intelligence, authors found that males were perceived of as more intelligent and likeable than females. Medium assertiveness for both males and females resulted in highest perceived intelligence and likeability. High assertiveness had a negative effect for ratings of female intelligence and a positive effect for male intelligence.

* Lapadat, Judy, and Maureen Seesahai. "Male versus Female Codes in Informal Contexts." *Sociolinguistics Newsletter,* 8, No. 3 (1977), 7-8. See item 862.

257. Larson, Carl E. "Speech Communication Research on Small Groups." *Speech Teacher,* 20 (1971), 89-107.

   This review of the research on small-group communication refers to some studies that found sex differences, two of them dating back to 1941, one that females became more accurate in a problem-solving task after interaction, and another that both sexes made greater attitudinal changes in mixed groups than in single-sex groups, though men made larger shifts.

* Leighton, Lennard A., Gray E. Stollak, and Lucy R. Ferguson. "Patterns of Communication in Normal and Clinic Families." *Journal of Consulting and Clinical Psychology,* 36 (1971), 252-256. See item 353.

* Leventhal, Gloria, Marsha Lipshultz, and Anthony Chiodo. "Sex and Setting Effects on Seating Arrangement." *Journal of Psychology,* 100 (1978), 21-26. See item 1172.

* Lewis, Benjamin F. "Group Silences." *Small Group Behavior,* 8 (1977), 109-120. See item 1291.

258. Lindskold, Svenn, and Michael G. Collins. "Inducing Cooperation by Groups and Individuals: Applying Osgood's GRIT Strategy." *Journal of Conflict Resolution,* 22 (1978), 679-690.

   Sixty-four female and 64 male undergraduates opposed one of four programmed strategies in a 30-trial Prisoner's Dilemma game. The strategies included a Graduated and Reciprocated Initiatives in Tension-Reduction (GRIT), a strategy involving a general statement of intent, specific announcements of choices, and some retaliation to exploitation. Other strategies were a competitive one in which announcements were used deceitfully, a tit-for-tat strategy without any verbal communication, and a 50% cooperative control strategy. For both groups and individuals the GRIT strategy promoted more cooperation than any of the other three, although this difference vanished when all four strategies were met with consistent, unannounced cooperation. Females were more cooperative than males. The conclusion was that GRIT is an effective strategy with groups as well as with individuals.

259. Lindskold, Svenn, Douglas C. McElwain, and Marc Wayner. "Cooperation and the Use of Coercion by Groups and

Individuals." *Journal of Conflict Resolution,* 21 (1977), 531-550.

In two experiments, male and female undergraduates, either as individuals or as groups, participated in a Prisoner's Dilemma game in which they could communicate either threats of punishment for target noncooperation or promises of their own cooperation. In Experiment 1 (98 M, 101 F), they opposed a live target; in Experiment 2 (85 M, 83 F), they opposed a simulated target who was either cooperative or competitive in response to the subject's messages. The major finding was that groups more strongly preferred the use of threats than individuals did. Groups were more competitive than individuals at the outset in both experiments. In Experiment 2, individual females opposing a cooperative target were most cooperative and conciliatory, while men in groups opposing a competitive target were most competitive and coercive. Female targets in Experiment 1 were more cooperative when playing against individuals than against groups; there was no difference for men.

260. Lirtzman, Sidney, and Mahmoud Wahba. "Determinants of Coalition Behavior of Men and Women: Sex Roles or Situational Requirements?" *Journal of Applied Psychology,* 56 (1972), 406-411.

To determine if sex or situation would be more important in coalition formation, the authors compared the strategies of 48 females working in triads in a competitive game-playing situation with built-in risks with the strategies of males in earlier studies. The women used the same coalition strategies as the men, supporting situation, not sex, as the determining factor.

* Lord, Robert G., James S. Phillips, and Michael C. Rush. "Effects of Sex and Personality on Perceptions of Emergent Leadership, Influence, and Social Power." *Journal of Applied Psychology,* 65 (1980), 176-182. See item 609.

261. Lumsden, Gay, Delindus R. Brown, Donald Lumsden, and Timothy A. Hill. "An Investigation of Differences in Verbal Behavior Between Black and White Informal Peer Group Discussions." *Today's Speech,* 22, No. 4 (1974), 31-36.

Eight groups of undergraduates, four black and four white, two all-male and two all-female groups in each, met to discuss interracial dating, a topic on which they had previously been measured for attitude. Fifteen random statements from each group were analyzed on eight variables and the groups were then compared. Significant findings were that black males and white females made statements showing greater orientation than black females and white males. White females' statements were less opinionated than those of the other three groups, black females used more profanity than the other three groups, and blacks of both sexes used more humor. White females' statements were more abstract than black females' and white males' than black males'. Whites of both sexes revealed more multi-valued orientation, and black females were more negative toward interracial dating then the other three groups.

262. Mabry, Edward A. "Exploratory Analysis of a Developmental Model for Task-Oriented Small Groups." *Human Communication Research,* 2 (1975), 66-74.

To explore a conceptual model for task-oriented group development, Mabry observed minute by minute 150 female undergraduates divided into 30 five-women groups. Analysis disclosed a pattern of development that began with an extended adaptation phase, which took most of the first half of group interaction, and continued with an integration phase. The last quarter of the interaction featured goal-attainment themes.

263. McBride, Kevin J., and Rosina C. Lao. "The Effects of Locus of Control on Coalition Formation Among College Females." *Psychology of Women Quarterly,* 3 (1978), 203-206.

To show the influence of locus of control on coalition formation, 45 female undergraduates were placed in triads by locus of control: externals, mixed, and internals. Subjects played a dice game where they could form alliances or play individually. More females preferred to win by forming coalitions than by not forming them. External females formed fewer coalitions than internal ones.

* McLaughlin, Frank E., Eleanor White, and Barbara Byfield. "Modes of Interpersonal Feedback and Leadership Structure in Six Small Groups." *Nursing Research,* 23 (1974), 307-318. See item 572.

* McMillan, Julie R., A. Kay Clifton, Diane McGrath, and Wanda S. Gale. "Women's Language: Uncertainty or

Interpersonal Sensitivity and Emotionality." *Sex Roles,* 3 (1977), 545-559. See item 867.

264. Madsen, Daniel B. "Issue Importance and Group Choice Shifts: A Persuasive Arguments Approach." *Journal of Personality and Social Psychology,* 36 (1978), 1118-27.

    In two experimental studies, each using over 100 female undergraduates in either individual or group argument situation on a topic of either high or low importance, Madsen found, as predicted, that group discussion produces more agree shifts under both levels of importance, though greater in low-importance condition than in high.

* Maier, Norman R.F. "Male Versus Female Discussion Leaders." *Personnel Psychology,* 23 (1970), 455-461. See item 610.

265. Maier, Norman R.F., and Marshall Sashkin. "The Contributions of a Union Steward vs. a Time-Study Man in Introducing Change: Role and Sex Effects." *Personnel Psychology,* 24 (1971), 221-238.

    A total of 458 male and female undergraduates role-played in a changing-work-procedure problem with three workers, one foreman, and alternately a time-study person or a union steward, the latter roles alternated by sex. The presence of neither time-study person nor union steward significantly altered the type of decision reached, though the presence of a time-study person made the decision reached significantly more acceptable to the workers. Both male and female foremen maintained their dominance over the time-study person of either sex. Male foremen retained dominance with the union steward, especially with a female union steward. Female foremen, however, lost dominance to male union stewards, the condition which was most conducive to high-quality solutions.

266. Mamola, Claire. "Women in Mixed Groups: Some Research Findings." *Small Group Behavior,* 10 (1979), 431-440.

    This review of research on women in groups, dating from 1949 through the late 1970s, reveals some contradictions. While some research indicates that women in mixed groups are reluctant to assume leadership roles, other research reveals that they may be more inclined to lead if the problem solution is given and that their abilities as supervisors are similar to males (though they advance less rapidly). Female followers of female leaders are only mildly positive about task satisfaction. Females exhibit more accommodation strategies in games.

267. Marr, Theodore J. "Conciliation and Verbal Responses as Functions of Orientation and Threat in Group Interaction." *Speech Monographs,* 41 (1974), 6-18.

    This study used 56 undergraduates in consensus-seeking discussions to investigate the interaction of level of orientation (verbal statement of fact or procedure to facilitate conflict resolution), level of threat (antagonism or unwillingness to consider alternatives), and sex of participant. High orientation led to a greater amount of conciliatory behavior than low orientation, and varying levels of threat did not significantly influence conciliatory behavior, although they did interact with levels of orientation. Females had significantly greater conciliatory behavior. Since all subjects knew that only consensus would bring a reward, Marr concluded that the "males were less logical than the females."

268. Marshall, Joan E., and Richard Heslin. "Boys and Girls Together: Sexual Composition and the Effect of Density and Group Size on Cohesiveness." *Journal of Personality and Social Psychology,* 31 (1975), 952-961.

    One hundred forty-two female and 142 male undergraduates in small or large rooms, crowded or not, mixed sex or unisex, performed a problem-solving task and then evaluated the experience. Density depressed general feelings of members, but had no effect on attitude toward group or on behavior. Small-size groups were more cohesive than large for same-sex groups, but not for mixed-sex ones. In general, males preferred mixed-sex groups. Females were favorable to mixed-sex groups if the groups were large or crowded, but to same-sex groups if small or uncrowded.

269. Maslach, Christina. "Social and Personal Bases of Individuation." *Journal of Personality and Social Psychology,* 29 (1974), 411-425.

    Forty female and forty male undergraduates game playing in groups of four were given both verbal and nonverbal opportunities to make themselves in some manner different from the rest of the group. When subjects anticipated positive rewards, they made more attempts to individuate than when rewards were expected to be negative. Though males and females were alike in that respect, they differed in that females' behavior showed a consistent pattern when individuating (less likely to smile or joke, talked less often but longer than males, whose behavior was not patterned). Males more often took a leadership role in games, females the consultant role. Females generally were more expressive nonverbally.

* Mayes, Sharon S. "Women in Positions of Authority: A Case Study of Changing Sex Roles." *Signs: Journal of Women in Culture and Society,* 4 (1979), 556-568. See item 611.

270. Meeker, B.F., and P.A. Weitzel-O'Neill. "Sex Roles and Interpersonal Behavior in Task-Oriented Groups." *American Sociological Review,* 42 (1977), 91-105.

    The theory that sex differences in behavior in a variety of task-oriented situations may be seen as the result of status processes is discussed. Since men have higher status than women, men are expected to be more competent and more competitive; therefore, dominating behavior is legitimate for men but not for women. Empirical studies of sex roles as they relate to task appropriateness, group problem solving, conflict, dominating behavior, and role expectations are reviewed in support of this theory. A three-page bibliography is included.

    Mehrabian, Albert, and Shirley G. Diamond. "Seating Arrangement and Conversation." *Sociometry,* 34 (1971), 281-289. See item 1177.

271. Mehrabian, Albert, and Sheldon Ksionzky. "Factors of Interpersonal Behavior and Judgment in Social Groups." *Psychological Reports,* 28 (1971), 483-492.

    A sociometric questionnaire was devised to administer to a closely knit group of 22 males and 18 females to classify each other's positive and negative reinforcing qualities. The results of a factor analysis are discussed, and correlations of the sociometric measure, personality measures, and sex revealed males less affiliative and considerably more negatively reinforcing than females.

272. Messé, Lawrence A., Joel Aronoff, and John P. Wilson. "Motivation as a Mediator of the Mechanisms Underlying

Role Assignments in Small Groups." *Journal of Personality and Social Psychology,* 24 (1972), 84-90.

Twenty-four triads of one male and two female undergraduates, homogeneous (based on pretests) in concern for safety or esteem needs, met for task discussions. Males became leaders in safety groups more often than in esteem groups, and there was a higher correlation between "suggests solutions" scores and leadership in esteem groups than in safety groups. Some influence of seating position on role differentiation was also found.

273. Miller, Charles E., and Patricia D. Anderson. "Group Decision Rules and the Rejection of Deviants." *Social Psychology Quarterly,* 42 (1979), 354-363.

This study used 60 groups of four female undergraduates and a female confederate in group discussion of appropriate sentence for a juvenile delinquent in which confederate always played a deviant role and in which group decisions were by majority vote, unanimity, or dictatorship. When group decision was unaffected by deviant, she was rejected only weakly. But when deviant's decision affected or even determined the group decision, she was strongly rejected, especially under dictator condition.

274. Mindock, Richard. "Risk Taking as a Function of an Individual's Impression of the Power Situation." *Psychological Reports,* 31 (1972), 471-474.

In an experiment designed to test the validity of a game board as a measure of risk-taking behavior, nine male and nine female undergraduates played games, three in each of three different levels of power. The number of risks taken was inversely related to the degree of power (most power, fewest risks). No sex differences were found.

275. Minton, Henry L., and Arthur G. Miller. "Group Risk Taking and Internal-External Control of Group Members." *Psychological Reports,* 26 (1970), 431-436.

Same-sex groups of six, internals, externals, or mixed based on test scores on an internal-external locus of control measure, problem-solved individually and then as groups. Female groups reached consensus significantly faster than male groups, but there were no significant differences by sex on risky shift or by locus of control and risky shift.

276. Moore, James C., Jr., Eugene B. Johnson, and Martha S.C. Arnold. "Status Congruence and Equity in Restricted Communication Networks." *Sociometry,* 35 (1972), 519-537.

In four-member task groups varied by educational status and by the presence and educational status of an assigned leader, 156 female first-year and graduate students revealed that status incongruence led to a decline in productivity and to less satisfaction of the group members. Leadership seemed not to be the primary predictor of the efficiency of the groups.

277. Nemeth, Charlan, Jeffrey Endicott, and Joel Wachtler. "From the '50s to the '70s: Women in Jury Deliberations." *Sociometry,* 39 (1976), 293-304.

Sex differences in deliberations in mock jury cases were analyzed for verdict, amount and nature of discussion participation, persuasiveness, and perceptions of the decision-making process. In the first study (28 groups of six with varying sex ratios), males offered more opinions, suggestions, and information, but in the second study (17 males and 19 females) no such differences emerged. Despite the similarities of males and females in verdict, interaction style, and persuasiveness, males were perceived as more independent, rational, strong, confident, influential, and leader-like than females were.

278. O'Connell, Agnes N. "Effects of Manipulated Status on Performance, Goal Setting, Achievement Motivation, Anxiety, and Fear of Success." *Journal of Social Psychology,* 112 (1980), 75-89.

Eighty female and 40 male undergraduates were tested in same-sex or mixed-sex groups of ten under no fear or fear-of-success arousal conditions to determine the effects of manipulated status on various performance and personality factors. In same-sex competition, those assigned to high status improved in performance while those assigned to low status did not. In mixed-sex competition under fear-of-success condition, both high- and low-status subjects improved. Sex differences included faster reaction time for males and higher personal goals set by males.

279. O'Day, Rory. "Individual Training Styles: An Empirically Derived Typology." *Small Group Behavior,* 7 (1976), 147-182.

The differences in training style among four trainers,

one female and three males, were measured by the Training Style Scoring System during sensitivity-training group sessions. The differences in styles were related to the trainers' interpersonal orientations and to the changes in trainers' perceptions of each other and of trainees' trainer. Details of these differences are given for each trainer leading to a typology of styles. The female trainer had the only negative change in rating from the group members.

* Parlee, Mary B. "Psychology and Women." *Signs: Journal of Women in Culture and Society,* 5 (1979), 121-133. See item 612.

280. Patterson, David L., and Stanley J. Smits. "Communication Bias in Black-White Groups." *Journal of Psychology,* 88 (1974), 9-25.

    T-groups of two black and two white females and two black and two white males, all graduate students, met in succeeding years, one five times, the other eight times, all sessions lasting over an hour, with a white male leader who did not actively participate. An analysis of the observed and videotaped sessions both statistically and through content analysis supported the hypothesis of a difference by race in percentage of remarks directed to members of the same race (blacks directed more comments to blacks than whites to whites), but not a hypothesis for a difference by sex.

* Patterson, Miles L., Carl E. Kelly, Bruce A. Kondracki, and Linda J. Wulf. "Effects of Seating Arrangement on Small-Group Behavior." *Social Psychology Quarterly,* 42 (1979), 180-185. See item 1179.

281. Patterson, Miles L., and Russell E. Schaeffer. "Effects of Size and Sex Composition on Interaction Distance, Participation, and Satisfaction in Small Groups." *Small Group Behavior,* 8 (1977), 433-442.

    The effects of the size and sex compositon of small groups on use of space, participation, and group satisfaction were investigated. Subjects were 270 male and female undergraduates who met in groups of four, six, or eight, either all male, all female, or mixed. A total of 45 groups, five in each of the nine conditions, was observed for seating positions and interaction. Sex composition of the groups significantly affected the distance, with female groups interacting more closely in dyads and in larger groups than males. Size of the groups had no significant effect on distance but did on satisfaction with the group. As group size increased, ratings of the pleasantness of the discussion, being at ease, and feeling a part of the group decreased. Individual participation decreased as group size increased.

* Paulus, Paul B., Angela B. Annis, John J. Seta, Janette K. Schkade, and Robert W. Matthews. "Density Does Affect Task Performance." *Journal of Personality and Social Psychology*, 34 (1976), 248-253. See item 1181.

* Pedersen, Darhl M. "Factors Affecting Personal Space Toward a Group." *Perceptual and Motor Skills*, 45 (1977), 735-743. See item 1182.

282. Phillips, James L., and Steven G. Cole. "Sex Differences in Triadic Coalition Formation Strategies." In *Studies of Conflict, Conflict Reduction, and Alliance Formation*. Eds. James L. Phillips and Thomas L. Conner. East Lansing: Michigan State University, 1970, pp. 154-180.

Ninety female and 90 male undergraduates participated in a game in which it was possible to make coalitions with one of the two others participating in the game and, in some conditions, with each separately. No difference between the sexes either in number of coalitions formed or in timing of forming them appeared. The accommodative-exploitative interpretation of sex differences in coalition formation in groups, therefore, received no support.

283. Piliavin, Jane A., and Rachel R. Martin. "The Effects of the Sex Composition of Groups on Style of Social Interaction." *Sex Roles*, 4 (1978), 281-296.

R. F. Bales's revised interaction category analyses (*Personality and Interpersonal Behavior*. New York: Rinehart & Winston, 1970) were done of audiotapes of 77 four-person discussion groups, 46 mixed sex, 15 female, and 16 male groups, all undergraduates, in 35-minute task discussions. Results showed large sex differences, regardless of group composition, in the direction of traditional sex roles, although mixed-sex groups had less sex-role stereotypic behavior. The strongest, clearest finding was that the behavior of individuals in groups was determined more by sex than by the composition of the group. Females engaged in more socioemotional behaviors than males, who engaged in more task behavior. Interacting in mixed-sex groups affected females, and to some extent, males, in the direction of moderating the differences found between the sexes when they worked in same-sex groups.

* Ragsdale, J. Donald. "Relationships Between Hesitation Phenomena, Anxiety, and Self-Control in a Normal Communication Situation." *Language and Speech,* 19 (1976), 257-265. See item 1242.

284. Richardson, James T., John R. Dugan, Louis N. Gray, and Bruce H. Mayhew, Jr. "Expert Power: A Behavioral Interpretation." *Sociometry,* 36 (1973), 302-324.

   Nineteen male and 21 female triads completed word tasks, either taking turns or spontaneously, and with or without a perceived expert present. Little difference attributable to sex occurred in spontaneous groups, but in taking-turns groups, females accepted fewer words from cohorts than males did and paid less attention to the point value of a word in rejecting it than males. The female taking-turns groups also were more influenced by the expert in their proportion of compliance.

285. Robson, R.A.H. "The Effects of Different Group Sex Composition on Support Rates and Coalition Formation." *Canadian Review of Sociology and Anthropology,* 8 (1971), 244-262.

   Fifty-two female and 51 male undergraduates formed coalitions in triads of various sex compositions and constructed a dramatic story from three Thematic Apperception Test pictures. Analysis indicated that females were more supportive, formed more coalitions, and distributed their support more equally among others when interacting with members of the same sex than males did. In the all-male groups, the least active member became an isolate; in the all-female group, the least active member received more support than any other group member. The typical coalition pattern in a male group was a coalition between two, with the third being an isolate; in the female groups, coalitions developed between all three members of the group. In mixed-sex groups, the effect of interacting with members of the opposite sex on both men and women made their behavior more like the others'.

* Ross, Michael, Bruce Layton, Bonnie Erickson, and John Schopler. "Affect, Facial Regard, and Reactions to

Crowding," *Journal of Personality and Social Psychology,* 28 (1973), 69-76. See item 1302.

286. Ruble, Diane N., and E. Tory Higgins. "Effects of Group Sex Composition on Self-Presentation and Sex-Typing." *Journal of Social Issues,* 32, No. 3 (1976), 125-132.

   The thesis of this article is that the sex composition of a group affects the sex-role awareness and sex-related responses of its members even when there is no actual or anticipated verbal interaction among group members. Support for the thesis is made through a review of literature and a report of two studies which revealed that the "mere presence" of certain proportions of females may be sufficient to affect awareness and responses.

* Ruch, Libby O., and Rae R. Newton. "Sex Characteristics, Task Clarity, and Authority." *Sex Roles,* 3 (1977), 479-494. See item 616.

287. Rumsey, Michael G., Elizabeth R. Allgeier, and Carl H. Castore. "Group Discussion, Sentencing Judgments, and the Leniency Shift." *The Journal of Social Psychology,* 105 (1978), 249-257.

   Two experimental studies (N=60, 160) examined the effects on same-sex group discussion on sentencing of a defendant when the case was systematically manipulated. Both sexes revealed a shift toward leniency. In the first experiment, only female subjects judging a negative defendant failed to produce this shift. In the second, in the defendant-salient condition, males moved toward leniency while females shifted slightly. In victim-salient condition, males moved little, while females shifted sharply toward leniency.

288. Sashkin, Marshall, and Norman R.F. Maier. "Sex Effects in Delegation." *Personnel Psychology,* 24 (1971), 471-476.

   This replication of a 1969 study of a changing-work-procedure problem used all female undergraduates (N=240). Three workers and a foreman, instructed either to encourage worker participation in the solution or restricted from doing so, reached a conclusion as to work procedures for the future. There were no significant differences by foreman instruction on quality of solution, but acceptance of the decision by workers, compared to earlier all-male study, was less, mainly because of low acceptance under the restricted condition.

* Schaible, Todd D., and Alfred Jacobs. "Feedback III: Sequence Effects: Enhancement of Feedback Acceptance and Group Attractiveness by Manipulation of the Sequence and Valence of Feedback." *Small Group Behavior,* 6 (1975), 151-173. See item 655.

289. Schlenker, Barry R. "Self-Presentation: Managing the Impression of Consistency when Reality Interferes with Self-Enhancement." *Journal of Personality and Social Psychology,* 32 (1975), 1030-37.

    One hundred and twenty female and male college students were led to expect participating in a group task where their individual performance would be revealed or not and where they were led to believe they would do well or poorly on the task. Before the task, each met in same-sex groups of four and exchanged information about themselves. Factor analysis of these revelations showed that under revealed-performance expectation, self-presentation was consistent with expected performance; under no-revelation condition, self-presentations were more favorable. Females perceived themselves as interpersonally oriented; males, task-oriented, except under revealed performance condition, when their self-ratings of interpersonal traits increased.

290. Schlenker, Barry R., and Marc Riess. "Self-Presentations of Attitudes Following Commitment to Proattitudinal Behavior." *Human Communication Research,* 5 (1979), 325-334.

    Under conditions of choice or no choice freedom to decide, 90 female subjects, in groups of three to five, committed themselves to argue for an action and then completed a measure of attitude toward that action. The results failed to support self-perception predictions of more favorable attitudes under choice rather than no-choice conditions.

* Schneier, Craig E. "The Contingency Model of Leadership: An Extension to Emergent Leadership and Leader's Sex." *Organizational Behavior and Human Performance,* 21 (1978), 220-239. See item 617.

* Schneier, Craig E., and Kathryn M. Bartol. "Sex Effects in Emergent Leadership." *Journal of Applied Psychology*, 65 (1980), 341-345. See item 618.

291. Shannon, John, and Bernard Guerney, Jr. "Interpersonal Effects on Interpersonal Behavior." *Journal of Personality and Social Psychology*, 26 (1973), 142-150.

    The spontaneous conversation of 14 groups of six college women was analyzed for response behavior. Findings supported the existence of stimulus-response bonds in interpersonal reflexes; for example, docile-dependent behavior tended to provoke leadership-advice and acceptance-assistance responses; and self-enhancing-competitive behavior tended to provoke resistance-distrust, self-effacement-submission, and docility-dependence responses.

* Sharf, Barbara F. "A Rhetorical Analysis of Leadership Emergence in Small Groups." *Communication Monographs*, 45 (1978), 156-172. See item 619.

292. Shaw, Marvin E. *Group Dynamics: The Psychology of Small Group Behavior*. New York: McGraw-Hill Book Co., 1971.

    In writing of the personal environment of groups (Chapter 6), Shaw briefly reviews sex differences arising from differences in sex roles, personality, nonverbal communication, especially eye contact, and conformity. In reviewing research on same-sex and mixed-sex groups, Shaw notes that research is not conclusive: sometimes same-sex groups are more efficient and sometimes mixed-sex groups are. More conformity is found in mixed-sex than in same-sex groups.

293. Shaw, Marvin E., and Blaze Harkey. "Some Effects of Congruency of Member Characteristics and Group Structure Upon Group Behavior." *Journal of Personality and Social Psychology*, 34 (1976), 412-418.

    Same-sex triads, 15 of each sex, varied for congruency or noncongruency of personal characteristics and with an assigned leader or not, solved problems. Congruent groups performed more effectively than noncongruent. Male leaders evaluated others in group higher than male followers did in both conditions, although higher for noncongruent. Female followers judged leaders more highly in noncongruent condition. Male leaders had significantly more confidence in their decisions than female leaders had. Females preferred groups with leader in noncongruent situation, males in congruent. Males preferred groups over individuals; females did not.

* Silbergeld, Sam, Elizabeth S. Thune, and Ronald W. Manderscheid. "The Group Therapist Leadership Role: Assessment in Adolescent Coping Courses." *Small Group Behavior,* 10 (1979), 176-199. See item 576.

294. Smith, Darrell, and Roger Miller. "Personal Growth Groups: A Comparison of the Experiences of Anglo and Mexican Americans." *Small Group Behavior,* 10 (1979), 263-270.

    To test the hypothesis that similarity of language between group leaders and members alone would not add significantly to positive gain from group process, an Anglo female, an Anglo male, and a Puerto Rican male, all doctoral students in counseling psychology, led 26 female and nine male Mexican American graduate students in five groups designed to enhance personal growth. An opinionnaire and a questionnaire assessed group members' attitudes about membership in their groups. The language variable influenced group members' preferences for a leader and the subsequent attitude toward the leader. The study also indicated that the sex of the group leader may be a major influence. The Anglo female leader effected a more positive influence, whether leading an Anglo or a Mexican-American group, than either of the male leaders.

* Smith, Edward D., and Anita Hed. "Effects of Offenders' Age and Attractiveness on Sentencing by Mock Juries." *Psychological Reports,* 44 (1979), 691-694. See item 1126.

295. Smith, E. Kim. "Effect of the Double-Bind Communication on the Anxiety Level of Normals." *Journal of Abnormal Psychology,* 85 (1976), 356-363.

    Four groups of 36 female college sophomores, balanced for high, medium, and low anxiety, were assigned randomly to punishment (white noise) or no punishment condition, given with contradictory or noncontradictory informative stimuli. The subjects were measured for changes in anxiety level on five tests. The group in both punishment and contradictory information conditions experienced significantly more anxiety than the other three groups, with the Mahl Speech Index the clearest measure of anxiety changes. Two hours after the experiment began, the Mahl Index revealed subjects in the "double bind," contradictory-information condition, had even greater anxiety, indicating their inability to adapt, while those who experienced only punishment gave evidence of adapting.

296. Smith, Gene F., and Peter Murdock. "Performance of Informed versus Noninformed Triads and Quartets in the 'Minimal Social Situation.'" *Journal of Personality and Social Psychology,* 15 (1970), 391-396.

In a problem-solving situation, 241 female undergraduates were placed in triads or quartets and were either informed or not of the effect of their own action on the others. Triads reached solution significantly more often than quartets, though quartets showed greater improvement in pre-solution trials. Information on the effect of individual action did not significantly affect either size group, although it improved performance in a subsequent study with dyads.

297. Smith, Kay H. "Changes in Group Structure through Individual and Group Feedback." *Journal of Personality and Social Psychology,* 24 (1972), 425-428.

In this study using four reinforcement conditions with ten four-person discussion groups of undergraduate females, entirely automated feedback was effective in changing rates of participation and perceived group structure. Individual feedback was more effective than group feedback, and was more effective if it was perceived as applying to individual only rather than to the group.

298. Stang, David J. "Effects of Interaction Rate on Ratings of Leadership and Liking." *Journal of Personality and Social Psychology,* 27 (1973), 405-408.

Thirty college females heard three scripts manipulated for levels and length of interaction of participants and then rated the participants for liking and leadership. Leadership rating increased as interaction rate increased, while liking rating was greater for medium-length parts than for either long or short parts.

299. Stebbins, Charles A., Bryan R. Kelly, Alexander Tolor, and Mary-Ellen Power. "Sex Differences in Assertiveness

in College Students." *Journal of Psychology,* 95 (1977), 309-315.

Eighty-one undergraduate males and females completed an assertion measure and then were placed in same-sex groups of three plus a male or female confederate and put in situations in which assertive behavior was called for. Females scored significantly higher on the assertion measure than males. In the first behavioral test, those who asserted themselves scored significantly higher on the assertion measure, and each sex was more assertive towards members of own sex than toward the opposite sex. In the second behavioral test, which required reporting the cheating of the confederate in the group, no one, male or female, reported it. In fact, almost half the male subjects aided the female cheater, though none of the female subjects aided the male cheater.

* Stein, R. Timothy, and Tamar Heller. "An Empirical Analysis of the Correlations Between Leadership Status and Participation Rates Reported in the Literature." *Journal of Personality and Social Psychology,* 37 (1979), 1993-2002. See item 621.

* Steinbacher, Roberta, and Faith D. Gilroy. "Persuasibility and Persuasiveness as a Function of Sex." *The Journal of Social Psychology,* 100 (1976), 299-306. See item 700.

300. Stephan, Cookie. "Sex Prejudice in Jury Simulation." *Journal of Psychology,* 88 (1974), 305-312.

Using 84 male and 101 female college students judging either individually or in groups a man or a woman accused of murdering a spouse, Stephan found that subjects were less likely to find same-sex defendants guilty than opposite-sex defendants. Female defendants were not sentenced more leniently, as predicted. Female jurors found reaching a decision more difficult, felt more empathy, and more often mentioned psychiatric care than male jurors. Groups reached decisions more quickly than individuals, and males gave longer sentences in group conditions while females gave longer ones in individual conditions.

301. Taylor, Shelley E., Susan T. Fiske, Nancy L. Etcoff, and Audrey J. Ruderman. "Categorical and Contextual Bases

of Person Memory and Stereotyping." *Journal of Personality and Social Psychology,* 36 (1978), 778-793.

Three studies used male and female undergraduates in a memory test of material from tapes and slides of small-group discussions manipulated for sex and race. Information was encoded by sex and race, but no difference between male and female subjects in error rate for opposite sex occurred, as predicted. Males in groups were rated as significantly more influential, confident, analytic, and negative and significantly less warm and sensitive than females in the experiment in which male and female discussants made identical statements. When one sex was a clear minority in the group, that sex was seen as having a stronger personality and being more assertive and confident, but being less warm and pleasant and more negative.

302. Thune, Elizabeth S., Ronald W. Manderscheid, and Sam Silbergeld. "Status or Sex Roles as Determinants of Interaction Patterns in Small, Mixed-Sex Groups." *Journal of Social Psychology,* 112 (1980), 51-65.

The interaction patterns of two mixed-sex, research therapy groups of ten (one of teachers, one of husband-wife pairs) over 15 sessions were analyzed using data from the Hill Interaction Matrix, which scores for both style and content. Generally the couples' group had differences between the sexes in instrumental and expressive verbal behavior, while the teachers' group did not. The data were interpreted to mean that status roles were more influential than sex roles in verbal behavior in mixed-sex groups.

* Tindall, Jeffry H., Linda Boyler, Pat Cline, Paul Emberger, Sharon Powell, and Joseph Wions. "Perceived Leadership Rankings of Males and Females in Small Task Groups." *Journal of Psychology,* 100 (1978),13-20. See item 622.

303. Vinacke, W. Edgar, Robert Mogy, William Powers, Charles Langan, and Robert Beck. "Accommodative Strategy and Communication in a Three-person Matrix Game." *Journal of Personality and Social Psychology,* 29 (1974), 509-525.

Forty-eight triads of male and female undergraduates in which the members were all high in exploitativeness or all high in accommodativeness, or mixed, played a strategy game (explained in detail) under conditions of verbal communication permitted or not. Significant effects for all variables and their interactions were found. Sex of subject was related to coalition choices, to expected outcome, to actual outcome, and to score. Among other findings, female accommodative triads preferred a coalition of all three members, females anticipated equal payoffs more than males did, female triads had more mutually cooperative payoffs, and female triads had higher mean outcomes.

304. Wahrman, Ralph. "Status, Deviance, Sanctions, and Group Discussion." *Small Group Behavior,* 8 (1977), 147-168.

The seriousness of three mild and three serious behaviors of a deviant person was rated by 72 fraternity and 72 sorority members either individually before the deviant was identified as a high or low-status member of their own groups, or individually after identification, or as groups after discussion. Males were less stable in their judgments of high-status deviants and females less stable in their judgments of low-status deviants. Mild deviance was rated more leniently after identification and still more leniently after discussion if the deviant had high status. If the deviant had low status, the deviant's behavior was rated more serious after identification and still more serious after discussion. Serious deviance was rated more leniently after identification regardless of the deviant's status. Men were more changeable than women after both identification and discussion. Discussion of sanctions led to milder sanctions regardless of sex of deviant, status of the deviant, or seriousness of the deviant's behavior.

305. Wall, James A., Jr. "Effects of Sex and Opposing Representative's Bargaining Orientation on Intergroup Bargaining." *Journal of Personality and Social Psychology,* 33 (1976), 55-61.

Teams of two representatives and two constituents who directed their negotiations were formed to bargain over wages, all teams of one sex only, using 132 undergraduates in all. Female constituents were more cooperative than male constituents, and male outsiders (opposing management team) conceded more than female outsiders, though male representatives ended with significantly higher demands. Both male and female representatives arrived at about the same number of agreements, but females took less time.

306. Wall, James A., Jr. "The Intergroup Bargaining of Mixed-Sex Groups." *Journal of Applied Psychology*, 62 (1977), 208-213.

A simulated three-person bargaining session used undergraduate males and females (total N=216) as union member, management representative, and union representative. Though no significant differences in demands or concessions were found between all-male, all-female, and mixed groups, the number of deadlocks was greater in mixed-sex groups, a result observed in industry as well. Both male and female groups reached agreements significantly more often than mixed groups.

307. Wallach, Michael A., and Jerome Mabli. "Information versus Conformity in the Effects of Group Discussion on Risk Taking." *Journal of Personality and Social Psychology*, 14 (1970), 149-156.

Eighteen all-male and 18 all-female triads composed of a conservative minority and a risky majority or vice versa made individual and then group decisions. From individual judgments to group judgments, the conservatives showed shifts to greater risk-taking, whether in majority or minority; the risk-takers showed no significant shift. No sex difference in these findings emerged.

* Welsh, M. Cay. "Attitudinal Measures and Evaluation of Males and Females in Leadership Roles." *Psychological Reports*, 45 (1979), 19-22. See item 623.

308. Wheelan, Susan A. "Effect of Personal Growth and Assertive Training Classes on Female Sex-Role Self-Concept." *Group and Organization Studies*, 3 (1978), 239-244.

One hundred eighty-six female undergraduates, enrolled in either 10-week personal growth classes or assertive training classes, completed the Bem Sex-Role Inventory before the classes began and again at the ninth week. Females in the assertive training classes increased their acceptance of masculine characteristics; females in the personal growth classes neither increased their acceptance of masculine characteristics nor reinforced their acceptance of feminine characteristics.

309. White, Sam E., John E. Dittrich, and James R. Lang. "The Effects of Group Decision-Making Process and Problem-Situation Complexity on Implementation Attempts." *Ad-

ministrative Science Quarterly, 25 (1980), 428-440.

The relationship between problem-solving techniques used in a group and attempts at implementing the group's ideas when the participants returned to their home organizations was investigated using 64 female and one male registered nurse administrators in a combination laboratory-field training situation. Three different group problem-solving techniques were used for dealing with three types of managerial problems: 1) an interactive process, 2) a nominal-group process; and 3) a structured discussion process. Structure in group decision-making processes led to increased rates of implementation attempts. There was a significant complexity-by-process interaction effect among the decision-making processes, which supported the conclusion that the type of group decision-making process and the problem-situation complexity should be considered in order to increase the number of implementation attempts.

310. Williams, J. Sherwood, Louis N. Gray, and Maxmilian H. von Broembsen. "Proactivity and Reinforcement: The Contingency of Social Behavior." *Small Group Behavior,* 7 (1976), 317-330.

    Differences among individuals on attempted influence in group decision making were examined. Ten male and eleven female same-sex triads formed words from a set of 13 letter-faced dice for a monetary reward. Male groups formed a differentiated role structure with a clearly defined task specialist. Female groups did not, but they generally had better total scores than the male groups, leading the authors to conclude that role differentiation is not necessarily a more efficient response to problem-solving.

311. Willis, Frank N., and Sharon J. Williams. "Simultaneous Talking in Conversation and Sex of Speakers." *Perceptual and Motor Skills,* 43 (1976), 1067-70.

    In three field settings, a high school discussion group, a university faculty office, and a university student union cafeteria, simultaneous talking was observed and classified as to being in agreement or not with the speaker or irrelevant. Simultaneous talking occurred in 18.6% of the utterances, and women were more likely to be interrupted, especially by men. Female interruptions were more likely to agree with a male speaker;

both male and female interruptors tended to disagree with a female speaker.

312. Winship, Barbara J., and Jan D. Kelley. "A Verbal Response Model of Assertiveness." *Journal of Counseling Psychology*, 23 (1976), 215-220.

   Twenty-five female nursing students were assigned randomly to an assertive training group, an attention control group, or a no-treatment group. On the posttreatment measures, a self-report scale, four written responses, and verbal responses to two role-playing situations, the subjects in the assertive training group revealed more assertive behavior.

313. Wolman, Carol, and Hal Frank. "The Solo Woman in a Professional Peer Group." *American Journal of Orthopsychiatry*, 45 (1975), 164-171.

   Case studies are given of six groups of peers, each with a lone woman member (size of groups not given). Three groups were unstructured sensitivity-training groups, whose goal was learning about group function by participation, and three were first-year psychiatric resident work groups. Some groups were recorded, others observed first-hand, and all participants completed various questionnaires and were interviewed. In four of the groups the lone woman became a deviant in the group; in one group an isolate by choice; and in one a low-status regular member. All became anxious or depressed in their efforts to become regular status members. Feminine coping mechanisms made the lone woman more deviant, and masculine coping mechanisms were seen as threatening, so she was isolated even more. Suggestions for counteracting the lone woman problem are made.

314. Wolosin, Robert J. "Cognitive Similarity and Group Laughter." *Journal of Personality and Social Psychology*, 32 (1975), 503-509.

   Using 12 male and 15 female groups of four of varying degrees of similarity on pretest on aggression, Wolosin found that for males only the greater the cognitive similarity, the more frequent the laughter. For both sexes cognitive similarity was associated with a pleasant group atmosphere, relaxed style of interaction, and fewer awkward silences.

* Woolfolk, Robert L., and Anita E. Woolfolk. "Effects of Teacher Verbal and Nonverbal Behaviors on Student Perceptions and Attitudes." *American Educational Research Journal,* 11 (1974), 297-303. See item 526.

315. Wright, Fred. "The Effects of Style and Sex of Consultants and Sex of Members in Self-Study Groups." *Small Group Behavior,* 7 (1976), 433-456.

    Self-study groups, as distinct from sensitivity-training groups, were examined for group level processes and interactions between group members and authority figures. Four male and four female trained consultants adopted either a reciprocating or nonreciprocating style with 38 female and 43 male undergraduates. Female consultants were more verbal, more peer-oriented (as opposed to authority-oriented), and more positive toward peers with the nonreciprocating style. Males had an opposite pattern, more verbal, more peer-oriented, and more positive toward peers with the reciprocating style. Subjects' responses to the situations in the group sessions were indirect, and female consultants seemed to generate more extreme reactions than male consultants. Female subjects seemed to be most extreme in responding to the female consultants.

* Yerby, Janet. "Attitude, Task, and Sex Composition as Variables Affecting Leadership in Small Problem Solving Groups." *Speech Monographs,* 42 (1975), 160-168. See item 626.

* Yockey, Jamie M. "Role Theory and the Female Sex Role." *Sex Roles,* 4 (1978), 917-927. See item 77.

IN THE FAMILY

316. Albrecht, Terrance L., and Ralph E. Cooley. "Androgyny and Communication Strategies for Relational Dominance: An Empirical Analysis." In *Communication Yearbook 4.* Ed. Dan Nimmo. New Brunswick, N.J.: Transaction Books, 1980, pp. 699-719.

    To investigate how individuals use strategies to gain dominance in interpersonal relationships, 96 community married couples completed independently a questionnaire on family communication patterns, both actual and ideal, and then were interviewed together on four topics concerning their life. From the questionnaires, a discrepancy score was obtained, and the five husbands and five wives at both the high and the low ends of the discrepancy scores were used for analysis of the transcript of their interviews. High discrepancy subjects and their spouses attempted dominance more than low discrepancy subjects and their spouses. High discrepancy subjects used interruption most often to dominate, while low discrepancy subjects used more the strategy of simultaneous speech. Spouses of high discrepancy subjects reciprocated their spouse's behavior; both tended to be unsupportive and more interruptive. Spouses of low discrepancy subjects displayed opposite behavior; when the subject was unsupportive and interruptive, the spouse was generally supportive and noninterruptive.

317. Alexander, James F. "Defensive and Supportive Communications in Normal and Deviant Families." *Journal of Consulting and Clinical Psychology,* 40 (1973), 223-231.

Videotapes of 20 normal and 20 deviant (runaway male or female child) families in discussion and settling-differences tasks revealed that deviant families manifested defensive communication and normal families supportive communication in all possible dyad combinations. Reciprocity and feedback were also found, supporting the idea of families operating as systems. No sex of parent or sex of child differences were found except that female runaway families exhibited a higher rate of defensive behavior.

318. Beier, Ernst G., and Daniel P. Sternberg. "Subtle Cues Between Newly Weds." *Journal of Communication,* 27 (Summer 1977), 92-97.

Videotapes of 51 newly married couples revealed significant differences in nonverbal behavior. Wives touched both self and spouse more and smiled more than husbands did. Husbands talked more and sat in more open arm and leg positions. Observation, but not statistical analysis, showed that couples reporting least discord in marriage displayed more interpersonal closeness, that is, sat closer, looked at each other longer and more frequently, touched each other more often, touched themselves less, and held legs in more open position. For a follow-up study, see item 375.

319. Billings, Andrew. "Conflict Resolution in Distressed and Nondistressed Married Couples." *Journal of Con-

sulting and Clinical Psychology, 47 (1979), 368-376.

This study compared the communication interaction of 12 maritally distressed and 12 nondistressed couples while they engaged in conflict resolution discussion. Distressed couples made significantly more negative and fewer positive cognitive and problem-solving statements and reciprocated more negative communication.

320. Birchler, Gary R., Robert L. Weiss, and John L. Vincent. "Multimethod Analysis of Social Reinforcement Exchange Between Maritally Distressed and Nondistressed Spouse and Stranger Dyads." *Journal of Personality and Social Psychology,* 31 (1975), 349-360.

    Volunteer married couples self-reported as either experiencing marital distress or as being happily married and stranger couples, 24 couples in all, were observed in at-home interactions and laboratory problem solving tasks and conversations. The authors found distressed couples made fewer positive reinforcements, made more negative ones, had more conflicts, and shared fewer recreational activities. Especially noticeable was the lack of exchange of positive social reinforcement in distressed couples in the problem-solving laboratory task.

    Bugental, Daphne, Jaques W. Kaswan, and Leonore R. Love. "Perception of Contradictory Meanings Conveyed by Verbal and Nonverbal Channels." *Journal of Personality and Social Psychology,* 16 (1970), 647-655. See item 1262.

321. Bugental, Daphne E., Leonore R. Love, and Robert M. Gianetto. "Perfidious Feminine Faces." *Journal of Personality and Social Psychology,* 17 (1971), 314-318.

    This study used ratings of verbal and nonverbal (smiling) behavior of parents by 20 normal and 20 disturbed children. Fathers' smiles were associated with friendly verbal messages. Mothers smiled, however, even when a verbal message was not positive. White middle-class mothers smiled more than lower-class ethnic mothers. No significant differences were found between mothers of disturbed and normal children.

322. Bugental, Daphne E., Leonore R. Love, Jaques W. Kaswan, and Carol April. "Verbal-Nonverbal Conflict in Parental Messages to Normal and Disturbed Children." *Journal of*

Abnormal Psychology, 77 (1971), 6-10.

Analyzing videotapes of parent-child communication of 20 families with a disturbed child aged eight to ten and ten "normal" families, the authors found mothers of disturbed children produced significantly more conflicting messages, including between verbal content and facial expression and between verbal content and tone of voice, than normal mothers did. No differences between fathers and children were found.

323. Burke, Ronald J., and Tamara Weir. "Patterns in Husbands' and Wives' Coping Behaviors." *Psychological Reports,* 44 (1979), 951-956.

Eighty-five married couples separately completed a questionnaire on their typical coping behavior in stressful situations. Husbands were found more likely to use problem-solving and talking with others, while wives were more likely to use distraction/depression and prayer and meditation. Intercorrelations of eight coping behaviors indicated that husbands and wives did not use the same strategies in coping, but complementary ones, an active/passive pattern or an "other-abused"/ "self-abused" pattern.

324. Centers, Richard, and Bertram H. Raven. "Conjugal Power Structure: A Re-Examination." *American Sociological Review,* 36 (1971), 264-278.

Data were gathered from interviews with 776 husbands and wives to determine their relative power in the marriage. Husband power was greatest among Oriental couples and least among Negro couples. Husband power decreased with age, with length of marriage, and was less in a second marriage, but increased with occupational status and educational level. Husband-dominant families tended to show high authoritarianism scores for both husbands and wives. Least marital satisfaction was associated with wife dominance.

* Chariter, Jan, and Myron R. Chartier. "Perceived Parental Communication and Self-Esteem: An Exploratory Study." *Western Speech,* 39 (1975), 26-31. See item 10.

325. Courtright, John A., Frank E. Millar, and L. Edna Rogers-Millar. "Domineeringness and Dominance: Replication and Expansion." *Communication Monographs,* 46 (1979), 179-192.

From self-report data and from interviews with 86 middle-class, white midwestern married couples, measures of domineering (individual message) and dominance (in couple interactions) were obtained and then correlated with a number of variables. Domineering expressions were unrelated to the frequency of being the dominant partner. The number of questions asked by the wife was negatively related to her dominance score; the proportion of assertions made by the wife decreased as husband domineeringness increased. The more domineering the spouse, the fewer support statements by either spouse. Wife's domineeringness was associated with less communication and less marital satisfaction of wife. Husband's dominance correlated positively with his satisfaction, but not his wife's.

326. Cromwell, Ronald E., and David H. Olson, eds. *Power in Families*. New York: Halsted Press, 1975.

    This collection of thirteen articles on power in families includes sections on conceptual and theoretical issues and methodological and substantive research. Each section is prefaced by an overview.

 * Dale, Philip S. "Hesitations in Maternal Speech." *Language and Speech,* 17 (1974), 174-181. See item 1227.

327. Doane, Jeri A. "Family Interaction and Communication Deviance in Disturbed and Normal Families: A Review of Research." *Family Process,* 17 (1978), 357-376.

    This review of 80 family interaction studies focusing on how the disturbed family's interaction differs from that in the nondisturbed family includes a section on the deviant styles of communication in the disturbed family, especially mother-conflicting messages (friendliness or approval in one channel and unfriendliness or disapproval in another).

328. Doherty, William J., and Robert G. Ryder. "Locus of Control, Interpersonal Trust, and Assertive Behavior Among Newlyweds." *Journal of Personality and Social Psychology,* 37 (1979), 2212-22.

    Correlations of responses of 86 married couples to measures of locus of control, trust for other, and the Inventory of Marital Conflicts, which requires both individual and couple responses, revealed that internal locus-of-control husbands were more assertive than external, that external, high-trust husbands were least assertive, and internal, low-trust wives were highly assertive. No separate locus-of-control effect was found for wives.

329. Downs, Philip E. "Intrafamily Decision Making in Family Planning." *JBR: Journal of Business Research*, 5 (1977), 63-74.

    This study reported the decision-making process of 58 husbands and their pregnant wives about a future contraceptive method. The subjects first individually and then jointly (with discussion) ranked preferences for 12 contraceptive methods. As wives made salient the side effects of various methods, they influenced their husbands. Condoms became a compromise preferred technique in joint decision making.

* Duckworth, Douglas H. "Personality, Emotional State, and Perception of Nonverbal Communication." *Perceptual and Motor Skills*, 40 (1975), 325-326. See item 1271.

* Dumas, Bethany K. "Male-Female Conversational Interaction Cues: Using Data From Dialect Surveys." In *The Sociology of the Languages of American Women*. Eds. Betty L. Dubois and Isabel Crouch. San Antonio, Tex.: Trinity University, 1976, pp. 41-52. See item 112.

330. Elrod, Mimi M., and Sedahia J. Crase. "Sex Differences in Self-Esteem and Parental Behavior." *Psychological Reports*, 46 (1980), 719-727.

    The relationship of parental behavior to the self-esteem of their 4- or 5-year-old sons or daughters was examined by a test of self-esteem given to 49 male and 45 female children and a self-inventory questionnaire given to their parents. Mothers reported interacting with sons and daughters more than fathers did, and fathers interacted more with sons than with daughters. Mothers interacted more similarly with either sex than fathers. Boys were found to have significantly higher self-esteem, and the same behavior in different parent-child combinations can either enhance or diminish self-esteem.

331. Epstein, Norman, and Elizabeth Jackson. "An Outcome Study of Short-Term Communication Training with Married Couples." *Journal of Consulting and Clinical Psychology*, 46 (1978), 207-212.

    Three groups of five couples each were given communication training or insight training for five sessions over three weeks or no training. Communication training produced a significant increase in assertive requests, a decrease in attacks, and an increase in spouse-rated empathy over other groups. Both treatment groups reported fewer disagreements after treatment.

332. Fishman, Pamela. "Interaction: The Work Women Do." *Social Problems,* 25 (1978), 397-406. See also item 333.

    This study of at-home, everyday conversations transcribed from 52 hours of tape recordings of three couples revealed an unequal distribution of work in conversation. Women more actively engaged in insuring conversation; they asked more questions, used more attention beginnings, did more support work while the men talked, and more actively maintained and continued conversations. Though women did the work necessary for interaction to occur, men controlled the conversation.

333. Fishman, Pamela M. "What Do Couples Talk About When They're Alone?" In *Women's Language and Style* (item 808), pp. 11-22. See also item 332.

    An examination of ten transcribed hours of 52 recorded hours of the at-home conversation of three couples (age range 25-35), all professionally oriented and all sympathetic to the women's movement, revealed that women raised 62% of the total topics raised, but only 38% of the topics resulted in successful conversations, while all of the topics raised by men were successful. Devices to secure attention and signs of topic failure were analyzed using the transcript data. Since women try more often to start conversations and have so many attempts fail, these devices seem to be features of women's talk. The same features are used by men, however, in interpersonal situations in which their conversational attempts are also ignored.

334. Fitzpatrick, Mary A., and Patricia Best. "Dyadic Adjustment in Relational Types: Consensus, Cohesion, Affectional Expression, and Satisfaction in Enduring Relationships." *Communication Monographs,* 46 (1979), 167-178.

    Sixty-eight couples, not from an academic community, completed dyadic adjustment and relational dimensions measures, the latter a measure to determine traditional, independent, separate, and separate/traditional couples.

Multivariant analysis of variance and discriminant analysis revealed that relational types can be discriminated by certain measures of dyadic adjustment. Traditional couples were higher on expression of affection, independent couples were lower on consensus, but not to the detriment of cohesiveness. Separate couples had high consensus, but were significantly lower on cohesiveness. Separate/traditional couples were low on consensus but high on satisfaction and expressing affection. Couples who agreed on their relational definition had more consensus and cohesiveness, but couples who disagreed were more satisfied with their relationships and expressed affection more. All were about equal in satisfaction.

335. Fox, Greer L., and Judith K. Inazu. "Patterns and Outcomes of Mother-Daughter Communication About Sexuality." *Journal of Social Issues,* 36, No. 1 (1980), 7-29.

This study, drawing from a sample survey of 449 black and white mother-teenage daughter dyads, examined patterns, correlates, and consequences of direct verbal communication about sex. While mothers and daughters reported frequent discussion of sex-related topics, they differed in terms of how comfortable they felt talking with each other, what roles each played in initiating discussions, and whether they desired more frequent future discussions.

336. Fraser, Colin, and Naomi Roberts. "Mothers' Speech to Children of Four Different Ages." *Journal of Psycholinguistic Research,* 4 (1975), 9-16.

Thirty-two mother-child pairs, with children ages 1-1/2, 2-1/2, 4, or 6 years old, were recorded in model-building and story tasks. Analysis of amount of speech, length of units, disfluencies, syntactic complexity, and richness of vocabulary revealed no sex or order of birth of child effects but did reveal task and age effects. In general, with increasing age of child, but especially between 1-1/2 and 2-1/2, the mothers spoke more, in longer, syntactically more complex sentences, and with more diversified vocabulary. In general, the same characteristics were found more in the story than in the model-building task.

* Gilbert, Shirley J. "Self Disclosure, Intimacy and Communication in Families." *The Family Coordinator,* 25, No. 3 (1976), 221-231. See item 732.

337. Gillespie, Dair L. "Who Has the Power? The Marital Struggle." In *Female Psychology: The Emerging Self.* Ed. Sue Cox. Chicago: Science Research Associates, 1976. Pp. 192-211.

Pointing out as inadequate research on power in marriages that does not account for hidden power (power to prevent others from doing what they want) as well as overt power, Gillespie reviews sources of marital power. Among them are socialization patterns, legal rights, economic sources, participation in organizations, education, and physical coercion, all of which favor the male. The connection between husband power and suburbanization, race, and family life cycles are also discussed.

338. Givens, David B. "Contrasting Nonverbal Styles in Mother-Child Interaction: Examples from a Study of Child Abuse." *Semiotica,* 24, No. 1/2 (1978), 33-47.

An analysis of the nonverbal behavior of fourteen mothers, half of them abusive parents, in videotaped task interactions with their 2- to 2-1/2-year-old children, revealed that abusive mothers more frequently used rough instrumental touching, especially the "grab-away," used less noninstrumental touching, and used over-high vocal pitch more than the control mothers, who used over-soft voices. All of the abusive mothers gave verbal instructions in a low-pitched, over-loud voice; no control mother did. In general, the maternal behavior put the child in a double-bind situation, provoking negative behavior and then responding negatively to it.

339. Gleason, Jean B. "Sex Differences in the Language of Children and Parents." In *Language, Children, and Society: The Effect of Social Factors in Children Learning to Communicate.* Eds. Olga Garnica and Martha L. King. Oxford: Pergamon, 1979, pp. 149-157.

Research in sex differences in the language of parents and children is reviewed. The differences reviewed for children include performance and neurological data, inborn and social-training differences, and neuroanatomical evidence of differences in the brains of male and female children. For parents the differences reviewed include their language, differences in addressing male and female children, and differences in their expectations of them.

340. Goldberg, Judy H., and Alvin A. Goldberg. "Family Communication." *Western Speech Communication,* 40 (1976), 104-110.

    This article describes a family-communication course approached from a systems theory point of view, which includes total family communication, marital communication, and parent-child communication.

341. Greif, Esther B. "Sex Differences in Parent-Child Conversations." *Women's Studies International Quarterly,* 3 (1980), 253-258.

    Sex differences in the use of interruptions and simultaneous speech during conversations between parents and preschool children were examined. Participants were 16 children, ages two to five, and both their parents; each parent-child pair engaged in semi-structured play for 30 minutes. Fathers interrupted more and spoke simultaneously more than mothers did. Both parents were more likely to interrupt and to speak simultaneously with daughters than with sons. Results are discussed in relation to the power differences between men and women and in reference to the socialization of children into gender roles.

342. Hadley, Trevor R., and Theodore Jacob. "The Measurement of Family Power: A Methodological Study." *Sociometry,* 39 (1976), 384-395.

    Taped interactions and self-reports of eleven mother, father, and high-school age sons were analyzed to determine the relationship of various measures of family power. Results included a positive relationship between attribution of power measure and decision measure for fathers and for sons, but not for mothers. No mother perceived of the family power hierarchy as anything other than a father-mother-son structure.

343. Harmon, Dana, and Kate L. Kogan. "Social Class and Mother-Child Interaction." *Psychological Reports,* 46 (1980), 1075-84.

    The authors review and critique studies from 1965 on social class as a variable in mother-child interaction. In their own study of 96 mother-child pairs, all white (to avoid compounding social class with ethnic differences) and stratified by social class based on the Hollingshead Two Factor Index (educational level and category of employment), social class was not a factor in controlling, lead-taking, or adult-structuring. The authors conclude that social class is not a reliable predictor of differences in mother-child interaction.

344. Harrison, Algea O., and Joanne H. Minor. "Interrole Conflict, Coping Strategies, and Satisfaction among Black Working Wives." *Journal of Marriage and the Family,* 40 (1978), 799-805.

    One hundred and four black working wives and mothers responded to a questionnaire to determine how satisfied they were with their role performance and their coping strategies for dealing with marital conflict. The type of conflict (wife-worker, mother-worker, mother-wife) influenced the strategy used, but coping strategy did not relate to satisfaction with role performance. Professional and nonprofessional women differed in their degree of worker satisfaction, and husband's approval did not affect worker satisfaction.

345. Hawkins, James L., Carol Weisberg, and Dixie L. Ray. "Marital Communication Style and Social Class." *Journal of Marriage and the Family,* 39 (1977), 479-490.

    The relationship between social class and style of marital communication was studied in 171 white married couples. Four interaction styles were employed: conventional (closed, low disclosure), controlling (closed, high disclosure), speculative (open, low disclosure), and contactful (open, supportive). The higher the social class of the couples, the more the contactful style was preferred and the less the conventional style. No class differences in preference for speculative style was found. The more education a husband had, the more the couple preferred contactful communication. All, regardless of class, seemed to value talking things over calmly (speculative style) and to detest pure power (controlling style). All couples regardless of class espoused an ideal of intimacy (respectful confrontation of feelings). The majority of couples at all levels believed that they usually dealt with emotional issues in speculative and contactful style. In a tape-recorded discussion on an emotional issue, however, only the best educated couples were able to string together substantial numbers of speculative and contactful speeches while managing to inhibit the appearance of long strings of controlling speeches.

346. Hawkins, James L., Carol Weisberg, and Dixie W. Ray. "Spouse Differences in Communication Style: Preference, Perception, Behavior." *Journal of Marriage and the Family*, 42 (1980), 585-593.

One hundred seventy-one married couples were interviewed individually and then together in order to discover their preferences for and beliefs about communication style in their marriages. Each person was asked to respond to a set of six critical incidents in one of four communication styles: conventional, controlling, speculative, or contactful. Then the couples were brought together and asked to participate in four 5-minute audiotaped discussions. Men and women had differences in what they preferred from the husband as a communicator: wives preferred to see less controlling communication behavior in their husbands than the husbands preferred to see in themselves. The wives also valued contactful style in their husbands more than the husbands did for themselves. Men valued conventional behavior in the wives less than their wives did, and husbands wanted more speculative behavior from their wives than the wives preferred to give. Spouses seemed to be in agreement on the value of a conventional style in the husband, as well as on the negative value of a controlling style and the positive value of a contactful style in the wife. Analysis of the audiotaped discussions revealed that the spouses used about the same proportions of styles, generally about two-thirds of the time the less-valued styles and only one-third of the time the styles they valued.

347. Henderson, Dorothy. "Contextual Specificity, Discretion and Cognitive Socialisation: With Special Reference to Language." *Human Context*, 3 (1971), 460-532.

One hundred London mothers, both middle class and working class, were interviewed twice and the contextual use of their language to their seven-year-old children analyzed. Compared with working class mothers, middle class mothers used abstract definitions, explicit rather than implicit "concrete" definitions. They avoided evasive answers to questions and emphasized language in the transmission of moral principles. Implications of these differing "teaching" styles for education are made.

348. Hershey, Sibilla, and Emmy Werner. "Dominance in Marital Decision Making in Women's Liberation and Non-Women's

Liberation Families." *Family Process*, 14 (1975), 223-233.

Fourteen "traditional" couples and 14 couples in which the wife was part of a women's liberation organization were interviewed by a female investigator first alone, then together, in a modified version of the Revealed Differences Technique of decision making. Analyses of the tapes of the interviews revealed two significant differences: women's liberation wives spoke first and spoke longer than traditional wives. The husbands' total speaking time in both groups did not differ. Analysis of the content of the women's responses revealed women's liberation wives were more self-reliant, and traditional wives were more passive and dependent.

349. Hofmann, Joanne, and John M. Panagos. "Mothers' and Non-Mothers' Semantic Adaption to Deviant Speech." *Language and Speech*, 16 (1973), 396-404.

Ten mothers of children with deviant speech were matched with ten non-mothers and their responses to the recorded verbal directions of a deviant-speaking child analyzed. Results indicated that maternal experience did not influence comprehension or performance.

* Holzman, Mathilda. "The Use of Interrogative Forms in the Verbal Interaction of Three Mothers and Their Children." *Journal of Psycholinguistic Research*, 1 (1972), 311-336. See item 839.

350. Jacob, Theodore. "Family Interaction in Disturbed and Normal Families: A Methodological and Substantive Review." *Psychological Bulletin*, 82 (1975), 33-65.

This review of 57 direct observation studies of interaction in normal and disturbed families includes sections on dominance, conflict, affect, and communication clarity in which sex differences have been found. Jacob notes, however, that although the sex of the child has been shown to affect interaction patterns significantly, most of the studies did not use sex as a variable. Over 100 references are listed.

351. Jacob, Theodore. "Verbal Activity of Middle- and Lower-Class Parents When Teaching Their Child." *Psychological Reports*, 40 (1977), 575-578.

In a proverb-teaching task with parents and son, 44 triads in all, middle-class fathers spoke more than middle-class mothers; lower-class mothers spoke more than lower-class fathers.

352. Lamb, Michael E. "Father-Infant and Mother-Infant Interaction in the First Year of Life." *Child Development,* 48 (1977), 167-181.

Twenty infants, at ages seven, eight, twelve, and thirteen months, were observed interacting at home with their parents by a male observer who taped his account of the behavior while a female assistant interacted with the family as a visitor. Infants showed no preference for either parent in attachment display, but responded more positively to father-infant play. Mothers held the infant most often for care-taking functions, fathers for playing. Lamb argues that this differing early interaction may involve experiences for the infant such that the parents have different influences on personality development.

353. Leighton, Lennard A., Gray E. Stollak, and Lucy R. Ferguson. "Patterns of Communication in Normal and Clinic Families." *Journal of Consulting and Clinical Psychology,* 36 (1971), 252-256.

Tape recordings of eight normal families (parents and at least two children) and seven clinic families (same) interacting as a family unit were codified for total times speaking, total and average duration, interruptions, etc. Authors found more conflict in clinic families. Normal families were characterized by father dominance accepted by others while clinic families were characterized by mother dominance unaccepted by others.

354. Lewis, Michael, and Roy Freedle. "Mother-Infant Dyad: The Cradle of Meaning." In *Communication and Affect, Language and Thought*. Eds. Patricia Pliner, Lester Krames, and Thomas Alloway. New York: Academic Press, 1973, pp. 127-155.

For this study of the communication of mother-infant dyads, 80 such dyads of blacks and whites, all socioeconomic levels, were observed when the infants were between 11 and 13 weeks old. Data were analyzed by frequency distribution of verbal and nonverbal behavior in the 2-hour observation, by simultaneous behavior within a 10-second unit, and by direction (initiator/ responder) of interactions. The authors conclude that the communication network "is a nonrandom, sequential and situationally determined system ... reminiscent of the more formal linguistic properties--especially the semantic ones--found at later ages" (p. 151).

355. Mack, Delores E. "The Power Relationship in Black Families and White Families." *Journal of Personality and Social Psychology,* 30 (1974), 409-413.

    This study of the power relationship in marriage used 80 married couples varied equally by race and by middle and working class. These couples completed a family power questionnaire individually, jointly, and then had a discussion with a joint statement, and, finally, a bargaining session. Working-class husbands were significantly more powerful than middle-class husbands on the questionnaire. No other significant class or sex differences were found, however.

356. Mandelcorn, Berenice S., and R.O. Pihl. "Maternal Expectation and the Mother-Child Interaction." *Psychological Reports,* 47 (1980), 307-317.

    The effect of maternal expectancies on the interaction between 37 mother-daughter and 37 mother-son pairs (all children 9-1/2 years old) was analyzed through questionnaire and observation during motor and verbal tasks. The many sex differences led authors to conclude that there is "a totally different quality of relationship" between the two sets of pairs. Mothers of girls evaluated them higher intellectually now but had lower expectations for them for the future. Mothers of boys were more accurate in assessing their son's intellectual abilities. Girls' mothers with high expectancy approved little and disapproved a lot, while boys' mothers said little but gave help in the tasks if they had low expectancy for their sons. Boys' mothers with high expectations displayed high approval, while girls' mothers with low expectations gave high approval.

357. Matteson, Roberta. "Adolescent Self-Esteem, Family Communication, and Marital Satisfaction." *Journal of Psychology,* 86 (1974), 35-47.

    From a pool of 111 ninth graders, ten male and ten female adolescents with high self-esteem and a like number with low self-esteem were selected. These subjects and their parents completed questionnaires on communication and marital adjustment. Low self-esteem adolescents perceived family communication as less facilitative. Parents of such subjects also perceived less facilitative marital communication and rated their marriages less satisfying. But these parents did not perceive their communication with the adolescent as the adolescent did, while high self-esteem adolescents and their parents were congruent in their perceptions of family communication. No sex differences were reported.

358. Meyer, John P., and Susan Pepper. "Need Compatibility and Marital Adjustment in Young Married Couples." *Journal of Personality and Social Psychology,* 35 (1977), 331-342.

    The Personality Research Form, a marital adjustment-scale, and a questionnaire reporting self, ideal self, spouse, and ideal spouse items, were completed by 66 married couples. All couples tended to be similar in ideal ratings, but well-adjusted spouses were more similar than poorly adjusted ones in self and spouse ratings.

359. Millar, Frank E., L. Edna Rogers-Millar, and John A. Courtright. "Relational Control and Dyadic Understanding: An Exploratory Predictive Regression Model." *Communication Yearbook 3.* Ed. Dan Nimmo. New Brunswick, N.J.: Transaction Books, 1979, pp. 213-224.

    The effects of domineeringness and dominance on spouses' ability to predict accurately each other's responses was investigated with 86 white husband and wife dyads who participated in a two-hour structured interview. Analysis of the interviews revealed that the degree of understanding was positively but curvilinearly related to the dominance structure existing in the dyad. The more one spouse occupied a dominant position over the other, the less each spouse understood the other on common family/household tasks. The more equivalence in verbal dominance, the more understanding manifested on these issues. Domineering messages served to decrease the odds of establishing a rigid dominance pattern. A couple's domineeringness ratio was positively and curvilinearly related to the husband's degree of understanding but was unrelated to the wife's, and the wife's degree of understanding was negatively and linearly related to her husband's degree of submissiveness.

* Morton, Teru L. "Intimacy and Reciprocity of Exchange: A Comparison of Spouses and Strangers." *Journal of*

Personality and Social Psychology, 36 (1978), 72-81. See item 145.

360. Noller, Patricia. "Misunderstandings in Marital Communication: A Study of Couples' Nonverbal Communication." *Journal of Personality and Social Psychology,* 39 (1980), 1135-48.

    Each partner of 48 married couples (some students, some community adults) sent and received a standard set of ambiguous messages. The messages could be interpreted as positive, neutral, or negative depending on the accompanying nonverbal communication. Females were better encoders than males, particularly in sending positive messages. Couples with high marital adjustment communicated more effectively, especially the husbands who sent clearer messages and made fewer errors. A higher percentage of errors on females' messages was attributable to problems of their spouses' decoding.

361. O'Neill, Michael S., and James F. Alexander. "Family Interaction Patterns as a Function of Task Characteristics." *Journal of Applied Social Psychology,* 1 (1971), 163-172.

    In two experiments using eight married college couples and 21 married community couples, dominance patterns occurring during different tasks were observed. The husband dominated more on three sets of tasks, the wife on three other tasks, and on two tasks they shared dominance. Authors conclude that family dominance patterns depend on task.

362. Pakizegi, Behnaz. "The Interaction of Mothers and Fathers With Their Sons." *Child Development,* 49 (1978), 479-482.

    Twenty first-born three-year-old boys interacted in dyads with each parent in a play situation. Analysis of the tapes revealed that the parents' behavior was child-centered while the child's behavior was self-centered. No significant differences were found in the behavior of mothers and fathers toward their sons.

363. Pollitt, Ernesto, Aviva W. Eichler, and Chee-Khoon Chan. "Psychosocial Development and Behavior of Mothers of Failure-to-Thrive Children." *American Journal of Orthopsychiatry,* 45 (1975), 525-537.

    Data on recollected childhood, marital history, and

relationships with the child were gathered via questionnaire, open-ended interviews, and observation of 19 mothers of non-thriving children and 19 matched control mothers. Comparisons indicated that, despite stressful backgrounds, most of the mothers of failure-to-thrive children were free of severe psychopathology. The strongest statistical differences were found in the scores on the Mother-Child Interaction Checklist. The control group mothers were more likely to have frequent verbal and physical contacts with their children, often positively reinforcing and warm. The mothers of failure-to-thrive children related less often to their children, were less affectionate, and were more prone to use physical punishment.

364. Prorok, Elza M.S. "Mother-Child Verbal Interchange: A Descriptive Study of Young Children's Verbal Behavior." *Journal of Psycholinguistic Research,* 9 (1980), 451-471.

Analysis of at-home and in-playroom observations of the verbal interactions of 5 English mothers and their first-born children aged about 21 months revealed that mothers had shorter pauses and that the amount of child verbalization was positively correlated to the proportion of the mother's output of immediate responses to the child, not to her total verbal output.

365. Rappaport, Alan F., David Payne, and Anne Steinmann. "Marriage as a Factor in the Dyadic Perception of the Female Sex Role." *Psychological Reports,* 27 (1970), 283-284.

Male-female differences in concepts of "man's ideal woman" and "woman's ideal woman" were computed for 45 married and 45 dating couples who completed the Inventory of Female Values. Married couples exhibited no more consensus than dating couples. For both, the greatest difference occurred in what each sex perceived as the "man's ideal woman."

366. Rausch, Harold L., William A. Barry, Richard R. Hertel, and Mary A. Swain. *Communication, Conflict, and Marriage.* San Francisco: Jossey-Bass, 1974.

A theory of communication as it applies to husband and wife interchange is presented along with discussion of conflict and coping strategies and a coding system for interpersonal conflict.

* Redlinger, Wendy. "Mothers' Speech to Children in Bilingual Mexican-American Homes." In *The Sociology of The Languages of American Women*. Eds. Betty L. Dubois and Isabel Crouch. San Antonio, Texas: Trinity University, 1976, pp. 119-130. Rpt. in *International Journal of the Sociology of Language*, 17 (1978), 73-82. See item 882.

367. Riskin, Jules, and Elaine E. Faunce. "An Evaluative Review of Family Interaction Research." *Family Process*, 11 (1972), 365-455.

    This critical review of research on family interaction since 1960 includes couple and small-group research and mother-child studies. Included are a 26-page glossary and an 18-page list of references.

368. Rogers-Millar, L. Edna, and Frank E. Millar, III. "Domineeringness and Dominance: A Transactional View." *Human Communication Research*, 5 (1979), 238-246.

    A definition and the dimensions of interpersonal power were examined. Analysis of interviews and questionnaires of 45 husband and wife dyads concerning their marital relationship suggested that domineeringness and dominance are different phenomena and that different patterns of satisfaction and interaction style are associated with these two dimensions. Domineering behavior of the wife was associated with lower levels of satisfaction and higher levels of role strain. Husband domineering behavior was associated with more nonsupportive statements and shorter discussion time. Domineering behavior of both husband and wife correlated with more successful talk-overs and more flexible transaction patterns. Dominance, especially husband dominance, was related to higher levels of satisfaction, lower levels of role strain, more supportive statements, and fewer nonsupportive statements.

369. Scanzoni, John. "An Historical Perspective on Husband-Wife Bargaining Power and Marital Dissolution." In *Divorce and Separation*. Eds. George Levinger and Oliver C. Moles. New York: Basic Books, 1979, pp. 20-36.

    This theoretical essay on divorce relies on the cost-reward theory and uses a sociological approach to historical evidence in showing that the relative bargaining power of women in marriage has increased since the 17th century.

370. Scanzoni, John. *Sex Roles, Women's Work, and Marital Conflict*. Lexington, Mass.: D.C. Heath, 1978.

Examined are the influences of changing sex roles on the preferences, work goals, and interests of women, especially of egalitarian women, and the effect of those changes on conflict and its resolution in the family. An eclectic version of the cost-reward theory of interpersonal behavior is used. Two chapters deal specifically with strategies in marital conflict and women's weaker power in bargaining. A list of references is included.

371. Scanzoni, John H. *Sexual Bargaining: Power Politics in the American Marriage*. Englewood Cliffs, N.J.: Prentice-Hall, 1972.

This review of bargaining within marriage is based on the premise that both males and females seek rewards, that reward-seeking generates social exchange, and that social exchange generates conflict. Both positive and negative consequences of conflict are discussed.

372. Schuham, Anthony L. "Activity, Talking Time, and Spontaneous Agreement in Disturbed and Normal Family Interaction." *Journal of Abnormal Psychology*, 79 (1972), 68-75.

Fourteen families with a disturbed child, matched with 14 families with a normal child, interacted to reach agreement on four items on which they had disagreed on a previously completed questionnaire. Normal families had longer discussion times, and parents talked more than the child. In these normal families, the parents initiated more interaction than the children; in disturbed families the father initiated more than either mother or child. Normal families had significantly greater spontaneous agreement level than disturbed families. In partial agreement situations, normal families differed significantly in having more instances of parents agreeing while disturbed families had more parent-child agreements.

373. Shafer, Robert E. "The Work of Joan Tough: A Case Study in Applied Linguistics." *Language Arts*, 55 (1978), 308-314, 372.

Commenting on the works of British educator Joan Tough, Shafer notes that in *Focus on Meaning: Talking to Some Purpose With Young Children* (1973), she described the difference between middle-class elaborated and working-class restricted codes. Working-class mothers often responded to questions with comments about their own concerns, not the child's; eventually, the child is conditioned not to question. Middle-class mothers stimulate curiosity by responding to their children's questions. Tough developed a classification system of language uses, and in a later book, *Listening to Children Talking: A Guide to the Appraisal of Children's Use of Language* (1976), she showed teachers how to use the system to detect children's levels of use and how to help to equalize the differences.

374. Slevin, Kathleen F., and Jack Balswick. "Children's Perceptions of Parental Expressiveness." *Sex Roles*, 6 (1980), 293-299.

To investigate the differences between sons' and daughters' perceptions of their mothers' and fathers' expressiveness of several emotions, both verbally and nonverbally, 578 male and 656 female high school students responded to a 16-item Likert-type Perceived Parental Expressiveness Scale. Fathers were perceived as less expressive of all emotions except physical anger by both sons and daughters; mothers were perceived by both sons and daughters as more expressive, particularly verbally, than fathers.

375. Sternberg, Daniel P., and Ernst G. Beier. "Changing Patterns of Conflict." *Journal of Communication*, 27 (Summer 1977), 97-100.

A follow-up questionnaire survey of 51 couples used in a newlywed nonverbal behavior study (see item 318) revealed that wives were significantly more unhappy nine months later, that topics of disagreement shifted to include sex for both partners, and that conflict in the marriage was increasing (approaching significance).

* Stolte, Karen M., and Paul G. Friedman. "Patients' Perceptions of Touch During Labor." *Journal of Applied Communications Research*, 8 (1980), 10-21. See item 1216.

376. Tallman, Irving, and Gary Miller. "Class Differences in Family Problem Solving: The Effects of Verbal Ability, Hierarchial Structure, and Role Expectations." *Sociometry*, 37 (1974), 13-37.

Testing with 115 middle- and working-class families who

used elaborated or restricted speech codes as they problem-solved with either the husband or wife as decision-maker, the authors posited four hypotheses: that middle-class families would be better problem solvers than working-class, that verbal ability would influence problem-solving (a bean-bag game with special rules), that role expectations would account for class differences in problem solving (better if father-led family for working-class and egalitarian if middle class), and the combination of open communication and normative role expectations would account for the better performance of middle-class families. Results supported hypotheses one and three and partially supported hypothesis four.

* Tesser, Abraham. "Self-Esteem Maintenance in Family Dynamics." *Journal of Personality and Social Psychology*, 39 (1980), 77-91. See item 68.

* Thune, Elizabeth S., Ronald W. Manderscheid, and Sam Silbergeld. "Status or Sex Roles as Determinants of Interaction Patterns in Small, Mixed-Sex Groups." *Journal of Social Psychology*, 112 (1980), 51-65. See item 302.

377. Toler, Sue A., and Nicholas W. Bankson. "Utilization of an Interrogative Model to Evaluate Mothers' Use and Children's Comprehension of Question Forms." *Journal of Speech and Hearing Disorders*, 41 (1976), 301-314.

    An analysis of the question-response interaction of three mother-preschool child pairs revealed that the question forms used most frequently were the who interrogative, the auxiliary with no infinitive, and tag questions.

378. Tulkin, Steven R., and Jerome Kagan. "Mother-Child Interaction in the First Year of Life." *Child Development*, 43 (1972), 31-41.

    Mothers with first-born ten-month-old daughters, 30 middle-class and 26 working-class, were observed at home. Social-class differences were small in physical contact, nonverbal interactions, and in prohibitions, but middle-class mothers had more frequent verbal behavior of every type than working-class mothers, who, perhaps, believed their infants were incapable of communicating.

* Waterman, Jill. "Family Patterns of Self-Disclosure." In *Self-Disclosure: Origins, Patterns, and Implications of Openness in Interpersonal Relationships*. Gordon J. Chelune and Associates. San Francisco: Jossey-Bass Publishers, 1979, pp. 225-242. See item 766.

379. West, Candace, and Don H. Zimmerman. "Women's Place in Everyday Talk: Reflections on Parent-Child Interaction." *Social Problems*, 24 (1977), 521-529.

    An examination of five parent-child verbal interactions in a physician's office revealed 14 interruptions in 17 exchanges; 12 of the 14 were interruptions by adults. The authors conclude that the pattern of interruptions in male-female interchange and those observed in the adult-child transactions had "striking similarities."

380. Willmington, S. Clay, and James A. Anderson. "An Investigation of the Relationship among the Speech Behaviors of Elementary School Children, Their Teachers, and Their Parents." *Elementary English*, 49 (1972), 179-183.

    To determine whether parents or teachers serve as dominant models for school children, oral questionnaires were administered to 30 third- and 33 sixth-graders, about half in public school and half in a laboratory school, to their teachers, and to their parents, all in private sessions. Scores of agreement between student-teacher, student-mother, and student-father revealed that laboratory school students agreed more than public school students with their parents. All students agreed significantly more with their mothers than their fathers or teachers on home-related items.

381. Wilton, Keri, and Ann Barbour. "Mother-Child Interaction in High-Risk and Contrast Preschoolers of Low Socioeconomic Status." *Child Development*, 49 (1978), 1136-45.

    Mothers of ten high-risk preschoolers (older siblings already identified as cultural-familial retardants) and ten contrast preschoolers (older siblings enrolled in regular classes), of two age groups, were observed interacting with their children. Mothers of older (30-46 months) high-risk children had less interaction, did less didactic teaching, showed less encouragement, and were less successful in attempts to control their children than mothers of the contrast group. Differences were not found in interaction with the younger (12-27 months) children.

382. Winter, William D., Antonio J. Ferreira, and Norman Bowers. "Decision-Making in Married and Unrelated Couples." *Family Process,* 12 (1973), 83-94.

The decision-making performance of 20 married and 20 unrelated couples, all undergraduates, was compared using the Ferreira-Winter Questionnaire technique. Married couples showed greater spontaneous agreement with each other prior to discussion, less politeness, more intrusive interruptions, and a lesser exchange of explicit information.

383. Young, David M., Kim M. Korner, J.D. Gill, and Ernst G. Beier. "'Beneficial' Aggression." *Journal of Communication,* 27 (Summer 1977), 100-103.

Twenty-three young couples played a padded pillow fight "game" and completed a marital discord questionnaire. Husbands and wives agreed on topics of marital conflict and on resultant unhappiness. Wives', but not husbands', frequency of blows in the game and the frequency and intensity of wives' blows to husbands were negatively related to length of marriage: the longer the marriage, the less "aggressive" the wife's behavior. Husbands rating marriage low on disagreement and unhappiness were significantly more likely to have wives who hit harder in the game bout.

IN PUBLIC

* Anderson, Judith, "Sexual Politics: Chauvinism and Backlash?" *Today's Speech,* 21, No. 4 (1973), 11-16. See item 482.

* Auer, J. Jeffery. "The Image of the Right Honourable Margaret Thatcher." *The Central States Speech Journal,* 30 (1979), 289-310. See item 483.

384. Baldwin, Sandra F., and Theodore Clevenger, Jr. "Effect of Speakers' Sex and Size of Audience on Heart-Rate Changes during Short Impromptu Speeches." *Psychological Reports,* 46 (1980), 123-130.

Ten male and 10 female undergraduates were measured for heart rate as they spoke impromptu before an audience of 21 (normal) or of 3 (very small). Both sexes revealed a heart-rate pattern of aroused heart rate prior to the speech, reaching a peak just prior to it, followed by a drop just before the end of the speech, and a substantial drop a minute after the end. Females, however, had significantly higher arousal rates, including pre- and post-speech and during the speech. They exhibited less post-speech drop in heart rate. Before the very small audience, they had earlier anticipatory arousal than males, who had a stronger confrontation arousal (just prior to speech) than females. Both sexes had higher arousal rates for the small audience than for the normal-sized one.

* Barclay, Martha T. "Distaff Campaigning in the 1964 and 1968 Presidential Elections." *The Central States Speech Journal,* 21 (1970), 117-122. See item 484.

385. Baxandall, Rosalyn, Linda Gordon, and Susan Reverby. "Boston Working Women Protest, 1869." *Signs: Journal of Women in Culture and Society,* 1 (1976), 803-808.

    After a brief background, the text of a speech by a Miss Phelps given at a citywide convention in Boston is used to reveal the complexity of the working women's response to the cruelties of industrialization.

386. Bock, Douglas G., and E. Hope Bock. "The Effects of Sex on the Experimenter, Expectancy Inductions, and Sex of the Rater on Leniency, Halo, and Trait Errors in Speech Rating Behavior." *Communication Education,* 26 (1977), 198-306.

    The effects of sex of speaker, positive or negative expectancy, and sex of 103 college undergraduates on the types of rating errors--leniency (too hard or too easy on all), halo (expectancy for a particular speaker), and trait (too hard or too easy on a particular category of the rating scale)--were examined. Results showed an opposite sex effect on leniency errors such that, regardless of expectancy, in the presence of a male experimenter, female raters were too hard on everyone, and in the presence of a female experimenter, male raters were too hard on everyone. Sex of experimenter and sex of rater interacted in different patterns for halo errors. For trait errors, the sex of the rater was a major variable for both content and delivery traits.

387. Bock, Douglas G., and Margaret E. Munro. "The Effects of Organization, Need for Order, Sex of the Source, and

Sex of the Rater on the Organization Trait Error." *Southern Speech Communication Journal*, 44 (1979), 364-372.

To investigate the effects of an organized vs. a disorganized speech, the need for order, the sex of the source, and the sex of the rater on organization trait error, 150 male and female undergraduates took pre- and post-tests measuring their need for order (Edwards' Personal Preference Inventory) and evaluated an organized or unorganized, male- or female-written speech. Organized speeches received more positive trait errors on organization (organization judged leniently) than unorganized speeches. Males with a high need for order made more of these positive trait errors than males with a low need for order or females with a high-need order. Male sources received more positive trait errors than female sources.

388. Bock, Douglas G., Larry Powell, James T. Kitchens, and James W. Flavin. "The Influence of Sex Differences in Speech Evaluation: Situational and Media Effects." *Communication Education*, 26 (1977), 143-153.

One of two studies investigated the interaction of sex and the following effect (superior speaker after average one or vice versa) on the speech evaluations of 72 male and 82 female undergraduates, and the second investigated the interaction of media and sex on trait errors in evaluation (tendency to judge speech effectiveness on personal bias about one ingredient of the speech) by 37 listeners of a live speech, 35 viewers of a live television speech, and 31 viewers of a videotaped speech. Superior speakers of both sexes had their ratings enhanced by the following effect when they followed an average speaker, while the average female speaker had her rating enhanced following either an average or a superior speaker. Female raters made more rating errors than male raters. Authors conclude that sex of rater is an important variable in analyzing rating results, perhaps because females, according to previous research, are more persuasible.

* Bosmajian, Haig A. "The Abrogation of the Suffragists' First Amendment Rights." *Western Speech*, 38 (1974), 218-232. See item 459.

* Bostrom, Robert N., John R. Basehart, and Charles M. Rossiter, Jr. "The Effects of Three Types of Profane

Language in Persuasive Messages." *Journal of Communication,* 23 (Dec. 1973), 461-475. See item 803.

389. Brake, Robert J., and Robert D. Neuleib. "Famous Women Orators: An Opinion Survey." *Today's Speech,* 21, No. 4 (1973), 33-37.

   An opinion survey concerning famous women speakers compared to a survey done in 1967 revealed greater current identification of the women, and greater attention to the diversity of their issues, their types of discourse, and the time periods in which they lived. Two tables quantify the citations and percentages of women orators named.

* Campbell, Karlyn K. "The Rhetoric of Women's Liberation: An Oxymoron." *Quarterly Journal of Speech,* 59 (1973), 74-86. See item 460.

390. Campbell, Karlyn K. "Stanton's 'The Solitude of Self': A Rationale for Feminism." *Quarterly Journal of Speech,* 66 (1980), 304-312.

   In this rhetorical analysis of Elizabeth Cady Stanton's farewell address to the National American Women Suffrage Association in 1892, the ideology of nineteenth-century feminism and the tone and style of the speech itself are examined. The speech is found to be a "rhetorical act in the lyric mode."

391. Conville, Richard L. "Linguistic Nonimmediacy and Attribution of Communicator's Attitudes." *Psychological Reports,* 36 (1975), 951-957.

   Fifteen students in a rhetoric class rated transcripts of 200-word sections of six speeches delivered by other rhetoric students selected to represent high, middle, and low communicator anxiety levels and both sexes. Separate analyses revealed that anxiety and nonimmediacy (degree of verbal indirectness in referring to self) were positively correlated (.81). Raters found those with low nonimmediacy to have a more positive attitude toward themselves and communication topic.

392. Conville, Richard L. "Linguistic Nonimmediacy and Communicators' Anxiety." *Psychological Reports,* 35 (1974), 1107-14.

   Tapes of speeches of six male and female undergraduates were analyzed for degree of verbal indirectness used to refer to self (nonimmediacy), with a speaker of each sex representing one of three levels of speech anxiety. Regardless of sex, the most anxious speakers produced the most nonimmediate language. A positive linear relationship was found between nonimmediacy scores and anxiety scores.

* Coughlin, Elizabeth M., and Charles E. Coughlin. "Convention in Petticoats: The Seneca Falls Declaration of Woman's Rights." *Today's Speech,* 21, No. 4 (1973), 17-23. See item 461.

* Dees, Diane. "Bernadette Devlin's Maiden Speech: A Rhetoric of Sacrifice." *Southern Speech Communication Journal,* 38 (1973), 326-339. See item 486.

393. Deffenbacher, Jerry L., and Dennis Payne. "Relationship of Apprehension about Communication to Fear of Negative Evaluation and Assertiveness." *Psychological Reports,* 42 (1978), 370.

    A series of measures of communication apprehension, fear of negative evaluation, and self-expression was given to 43 male and 261 female elementary education majors. Correlation analysis revealed that those who were apprehensive about speaking before others were also more fearful of negative evaluations and were less assertive in social situations. No sex differences emerged in any of the correlations.

394. Droppleman, Leo F., and Douglas M. McNair. "An Experimental Analog of Public Speaking." *Journal of Consulting and Clinical Psychology,* 36 (1971), 91-96.

    Eight men and four women, all college graduates, in a laboratory setting recorded a three-minute speech; the authors found a consistent and parallel level of response to the stress within and between subjects on physiological (finger sweat) and psychological (reported stress) measures from baseline to anticipation of speech, to speech, to post-speech measure.

* DuBoise, Ellen, ed. "On Labor and Free Love: Two Unpublished Speeches of Elizabeth Cady Stanton." *Signs: Journal of Women in Culture and Society,* 1 (1975), 257-268. See item 462.

* Eble, Connie C. "Girl Talk: A Bicentennial Perspective." In *Views of Language.* Eds. Reza Ordoubadian and

Walburga von Raffler-Engel. Murfreesboro, Tenn.: Inter-University Publishing, 1975, pp. 77-86. See item 815.

395. Farley, Frank H., Arie Cohen, Joel Goldberg, and Yoel Yinon. "Fears in American and Israeli Women." *Journal of Social Psychology,* 106 (1978), 17-24.

    A questionnaire survey of 66 age-matched pairs of American and Israeli women revealed that American women reported among their ten most feared stimuli feeling rejected by others, failure, speaking in public, and feeling disapproved of.

* Farrell, Thomas B. "Political Conventions as Legitimation Ritual." *Communication Monographs,* 45 (1978), 293-305. See item 487.

396. Farrell, Thomas J. "The Female and Male Modes of Rhetoric." *College English,* 40 (1979), 909-921.

    Farrell explains the feminine rhetorical mode as one of "indirection" as opposed to the male "direct" mode of beginning with a statement much like a final conclusion. Both spoken and written examples, from Elizabeth I of England to contemporary journalists, are included. The features and advantages of both modes are examined in this "descriptive and exploratory" essay.

397. Fischli, Ronald. "Anita Bryant's Stand Against 'Militant Homosexuality': Religious Fundamentalism and the Democratic Process." *The Central States Speech Journal,* 30 (1979), 262-271.

    Anita Bryant's opposition to the Gay Liberation Alliance is analyzed and the rhetorical arguments and stragegies of Bryant's Save Our Children organization evaluated. Fischli contends that Bryant's strategy of linking child exploitation to homosexuality belied her fundamentalist reasoning and that her presumption of the inherent moral supremacy of fundamentalist doctrine contradicts the First Amendment.

* Fong, M.S. "The Early Rhetoric of Women's Liberation: Implications for Zero Population Growth." *Journal of Marriage and the Family,* 38 (1976), 127-140. See item 463.

* Foss, Sonja K. "The Equal Rights Amendment Controversy: Two Worlds in Conflict." *Quarterly Journal of Speech,* 65 (1979), 275-288. See item 464.

* Foss, Sonja K. "Teaching Contemporary Feminist Rhetoric: An Illustrative Syllabus." *Communication Education,* 27 (1978), 328-335. See item 466.

398. Freimuth, Vicki S. "The Effects of Communication Apprehension on Communication Effectiveness." *Human Communication Research,* 2 (1976), 289-298.

    To investigate the hypothesis that physiological, psychological, and verbal behavior indices of communication apprehension can predict comprehension, perception of speaker credibility, and ratings of speech effectiveness, measures of all the indices were taken of 85 undergraduates who were videotaped as they expressed their views on women's liberation. One minute of each videotape was evaluated for comprehension, source credibility, and speech effectiveness by 81 female and 89 male undergraduates. The indices of communication apprehension could predict all the communication effects except one, perception of character. An analysis of data on the ratings of speech effectiveness revealed that women comprehended more than men, and the message was more comprehensible if it was delivered by a woman. Sex may have had a significant influence because the topic was sex-related.

399. Friedrich, Gustav W. "An Empirical Explication of a Concept of Self-Reported Speech Anxiety." *Speech Monographs,* 37 (1970), 67-72.

    The inventory portion of Gilkinson's Personal Report of Confidence as a Speaker was given to 366 undergraduates. An analysis of variance showed sex differences on self-reported speech anxiety, with females indicating more anxiety. A factor analysis revealed dimensions of speech anxiety, exhibitionism, and reticence as the most salient for both males and females; females' responses also generated a physical manifestations factor.

* Frye, Jerry K., and Franklin B. Krohn. "An Analysis of Barbara Jordan's 1976 Keynote Address." *Journal of Applied Communications Research,* 2 (1977), 73-82. See item 489.

400. Gearhart, Sally M. "The Womanization of Rhetoric." *Women's Studies International Quarterly,* 2 (1979), 195-201.

   Gearhart argues that those who have been studying the theory, practice, and criticism of public discourse have been advocates and mentors of violence and that a female model of communication is not only the antidote to such violence but also the necessary alternative to self-destruction as a species.

* Gonchar, Ruth M., and Dan F. Hahn. "Political Rhetoric: A Reassessment of Critical Methodologies." *Journal of Applied Communications Research,* 6 (1978), 55-63. See item 490.

* Gruber, Kenneth J., and Jacquelyn Gaebelein. "Sex Differences in Listening Comprehension." *Sex Roles,* 5 (1979), 299-310. See item 639.

* Hancock, Brenda R. "Affirmation by Negation in the Women's Liberation Movement." *Quarterly Journal of Speech,* 58 (1972), 264-271. See item 467.

401. Hayes, Michael T., and Joe McAdoo. "Debate Performance: Differences Between Male and Female Rankings." *The Journal of the American Forensic Association,* 8 (1972), 127-131.

   This study used 1,141 college debate ballots to test the hypothesis of a significant difference by sex between the expected and observed frequencies of speaker rankings awarded by judges to male and female debaters. The hypothesis was upheld: females as a group were rated proportionately higher in abilities.

402. Heisch, Allison. "Queen Elizabeth I: Parliamentary Rhetoric and the Exercise of Power." *Signs: Journal of Women in Culture and Society,* 1 (1975), 31-55.

   This study examines the use of language by Queen Elizabeth I in her speeches and the strategies revealed in them.

* Hope, Diane S. "Redefinition of Self: A Comparison of the Rhetoric of the Women's Liberation and Black Liberation Movements." *Today's Speech,* 23, No. 1 (1975), 17-25. See item 468.

403. Hudson, Lee. "Belting the Bible: Madalyn Murray O'Hair vs. Fundamentalism." *Western Speech,* 36 (1972), 233-240.

The rhetoric and strategies used in a televised debate between Dr. Carl McIntire, fundamentalist minister, and Madalyn Murray O'Hair, militant atheist, are analyzed.

404. Infante, Dominic A., and Jeanne Y. Fisher. "Anticipated Credibility and Message Strategy Intentions as Predictors of Trait and State Speech Anxiety." *The Central States Speech Journal,* 29 (1978), 1-10.

The pre-speech delivery perceptions of 46 male and 41 female undergraduates of their credibility and of various message strategies were assessed via a questionnaire as predictors of speech anxiety. The strongest predictors of trait speech anxiety were expectations of how receivers would perceive their expertise and speaking on a controversial topic. Expectations about dynamism and intentions to present a two-sided message best predicted state speech anxiety. There were no sex differences for any of the measured variables, including for speech anxiety, which previous research had observed to be higher in females than males.

405. Infante, Dominic A., and Jeanne Y. Fisher. "The Influence of Receivers' Attitudes, Audience Size, and Speakers' Sex on Speakers' Pre-Message Perceptions." *The Central States Speech Journal,* 25 (1974), 43-49.

To determine the effects of audience size and attitude on anxiety, 172 male and female undergraduates prepared a pro-policy speech for an audience manipulated for size and attitude toward both the speaker and his message, and then completed an anxiety measure. Of the manipulated variables, only sex resulted in a significant finding: females perceived a higher probability of failure than males and were more anxious.

406. Jensen, Keith. "Self-Reported Speech Anxiety and Selected Demographic Variables." *The Central States Speech Journal,* 27 (1976), 102-108.

In this two-part study using 420 male and female undergraduates to examine the effects of age, training, experience, sex, and birth order on self-reported speech anxiety, no evidence was found to suggest a relationship between sex and anxiety, as previous research had found.

* Judd, Larry R., and Carolyn B. Smith. "The Relationship of Age, Educational Classification, Sex, and Grade to Self Concept and Ideal Self Concept in a Basic Speech Course." *Communication Education,* 26 (1977), 289-297. See item 29.

407. Kendall, Kathleen E. "Do Real People Ever Give Speeches?" *The Central States Speech Journal,* 25 (1974), 233-235.

    The frequency of speechmaking on the part of blue collar workers and their families was correlated with their education, age, income, and sex. Interviews revealed that 46.5% said they had given at least one speech to ten or more people in the past two years. No significant correlations between the respondents' income level and sex and their frequency of speechmaking was found.

408. Kendall, Kathleen E., and Jeanne Y. Fisher. "Frances Wright on Women's Rights: Eloquence Versus Ethos." *Quarterly Journal of Speech,* 60 (1974), 58-68.

    A rhetorical analysis of Scotswoman Wright's failure to persuade American audiences in her speeches of 1828-1830 is made.

409. Kibler, Robert J., Larry L. Barker, and Donald J. Cegala. "Effect of Sex on Comprehension and Retention." *Speech Monographs,* 37 (1970), 287-292.

    Audio-taped speeches, identical except for sex of speaker, were heard by 216 college undergraduates and 118 high school students, who responded to a comprehension test immediately after and three weeks later. Analysis of variance of the results showed that sex of speaker did not significantly alter perceptions of speaker effectiveness. Furthermore, neither sex of speaker nor sex of audience affected comprehension or retention, a finding contrary to some earlier research.

410. Kramer, Cheris. "Women's and Men's Ratings of Their Own and Ideal Speech." *Communication Quarterly,* 26, No. 2 (Spring 1978), 2-11.

    A study of 466 high school and college students sought to determine male and female ratings for an ideal speaker, the discrepancy between self and ideal ratings, and the difference between stereotypically assigned male and female speech characteristics and the ideal. Except for the characteristic *deep voice*, which men thought important, women and men agreed on ratings for an ideal speaker. Male speech was significantly different from the ideal on 41 characteristics, females on 34. Though both sexes saw discrepancies between their self and ideal ratings, the discrepancies differed between the sexes only in isolated cases. Kramer suggests that before females assume that male speech is the best model they might benefit from considering the positive qualities of female speech.

* Linkugel, Wil A. "The Rhetoric of American Feminism: A Social Movement Course." *Speech Teacher,* 23 (1974), 121-130. See item 469.

411. McCroskey, James C. "The Implementation of a Large-Scale Program of Systematic Desensitization for Communication Apprehension." *Speech Teacher,* 21 (1972), 255-264.

    An analysis of variance of pre- and post-treatment scores of 541 undergraduates on a self-report of speech apprehension and sex of subject and type of treatment (classroom vs. laboratory training in apprehension reduction vs. no-training) revealed significant differences. Training, whether by males or females, in the classroom and training in the laboratory by male instructors resulted in more improvement than non-training. Males improved more than females.

412. McDowell, Earl E., and Carlene E. McDowell. "An Investigation of Source and Receiver Apprehension at the Junior High, Senior High and College Levels." *The Central States Speech Journal,* 29 (1978), 11-19.

    This investigation analyzed source and receiver apprehension at the junior high (51 M and 37 F), senior high (34 M and 57 F), and college levels (30 M and 38 F). Results of the Personal Report of Communication Apprehension questionnaire indicated that across educational levels males were more apprehensive about meeting new acquaintances and felt their posture strained. Females experienced significantly more anxiety during pre-speech preparation and during delivery and were more tense when interacting in class. The Receiver Apprehension Test results indicated that across educational levels males were significantly more apprehensive than females and found it difficult to concentrate on instructions, ideas, and new information. Females felt more anxious when listening to males.

* McDowell, Margaret B. "The New Rhetoric of Woman Power." *The Midwest Quarterly,* 12 (1971), 187-198. See item 470.

413. McEdwards, Mary G. "American Values: *Circa* 1920-1970." *Quarterly Journal of Speech,* 57 (1971), 173-180.

    This essay on three salient features of American rhetoric from 1920-70 includes discussion of the rhetoric of masculinity and references to the feminization of males through the public school system.

414. McFarlin, Annjennette S. "Hallie Quinn Brown: Black Woman Elocutionist." *Southern Speech Communication Journal,* 46 (1980), 72-82.

    This study of Hallie Q. Brown, a prominent elocutionist, teacher, and political leader (1850-1950), notes the importance of her speaking, performing, writing, and political involvement.

* Mansfield, Dorothy M. "Abigail S. Duniway: Suffragette with Not-so-common Sense." *Western Speech,* 35 (1971), 24-29. See item 472.

* Mulac, Anthony. "Effects of Obscene Language upon Three Dimensions of Listener Attitudes." *Communication Monographs,* 43 (1976), 300-307. See item 872.

415. Mulac, Anthony, and A. Robert Sherman. "Relationships among Four Parameters of Speaker Evaluation: Speech Skill, Source Credibility, Subjective Speech Anxiety, and Behavioral Speech Anxiety." *Speech Monographs,* 42 (1975), 302-310.

    Twenty-one male and 21 female undergraduates completed measures of speech anxiety and had videotaped their speeches delivered at the beginning and toward the end of their speech communication course. Independent raters judged speech skills, source credibility, and behavioral speech anxiety according to standard measures. In initial speeches males showed significant positive correlation between speech skill and credibility and significant negative correlation between speech skill and source credibility and between subjective and behavioral anxiety. Correlations for females were in that direction, but were not statistically significant. Improvement scores showed males progressed significantly more than females on speech skill and behavioral speech anxiety, while females improved significantly only on one of the dimensions of speech credibility, trustworthiness.

* Pinola, Mary, and Nancy E. Briggs. "Martha Wright Griffiths: Champion of Women's Rights Legislation." *The Central States Speech Journal*, 30 (1979), 228-240. See item 473.

416. Porter, D. Thomas. "Self-Report Scales of Communication Apprehension and Autonomic Arousal (Heart Rate): A Test of Construct Validity." *Speech Monographs*, 41 (1974), 267-276.

    Twenty-four female and 21 male undergraduates completed various fear and anxiety measures and then delivered a three-minute speech for videotaping while they had heart sensors attached. Analysis revealed that only the items measuring communication fear (not communication anxiety) predicted autonomic arousal, hence communication apprehension. Females reported more fear, and their heart rates were higher and increased at a faster rate than males' in the public speaking situation.

* Reynolds, Beatrice K. "An Interview with Ti-Grace Atkinson: Her Speeches and Speechmaking." *Today's Speech*, 21, No. 4 (1973), 3-10. See item 475.

417. Ritter, Ellen M. "Elizabeth Morgan: Pioneer Female Labor Agitator." *The Central States Speech Journal*, 22 (1971), 242-251.

    This analysis of the rhetoric of Elizabeth Morgan in her efforts to improve the working conditions of Chicago women in the 1890s reveals that she was more successful when she switched from vituperative rhetoric to more credible appeals based directly on a description of the working conditions. Her rhetoric resulted in a House of Representatives' Committee on Manufacturers investigation in Chicago and, eventually, the 1893 State Factory Law.

418. Roever, James E. "Audience Perception of Speaker Training: An Expectancy Artifact in Communication Research." *The Central States Speech Journal*, 27 (1976), 47-55.

    Two experiments tested the hypothesis that students would rate speeches of their peers significantly higher if the raters thought the speakers had completed a course in public speaking. In the first experiment, nine female undergraduates' speeches were rated by 144 female undergraduates; raters evaluated higher those speakers they thought had had a public speaking course. In the second experiment, four of the original speeches, two rated high and two rated low, were evaluated by 15 male and 41 female undergraduates. The hypothesis was again validated.

419. Scholten, Pat C. "Exploitation of Ethos: Sara Winnemucca and Bright Eyes on the Lecture Tour." *Western Journal of Speech Communication,* 41 (1977), 233-244.

This account gives the nature and the effect of the rhetorical strategies of two Indian women, Sara Winnemucca and Bright Eyes. They made separate lecture tours between 1878 and 1884 on behalf of Indian rights. Sarah and Bright Eyes used the rhetorical strategies of ethos and pathos by appealing to the audiences' romantic image of the Indian maiden through their appearance, dress, and speech. In addition, they appealed to the audiences' Christian values.

* Scott, Kathryn P. "Perceptions of Communication Competence: What's Good for the Goose Is Not Good for the Gander." *Women's Studies International Quarterly,* 3 (1980), 199-208. See item 889.

* Scott, Robert L. "The Conservative Voice in Radical Rhetoric: A Common Response to Division." *Speech Monographs,* 40 (1973), 123-135. See item 477.

420. Sigall, Harold. "Effects of Competence and Consensual Validation on a Communicator's Liking for the Audience." *Journal of Personality and Social Psychology,* 16 (1970), 251-258.

In a laboratory, mock speaker-audience situation, 70 undergraduate females who felt strongly on the issue of automobile safety standards were assigned randomly to low or high involvement in preparing a speech or to an effort condition. The audience response was manipulated either to agree but change slightly or to disagree but change considerably in the speaker's direction. Liking for audience was greatest under both agreement and large change conditions, and was greater for an agreeing audience (small change) than a disagreeing one (large change) when involvement was low, and the reverse when involvement was high.

* Silverman, Ellen-Marie, and Catherine H. Zimmer. "Speech Fluency Fluctuations During the Menstrual Cycle." *Journal of Speech and Hearing Research*, 18 (1975), 202-206. See item 1249.

* Solomon, Martha. "The 'Positive Woman's' Journey: A Mythic Analysis of the Rhetoric of STOP ERA." *Quarterly Journal of Speech*, 65 (1979), 262-274. See item 478.

* Solomon, Martha. "The Rhetoric of STOP ERA: Fatalistic Reaffirmation." *Southern Speech Communication Journal*, 44 (1978), 42-59. See item 479.

* Thompson, Wayne N. "Barbara Jordan's Keynote Address: Fulfilling Dual and Conflicting Purposes." *The Central States Speech Journal*, 30 (1979), 272-277. See item 495.

* Thompson, Wayne N. "Barbara Jordan's Keynote Address: The Juxtaposition of Contradictory Values." *Southern Speech Communication Journal*, 44 (1979), 223-232. See item 496.

421. Trautmann, Fredrick. "Harriet Beecher Stowe: Public Readings in the Central States." *The Central States Speech Journal*, 24 (1973), 22-28.

    This account of Harriet Beecher Stowe's reading tour of the Central States in 1873 notes her success in overcoming obstacles of inexperience, unfavorable settings, and travel difficulties.

422. Wood Sally M. "Questions I Should Have Answered Better: A Guide to Women Who Dare to Speak Publicly." In *Voices from Women's Liberation*. Ed. Leslie B. Tanner. New York: Signet Books, 1970, pp. 142-153.

    A first-hand account of the reactions of and questions from audiences at the beginning of the Women's Liberation Movement by a speaker for that movement is given.

* Woodall, W. Gill, Judee K. Burgoon, and Norman N. Markel. "The Effects of Facial-Head Cue Combinations on Interpersonal Evaluations." *Communication Quarterly*, 28 (Summer 1980), 47-55. See item 1089.

* Zacharis, John C. "Emmeline Pankhurst: An English Suffragette Influences America." *Speech Monographs*, 38 (1971), 198-206. See item 481.

IN ORGANIZATIONS

BUSINESS

423. Athanassiades, John C. "An Investigation of Some Communication Patterns of Female Subordinates in Hierarchical Organizations." *Human Relations*, 27 (1974), 195-209.

   This study focused on the distortion of upward communication by female subordinates and its relation to the female subordinate's achievement and security needs. The subjects were 25 female and 25 male business employees who responded to a set of questions measuring perceptions of discrimination against females, autonomy in organizations, and perceptions of self-esteem. Subordinates of both sexes were aware of the existence of job-discrimination against women. An inverse relationship between perceived autonomy and the distortion of upward communication for the female subordinate emerged such that the less autonomous she felt, the more likely she was to distort upward communication. No significant relationship between the female subordinate's perception of discrimination, autonomy, and her self-image was found.

424. Baird, John E., Jr., and Patricia H. Bradley. "Styles of Management and Communication: A Comparative Study of Men and Women." *Communication Monographs*, 46 (1979), 101-111.

   A questionnaire of managerial communication behavior was given to 150 employees, 50 each from a hospital, the clerical department of a manufacturing company, and the production line of a manufacturing company. T-tests revealed different leadership styles for men and women; women gave more information, stressed interpersonal relations, were receptive to ideas, encouraged effort, and showed concern and were attentive to others. Men were more dominant, quick to challenge others, and directed conversations more. The authors conclude that the female behaviors "seem more conducive" to morale.

425. Baron, Alma S. "Communication Skills for the Woman Manager--A Practice Seminar." *Personnel Journal*, 59

(1980), 55-58, 63.

A seminar to improve communication skills needed by women in management is described. It included practice with parliamentary procedure, networking through telephoning, and role playing difficult situations of actual work-related cases.

426. Bartol, Kathryn M., and D. Anthony Butterfield. "Sex Effects in Evaluating Leaders." *Journal of Applied Psychology*, 61 (1976), 446-454.

    Two hundred fifty-five male and 57 female business students evaluated male and female managers using one of four managerial styles. Data were presented in story form, with sex of manager and style of management systematically manipulated. Female managers were evaluated significantly more favorably than males on the consideration style of management (emphasis on interpersonal satisfaction within a division), while male managers were evaluated significantly more favorably on the initiating-structures style (emphasis on clarity of organizing division responsibilites). Sex of manager had no significant influence on the production-emphasis or the tolerance-for-freedom styles of management.

* Bednarek, Frank, Louis Benson, and Husain Mustafa. "Identifying Peer Leadership in Small Work Groups." *Small Group Behavior*, 7 (1976), 307-316. See item 198.

427. Brenner, Otto C., and W. Edgar Vinacke. "Accommodative and Exploitative Behavior of Males versus Females and Managers versus Nonmanagers as Measured by a Test of Strategy." *Social Psychology Quarterly*, 42 (1979), 289-293.

    A survey of 264 adults in New York business firms using Vinacke's Test of Strategy found that males were more exploitative, females more accommodating. Though not statistically significant, managers tended to be more exploitative, nonmanagers accommodative.

* Brown, Stephen M. "Male Versus Female Leaders: A Comparison of Empirical Studies." *Sex Roles*, 5 (1979), 595-611. See item 595.

* Chapman, J. Brad. "Comparison of Male and Female Leadership Styles." *Academy of Management Journal*, 18 (1975), 645-650. See item 596.

428. Deaux, Kay. "Self-Evaluations of Male and Female Managers." *Sex Roles*, 5 (1979), 571-580.

Two separate samples of 70 males and 64 females holding first-level management positions in United States organizations completed questionnaires which asked for self-evaluation on a number of job-related characteristics and for attribution of causality for successful and unsuccessful job experiences. As in previous research, males evaluated their performance more favorably than females and rated themselves as having more ability and greater intelligence. Males also saw ability as more responsible for their success than did women, but the sexes did not differ in attributions to luck, effort, or task.

429. DiMarco, Nicholas, and Susan E. Whitsitt. "A Comparison of Female Supervisors in Business and Government Organizations." *Journal of Vocational Behavior*, 6 (1975), 185-196.

A group of 51 female first- and second-level supervisors in government and a group of 24 counterparts in private business, not different from each other in age, organization tenure, and supervisory tenure, were given a battery of questionnaires on life style, organizational structure, interpersonal needs, and leadership style. The government group perceived their organization as largely bureaucratic; the business group perceived theirs as largely collaborative. The government group had a significantly higher formalistic life style, had a lower need for affection and a higher need for control, and were lower on consideration and higher on structure in leadership style than the business group.

430. Dipboye, Robert L., and Jack Wiley. "Reactions of College Recruiters to Interviewee Sex and Self-Presentation Style." *Journal of Vocational Behavior*, 10 (1977), 1-12.

Sixty-six male college recruiters evaluated from videotaped interviews and resumes the qualifications and employability of either a male or female applicant for a supervisory position. Half of the applicants presented themselves passively and half moderately aggressively. The moderately aggressive female was rated as favorably as the moderately aggressive male and the passive male was rated as negatively as the passive female. Recruiters were as willing to hire a moderately aggressive female as they were the moderately aggressive male, and they perceived the female's overall qualifications and her experiences and training as superior to that of the male's.

431. Haccoun, Dorothy M., Robert R. Haccoun, and George Sallay. "Sex Differences in the Appropriateness of Supervisory Styles: A Nonmanagement View." *Journal of Applied Psychology*, 63 (1978), 124-127.

    Sixty male and female blue-collar workers evaluated male and female supervisors in hypothetical situations, systematically displaying directive, rational, or friendly supervisory styles. An analysis of variance showed that all workers perceived the male supervisors more favorably, and preferred friendly, rational, and directive styles, in that order. Worker/sex differences indicated that least preferred of all was a female directive supervisor.

432. Heilman, Madeline E., and Lois R. Saruwatari. "When Beauty Is Beastly: The Effects of Appearance and Sex on Evaluations of Job Applicants for Managerial and Nonmanagerial Jobs." *Organizational Behavior and Human Performance*, 23 (1979), 360-372.

    To determine the effects of both appearance and sex on the evaluations of applicants for managerial and nonmanagerial positions, 22 female and 23 male advanced undergraduates evaluated the applications with accompanying photographs of either a male or female applying for either a managerial or a nonmanagerial job. Attractiveness consistently proved to be an advantage for males but for females only for a nonmanagerial position, a finding that affected ratings of qualifications, recommendations for hiring, suggested starting salary, and rankings of hiring preferences. Additional results indicated that attractiveness exaggerated perceptions of gender-related attributes.

433. Heinen, J. Stephen, Dorothy McGlauchlin, Constance Legeros, and Jean Freeman. "Developing the Woman Manager." *Personnel Journal*, 54 (1975), 282-286, 297.

    This essay-report by a professor of managerial communication and three consultants notes their assessment of the needs of potential women managers on which they based their development of a three-day training program (for women only) to raise self-esteem, to manage interpersonal conflict, to develop leadership skills, and to plan careers.

434. Helmich, Donald L. "Male and Female Presidents: Some Implications of Leadership Style." *Human Resource Management,* 13, No. 4 (1974), 25-26.

    Questionnaires on leadership style were completed by 112 male corporate presidents and 69 female presidents. Male presidents were better able to differentiate positive characteristics of their least-preferred coworker and were thus more employee-oriented as a group than were their female counterparts.

435. Huck, James R., and Douglas W. Bray. "Management Assessment Center Evaluations and Subsequent Job Performance of White and Black Females." *Personnel Psychology,* 29 (1976), 13-30.

    A sample of 91 white and 35 black nonmanagement women who attended a Bell System assessment center and were subsequently promoted to first-level supervisory jobs was compared with a group of 479 black and white women who had attended and either not been promoted or promoted to jobs other than those of the first group. Assessment-center judgments were found to be good predictors, especially the Overall Assessment Rating. A factor analysis of 16 assessment dimensions of the promoted sample yielded four factors: Interpersonal Effectiveness (including group problem solving), Administrative Skills (including decision making), Sensitivity, and Effective Intelligence. Some differences between the black and white groups emerged, but no significant correlations of the Overall Assessment Rating with Potential for Advancement or with Overall Job Performance did.

436. Humphreys, Luther W., and William A. Shrode. "Decision-Making Profiles of Female and Male Managers." *MSU Business Topics,* 26, No. 4 (1978), 45-51.

    To compare decision-making styles of male and female commercial bank managers, 60 female managers and 59 male managers responded to a questionnaire in which they ranked task, personnel, budgetary, information, and conceptual decisions. More similarities than differences were found in the profiles of the female and male managers. Female managers spent more of their time making task decisions while they considered conceptual decisions the most important. They experienced the least difficulty in making task decisions, but they preferred personnel decisions. Budgetary decisions were the most difficult for them and the least preferred. Male managers also spent more time in making task decisions, but they considered personnel decisions most important. They preferred conceptual decisions and considered them most difficult. Budgetary decisions were also the least preferred by the male managers.

* Inderlied, Sheila D., and Gary Powell. "Sex-Role Identity and Leadership Style: Different Labels for the Same Concept?" *Sex Roles,* 5 (1979), 613-625. See item 606.

437. Infante, Dominic A., and William I. Gorden. "Subordinate and Superior Perceptions of Self and One Another: Relations, Accuracy, and Reciprocity of Liking." *Western Journal of Speech Communication,* 43 (1979), 212-223.

To investigate superior-subordinate perceptions of participation in decision-making, degree of supervision, and after-hours work, questionnaires were completed by 241 female secretaries and their immediate supervisors, 34 females, 205 males, and 2 sex not identified. Both superiors and subordinates had inaccurate beliefs about how they were perceived, and they differed in perceptions of subordinate participation in decision-making and in degree of supervision. Favorable perception of the traits of the other influenced the ratings of the other. Each rated the other more highly when perceived to be liked. Subordinates estimated their participation in decision making was higher and felt they were supervised less than superiors did. Based on their limited responses, the less secretive and dynamic secretary was more likely to be asked to work after hours.

438. Jablin, Frederic M. "Subordinate's Sex and Superior-Subordinate Status Differentiation as Moderators of the Pelz Effect." In *Communication Yearbook 4.* Ed. Dan Nimmo. New Brunswick, N.J.: Transaction Books, 1980, pp. 349-366.

Using 283 insurance and manufacturing employees who responded to a questionnaire, Jablin replicated earlier studies that showed a positive linear association between a subordinate's satisfaction and openness with his/her supervisor and the supervisor's strategic and work-related influence; he added an investigation of the effect of the subordinate's sex and subject's perception of supervisor-subordinate status. If male and female subordinates perceived their supervisors as being low in supportiveness, there was no sex difference in their perceptions of the levels of openness and satisfaction. If they perceived their supervisor as high in supportiveness, females were significantly more open and satisfied with their supervisors than males. Females also perceived more status difference between themselves and their supervisors.

439. Kanter, Rosabeth M. "Some Effects of Proportions on Group Life: Skewed Sex Ratios and Responses to Token Women." *American Journal of Sociology*, 82 (1977), 965-990.

Forty male and 16 female managers in the sales force of a large industrial corporation were interviewed and observed in sales-training groups and at informal social gatherings for approximately 100 hours. Analysis of the data of these sex-skewed groups showed that the women (tokens) stood out vividly, that group culture became polarized, and that individual characteristics of the token women were distorted to bring them into line with stereotpyes. Extensive discussion leading to a framework for interaction dynamics of groups with tokens is included.

440. Larwood, Laurie, Linda M. Radford, and Dale Berger. "Do Job Tactics Predict Success? A Comparison of Female with Male Executives in 14 Corporations." *Academy of Management Proceedings* (1980), 386-390.

This research compared job tactics (potential strategies) of 98 females and 96 males at low and high levels of management and from line and staff positions in large manufacturing organizations. Job tactics, situation, and background were found to predict success. Questionnaire data showed that men and women differed in their evaluations of the importance of some tactics, as well as in their descriptions of success. A factor analysis of the 82 tactic items resulted in seven factors: abilities (expressing oneself clearly, meeting deadlines); public appearances (attending worship, not divorcing); vigilance (keeping what is yours, demanding what you deserve); sex role (appearing feminine, learning from male models); politics (having a sponsor, willing to express disagreement); compliance (not complaining, advocating company policy); education (having an advanced degree and a good academic record). The most notable sex differences in tactics were that women were more willing to use femininity, to learn from both male and female models, and to endorse other role-identified traits.

441. Larwood, Laurie, Marion M. Wood, and Sheila D. Inderlied. "Training Women for Management: New Problems, New Solutions." *Academy of Management Review*, 3 (1978), 584-593.

    This discussion of the problems associated with training women for management includes material on both interior and exterior barriers, the lack of role models, and the pre-employment socialization and training, including leadership and communication barriers. Examples of programs designed to effect change are presented.

442. Mai-Dalton, Renate R., Shirley Feldman-Summers, and Terence R. Mitchell. "Effect of Employee Gender and Behavioral Style on the Evaluations of Male and Female Banking Executives." *Journal of Applied Psychology*, 64 (1979), 221-226.

    One hundred and twenty-two male and female banking executives evaluated a manager, male or female, behaving in a conflict situation either in a calm manner or an angry manner. The calm, unemotional behavior was evaluated more effective, but angry behavior was evaluated more favorably if used by a female than by a male manager.

443. Massengill, Douglas, and Nicholas DiMarco. "Sex-Role Stereotypes and Requisite Management Characteristics: A Current Replication." *Sex Roles*, 5 (1979), 561-570.

    A survey of 160 adults in organizations to determine stereotypes of men, women, and successful managers revealed a moderately high degree of similarity between stereotypes of men and managers, but none between men and women nor women and managers for male respondents. Female respondents perceived a moderately high similarity between men and managers and a slight degree of similarity between women and both men and managers.

444. Matteson, Michael T. "Attitudes toward Women as Managers: Sex or Role Differences?" *Psychological Reports*,

39 (1976), 166.

A survey of 69 female and 39 male managerial-level employees in health services on their attitudes toward women managers revealed that females had more favorable attitudes than males. A negative relation between number of years of work experience and attitude score suggested that the longer one works, the more negative the attitude toward women in management becomes.

445. Osborn, Richard N., and William M. Vicars. "Sex Stereotypes: An Artifact in Leader Behavior and Subordinate Satisfaction Analysis?" *Academy of Management Journal*, 19 (1976), 439-449.

To determine if female managers behaved differently toward subordinates than male managers, and if they had a different effect on their subordinates, 73 male and female employees and first-level supervisors in two mental health organizations answered questionnaires in small group sessions. No consistent effect of leader sex on either leader behavior or subordinate satisfaction appeared. The results fit a pattern of research evidence that shows sex stereotypes may be important in some laboratory settings but not in long-term situations.

446. Petty, M.M., and Robert H. Miles. "Leader Sex-Role Stereotyping in a Female-Dominated Work Culture." *Personnel Psychology*, 29 (1976), 393-404.

Correlations of various measures of the job satisfaction of 226 male and female subordinates of 41 female and 10 male directors of county-level social service organizations were made to investigate sex-role stereotyping. Satisfaction with supervisor correlated with initiating structure for male supervisors and with consideration for female supervisors; sex of subordinate made no difference. Individual work motivation correlated more positively with leader initiating structure with male than with female supervisors, especially for female subordinates.

447. Petty, M.M., Charles A. Odewahn, Nealia S. Bruning, and Terry L. Thomason. "An Examination of the Moderating Effects of Supervisor Sex and Subordinate Sex Upon the Relationships Between Supervisory Behavior and Subordinate Outcomes in Mental Health Organizations." *Academy of Management Proceedings* (1977), 408-412.

Employees in mental health organizations (432 F, 160 M)

evaluated their supervisors for consideration, participation, initiating structure, and production emphasis. Male subordinates did not have differential expectations for male and female supervisors, but female subordinates expected their female supervisors to be more considerate and allow more participation.

448. Renwick, Patricia A. "The Effects of Sex Differences on the Perception and Management of Superior-Subordinate Conflict: An Exploratory Study. *Organizational Behavior and Human Performance,* 19 (1977), 403-415.

Forty female and 55 male management personnel responded to a questionnaire on the perception and management of superior-subordinate conflict; 30 of the females were supervised by males and 10 by females (data was analyzed separately on these groups) and all males were supervised by males. No support was found for the popular belief that women would be less assertive than men in dealing with differences and disagreements or any more or less cooperative than men. Both male and female subordinates described themselves as most likely to rely on compromise, confrontation, and smoothing in that order to manage superior-subordinate conflict; neither sex was likely to withdraw from such differences and disagreements. Differences emerged between the perceptions of male-supervised males and females concerning the behavior of their supervisors, but preliminary analyses suggested that the sex of supervisor was unrelated to female subordinates' perceptions of conflict management.

449. Rosen, Benson, and Thomas H. Jerdee. "Effects of Employee's Sex and Threatening Versus Pleading Appeals on Managerial Evaluations of Grievances." *Journal of Applied Psychology,* 60 (1975), 442-445.

In a simulated exercise over 100 bank employees (73 M, 28 F) evaluated complaints manipulated by appellant's sex and mode of approach, but otherwise identical, on scales of justification and favorableness of reaction. The male appellant was favorably received with a pleading appeal, and fairly well received with a threatening one. The female appellant was favorably received with a threatening appeal and much less well received with a pleading one.

450. Rosen, Benson, and Thomas H. Jerdee. "The Influence of Sex-Role Stereotypes on Evaluations of Male and Female

Supervisory Behavior." *Journal of Applied Psychology*, 57 (1973), 44-48.

Ratings by 134 male and 24 female business students and 83 male and 15 female bank supervisors were made of the effectiveness of a male or female supervisor employing one of four leadership styles with subordinates of one sex or mixed sexes. Though no significant difference by sex on the evaluations of the effectiveness of supervision was found, certain supervisory styles were related to sex. A reward style was rated more effective for male managers than female, and a friendly-dependent style was rated more effective for either sex supervisor when used with subordinates of the opposite sex. Threat style was rated low for both sex supervisors; helping style, high for both.

451. Schein, Virginia E. "Relationships Between Sex Role Stereotypes and Requisite Management Characteristics Among Female Managers." *Journal of Applied Psychology*, 60 (1975), 340-344.

Replicating her 1973 study with males, Schein found that 167 female managers in insurance companies perceived successful managers as having characteristics commonly found in men in general but not in women in general. Schein speculates that females may have to accept stereotypical male characteristics as a basis for success in management. She notes that female managers did see some characteristics, normally sex stereotyped, as equally characteristic of men and women in general. These characteristics deal with emotionality and with rational thinking.

452. Schwartz, Felice N. "'Invisible' Resource: Women for Boards." *Harvard Business Review*, 58 (1980), 6-8, 12.

This article discusses identifying and selecting the best of the unknown but talented pool of women candidates for board membership. Included in the article are quotations from current female board members who reflect on their contributions; frequently they commented that asking questions and analyzing were their chief contributions.

453. Simas, Kathleen, and Michael McCarrey. "Impact of Recruiter Authoritarianism and Applicant Sex on Evaluation and Selection Decisions in a Recruitment Interview

Analogue Study." *Journal of Applied Psychology*, 64 (1979), 483-491.

Videotaped simulated interviews of both male and female applicants for entry-level management positions were evaluated by 144 male and female personnel officers of high, moderate, or low authoritarianism. High authoritarian officers, whether male or female, preferred hiring male applicants and tended to overevaluate male compared to female applicants. In a semantic differential, all personnel officers rated male applicants significantly higher in potency items (ruggedness, dominance, aggression) than female applicants.

454. Stead, Bette A., ed. *Women in Management*. Englewood Cliffs, N.J.: Prentice-Hall, 1978.

Seven articles explore myths and stereotypes that have hindered women in management. Three others identify language barriers, one specifies a non-sexist language guide, and another lists job title changes designed to eliminate sexism. Three articles explore women's leadership style and motivation. A 22-page annotated bibliography is included.

* Sterrett, John H. "The Job Interview: Body Language and Perceptions of Potential Effectiveness." *Journal of Applied Psychology*, 63 (1978), 388-390. See item 1308.

* Stevens, Betsy. "Improving Communication With Clerical Workers: The Non-Sexist Directive." *Personnel Journal*, 56 (1977), 170-172. See item 961.

455. Terborg, James R. "Women in Management: A Research Review." *Journal of Applied Psychology*, 62 (1977), 647-664.

A review of research from 1974 to 1976 (100 articles) covers such topics as self-concept and career choice, blocked career pathways, stereotyping, and socialization. Recommendations for research are included.

456. Waetjen, Walter B., James M. Schuerger, and Eleanor B. Schwartz. "Male and Female Managers: Self-Concept, Success, and Failure." *Journal of Psychology*, 103 (1979), 87-94.

From two large multinational corporations, 14 male and 14 female managers, half rated successful, half unsuccessful by their supervisors, completed a self-concept as manager measure. Analysis of variance and t-tests revealed that the highest self-concepts were those of unsuccessful female managers, followed by successful male, successful female, and unsuccessful male managers. The anomaly of the unsuccessful female manager's high self-concept is interpreted as a problem of these managers being in a protected environment (Affirmative Action programs) which includes encouragement but no feedback on performance.

* Wexley, Kenneth N., and Peter J. Hunt. "Male and Female Leaders: Comparison of Performance and Behavior Patterns." *Psychological Reports,* 35 (1974), 867-872. See item 624.

457. Wood, Marion M. "What Does It Take for a Woman to Make It in Management?" *Personnel Journal,* 54 (1975), 38-41, 66.

    From nearly 100 interviews of women in management, from trainee to company president, ten characteristics necessary for success in management were noted: competence, education, realism, aggressiveness, self-confidence, career-mindedness, femininity, a strategy, support of an influential male, and uniqueness.

* Young, Jerald W. "The Subordinate's Exposure of Organization Vulnerability to the Superior: Sex and Organizational Effects." *Academy of Management Journal,* 21 (1978), 113-122. See item 767.

POLITICAL

Feminist Movement

458. Barber, Sharla, Brenda Hancock, and Bonnie Spillman. "Rhetoric of Feminism." *Female Studies,* 7 (1973), 109-110.

    The syllabus and bibliography for a course on the rhetoric of feminism are presented.

* Blakar, Rolv M. "How Sex Roles Are Represented, Reflected and Conserved in the Norwegian Language." *Acta Sociologica,* 18 (1975), 162-173. See item 923.

459. Bosmajian, Haig A. "The Abrogation of the Suffragists' First Amendment Rights." *Western Speech*, 38 (1974), 218-232.

    This analysis of the treatment of the suffragists includes some analysis of their rhetorical symbolic strategies as well.

460. Campbell, Karlyn K. "The Rhetoric of Women's Liberation: An Oxymoron." *Quarterly Journal of Speech*, 59 (1973), 74-86.

    Analysis of the substance and the style of women's liberation rhetoric reveals that it constitutes a distinctive genre, characterized metaphorically by the oxymoron, figure of paradox and contradictions. To begin with, rhetors are seen as self-reliant, self-confident, and independent, all traditionally non-female qualities. The distinctive stylistic features of the rhetoric includes emphasis on affective proofs and personal testimony, self-disclosure and self-criticism, and autonomous decision-making.

461. Coughlin, Elizabeth M., and Charles E. Coughlin. "Convention in Petticoats: The Seneca Falls Declaration of Woman's Rights." *Today's Speech*, 21, No. 4 (1973), 17-23.

    The First Woman's Rights Convention (1848) is discussed in light of the rhetorical tensions it produced.

*   Crowley, Sharon. "The Semantics of Sexism." *ETC.*, 4 (1973), 407-411. See item 931.

462. DuBoise, Ellen, ed. "On Labor and Free Love: Two Unpublished Speeches of Elizabeth Cady Stanton." *Signs: Journal of Women in Culture and Society*, 1 (1975), 257-268.

    A brief background to and the text of two previously unpublished speeches by Elizabeth C. Stanton are given.

463. Fong, M.S. "The Early Rhetoric of Women's Liberation: Implications for Zero Population Growth." *Journal of Marriage and the Family*, 38 (1976), 127-140.

    Examining the policies concerning sex, contraception, abortion, and child care advocated in the rhetoric from 1967 to 1971 of women in the Liberation Movement, Fong concludes that women's liberation was intimately linked to zero population growth in all factors affecting reproduction, including child rearing and child care.

464. Foss, Sonja K. "The Equal Rights Amendment Controversy: Two Worlds in Conflict." *Quarterly Journal of Speech,* 65 (1979), 275-288.

An analysis of the settings, characters, actions, and motivations of each side in the ERA controversy reveals that each side creates its own world view. These views reveal "little common ground on which traditional argumentation can occur." Foss concludes that "each side's rhetoric is not only a threat to the other's way of making sense of the world, but also is a reason to defend strongly their particular world."

465. Foss, Sonja K. "The Feminists: A Rhetorical Analysis of the Radical Feminist Movement." *University of Michigan Papers in Women's Studies,* 2 (1976), 79-95.

466. Foss, Sonja K. "Teaching Contemporary Feminist Rhetoric: An Illustrative Syllabus." *Communication Education,* 27 (1978), 328-335.

An outline for a course on the rhetoric of the feminist movement, including its history, the radical wing, the ERA and abortion issues, language, and family and child care is presented. Sources, lecture summaries, and sample discussion questions are included.

* Gregersen, Edgar A. "Sexual Linguistics." In *Language, Sex, and Gender*. Eds. Judith Orasanu, Mariam K. Slater, and Lenore L. Adler. New York: New York Academy of Sciences, 1979, pp. 3-19. See item 830.

467. Hancock, Brenda R. "Affirmation by Negation in the Women's Liberation Movement." *Quarterly Journal of Speech,* 58 (1972), 264-271.

This analysis of the rhetoric of the feminist movement concludes that the "man-hating" element not only released frustration and guilt but also led to an identification of female characteristics as the antithesis of male characteristics, thereby giving women a new identity.

468. Hope, Diane S. "Redefinition of Self: A Comparison of the Rhetoric of the Women's Liberation and Black

Liberation Movements." *Today's Speech,* 23, No. 1 (1975), 17-25.

A comparison of the women's and black liberation movements reveals that both groups have generated a rhetoric redefining the self; rhetors of both use the other's oppression as metaphor. Rhetorical analysis reveals three significant differences, however: the black movement assumes a sexist society while the women's movement attempts to alter white racism; black rhetors can assume an audience, but feminist rhetors must create one; and black rhetoric generates a counter-movement, while feminist rhetoric generates backlash, ridicule, or silence.

* Jacobson, Marsha B. "A Rose by Any Other Name: Attitudes Toward Feminism as a Function of Its Label." *Sex Roles,* 5 (1979), 365-371. See item 1007.

* Jacobson, Marsha B., and Walter Koch. "Attributed Reasons for Support of the Feminist Movement as a Function of Attractiveness." *Sex Roles,* 4 (1978), 169-174. See item 1109.

469. Linkugel, Wil A. "The Rhetoric of American Feminism: A Social Movement Course. *Speech Teacher,* 23 (1974), 121-130.

    A detailed description of the goals and units of a course in the rhetoric of feminism in America is given. It uses an historical approach and calls for rhetorical analysis of speeches from Lucretia Mott to Betty Friedan and of essays of both pro- and anti-feminists.

470. McDowell, Margaret B. "The New Rhetoric of Woman Power." *The Midwest Quarterly,* 12 (1971), 187-198.

    General questions on the rhetoric of women's liberation found in speeches and writings of its members as well as in media assumptions about women are explored. Various branches of the movement are analyzed and the language, particularly militarist vocabulary, examined.

471. McPherson, Louise. "Communication Techniques of the Women's Liberation Front." *Today's Speech,* 21, No. 2 (1973), 33-38.

    In this essay on the communication techniques of the Women's Liberation Front, which included setting up their own press, KNOW, Inc., and refusing interviews with traditional media, McPherson asserts that the techniques aimed at changing social structure were more effective than those which aimed at changing social attitudes.

472. Mansfield, Dorothy M. "Abigail S. Duniway: Suffragette with Not-so-common Sense." *Western Speech,* 35 (1971), 24-29.

    This essay discusses the common sense and good humor of 1870s suffragette Abigail Duniway by looking at selected speeches.

473. Pinola, Mary, and Nancy E. Briggs. "Martha Wright Griffiths: Champion of Women's Rights Legislation." *The Central States Speech Journal,* 30 (1979), 228-240.

    The strategies employed by Congresswoman Martha Griffiths in her efforts to obtain women's rights legislation are analyzed using a four-fold typology developed by Walter R. Fisher. Analysis of Griffiths' rhetoric reveals predominant motives of affirmation and subversion.

474. Polk, Barbara B. "Male Power and the Women's Movement." *Journal of Applied Behavioral Science,* 10 (1974), 415-431.

    The power relationship between females and males is analyzed using four major perspectives: sex role socialization, differing feminine and masculine cultures, power analysis, and economic relationships. These perspectives suggest the sources of male power are normative, institutional, reward, expertise, psychological, and physical. To change the power relationships various segments of the women's movement urge various strategies, including desocialization or resocialization of oneself; changing personal interactions; resocializing others, especially through the media; changing male dominance of insitutions; and building alternate insitutions. The problems of coordinating these various strategies and of leadership in the movement are also discussed.

475. Reynolds, Beatrice K. "An Interview with Ti-Grace Atkinson: Her Speeches and Speechmaking." *Today's Speech,* 21, No. 4 (1973), 3-10.

    This article includes excerpts from a 1973 two and one-half hour interview with Ti-Grace Atkinson, active in NOW and one of the founders of The Feminists. It includes a section on her speechmaking.

In Organizations

476. Rosenwasser, Marie J. "Rhetoric and the Progress of the Women's Liberation Movement." *Today's Speech*, 20, No. 3 (1972), 45-56.

    This essay reviews the growth of the women's liberation movement through a five-stage structure of a movement from genesis to action to conversion to revision to success. Analysis of the language, goals, and strategies of leading rhetors and organizations leads Rosenwasser to determine the movement is in the third stage and to suggest probable changes to come.

477. Scott, Robert L. "The Conservative Voice in Radical Rhetoric: A Common Response to Division." *Speech Monographs*, 40 (1973), 123-135.

    In this analysis of radical rhetoric of the late 1960s and early 1970s, including examples from the women's liberation movement, Scott argues that, by appealing to well-established values, the rhetoric really reflects a conservative impulse.

478. Solomon, Martha. "The 'Positive Woman's' Journey: A Mythic Analysis of the Rhetoric of STOP ERA." *Quarterly Journal of Speech*, 65 (1979), 262-274.

    An analysis of the rhetoric of the Stop ERA group, primarily of Phyllis Schlafly, shows that it draws its structure patterns from the romantic quest myth and its characteristics to describe both supporters and opponents from elements of Jung's mother archetype. Hence, it is "especially potent and appealing."

479. Solomon, Martha. "The Rhetoric of STOP ERA: Fatalistic Reaffirmation." *Southern Speech Communication Journal*, 44 (1978), 42-59.

    This study of the Stop ERA rhetoric examines the image which the group has developed of its opponents, the image it has projected of its supporters, the ideological framework indicated by these images, and their rhetorical implications. Solomon concludes that, although the movement's ideology is implicitly fatalistic and manipulative, its reaffirmation of traditional perspectives and its appeal to the need for personal security make it extremely effective rhetorically.

480. Thorne, Barrie. "Women in the Draft Resistance Movement: A Case Study of Sex Roles and Social Movements." *Sex*

Roles, 1 (1975), 179-195.

This case study, based on participant observation, explores the factors which led women in the draft-resistance movement in Boston in the late 1960s to turn toward and help found a Women's Liberation group. It covers the strategies and tactics of the resistance movement, including risk taking, confrontation, and communication networks, and how these strategies differed for male and female participants.

* Weisman, Martha. "Rhetoric of Women Activists in the United States." *Female Studies*, 7 (1973), 111-112. See item 909.

481. Zacharis, John C. "Emmeline Pankhurst: An English Suffragette Influences America." *Speech Monographs*, 38 (1971), 198-206.

    This essay-analysis of the influence of the 1909, 1911, and 1913 trips to America of Mrs. Pankhurst includes a rhetorical analysis of her speeches, especially of her credibility and ethos.

Political Parties

482. Anderson, Judith. "Sexual Politics: Chauvinism and Backlash?" *Today's Speech*, 21, No. 4 (1973), 11-16.

    This analysis of the audience images of contemporary women politicians classifies them by temperament (the psychological dimension), role (the sociological dimension), and status (the political dimension). Anderson's findings result in a qualified "yes" to the question raised in the title of the article.

483. Auer, J. Jeffery. "The Image of the Right Honourable Margaret Thatcher." *The Central States Speech Journal*, 30 (1979), 289-310.

    Auer's review of the career, particularly the British general election campaign in 1979, of Margaret Thatcher identifies the salient elements of her image as her cultural identification, her dialect and language choices, her persuasive messages, her sex, and her sense of conviction.

484. Barclay, Martha T. "Distaff Campaigning in the 1964 and 1968 Presidential Elections." *The Central States*

Speech Journal, 21 (1970), 117-122.

A comparison of the campaign techniques of Mrs. Lyndon Johnson, Mrs. Barry Goldwater, Mrs. Hubert Humphrey, and Mrs. Richard Nixon reveals that Mrs. Johnson and Mrs. Humphrey made informal and formal appeals directly to the public while Mrs. Goldwater and Mrs. Nixon supported their husbands mainly by their presence.

* Carlson, James M. "Politics and Interpersonal Attraction." *American Politics Quarterly,* 7 (1979), 120-126. See item 773.

485. Carroll, Berenice A. "Political Science, Part I: American Politics and Political Behavior." *Signs: Journal of Women in Culture and Society,* 5 (1979), 289-306.

   This essay reviews research in political science, including research on the differences between leadership characteristics of male and female politicians. Carroll concludes that political scientists have made few changes in the way they study women or define political activity. Forty-eight footnotes, many with multiple citations, are included.

486. Dees, Diane. "Bernadette Devlin's Maiden Speech: A Rhetoric of Sacrifice." *Southern Speech Communication Journal,* 38 (1973), 326-339.

   This study examines Devlin's 22 April 1969 speech to the British House of Commons by looking at her background, the history of the conflict in Northern Ireland, and the specific debate situation in the House of Commons on that day. Dees concludes that the speech was an outstanding example of parliamentary debate.

487. Farrell, Thomas B. "Political Conventions as Legitimation Ritual." *Communication Monographs,* 45 (1978), 293-305.

   This analysis of the rituals, including the speechmaking one, of both parties in the 1976 nominating conventions includes several paragraphs on Barbara Jordan's keynote address, which was found less important than her symbolic role within the ritual.

488. Fowler, Marguerite G., Robert L. Fowler, and Hani Van de Riet. "Feminism and Political Radicalism." *Journal of Psychology,* 83 (1973), 237-242.

In Organizations

A comparison of political attitudes of 50 feminists and 50 female peers revealed the feminists manifested more feminism and were more radical politically, though both groups shared opinions on several politically relevant issues, such as the potential influence of women's vote and the Vietnam war. Authors suggest that feminists are not different from peers, as stereotype would indicate, but that feminists are more vociferous.

489. Frye, Jerry K., and Franklin B. Krohn. "An Analysis of Barbara Jordan's 1976 Keynote Address." *Journal of Applied Communications Research,* 2 (1977), 73-82.

After a biographical sketch of Barbara Jordan, the authors describe the rhetorical situation, explain why she was selected, and analyze the rhetorical characteristics of her speech, particularly its organization and style.

490. Gonchar, Ruth M., and Dan F. Hahn. "Political Rhetoric: A Reassessment of Critical Methodologies." *Journal of Applied Communications Research,* 6 (1978), 55-63.

A new approach to critical methodology in political rhetoric using rhetorical biography, the speaker's purposes, the issues, the organization, and the style is proposed. Barbara Jordan's 1976 Democratic National Convention Keynote Address is examined using the authors' recommended critical method.

491. Jaquette, Jane S., ed. *Women in Politics.* New York: John Wiley & Sons, 1974.

This collection of essays exploring female participation in politics includes sections on interaction networks, sex stereotyping, and small groups. A selective topical bibliography, approximately 225 items, is included.

492. Linkugel, Wil A., and Dixie L. Coty. "Nixon, McGovern, and the Female Electorate." *Today's Speech,* 21, No. 4 (1973), 25-32.

This essay examines the campaign rhetoric of both Richard Nixon and George McGovern in the 1972 presidential campaign designed to sway women's votes. The authors note that McGovern's 25 October 1972 speech was "the most comprehensive address on issues of concern to women ever made by a major presidential candidate in the history of the country."

493. Phifer, Gregg. "Edith Bolling Wilson: Gatekeeper Extraordinary." *Speech Monographs,* 38 (1971), 277-289.

An account of Mrs. Wilson's intermediary role between ailing President Wilson and Congress, his advisors, and others is given. Since this period, October 1919 through April 1920, coincided with Congress' consideration of the League of Nations bill, her role was a crucial, but not a decisive, one.

494. Pugh, Evelyn L. "The First Woman Candidate for Parliament: Helen Taylor and the Election of 1885." *International Journal of Women's Studies,* 1 (1978), 378-390.

This account of the life of Helen Taylor concentrates on the campaign of 1885, which it depicts as an extraordinary achievement. Her unsuccessful endeavors in 1885 to get her name on the ballot were the first in a long line of continuing attacks against the male-dominated political establishment.

495. Thompson, Wayne N. "Barbara Jordan's Keynote Address: Fulfilling Dual and Conflicting Purposes." *The Central States Speech Journal,* 30 (1979), 272-277.

This article analyzes Jordan's keynote address to the 1976 Democratic Convention, attributing its success to her skillful handling of three sets of conflicting purposes: pleasing two unlike audiences; fulfilling the role expectations imposed on keynoters while avoiding triteness; and affirming blackness and womanliness while avoiding unfavorable stereotypes of each.

496. Thompson, Wayne N. "Barbara Jordan's Keynote Address: The Juxtaposition of Contradictory Values." *Southern Speech Communication Journal,* 44 (1979), 223-232.

The keynote address of Barbara Jordan at the 1976 National Democratic Party Convention is analyzed for the skillful use of appeals to the values of the immediate audience while not offending the values of the larger, viewing audience.

497. Tiffany, Sharon W. "Women, Power, and the Anthropology of Politics: A Review." *International Journal of Women's Studies,* 2 (1979), 430-442.

Tiffany questions the prevailing view of women and politics by examining the nature of power and authority and cross-cultural variations in female political participation. She asserts that women in most societies are politically active, although their means of expression and extent of formal participation frequently differ from men's.

498. Whalen, Ardyce C. "The Presentation of Image in Ella T. Grasso's Campaign." *The Central States Speech Journal,* 27 (1976), 207-211.

   The image-building process in Ella Grasso's 1974 gubernatorial campaign is examined with particular attention to the efforts made to overcome negative female stereotypes.

PROFESSIONS

Academic

   * Barron, Nancy. "Sex-Typed Language: The Production of Grammatical Cases." *Acta Sociologica,* 14 (1971), 24-42. See item 798.

499. Bate, Barbara. "Assertive Speaking: An Approach to Communication Education for the Future." *Communication Education,* 25 (1976), 53-59.

   Bate makes a case for assertiveness training as an approach to preparing for the changing lifestyles of men and women. Included are brief references to recent research in sex differences in assertiveness and assertive-training techniques.

   * Bate, Barbara. "Nonsexist Language Use in Transition." *Journal of Communication,* 28 (Winter 1978), 139-149. See item 919.

500. Berryman, Cynthia L. "Instructional Materials for Teaching a Course in 'Women and Communication.'" *Communication Education,* 28 (1979), 217-224.

   This description for a course in "Women and Communication" covers intrapersonal communication, between-sex communication, female group communication, and public communication. Both required and supplementary readings, films, instructional objectives, and suggested projects are included.

501. Brooks, Douglas M., and Barry J. Wilson. "Teacher Verbal and Nonverbal Behavior Expression Toward Selected Pupils." *Journal of Educational Psychology,* 70 (1978), 147-153.

Twelve teachers, sex not given, were observed interacting in the classroom situation with four groups of selected high school students--the accepted, the concerned, the indifferent, and the rejected. Neither verbally (questioning, responding, managing behavior, etc.) nor nonverbally (body movements and use of space) did a significant difference in teacher behavior toward the pupil groups emerge. However, teachers maintained greater average distance from the rejected pupils than from those in the other three groups.

502. Brophy, Jere, and Thomas L. Good. "Teacher Communication of Differential Expectations for Children's Classroom Performance: Some Behavior Data." *Journal of Educational Psychology,* 61 (1970), 365-374.

Four first-grade teachers (sex not specified) were observed in dyadic transactions with six students of both sexes ranked high and then with six ranked low in anticipated achievement. Analysis of the interactions revealed anticipated high achievement students received more praise and support, and that boys were interacted with more frequently with praise for work-related interactions and with criticism and disapproval for behavior-related interactions. Specifically, teachers praised highs more when correct and criticized less when incorrect than they did lows. Teachers were more persistent in eliciting responses from highs and gave feedback significantly more often to highs than to lows.

503. Bryant, Jennings, Paul Cominsky, and Dolf Zillmann. "Teachers' Humor in the College Classroom." *Communication Education,* 28 (1979), 110-118.

In this observational study of the humor used by 49 male and 21 female professors in their classrooms, frequency data revealed males tended to use humor more often per class (3.73 items) than females (2.49 items). Males tended to rely on stories, brief comments, or classic joke formats, and females on funny comments. Each sex showed balance between harmless and tendentious humor, but within the tendentious category females used sexual material more frequently than males. Though both groups used more spontaneous than "repeated" humor, the females' percentage was greater than males, and female humor was judged more closely related to the educational message. Males tended to use themselves more often in humor of disparagement.

504. Bryant, Jennings, Jon S. Crane, Paul W. Cominsky, and Dolf Zillmann. "Relationships between College Teachers' Use of Humor in the Classroom and Students' Evaluations of Their Teachers." *Journal of Educational Psychology*, 72 (1980), 511-519.

    Tape recordings of a class presentation in different courses were played to 70 students, who evaluated the teacher on competence, delivery, and effectiveness. The presentations were factor analyzed to identify key features of humor and the factors correlated with the students' evaluations. For male teachers, use of humor was positively related to appeal, delivery, and effectiveness. For female teachers, hostile humor was associated with enhanced appeal, especially when it had sexual connotations, but that was the only use of humor that enhanced ratings for female teachers. Males used more humor; females used more spontaneous humor. Sex stereotyping is posited as an explanation for the discrepancy in student ratings.

* Caproni, Valerie, Douglas Levine, Edgar O'Neal, Peter McDonald, and Gray Garwood. "Seating Position, Instructor's Eye Contact Availability, and Student Participation in a Small Seminar." *The Journal of Social Psychology*, 103 (1977), 315-316. See item 1043.

* Chaikin, Alan L., Edward Sigler, and Valerian J. Derlega. "Nonverbal Mediators of Teacher Expectancy Effects." *Journal of Personality and Social Psychology*, 30 (1974), 144-149. See item 1266.

* Cherry, Louise. "Teacher-Child Verbal Interaction: An Approach to the Study of Sex Differences." In *Language and Sex: Difference and Dominance*. Eds. Barrie Thorne and Nancy Henley. Rowley, Mass.: Newbury House Publishers, 1975, pp. 172-183. See item 104.

505. Cooper, Harris M. "Controlling Personal Rewards: Professional Teachers' Differential Use of Feedback and the Effects of Feedback on the Student's Motivation to Perform." *Journal of Educational Psychology*, 69

(1977), 419-427.

In three experiments involving six female kindergarten-through-second grade teachers interacting with students for whom they had low expectations of academic success, Cooper found that teachers' perceptions of and expectations for control over student performance were significantly related. When teachers stopped negative feedback to those who had been receiving most of it, the low achievers, those students initiated interactions with the teachers more frequently. Students' perceptions of the connection between effort and outcome was negatively related to amount of criticism received after seeking out the teacher. The findings provide an explanation for the self-fulfilling prophecy phenomenon.

* Dellacava, Frances A., and Madeline H. Engel. "Resistance to Sisterhood: The Case of the Professional Woman." *International Journal of Women's Studies,* 2 (1979), 505-512. See item 560.

506. Eakins, Barbara, and Gene Eakins. "Verbal Turn-Taking and Exchanges in Faculty Dialogue." In *The Sociology of the Languages of American Women* (item 1003), pp. 53-62.

An examination of the amount of talk, the interruptions, and the length of utterances occurring in seven tape-recorded faculty meetings revealed that males talked more often, spoke longer, made more interruptions of others' speech, and had their own speech interrupted less than women. These findings also obtained for status, with higher status persons behaving like male faculty, lower status more like female faculty.

507. Elmore, Patricia B., and Karen A. LaPointe. "Effect of Teacher Sex, Student Sex, and Teacher Warmth on the Evaluation of College Instructors." *Journal of Educational Psychology,* 67 (1975), 368-374.

Twenty-two pairs of courses, matched for level, one taught by a male, the other by a female, were evaluated by 838 college students on the Twenty Instructional Improvement Questionnaire. No interactions by faculty sex, student sex, and teacher warmth were found. Students rated teachers higher in effectiveness when they were perceived of as warm. When teachers rated themselves on warmth, sex differences occurred. Females received higher effectiveness ratings than males when they rated themselves low in warmth. Males who had rated themselves high in warmth received higher effectiveness ratings than those who had rated themselves low.

508. Feldman, Robert S., and Lawrence F. Donohoe. "Nonverbal Communication of Affect in Interracial Dyads." *Journal of Educational Psychology,* 70 (1978), 979-987.

    Thirty-six high- and low-prejudiced white female college students acted as teachers in an experimental teaching situation with two white and two black female college students in which feedback was controlled by requiring set responses to correct and incorrect student answers. Twenty black and 20 white female college students evaluated how pleased the teachers were with the students' performance by viewing videotaped samples. Analysis of variance revealed that both high- and low-prejudiced teachers were perceived as being significantly more pleased with a white than a black student, although the low-prejudiced teacher was significantly more pleased with a black student than the high-prejudiced teacher. A second similar experiment revealed that nonverbal behavior was more positive to a student of the teacher's own race, whether black or white, than to the other race.

* Foss, Sonja K. "Teaching Contemporary Feminist Rhetoric: An Illustrative Syllabus." *Communication Education,* 27 (1978), 328-335. See item 466.

509. Glenwick, David S., Sandra L. Johansson, and Jeffrey Bondy. "A Comparison of the Self-Image of Female and Male Assistant Professors." *Sex Roles,* 4 (1978), 513-524.

    To investigate role perceptions of 56 male and female assistant professors at two eastern universities in 1970 and 1975, a 22-item questionnaire concerning job roles, job duties, departmental issues, university issues, and personal roles was administered. Results showed few differences between males and females on specific job duties or in job roles, although men in 1975 showed a greater preference for discussion classes and research. A difference in perception of departmental and university issues was that women in 1975 showed a trend to keep silent in departmental meetings.

510. Good, Thomas L., and Jere E. Brophy. "Behavioral Expression of Teacher Attitudes." *Journal of Educational Psychology,* 63 (1972), 617-624.

With the Brophy-Good system, data on the dyadic interactions of nine female first-grade teachers with 270 students were collected and analyzed to determine the relationship between teacher behavior toward students about whom they held differing attitudes. Students toward whom the teachers were concerned received more opportunities to answer questions, their failures were responded to more favorably, and they were "pushed" more by the teacher than the other groups. Teachers tended to avoid contact with those in the "indifference" group (who also avoided contact with the teachers). With the "rejection" group, teachers also avoided contact; feedback, when given, was generally critical. Students toward whom the teacher was attached received more praise for academic work and less criticism, although not more praise per correct answer than the other groups.

511. Good, Thomas L., J. Neville Sikes, and Jere E. Brophy. "Effects of Teacher Sex and Student Sex on Classroom Interaction." *Journal of Educational Psychology,* 65 (1973), 74-87.

Eight male and eight female junior-high school teachers were observed during ten instructional hours in dyads with their students and the data coded using the Brophy-Good Coding System. Though several significant differences between male and female teachers were found, the frequency of such interaction was below chance expectation. Both sexes, however, clearly treated male students differently from female. High-achieving males received more favorable teacher treatment than any other group and low-achieving males the poorest treatment.

512. Harris, Mary B. "The Effects of Sex, Sex-Stereotyped Descriptions, and Institution on Evaluations of Teachers." *Sex Roles,* 2 (1976), 15-21.

Sixteen male and 16 female undergraduate students evaluated on a bipolar adjective scale 16 randomly ordered descriptions of teachers of both sexes with either masculine or feminine traits. Masculine teachers of both sexes were rated more positively on all variables except warmth. Female teachers were seen as warmer and more feminine than male teachers. Female subjects rated teachers as more intelligent than did male subjects. The difference in ratings of teachers with masculine-versus-feminine characteristics on the superiority and rehiring variables increased as the institutional level increased from nursery school to elementary school to high school to college.

513. Harris, Mary B. "Sex Role Stereotypes and Teacher Evaluations." *Journal of Educational Psychology,* 67 (1975), 751-756.

Eighty female and 70 male college students rated a male or female teacher of engineering or nursing who used either a masculine (active) or feminine (passive) style of teaching. Female students generally rated performance and rank higher than males did, and the masculine-style teacher higher than the feminine-style one. The male teacher was rated more masculine if labeled in engineering than if in nursing.

514. Hillman, Stephen B., and G. Gregory Davenport. "Teacher-Student Interactions in Desegregated Schools." *Journal of Educational Psychology,* 70 (1978), 545-553.

Data on teacher-student interactions from 306 classes involving elementary through high school teachers, male and female, black and white, were recorded using a version of the Brophy-Good Dyadic Interaction Observation System. Results indicated black students and males received a greater proportion of the classroom interactions, both positive (example, answering correctly) and negative (teacher criticism), than whites or females. Sex of teacher made no difference in these results.

515. Johnson, Fern, and Lynda Goldman. "Communication for Education for Women: A Case for Separatism." *Communication Education,* 26 (1977), 319-326.

This argumentative essay, citing research that reveals a male-dominant communication norm, calls for a course in interpersonal communication for women only. Suggestions for topics on areas such as perception and self-concept, stereotyping, assertiveness training, language, nonverbal communication, and public speaking are included.

516. Kaufman, Debra R. "Associational Ties in Academe: Some Male and Female Differences." *Sex Roles,* 4 (1978), 9-21.

For this study about friendship networks in academic

organizations, questionnaire data was collected and two-and-a-half hour personal interviews were held with 46 female and 32 male faculty members. Female faculty had larger, more integrated networks than their male colleagues. They tended to surround themselves with same-sex colleagues more than males, especially if unmarried. Unmarried female faculty had larger, more integrated, and more homogeneous networks than married women. It is suggested that isolation from informal male contacts leaves women at a professional disadvantage.

517. Kjerulff, Kristen H., and Milton R. Blood. "A Comparison of Communication Patterns in Male and Female Graduate Students." *Journal of Higher Education,* 44 (1973), 623-632.

    A questionnaire of 41 male and 27 female graduate students' communication with professors and peers revealed that female students saw their research advisors less frequently than male students, especially in out-of-office situations. They also viewed their relationships with the advisors as less relaxed, casual, equalitarian, friendly, and jocular.

* McMillan, Julie R., A. Kay Clifton, Diane McGrath, and Wanda S. Gale. "Women's Language: Uncertainty or Interpersonal Sensitivity and Emotionality?" *Sex Roles,* 3 (1977), 545-559. See item 867.

518. Powell, Douglas R. "Correlates of Parent-Teacher Communication Frequency and Diversity." *Journal of Educational Research,* 71 (1978), 333-341.

    The aim of this study was to identify parent- and teacher-related variables that are predictive of parent-teacher communication. Interview data from a sample of 212 parents (90.6% mothers) and 89 teachers (94.3% women) in 12 preschool programs revealed a strong relationship between communication frequency and diversity. Teacher role status, attitudes toward appropriate parent-teacher communication content, professional education and experience, and length of parental association with school were among the statistically significant predictors.

519. Purnell, Sandra E. "Sex Roles in Communication: Teaching and Research." *Western Speech Communication,* 40 (1976), 111-120.

    A course in the differences in male/female communication

is described, including the theoretical underpinnings and the major topics covered, namely family communication, small group communication, organizational communication, speaker-audience interaction, language and nonverbal codes, communication in mental health, and mass media.

520. Radecki, Catherine, and Joyce Jennings (Walstedt). "Sex as a Status Variable in Work Settings: Female and Male Reports of Dominance Behavior." *Journal of Applied Social Psychology,* 10 (1980), 71-85.

    A questionnaire survey of dominance behaviors both to and from opposite-sex co-workers and to and from opposite-sex superiors of 88 females and 69 males employed at three different levels in academic institutions revealed that expressed sexual intimacy (e.g., commenting on looks) follows the same continuum as traditional dominance behaviors (e.g., first name address).

521. Rothbart, Myron, Susan Dalfen, and Robert Barrett. "Effects of Teacher's Expectancy on Student-Teacher Interaction." *Journal of Educational Psychology,* 62 (1971), 49-54.

    In a simulated classroom situation, 13 female teacher trainees were observed in their interactions with 27 male and 25 female high school students, randomly assigned to high-expectancy or low-expectancy condition, for amount of attention, reinforcement they gave, their evaluation of the students, and the students' amount of talking. Though reinforcement was directed about equally to both high- and low-expectation students, the trainees were more attentive to the high-expectation students, who in turn talked more than low-expectation students, who were judged less intelligent, having less potential for success, and needing approval more.

522. Sprague, Jo. "The Reduction of Sexism in Speech Communication Education." *Speech Teacher,* 24 (1975), 37-45.

    In this essay review of sexism in education, recommendations for removing materials and/or methods that perpetuate sex role stereotyping are made.

523. Staton-Spicer, Ann Q., and Ronald E. Bassett. "Communication Concerns of Preservice and Inservice Elementary

School Teachers." *Human Communication Research*, 5 (1979), 138-146.

To identify their communication concerns, 227 prospective, student, and inservice elementary school teachers completed questionnaires. Prospective teachers expressed more concerns about self than about task or impact, student teachers expressed more task than impact or self concerns, and inservice teachers expressed more impact than self or task concerns. In each case each group's leading concern of the three was greater than for any of the other groups.

524. Sternglanz, Sarah H., and Shirley Lyberger-Ficek. "Sex Differences in Student-Teacher Interactions in the College Classroom." *Sex Roles*, 3 (1977), 345-352.

    Observation of 49 male and 11 female teachers and their interactions in 60 college classes with 870 female and 1,414 male students revealed sex differences. Male students engaged in proportionately more student-teacher interactions than female students in male-taught classes; there was no sex difference in female-taught classes. Neither male nor female professors appeared to respond differentially to male and female students.

* Swacker, Marjorie. "Women's Verbal Behavior at Learned and Professional Conferences." In *The Sociology of the Languages of American Women*. Eds. Betty L. Dubois and Isabel Crouch. San Antonio, Texas: Trinity University, 1976, pp. 155-160. See item 903.

525. Taylor, Marylee C. "Race, Sex, and the Expression of Self-Fulfilling Prophecies in a Laboratory Teaching Situation." *Journal of Personality and Social Psychology*, 37 (1979), 897-912.

    One hundred undergraduate females in teacher training were observed teaching "phantom" students manipulated for race, sex, and ability. Low-ability students were presented with less material, given less opportunity to respond, given more praise after success, and subjects teaching them showed less vocal nervousness. Subjects responded more favorably emotionally to high-ability black and low-ability white students. Although main effects for sex were negligible, subjects with high-ability female and low-ability male students gave them less praise feedback than any other sex-ability pairs, but they received more slip-of-tongue help than the other groups.

*   Thune, Elizabeth S., Ronald W. Manderscheid, and Sam Silbergeld. "Status or Sex Roles as Determinants of Interaction Patterns in Small, Mixed-Sex Groups." *Journal of Social Psychology,* 112 (1980), 51-65. See item 302.

*   Willmington, S. Clay, and James A. Anderson. "An Investigation of the Relationship among the Speech Behaviors of Elementary School Children, Their Teachers, and Their Parents." *Elementary English,* 49 (1972), 179-183. See item 380.

*   Wilson, LaVisa C. "Teachers' Inclusion of Males and Females in Generic Nouns." *Research in the Teaching of English,* 12 (1978), 155-161. See item 994.

526. Woolfolk, Robert L., and Anita E. Woolfolk. "Effects of Teacher Verbal and Nonverbal Behaviors on Student Perceptions and Attitudes." *American Educational Research Journal,* 11 (1974), 297-303.

    A female teacher taught a vocabulary lesson to four groups of 20 students (10 high self-esteem, 10 low) under one of four conditions--positive verbal and nonverbal behavior, positive verbal and negative nonverbal behavior, negative verbal and positive nonverbal behavior, and negative verbal and nonverbal behavior. Student measures of perception of teacher and attraction for her revealed a strong main effect for positive communication. The impact of the verbal channel on perception was greater than the nonverbal channel. Level of self-esteem had no significant effect.

527. Young, Stephen L. "Student Perceptions of Helpfulness in Classroom Speech Criticism." *Speech Teacher,* 23 (1974), 222-234.

    The responses of 309 college students to various kinds of criticism from both male and female instructors of speech communication were analyzed. Atomistic comments were perceived of as more helpful than holistic ones for all types of criticism. Both speech anxiety level and sex differences affected helpfulness perceptions, with students of female instructors rating criticism more helpful than students of male instructors, and female students rating criticism more helpful than male students. Female students of female instructors gave them the highest helpfulness ratings; male students of male instructors gave the lowest.

* Zammuto, Raymond F., Manual London, and Kendrith M. Rowland. "Effects of Sex on Commitment and Conflict Resolution." *Journal of Applied Psychology,* 64 (1979), 227-231. See item 796.

Counseling

528. Alagna, Frank J., Sheryle J. Whitcher, Jeffrey D. Fisher, and Edward A. Wicas. "Evaluative Reaction to Interpersonal Touch in a Counseling Interview." *Journal of Counseling Psychology,* 26 (1979), 465-475.

    Fifty-four female and 53 male undergraduates evaluated the effects of touching or not by a male or female counselor with whom they interviewed. Results indicated that touched clients evaluated the counseling experience more positively than nontouched clients, with stronger effects occurring in opposite-sex dyads.

529. Berman, Judith. "Counseling Skills Used by Black and White Male and Female Counselors." *Journal of Counseling Psychology,* 26 (1979), 81-84.

    The written responses of 15 black male, 24 black female, 21 white male, and 21 white female counselors with some training to culturally varied client vignettes were coded according to a counseling skills scoring system. Black counselors used significantly more active expression skills (directions, interpretations) than whites, while white counselors used significantly more attending (paraphrasing, questioning) skills than black counselors. Sex was relatively insignificant as a source of difference, with white males attending more than white females being the only significant sex difference.

530. Bloom, Larry J., Richard G. Weigel, and Gregory M. Trautt. "'Therapeugenic' Factors in Psychotherapy: Effects of Office Decor and Subject-Therapist Sex Pairing on the Perception of Credibility." *Journal of Consulting and Clinical Psychology,* 45 (1977), 867-873.

    Using 72 female and 72 male undergraduates evaluating impressions of a male or female psychologist after sitting in an office decorated traditionally or humanistically, authors found subjects perceived female therapist in traditional office as significantly more credible than in humanistic one, and just the reverse for male therapists.

* Bohart, Arthur C. "Role Playing and Interpersonal-Conflict Reduction." *Journal of Counseling Psychology,* 24 (1977), 15-24. See item 205.

531. Breisinger, Gary D. "Sex and Empathy Reexamined." *Journal of Counseling Psychology,* 23 (1976), 289-290.

    Replicating an earlier study on empathy, Breisinger used 21 female and 21 male graduate students in counselor education rating male and female clients seen on videotape. No overall significant difference in empathetic ability was found, and, unlike the earlier study, no difference in empathy with same or opposite sex was found either.

532. Cash, Thomas F., and Jo Anne Kehr. "Influence of Nonprofessional Counselors' Physical Attractiveness and Sex on Perceptions of Counselor Behavior." *Journal of Counseling Psychology,* 25 (1978), 336-342.

    Ninety-six female undergraduates evaluated nonprofessional counselors, presented on audiotape, varied only by sex and either physically anonymous or attractive or not (photograph included). Regardless of sex of subject or counselor, unattractive counselors were judged to have less desirable traits and to elicit weaker commitment and less optimistic expectations.

533. Feldstein, JoAnn C. "Effects of Counselor Sex and Sex Role and Client Sex on Clients' Perceptions and Self-Disclosure in a Counseling Analogue Study." *Journal of Counseling Psychology,* 26 (1979), 437-443.

    Thirty-five male and 39 female undergraduates were interviewed by a male or a female counselor, each either masculine (action oriented, cognitive, louder voice, less body lean) or feminine (responsive, supportive, softer voice, smiling) sex-typed. Analysis of post-interview questionnaire responses indicated that male subjects were more satisfied with the counseling process than female subjects and had greater satisfaction and regard for feminine counselors than the masculine ones, regardless of sex. By contrast, female clients expressed more satisfaction and regard for masculine counselors, regardless of sex. Male subjects had most self disclosure with feminine female counselors and least with masculine female counselors, while female subjects self disclosed most with feminine male counselors and least with masculine male counselors.

534. Fretz, Bruce R., Roger Corn, Janet M. Tuemmler, and William Bellet. "Counselor Nonverbal Behaviors and Client Evaluations." *Journal of Counseling Psychology,* 26 (1979), 304-311.

In the first of three studies, 104 female college students rated two male and two female counselors seen in a 10-minute videotape displaying either high or low levels of eye contact, body orientation, and forward lean. Subjects rated both male and female counselors as attractive and facilitative when they had higher levels of these nonverbal behaviors. In the second study, with scripts altered to provide low or moderate levels of the same nonverbal behaviors, 40 female undergraduates again preferred the higher-level counselors. In the third study, 18 female undergraduates met for a 10-minute session with a male counselor displaying either high or low levels of the nonverbal behaviors; this time no significant differences in ratings of attractiveness or facilitativeness were found.

535. Grantham, Robert J. "Effects of Counselor Sex, Race, and Language Style on Black Students in Initial Interviews." *Journal of Counseling Psychology,* 20 (1973), 553-559.

Videotapes of 37 black male and female first-semester college students being interviewed by black or white male or female counselors were analyzed for various measures and the data compared with the student's questionnaire responses. An analysis of variance indicated that the subjects preferred black counselors to white to a significant degree, and that they explored themselves in greater depth with female counselors, regardless of race. Comprehension of black "slang" was not a significant variable in any analysis.

536. Greenberg, Roger P. "Sexual Bias in Rorschach Administration." *Journal of Personality Assessment,* 36 (1972), 336-339.

To test further the finding in Rorschach testing that male interns elicit more responses from female clients than any other sex combination, three male interns, five female interns (mean ages 24.33 and 26.20) and three experienced male clinicians (mean age = 40.67) administered the Rorschach to four or five male and a like number of female patients, randomly selected from the patients each treated. A t-test for difference between the means of the numbers of responses elicited under each sex combination revealed that male interns obtained significantly more responses from female than male patients. No other significant cross-sex differences were found, including for the older male clinicians.

* Haase, Richard F. "The Relationship of Sex and Instructional Set to the Regulation of Interpersonal Interaction Distance in a Counseling Analogue." *Journal of Counseling Psychology,* 17 (1970), 233-236. See item 1159.

537. Halas, Celia. "All-Women's Groups--A View from Inside." *Personnel and Guidance Journal,* 52, No. 2 (1973), 91-95.

538. Harris, Sandra, and Joseph Masling. "Examiner Sex, Subject Sex, and Rorschach Productivity." *Journal of Consulting and Clinical Psychology,* 34 (1970), 60-63.

   Using 32 male and 9 female clinical psychology graduate students testing 64 male and female clients, authors found female subjects with male experimenter produced significantly more responses to a Rorschach test than any other sex combination.

539. Hayes, Kathryn E., and Patricia L. Wolleat. "Effects of Sex in Judgments of a Simulated Counseling Interview." *Journal of Counseling Psychology,* 25 (1978), 164-168.

   Forty graduate students, an equal number of each sex, rated an audiotaped counseling interview of a male or female client reading identical scripts. An analysis of variance with the scores on the Broverman Sex-Role Stereotype Questionnaire revealed that 16 of the 37 items were significantly different by sex of client, with the females having a higher mean score on all 16. She was seen as more stereotypically male (aggressive, independent, dominant, not influenceable). Interaction between subject sex and sex of client was not significant.

540. Heilbrun, Alfred B., Jr. "Female Preference for Therapist Initial Interview Style as a Function of 'Client' and Therapist Social Role Variables." *Journal of Counseling Psychology,* 18 (1971), 285-291.

   From the Adjective Check List, 71 female undergraduates completed the Masculinity-Femininity Scale and the

Counseling Readiness Scale and then rated preference for directive or nondirective responses of a male or female therapist, highly trained or not. Subjects scoring high on readiness for counseling preferred less directive interviewing from high-status therapists of either sex. Low-scoring subjects (ones most likely to leave therapy) preferred greater directive interviewing from male than from female high-status interviewer, but greater nondirectiveness from male than from female low-status therapists. These differences were found to be dependent on the preferences of feminine sex-role oriented subjects.

* Heilbrun, Alfred B., Jr. "History of Self-Disclosure in Females and Early Defection from Psychotherapy." *Journal of Counseling Psychology*, 20 (1973), 250-257. See item 736.

541. Heppner, Paul, and Steve Pew. "Effects of Diplomas, Awards, and Counselor Sex on Perceived Expertness." *Journal of Counseling Psychology*, 24 (1977), 147-149.

    Sixty-four undergraduates of both sexes were interviewed by a male or female counselor either with or without displays of expertness in office and then completed a semantic differential questionnaire on perceived expertness. Results were that the expertness displays significantly influenced expertness ratings, but sex of counselor did not.

542. Hersen, Michel. "Sexual Aspects of Rorschach Administration." *Journal of Projective Techniques and Personality Assessment*, 34 (1970), 104-105.

    The mean number of responses that five female and 14 male interns elicited from male and female patients matched for age and intelligence (number not given though all files for a 13-year period were examined), when subjected to $\underline{t}$-tests, revealed that male interns elicited significantly more responses from female patients than any other sex combination did.

543. Hill, Clara E. "Sex of Client and Sex and Experience Level of Counselor." *Journal of Counseling Psychology*, 22 (1975), 6-11.

    Twelve male and 12 female counselors, half experienced and half not, recorded a session with a male and a female client. Same-sex pairings discussed feelings more.

Females were judged to have explored themselves more than males, and clients of female counselors reported more satisfaction.

544. Hoffman, Mary A., and Gregory P. Spencer. "Effect of Interviewer Self-Disclosure and Interviewer-Subject Sex Pairing on Perceived and Actual Subject Behavior." *Journal of Counseling Psychology*, 24 (1977), 383-390.

    Sixteen female and 16 male undergraduates discussed their procrastination tendencies with either male or female counselors, who self-disclosed either positively or negatively about their own procrastination as undergraduates. After the interview, subjects in the positive disclosure condition expected to study more and did study more. They also perceived that they procrastinated significantly more after the interview than before. No significant interactions due to sex of either counselor or subject were found.

545. Hoffman-Graff, Mary A. "Interviewer Use of Positive and Negative Self-Disclosure and Interviewer-Subject Sex Pairing." *Journal of Counseling Psychology*, 24 (1977), 184-190.

    Interviews about procrastination between male and female counselors who used either positive or negative feedback and 36 male and 36 female undergraduates revealed that subjects saw the negative-feedback counselor as more empathetic, warm, and credible. Subjects with a negative-disclosing counselor perceived that they procrastinated significantly less after the interview than before; subjects with a positive-disclosing counselor perceived the opposite. Sex pairing of interviewer-subject had no significant effects.

546. Johnson, Marilyn. "Influence of Counselor Gender on Reactivity to Clients." *Journal of Counseling Psychology*, 25 (1978), 359-365.

    Forty experienced counselors, 20 of each sex, responded verbally to videotapes of one of four clients: angry male or female, depressed male or female. The responses were rated by two judges for sympathy, identification, defensiveness, and anger, and the counselors evaluated themselves on liking, attractiveness for counseling, empathy, and comfort. Only two significant counselor-sex effects were found: female counselors rated themselves as more empathetic than males did, and female counselors were rated by judges as being more angry than male counselors. This latter, surprising result seemed to be attributable mostly to female counselor response to the angry male client.

547. LaCrosse, Michael B. "Nonverbal Behavior and Perceived Counselor Attractiveness and Persuasiveness." *Journal of Counseling Psychology,* 22 (1975), 563-566.

Twenty female and 20 male undergraduates rated two female and two male counselors trained to respond with nonverbal affiliative (smiles, head nods, etc.) or unaffiliative behavior. Affiliative counselors were evaluated as more attractive and more persuasive than unaffiliative ones, with female affiliative counselors rated significantly greater in persuasiveness than male affiliative ones.

* Lerner, Harriet E. "Girls, Ladies, or Women? The Unconscious Dynamics of Language Choice." *Comprehensive Psychiatry,* 17 (1976), 295-299. See item 941.

548. Lewis, Kathleen N., and W. Bruce Walsh. "Physical Attractiveness: Its Impact on the Perception of a Female Counselor." *Journal of Counseling Psychology,* 25 (1978), 210-216.

Thirty female and 30 male college students, having viewed a videotape of a female actress playing a counselor, either physically attractive or not, evaluated the counselor on her traits and on their expectancies of her helpfulness on a variety of problems. While two control groups who listened to audio only did not differ in their ratings, in the experimental condition the attractive counselor was perceived more favorably by female subjects only, who found her significantly more competent, professional, interesting, relaxed, and assertive. They expected her to be more effective treating problems of general anxiety, shyness, sexual function, career choice, and inferiority.

549. Maslin, Audrey, and Jerry L. Davis. "Sex-Role Stereotyping as a Factor in Mental Health Standards Among Counselors-in-Training." *Journal of Counseling Psychology,* 22 (1975), 87-91.

Ninety graduate-level counselors-in-training, evenly divided by sex, completed a questionnaire about characteristics of a "healthy, mature, socially competent" male, female, or adult, sex unspecified. Female graduate students revealed a relatively uniform standard for all three conditions, while males did so for healthy males and adults but had another, more stereotyped, standard for females.

550. Merluzzi, Thomas V., Paul G. Banikiotes, and Joseph W. Missbach. "Perceptions of Counselor Characteristics: Sex, Experience, and Disclosure Level." *Journal of Counseling Psychology,* 15 (1978), 479-482.

    One hundred and twelve college students evaluated an expert or nonexpert male or female counselor from a biographical sketch and an interaction with a client for expertness, attractiveness, and trustworthiness. Female expert counselors were rated more expert than female nonexperts, though male expert and nonexpert did not differ. High-disclosing counselors were rated more attractive than low-disclosing ones, even nonexpert high-disclosing over expert low-disclosing. Low-disclosing female counselors, however, were rated more trustworthy than high-disclosing ones, but no difference for low- and high-disclosing males appeared.

551. Persely, George, James H. Johnson, and L.G. Hornsby. "Effects of Profession, Sex, and Prognostic Expectancies on Therapists' Comments in a Psychotherapeutic Analogue." *Psychological Reports,* 37 (1975), 455-459.

    Seven female and 13 male psychotherapists viewed a 30-minute videotape of a female patient presented to them with either a positive or negative prognosis. At specified intervals the 20 subjects responded in writing as they might in an actual session; after the tape, they also completed a questionnaire about the patient. No significant differences were found on any of the variables but sex; female therapists used significantly more positive comments and tended to have more reflections of feeling. Since females did not rate the patients significantly differently from males, results suggest female therapists may respond more warmly to patients in general.

552. Petro, Carole S., and James C. Hansen. "Counselor Sex and Empathic Judgment." *Journal of Counseling Psychology,* 24 (1977), 373-376.

    Practicing counselors (71 F, 102 M) used the Affective Sensitivity Scale and evaluated the affective state of males and females seen on the film associated with the scale. Both sexes were equally accurate in their empathetic judgments, and both sexes were more accurate in identifying feelings of males than of females. Sex or cross-sex pairing of counselor and stimulus person had no significant effects.

553. Rivero, Estela M., and Edward S. Bordin. "Initiative Behavior of Male and Female Therapists in First Interviews with Females." *Journal of Consulting and Clinical Psychology,* 48 (1980), 124-125.

Eleven male and 11 female therapists participated in two analogue psychotherapeutic interviews. One interview was with a female whom all interviewed, and the other with a female seen alone by each individual therapist. No significant differences by condition of interview or by sex of therapist in the therapists' initiative behavior were found.

* Safilios-Rothschild, Constantina. *Women and Social Policy*. Englewood Cliffs, N.J.: Prentice-Hall, 1974. See item 952.

554. Scher, Murray. "Verbal Activity, Sex, Counselor Experience, and Success in Counseling." *Journal of Counseling Psychology,* 22 (1975), 97-101.

Five female and 18 male counselors, both experienced and inexperienced, and 20 female and 16 male under- and graduate students were audiotaped in four sessions and the verbal activity measured. In addition, both groups responded to an outcome measure. Multiple linear regression analysis revealed that experience was significantly related to successful outcome, but neither sex nor verbal activity was. Female counselors and female clients talked more than males, and dyads of experienced counselors with male clients and inexperienced counselors with female clients reported greater success.

555. Sherman, Julia, Corinne Koufacos, and Joy A. Kenworthy. "Therapists: Their Attitudes and Information About Women." *Psychology of Women Quarterly,* 2 (1978), 299-313.

The scores of 184 male and female therapists (psychiatrists, psychologists, and social workers) on the Therapists' Information About Women Scale and the Therapists' Attitude Toward Women Scale revealed no significant differences by profession, but female therapists were significantly better informed, more liberal, and less stereotyped in their attitudes than male therapists.

556. Simons, Janet A., and Janet E. Helms. "Influence of Counselors' Marital Status, Sex, and Age on College and Non-College Women's Counselor Preferences." *Journal of Counseling Psychology,* 23 (1976), 380-386.

    Two studies, one with 32 college women and the other with 32 beauty salon customers, all women, in which male or female counselors were evaluated, revealed that both groups of women preferred female counselors, expected to be more comfortable with them, less anxious and more willing to disclose. Beauty salon customers preferred oldest counselors to youngest ones and married to unmarried, while college subjects preferred counselors in 35-45 or 55-65 age groups and single counselors.

557. Whiteley, John M., and John V. Flowers, eds. *The Counseling Psychologist,* 5, No. 4 (1975), entire issue.

    The issue is on assertion training with several articles specifically focused on such training for women.

Law

558. Coplin, Jane W., and John E. Williams. "Women Law Students' Descriptions of Self and the Ideal Lawyer." *Psychology of Women Quarterly,* 2 (1978), 323-333.

    The Adjective Check List was used to assess descriptions of self and of ideal lawyer of 73 female law students and 100 undergraduate females. Compared to the undergraduates, the law students exhibited more self-confidence and autonomy. The law students perceived the ideal lawyer to be more rational and less emotional than themselves. While both groups had "feminine" self-descriptions, the law students' perception of the ideal lawyer was "masculine."

559. Curtis, Rebecca C., Mark P. Zanna, and Woodrow W. Campbell, Jr. "Sex, Fear of Success, and the Perceptions and Performance of Law School Students." *American Educational Research Journal,* 12 (1975), 287-297.

    A questionnaire concerning fear of success and the perceptions and performance of 30 male and 24 female law school students revealed main effects for both sex and fear of success, but no interactions. Female students gave fewer responses in class and showed greater reluctance to reveal their grades. Findings characteristic of high fear-of-success respondents of both sexes included lower Law Aptitude Test scores and more frequent failure to volunteer answers in class when desiring to do so. The results indicated that women may be more likely than men to fear rejection, but not more likely to fear success.

560. Dellacava, Frances A., and Madeline H. Engel. "Resistance to Sisterhood: The Case of the Professional Woman." *International Journal of Women's Studies*, 2 (1979), 505-512.

Questionnaire data from 77 female lawyers and 243 female college professors in the New York City area focused on their perceptions of other non-professional groups. Professional women felt estranged from and marginal to other women. Professional women perceived other women as a negative reference group for two reasons: their perception of success required them to overconform to the expectations of the male professional world, and they had a need to see themselves as special and unique in order to deal with the internal conflict they experienced.

561. Lind, E. Allan, and William M. O'Barr. "The Social Significance of Speech in the Courtroom." In *Language and Social Psychology*. Eds. Howard Giles and Robert N. St. Clair. Baltimore, Md.: University Park Press, 1979, pp. 66-87.

The authors report on their three experiments to determine the effects of speech characteristics on judgments of court testimony. In the first, 46 male and 50 female subjects (presumably undergraduates) evaluated the effectiveness of testimony presented by either a male or a female witness in either a powerful or power-less style (intensifiers, hedges, questioning, and other features R. Lakoff [see item 858] mentions as characteristics of female speech).
Both male and female subjects found the witnesses using the powerful style more competent, trustworthy, attractive, dynamic, and convincing than the power-less style witnesses. In the second experiment, 82 male and female undergraduates and 43 male and female law

students evaluated either a male or female witness testifying in either fragmented (considered feminine) or narrative (masculine) styles. Undergraduates hearing the male witness and law students hearing the female witness rated the narrative testimony higher than the fragmented. In the third experiment, 38 male and 48 female undergraduates rated the effects of simultaneous talking of a male attorney and a male witness and of perseverance (taking over after simultaneous speech) or acquiescence (giving way). Both sexes saw the attorney as less in control when there was simultaneous talking than when there was not and perceived him as less intelligent and fair. Females thought the witness less likeable and competent and the attorney less skillful when the attorney persevered, while males thought the witness more likeable and competent and the attorney more skillful when the attorney acquiesced. See also items 820 and 1013.

* Safilios-Rothschild, Constantina. *Women and Social Policy*. Englewood Cliffs, N.J.: Prentice-Hall, 1974. See item 952.

Medical

* Aldag, Ramon J., and Arthur P. Brief. "Some Correlates of Women's Self-Image and Stereotypes of Femininity." *Sex Roles*, 5 (1979), 319-328. See item 1.

562. Ayres, H.J., Vera R. Brand, and Donald F. Faules. "An Assessment of the Flow of Communication in Nursing Teams." *Journal of Applied Communications Research*, 1 (1973), 75-90.

   This examination of communication in nursing teams at a Western medical center tested the hypothesis that information flows just as freely from supervisor to subordinate (downward communication) as from subordinate to supervisor (upward communication). Sixty nurses rank ordered communication about duties, problems, and trust. Downward communication flowed relatively freely, but upward communication did not. The authors concluded that the authoritarian character, the military-like discipline, and the concepts of sacrifice and selfless service which have long characterized nursing continue to be fostered.

563. Bartol, Kathryn M., and Max S. Wortman, Jr. "Male Versus Female Leaders: Effects on Perceived Leader Behavior and Satisfaction in a Hospital." *Personnel Psychology,* 28 (1975), 533-547.

A questionnaire survey was taken of 60 female and 124 male supervisory and non-supervisory employees of a psychiatric hospital on dimensions of leadership and on work satisfaction. No difference in leader behavior by sex was perceived except that female leaders were seen as higher on "initiating structure." Female subordinates rated leader's behavior higher than male subordinates did on all 12 subscales, significantly so on half of them. Sex of leader made no difference on subordinates' satisfaction with the job or with leader, although female subordinates indicated greater satisfaction than male subordinates.

* Bartol, Kathryn M., and Max S. Wortman, Jr. "Sex Effects in Leader Behavior Self-Descriptions and Job Satisfaction." *Journal of Psychology,* 94 (1976), 177-183. See item 592.

* Bartol, Kathryn M., and Max S. Wortman, Jr. "Sex of Leader and Subordinate Role Stress: A Field Study." *Sex Roles,* 5 (1979), 513-518. See item 593.

* Blass, Thomas, and Aron W. Siegman. "A Psycholinguistic Comparison of Speech, Dictation and Writing." *Language and Speech,* 18 (1975), 20-34. See item 1223.

564. Brief, Arthur P., Ramon J. Aldag, and Craig J. Russell. "An Analysis of Power in a Work Setting." *Journal of Social Psychology,* 109 (1979), 289-295.

This questionnaire survey of 122 registered nurses and 77 of their supervisors on an instrument measuring supervisor power, social distance, and subordinate performance revealed that those supervisors who saw themselves as relatively powerful maintained greater social distance than those who saw themselves as less powerful.

565. Burke, Ronald J., William Weitzel, and Tamara Weir. "Characteristics of Effective Employee Performance Review and Development Interviews: Replication and Extension." *Personnel Psychology,* 31 (1978), 903-919.

Replicating a 1969 study designed to examine effective employee review and development interview characteristics, authors used a questionnaire survey of 270 nursing staff of a large midwestern hospital, 94% female, 6% male. As in the earlier study, they found degree of subordinate participation, degree of helpfulness of supervisor, extent to which problems hindering performance were cleared up, and extent to which new performance targets were set were significantly related to satisfaction with review interview, with desire to improve, and with reported actual improvement. Two new variables found significantly related to interview satisfaction were influence in planning self-development and amount of threat (negatively).

566. Carpenter, Kay F., and Jerome A. Kroth. "Effects of Videotaped Role Playing on Nurses' Therapeutic Communication Skills." *Journal of Continuing Education in Nursing*, 7 (1976), 47-53.

    This study investigated the use of videotaped role playing as a method of teaching verbal and nonverbal therapeutic communication skills. Twelve female nurses were taught the skills in a videotaped role playing situation, 12 were taught in a non-videotaped situation, and 12 served as a control group without communication instruction. All subjects completed a therapeutic behavior questionnaire. All subjects taking the communication course scored significantly higher in perceived therapeutic behaviors than those not taking the course, and those in the videotape situation scored significantly higher than those not in the videotape situation.

* deWever, Margaret K. "Nursing Home Patients' Perception of Nurses' Affective Touching." *Journal of Psychology*, 96 (1977), 163-171. See item 1206.

* Ekman, Paul, and Wallace V. Friesen. "Detecting Deception from the Body or Face." *Journal of Personality and Social Psychology*, 29 (1974), 288-298. See item 1081.

567. Ekman, Paul, Wallace V. Friesen, and Klaus R. Scherer. "Body Movement and Voice Pitch in Deceptive Interaction." *Semiotica*, 16, No. 1 (1976), 23-27.

    Sixteen student nurses were videotaped in interviews that permitted honest behavior or that called for deceptive behavior, and their hand movements and pitch were analyzed. In the deception condition, use of illustrator hand movement significantly decreased, shrugs (symbolic gestures transmitting uncertainty) increased to near-significant level, and pitch increased significantly.

568. Gruenfeld, Leopold, and Saleem Kassum. "Supervisory Style and Organizational Effectiveness in a Pediatric Hospital." *Personnel Psychology*, 26 (1973), 531-544.

    Questionnaire data relating to consideration and leadership behavior obtained from 82 nurses in a pediatric hospital were correlated with satisfaction with supervision, patient care, and organizational coordination measures. Those who combined high levels of leader initiation and consideration provided significantly more satisfaction among subordinates and better patient care as seen by other nurses. The effectiveness of coordination of the organization, however, was primarily leader initiating and was unrelated to level of consideration.

569. Jain, Harish C. "Supervisory Communication and Performance in Urban Hospitals." *Journal of Communication*, 23 (1973), 103-117.

    A questionnaire survey of 312 service, technical, and professional employees of two hospitals (no information on sex of employees) was used to establish the relationship between the communication effectiveness of supervisors and their performance, both as perceived by subordinates. General findings were a positve correlation between effectiveness and performance, between amount of communication and performance, and between subordinates' communication satisfaction and performance.

570. Kolin, Philip C. "The Language of Nursing." *American Speech*, 48 (1973), 192-210.

    In this discussion, Kolin concludes that the language of nursing is a "blend of the banal and the medically exact," using many abbreviations, acronyms, clipped forms, and euphemisms. The number of subjects observed was not specified, and Kolin's assumption was that all nurses were female.

* Kutner, Nancy C., and Donna Brogan. "An Investigation of Sex-Related Slang Vocabulary and Sex-Role Orientation Among Male and Female University Students." *Journal of Marriage and the Family*, 36 (1974), 474-484. See item 855.

571. Leserman, Jane. "Sex Differences in the Professional Orientation of First-Year Medical Students." *Sex Roles*, 6 (1980), 645-660.

This article presents the findings from a 1975 survey of 244 male and 82 female first-year medical students on the relationship between sex and orientations relevant to current medical problems. On the one communication problem mentioned, humanizing physician-patient relationships, female students were more highly oriented than male students.

572. McLaughlin, Frank E., Eleanor White, and Barbara Byfield. "Modes of Interpersonal Feedback and Leadership Structure in Six Small Groups." *Nursing Research*, 23 (1974), 307-318.

Forty-three graduate nursing students (1 male) participated in one of six small groups in a study designed to determine the effects of the format on a group. Group 1 had a leader always present, Group 2 had a leader present every other meeting, Group 3 had a programmed tape format with a leader on call, Group 4 had the same with a leader present. These groups met for one and a half hours weekly during a semester. Groups 5 and 6 were marathon groups that met for eight hours twice during a semester; Group 5 had video feedback and Group 6 did not. All groups showed group process cohesiveness, although it declined in Groups 2, 4, and 5 toward the end. Development of the group was high in Groups 1, 3, and 4; evaluative feedback was more evident in Groups 1, 4, and 6. Lack of structure due to lack of leader always being present led more often to group member dissatisfaction and to reservation about the group process. Group 1 showed high productiveness and development as a group. Group 3 had a minimal amount of interpersonal revelation, exploration, or confrontation. Group 4 members reported great liking of the group and showed great productivity. Group 5 revealed little feedback that would have strengthened the group processes; Group 6 rated the group more positively during the second marathon than Group 4 did.

* Petty, M.M., Charles A. Odewahn, Nealia S. Bruning, and Terry L. Thomason. "An Examination of the Moderating Effects of Supervisor Sex and Subordinate Sex Upon the Relationships Between Supervisory Behavior and Subordinate Outcomes in Mental Health Organizations." *Academy of Management Proceedings* (1977), 408-412. See item 447.

* Pope, Benjamin, Aron W. Siegman, and Thomas Blass. "Anxiety and Speech in the Initial Interview." *Journal of Consulting and Clinical Psychology*, 35 (1970), 233-238. See item 153.

* Reich, Stephen, and Andrew Geller. "Self-Image of Nurses." *Psychological Reports*, 39 (1976), 401-402. See item 51.

573. Sheridan, John E., and Donald J. Vredenburgh. "Predicting Leadership Behavior in a Hospital Organization." *Academy of Management Journal*, 21 (1978), 679-689.

    Sheridan examined the factors in predicting the leadership behavior of 46 head nurses in a 560-bed metropolitan hospital; questionnaires were completed to provide data. Results indicated turnover among staff members, the leadership behavior of supervisor nurses, and administrative climate were variables that explained significant portions of variance in the measures of the head nurse's consideration and initiating structure behavior.

574. Sheridan, John E., and Donald J. Vredenburgh. "Structural Model of Leadership Influence in a Hospital Organization." *Academy of Management Journal*, 22 (1979), 6-21.

    A questionnaire on the leadership dimensions of initiating structure and consideration was given to 372 nursing employees at a large metropolitan hospital. Results indicated that the head nurse's consideration behavior had an inverse effect on her staff members' job-related tension and job performance. Her initiating structure behavior had a positive effect on employee terminations (19% of the sample terminated voluntarily), particularly in the structured task situations.

575. Sheridan, John E., and Donald J. Vredenburgh. "Usefulness of Leadership Behavior and Social Power Variables in Predicting Job Tension, Performance, and Turnover of Nursing Employees." *Journal of Applied Psychology*, 63 (1978), 89-95.

    Measures of job tension of 216 nurses who completed a leadership measure of their head nurse, ratings of the nurses from the head nurse, and data on employment termination one year later were correlated. Leader consideration was inversely associated with tension, termination, and job performance. Predictor variables explained a small but statistically significant portion of the variance.

576. Silbergeld, Sam, Elizabeth S. Thune, and Ronald W. Manderscheid. "The Group Therapist Leadership Role: Assessment in Adolescent Coping Courses." *Small Group Behavior,* 10 (1979), 176-199.

The study examined style and content, therapeutic quality, and changes in interaction patterns of two group therapists who served as leaders in an elective, experiential, interpersonal coping course for junior high school students. The group therapists were a male psychiatrist and a female psychiatric nurse. Subjects were 43 seventh, eighth, and ninth graders. Objectives of the coping courses were improvement of students' self-esteem, nonverbal communication, and ability to express feelings. Videotapes and audiotapes were used to gather data. The interactions of the two group therapists were assessed by means of the Hill Interaction Matrix procedure. Comparisons were made to discern leadership differences between counselor and non-counselor classes, to evaluate leaders' relative level of interactions within specific style and content categories, and to delineate changes over time. Generally, the therapists employed a similar style but different interactional content with the two types of student participants, those who volunteered and those who were referred by the school counselor.

577. Stein, Leonard I. "Male and Female: The Doctor-Nurse Game." In *Conformity and Conflict: Readings in Cultural Anthropology.* 4th ed. Eds. James P. Spradley and David W. McCurdy. Boston: Little, Brown, 1980, pp. 202-211.

The game of doctor-nurse communication, labeled "basically a transactional neurosis," involves transmission of advice for treatment from the nurse to the doctor without challenging the doctor's authority. Examples of such interactions, both positive and negative, are given and explanations for the genesis of the game and its preservation, including sex role stereotyping, are made.

578. Sterling, F.E. "Net Positive Social Approaches of Young Psychiatric Inpatients as Influenced by Nurses' Attire."

Journal of Consulting and Clinical Psychology, 48 (1980), 58-62.

To determine the effect of clothing of the staff on social approaches of the patients in a 28-bed psychiatric ward, two uniform-biased and two street-clothing biased nursing staff men and women participated in an eight-week study. For two-week intervals, they all wore white uniforms, then street clothing, again street clothing, and again white uniforms. Results were that positive social approaches increased when staff wore street clothing.

* Watson, Wilbur H. "The Meanings of Touch: Geriatric Nursing." *Journal of Communication,* 25 (Summer 1975), 104-112. See item 1219.

* Whitcher, Sheryle J., and Jeffrey D. Fisher. "Multidimensional Reaction to Therapeutic Touch in a Hospital Setting." *Journal of Personality and Social Psychology,* 37 (1979), 87-96. See item 1220.

579. White, Martha S. "Measuring Androgyny in Adulthood." *Psychology of Women Quarterly,* 3 (1979), 293-307.

    After critiquing trends in sex-difference studies, White suggests measuring androgynous competencies by using concepts of agency and communion. White tested this idea on 162 female and four male nurses who responded to a checklist of adjectives on agency and communion competency scales. Based on her critique and this experiment, White concludes that adult women high on both agentic (self-assertive qualities) and communion (union, receptivity, and altruism) competencies seem to have many advantages over those who are low in both competencies or who are competent in only one area.

* White, Sam E., John E. Dittrich, and James R. Lang. "The Effects of Group Decision-Making Process and Problem-Situation Complexity on Implementation Attempts." *Administrative Science Quarterly,* 25 (1980), 428-440. See item 309.

* Wilson, John P. "Coping-Defense Employment in Problematic Interpersonal Situations." *Small Group Behavior,* 9 (1978), 135-148. See item 74.

* Winship, Barbara J., and Jan D. Kelley. "A Verbal Response Model of Assertiveness." *Journal of Counseling Psychology*, 23 (1976), 215-220. See item 312.

* Wolman, Carol, and Hal Frank. "The Solo Woman in a Professional Peer Group." *American Journal of Orthopsychiatry*, 45 (1975), 164-171. See item 313.

GENERAL REFERENCES

580. Bartol, Kathryn. "The Sex Structuring of Organizations: A Search for Possible Causes." *Academy of Management Review*, 3 (1978), 805-815.

    Bartol reviews the literature on sex differences in three areas important to leadership--style, job satisfaction, and performance--and finds few differences between male and female leaders. Eighty-three references are included.

581. Daniels, Arlene K. "Development of Feminist Networks in the Professions." *Annals of the New York Academy of Sciences*, 323 (1979), 215-227.

    This discussion of the use of networks in the professions leads to argument for their use in helping to solve problems for women within organizations.

582. Day, David R., and Ralph M. Stogdill. "Leader Behavior of Male and Female Supervisors: A Comparative Study." *Personnel Psychology*, 25 (1972), 353-360.

    Male and female subordinates' descriptions of leader behavior and evaluations of the leaders as well as biographical information were collected from 37 male and 36 female civilian supervisors at Air Force bases who were matched for civil service level, kind of work, education, and years in position. No significant sex differences were found in subordinates' ratings of behavior or in effectiveness, but for males rapid advancement tended to go with being effective while for females effectiveness and advancement were unrelated.

583. Heilman, Madeline, and Kathy E. Kram. "Self-Derogating Behavior in Women--Fixed or Flexible: The Effects of Co-Worker's Sex." *Organizational Behavior and Human*

Performance, 22 (1978), 497-507.

Fifty male and 50 female insurance company employees participated in a joint decision-making task with a male or female and were given either positive or negative feedback about their dyad's performance. Women derogated themselves when working with males but only negligibly when working with females. When paired with a female, female subjects accepted more responsibility for success and less for failure, and reported greater confidence about their future performance. The coworker sex variable is interpreted as only one among many that can have an impact on a woman's perception of her competence.

584. Kanter, Rosabeth M. *Men and Women of the Corporation.* New York: Basic Books, 1977.

This ethnographic study of a corporation includes chapters on secretaries and wives of managers as well as ones on power in corporations and "tokens" in the corporation. Kanter analyzes secretaries' supportive and personal communication, the importance of their use of nonverbal displays, and their strategies for attaining recognition and control. The image of the corporate wife and her "people handling" tasks are discussed.

585. Kanter, Rosabeth M. "Women and the Structure of Organizations: Explorations in Theory and Behavior." In *Another Voice: Feminist Perspectives on Social Life and Social Science.* Eds. Marcia Millman and Rosabeth M. Kanter. Garden City, N.Y.: Anchor Press/Doubleday, 1975. Pp. 34-74.

After reviewing theories on managing that reflect a "masculine ethic," Kanter discusses women within the organization. Topics covered include behavior in single-sex and in mixed-sex groups, the lone woman in a male group (token), and leadership of women, all discussed in light of the structure of organizations.

586. Lincoln, James R., and Jon Miller. "Work and Friendship Ties in Organizations: A Comparative Analysis of Relational Networks." *Administrative Science Quarterly*, 24 (1979), 181-199.

To examine the effects of authority, education, sex, race, and branch assignment on the intraorganizational network among the members of five professional organizations, 314 subjects responded to a questionnaire survey.

Sex and race were found to have greater influence on friendship ties than on work ties. Women and nonwhites tended to be excluded from friendship networks, which are usually influential within organizations.

* Reich, Stephen, and Andrew Geller. "Self-Image of Social Workers." *Psychological Reports,* 39 (1976), 657-658. See item 52.

PART TWO
CHARACTERISTICS OF COMMUNICATION

LEADERSHIP

587. Adams, Major Jerome, and Jack M. Hicks. "Leader Sex, Leader Descriptions of Own Behavior, and Subordinates Description of Leader Behavior (Project Athena: West Point)." *International Journal of Women's Studies*, 3 (1980), 231-326.

This study examined the relationship between male and female leaders' descriptions of their own behavior and their followers' descriptions of the leader's behavior in traditionally male-oriented leadership positions in the Corps of Cadets at West Point. Five male and five female platoon leaders from the same unit described their behavior using the Fleishman Leadership Opinion Questionnaire, and their subordinates (no number given) rated their leader's behavior on the dimensions of consideration and structure. There were no significant differences between how male and female leaders described their own behavior. Subordinates saw female leaders as more considerate but saw no difference between the sexes in their use of structure (activities to accomplish the mission).

588. Alderton, Steven M., and William E. Jurma. "Genderless/ Gender-Related Task Leader Communication and Group Satisfaction: A Test of Two Hypotheses." *Southern Speech Communication Journal*, 46 (1980), 48-60.

The effects of gender of group leader and group member on leader communication and satisfaction of group participants were examined. Subjects were 72 male and female undergraduates completing an unstructured problem-solving task in triads with either a male or female leader and either male or female followers in all possible combinations. Group member satisfaction was ascertained by a post-discussion questionnaire and by content analysis of the recorded discussion. Group members were equally satisfied with male and female leaders as long as they had similar frequencies of task-oriented behavior. Female leaders agreed more with their male and female followers than male leaders did. Followers tended to disagree more with the same gender leaders than with opposite gender leaders; overall, there was a tendency for male and female group members to disagree more with female leaders than with male leaders.

589. Arnett, Matthew D., Richard B. Higgins, and Andre P. Priem. "Sex and Least Preferred Co-Worker Score Effects in Leadership Behavior." *Sex Roles,* 6 (1980), 139-152.

This study explored the impact of sex-role expectations upon leadership behavior and upon liking by subordinates of male and female managers in a simulated business problem (vacation policy exercises) where the managers were caught between the conflicting desires of their superior and their male and female subordinates. Measurements of leadership behavior and subordinate liking were taken from 67 female and 290 male undergraduate and graduate business students and tested against differences in the sex of the manager and scores on the Least Preferred Co-Worker Scale. Female managers, on the average, were not less well liked, nor were they more accommodative than male managers. Among managers classified as distinctly accommodative, females were not better liked than males; among managers classified as distinctly directive, females were significantly better liked than males. When under pressure to act in a directive manner, male and female managers behaved differently and in such a manner as to suggest that the females were less comfortable in this condition.

* Babinec, Carol S. "Sex, Communication Structures and Role Specification." *Sociological Focus,* 11 (1978), 199-210. See item 190.

* Baird, John E., Jr., and Patricia H. Bradley. "Styles of Management and Communication: A Comparative Study of Men and Women." *Communication Monographs,* 46 (1979), 101-111. See item 424.

590. Bartol, Kathryn M. "The Effect of Male versus Female Leaders on Follower Satisfaction and Performance." *Journal of Business Research,* 3 (1975), 33-42.

The satisfaction and performance of 23 female and 73 male undergraduates in 24 task groups playing executive games led by either a male or a female leader were investigated. Sex of leader made no difference on performance of the groups. Satisfaction levels on four of the five dimensions investigated appeared unrelated to either leader sex or sex composition of the group. Bartol concludes that women in leadership positions may not necessarily have detrimental effects on subordinate satisfaction and performance.

591. Bartol, Kathryn M. "Male Versus Female Leaders: The Effect of Leader Need for Dominance on Follower Satisfaction." *Academy of Management Journal,* 17 (1974), 225-233.

    A simulated business task game played by 100 female and male undergraduates was used to determine the relationship between the sex of the leader, the sex composition of the group, leader need for dominance, and follower satisfaction in five dimensions: task structure, leader action, group atmosphere, team interaction, and task conceptualization. Findings indicated significant relationships between the leader sex, group composition, and leader need for dominance, and the satisfaction with task structure and team interaction. The study did not support the view that female leaders with a high need for dominance adversely affect follower satisfaction. In satisfaction with team interaction, male follower groups were significantly more satisfied with high-need-for-dominance female leaders than with low-need-for-dominance female leaders. In other areas, differences related to female dominance need levels were nonsignificant.

   * Bartol, Kathryn. "The Sex Structuring of Organizations: A Search for Possible Causes." *Academy of Management Review,* 3 (1978), 805-815. See item 580.

   * Bartol, Kathryn M., and D. Anthony Butterfield. "Sex Effects in Evaluating Leaders." *Journal of Applied Psychology,* 61 (1976), 446-454. See item 426.

   * Bartol, Kathryn M., and Max S. Wortman, Jr. "Male Versus Female Leaders: Effects on Perceived Leader Behavior and Satisfaction in a Hospital." *Personnel Psychology,* 28 (1975), 553-547. See item 563.

592. Bartol, Kathryn M., and Max S. Wortman, Jr. "Sex Effects in Leader Behavior Self-Descriptions and Job Satisfaction." *Journal of Psychology,* 94 (1976), 177-183.

A questionnaire survey of 53 male and 19 female supervisory employees of a government psychiatric hospital revealed that females reported behaving with more consideration and tolerance of uncertainty and had more job satisfaction than males. However, on 10 of the 12 behavior categories, there were no sex differences, including on persuasiveness and role assumption.

593. Bartol, Kathryn M., and Max S. Wortman, Jr. "Sex of Leader and Subordinate Role Stress: A Field Study." *Sex Roles*, 5 (1979), 513-518.

Sixty female and 124 male full-time civil service supervisory and nonsupervisory employees in a psychiatric hospital were used to test, via questionnaires, the hypothesis that higher role conflict and role ambiguity would be associated with female than with male leaders when subordinate job level, age, and sex were controlled. A second hypothesis was that males working for females would perceive greater amounts of role conflict and role ambiguity than would any other sex-of-leader/sex-of-subordinate combination. Results indicated that little or no variance in role conflict and role ambiguity could be attributed to sex of leader. Role ambiguity tended to increase for persons at higher levels in the organization when their superiors were male rather than female.

* Bednarek, Frank, Louis Benson, and Husain Mustafa. "Identifying Peer Leadership in Small Work Groups." *Small Group Behavior*, 7 (1976), 307-316. See item 198.

594. Bormann, Ernest G., Jerie Pratt, and Linda Putnam. "Power, Authority, and Sex: Male Response to Female Leadership." *Communication Monographs*, 45 (1978), 119-155.

This case study gives details of a starting-from-the-beginning organization and analyzes the consequences when five divisions all emerged with female leadership. Male reaction was either withdrawal from active participation, attempted takeover of leadership (with subsequent loss of self-image at failure), or active, even influential, participation with no attempt at leadership. The discussion includes attention to sex-role stereotyping and to "shared fantasies," verbalizations that identify the rhetorical vision of the group.

595. Brown, Stephen M. "Male Versus Female Leaders: A Comparison of Empirical Studies." *Sex Roles*, 5 (1979), 595-611.

Thirty-two female leadership studies were analyzed using trait, style, and contingency leadership theories as a framework. The trait studies consistently supported the traditional view that women lack adequate leadership characteristics. Style and contingency studies were split as to whether women were effective or ineffective leaders: most student studies supported the traditional beliefs about women as leaders, while managerial studies did not support this typical female stereotyping. The possiblity of a socializing process modifying practicing managers' attitudes towards women is suggested.

* Burroughs, W., W. Schultz, and S. Autrey. "Quality of Argument, Leadership Votes, and Eye Contact in Three-Person Leaderless Groups." *The Journal of Social Psycology*, 90 (1973), 89-93. See item 212.

* Carroll, Berenice A. "Political Science, Part I: American Politics and Political Behavior." *Signs: Journal of Women in Culture and Society*, 5 (1979), 289-306. See item 485.

596. Chapman, J. Brad. "Comparison of Male and Female Leadership Styles." *Academy of Management Journal*, 18 (1975), 645-650.

    To investigate differences between male and female leadership styles, 146 male and 60 female military leaders and 49 male and 28 female supervisors responded to a semantic differential measuring the leader's perception of the least-preferred co-worker. Results indicated differences in leadership behaviors between male and female leaders but no differences in terms of style. Female leaders did not have a significantly higher need for fostering good interpersonal relationships and were not significantly more task oriented than the male leaders.

597. Chapman, J. Brad, and Fred Luthans. "The Female Leadership Dilemma." *Public Personnel Management*, 4 (1975), 173-179.

    The authors briefly review the research on the leadership style of women. The dilemma female leaders face is their acceptance by followers in an organizational setting, even when the organization in the abstract is supportive of them. Solutions offered are recruitment and placement, training, and organizational development.

* Day, David R., and Ralph M. Stogdill. "Leader Behavior of Male and Female Supervisors: A Comparative Study." *Personnel Psychology*, 25 (1972), 353-360. See item 582.

598. Denmark, Florence L. "Styles of Leadership." *Psychology of Women Quarterly*, 2 (1977), 99-113.

    This review article (36 studies) examines what kinds of leaders emerge in what kinds of groups, specifically the kinds of women leaders, their styles of leadership, and the effects of those styles on group behavior.

599. Downs, Cal W., and Terry Pickett. "An Analysis of the Effects of Nine Leadership-Group Compatibility Contingencies upon Productivity and Member Satisfaction." *Communication Monographs*, 44 (1977), 220-230.

    Women active in a civic organization were placed in 18 five-member groups representing three kinds of compatibility, based on Fundamental Interpersonal Relations Orientation-Behavior test scores. Each group was to complete a task under one of three leadership styles, one high on task and people, another high on task only, and the third unstructured. Measures of group satisfaction and on individual and group correct answers were taken. Analysis of variance revealed that the compatible-on-personal-interaction group with no leadership structure was the least productive, the same group with task leadership was more productive but least satisfied, but with a leader high on people and on task was more productive and more satisfied. For the compatible-on-task groups, no significant differences for either productivity or group satisfaction appeared, although they tended not to be satisfied with the unstructured leadership style. Likewise, there were no significant differences for the incompatible groups, although they seemed to produce somewhat better and be more satisfied with the unstructured leadership style.

600. Eagly, Alice H. "Leadership Style and Role Differentiation as Determinants of Group Effectiveness." *Journal of Personality*, 38 (1970), 509-524.

    Sixty groups of four or five, 33 male and 27 female, each containing one member in top and one in bottom quintile of scores on a leadership style instrument, participated in a task discussion. All participants completed measures on group success with task, on liking, and the Least Preferred Co-Worker Scale.

Liking for task leader did not affect ratings of group effectiveness. In male groups, task effectiveness was greater as the best-liked member score became greater, but not in female groups. In general, leadership style (based on LPC score) was related to effectiveness for males but not for females. Eagly concludes that the relationship between leadership style of best-liked member and group effectiveness is complex: if that person is oriented to interpersonal success, it appears that, if male, he will facilitate task success through reducing tensions and hostilities, or, if female, she will attain direct personal reward in the form of liking.

601. Eskilson, Arlene, and Mary G. Wiley. "Sex Composition and Leadership in Small Groups." *Sociometry*, 39 (1976), 183-194.

    Same- or mixed-sex triads (N = 144 undergraduates) problem-solved with a leader either appointed or achieved. No significant difference between performance and sex of leader emerged, although male leaders engaged in significantly more verbal leader-like behavior, and female leaders in significantly more positive affect behavior. Females who achieved leadership assumed both task and socioemotional leadership, while female appointed leaders performed minimal socioemotional leadership. Males showed no difference under leadership conditions. Leaders of same-sex groups, whether male or female, employed more directive behavior than leaders of mixed-sex groups.

602. Fenelon, James R., and Edwin I. Megargee. "Influence of Race on the Manifestation of Leadership." *Journal of Applied Psychology*, 55 (1971), 353-358.

    Four groups of fifteen pairs each of black and white college-age females systematically varied by race and by high or low levels of dominance took part in a game situation requiring a leader. In uniracial dyads, the high-dominance female tended to assume leadership, as expected. In biracial dyads, high-dominance white subjects tended not to assume leadership but high-dominance black subjects did. Cultural influences are offered as explanation.

* Flowers, Matie L. "A Laboratory Test of Some Implications of Janis's Groupthink Hypothesis." *Journal of Personality and Social Psychology*, 35 (1977), 888-896. See item 227.

603. Fowler, Gene D., and Lawrence B. Rosenfeld. "Sex Differences and Democratic Leadership Behavior." *Southern Speech Communication Journal,* 45 (1979), 69-78.

    The communication behavior of ten male and ten female democratic leaders as they conducted discussion in small groups (total N = 80 male and female undergraduates) was analyzed. Female leaders had more positive socioemotional behavior than males; males were more task-oriented. Personality characteristics attributed by followers to male democratic leaders were being more forceful, analytical, and utilitarian; to female democratic leaders they were being helpful, affectionate, desirous of unity, and desirous of stability.

* Gibbard, Graham S., and John J. Hartman. "The Oedipal Paradigm in Group Development: A Clinical and Empirical Study." *Small Group Behavior,* 4 (1973), 305-354. See item 236.

604. Ginter, Gary, and Svenn Lindskold. "Rate of Participation and Expertise as Factors Influencing Leader Choice." *Journal of Personality and Social Psychology,* 32 (1975), 1085-89.

    Seventy-two female undergraduates in four-person problem-solving groups varied by reputed expertise of a confederate member, expertness of comments of that member, and amount of talking by that member, picked a leader. Under reputed-expertise condition, amount of talking had no effect on choice of leader. Under no-expert-in-group condition, the amount of talking did influence the choice of leader, with a more talkative member more likely to be picked.

605. Gitter, A. George, Harvey Black, and John Walkley. "Nonverbal Communication and the Judgment of Leadership." *Psychological Reports,* 39 (1976), 1117-18.

    An analysis of variance using strong and weak levels of nonverbal communication, audio-visual and audio-only modes of presentation, and 55 subjects of both sexes indicated that the nonverbal manipulation made a significant difference on judgment of leadership. A factor analysis revealed that the factor "structure" (exciting, bold, strong, hard) was perceived significantly more by those viewing the strong nonverbal condition than those in the weak nonverbal condition. Sex and mode of presentation had no significant effect.

* Gruenfeld, Leopold, and Saleem Kassum. "Supervisory Style and Organizational Effectiveness in a Pediatric Hospital." *Personnel Psychology*, 26 (1973), 531-544. See item 568.

* Helmich, Donald L. "Male and Female Presidents: Some Implications of Leadership Style." *Human Resource Management*, 13, No. 4 (1974), 25-26. See item 434.

606. Inderlied, Sheila D., and Gary Powell. "Sex-Role Identity and Leadership Style: Different Labels for the Same Concept?" *Sex Roles*, 5 (1979), 613-625.

    This study used four different groups (undergraduates, business school graduate students, members of a professional association for home economists, and technical trainers in a large public utility company who had all been managers, total N = 505) responding to a questionnaire to investigate the relationship between leader behavior and sex-role identification. Subjects registered a strong preference for a "masculine" team manager. Although results supported a connection between masculine characteristics and structuring behavior of a leader, they did not uphold the hypothesis of a relationship between sex-role identity and leadership style.

607. Jacobson, Marsha B., and Joan Effertz. "Sex Roles and Leadership: Perceptions of the Leaders and the Led." *Organizational Behavior and Human Performance*, 12 (1974), 383-396.

    To investigate the effect of traditional sex roles on leadership performance, 36 male and 36 female undergraduates completed a dominoes-placement task in groups of three with the sex of the leader and followers varied factorially. Females in the leadership position were perceived by both sexes and by themselves as doing a better job than male leaders in a situation where the performance of both groups was equivalent. Males were judged more harshly than females when they were leaders but more leniently than females when they were followers. Contrary to prediction, males and females did not differ as to how much they enjoyed leadership, a finding contrary to other findings.

* Jain, Harish C. "Supervisory Communication and Performance in Urban Hospitals." *Journal of Communication*, 23 (1973), 103-117. See item 569.

608. Larwood, Laurie, and John Blackmore. "Sex Discrimination in Managerial Selection: Testing Predictions of the Vertical Dyad Linkage Model." *Sex Roles,* 4 (1978), 359-367.

This study investigated 60 undergraduates' behavior in soliciting volunteer leaders for a series of leadership experiments. The solicitation behavior was consistent with the vertical dyad linkage leadership model (in which the leader is involved in dyadic relationship with all of the group members as individuals), which predicted that ingroup members would share more responsibilities and benefits with the leader/manager than would outgroup members; members of the same sex were expected to be more frequently ingroup (acquaintances). Results showed that same-sex acquaintances were solicited more often than cross-sex acquaintances. Same-sex acquaintances were more frequently asked to volunteer on highly valued tasks and were more likely than non-acquaintances to agree to participate. The results are interpreted as demonstrating a bias in favor of aiding and promoting members of one's own sex in managerial situations.

* Larwood, Laurie, Marion M. Wood, and Sheila D. Inderlied. "Training Women for Management: New Problems, New Solutions." *Academy of Management Review,* 3 (1978), 584-593. See item 441.

609. Lord, Robert G., James S. Phillips, and Michael C. Rush. "Effects of Sex and Personality on Perceptions of Emergent Leadership, Influence, and Social Power." *Journal of Applied Psychology,* 65 (1980), 176-182.

In four-person groups, 54 male and 42 female undergraduates performed four tasks varying in output and process interdependence and then rated each other on measures of perceived leadership, social power, and influence.
Rater sex was significantly related to almost all of the dependent variables, with females giving higher ratings. In general, sex, locus of control, and least-preferred coworker measures accounted for significant amounts of variance in person perceptions, explaining between 17 and 44 percent of the variance.

610. Maier, Norman R.F. "Male Versus Female Discussion Leaders." *Personnel Psychology,* 23 (1970), 455-461.

Ninety-six groups of two male, two female undergraduates role-played in a changing-work-procedure problem where the leader received facts only about the workers' times or those facts plus a suggested solution. Female leaders in fact-plus-solution condition were just as persuasive as male leaders in having their solution adopted. In facts-only condition, however, female leaders accepted followers' solutions less conducive to productivity more readily than male leaders did.

* Mamola, Claire. "Women in Mixed Groups: Some Research Findings." *Small Group Behavior,* 10 (1979), 431-440. See item 266.

611. Mayes, Sharon S. "Women in Positions of Authority: A Case Study of Changing Sex Roles." *Signs: Journal of Women in Culture and Society,* 4 (1979), 556-568.

    The leadership behavior of male and female leaders in four small group conferences (220 university health-associated professionals) was observed for the dynamics of patriarchal relations, sex roles, and sex-role behavior. Six female-led and 12 male-led groups of 11 to 12 members each responded to questionnaires and were video- and audiotaped in discussion. The tapes were analyzed by the author and twelve experienced observers. Males in female-led groups expressed a fear of loss of control, overt anger, and fear of the female leader. Female-led groups were characterized by sex-role confusion, and single females assumed more traditional roles than married females. It was conjectured that the strong resistance to changing sex-role behavior occurred because of a fear of generating confusion. Leadership behaviors of females tended to weaken during the four conferences.

* Messé, Lawrence A., Joel Aronoff, and John P. Wilson. Motivation as a Mediator of the Mechanisms Underlying Role Assignments in Small Groups." *Journal of Personality and Social Psychology,* 24 (1972), 84-90. See item 272.

* Moore, James C., Jr., Eugene B. Johnson, and Martha S.C. Arnold. "Status Congruence and Equity in Restricted Communication Networks." *Sociometry,* 35 (1972), 519-537. See item 276.

* O'Day, Rory. "Individual Training Styles: An Empirically Derived Typology." *Small Group Behavior,* 7 (1976), 147-182. See item 279.

612. Parlee, Mary B. "Psychology and Women." *Signs: Journal of Women in Culture and Society,* 5 (1979), 121-133.

This review essay critiquing traditional psychological research on women includes research on leadership, language, and conversational interactions. Women were unlikely to be seen as leaders in a mixed-sex group and were identified as leaders only in all-female groups. Women spoke differently from men with more tentative intonations, more tag questions, and more qualifiers. Parlee found that the language of women is also used by someone (anyone) in a less powerful role when speaking to someone more powerful. Teachers' feedback was more negative to girls and focused on the intellectual quality of the work, while the feedback to boys, though negative, focused on form and not the intellectual aspect. In conversational interactions (means through which power is created in social interactions), women were interrupted and not allowed to manage the topic of conversation. Parlee proposes that the research used in studies of interactions should take into account the context and conceptual frameworks of the interactions. Approximately 50 studies are reviewed.

* Petty, M.M., and Robert H. Miles. "Leader Sex-Role Stereotyping in a Female-Dominated Work Culture." *Personnel Psychology*, 29 (1976), 393-404. See item 446.

613. Rendel, Margherita. "The Death of Leadership or Educating People to Lead Themselves." *Women's Studies International Quarterly*, 1 (1978), 313-325.

This report of a conference on "Educating Women for Leadership" contains a review of more than 33 studies on leadership, including sex differences in attitudes about and abilities in leadership. Factors that confine women to sex-stereotyped roles, especially lack of self-confidence, are considered.

614. Roger, D.B. "Personal Space, Body Image, and Leadership: An Exploratory Study." *Perceptual and Motor Skills*, 43 (1976), 25-26.

Personal space and boundary scores of 13 black female leaders and 13 black female nonleaders were investigated using measures simulated with doll placement and barriers and penetration responses to the Holtzman Inkblot Test. Results indicated that the mean personal space scores were significantly lower for the leaders on both behavioral and simulated measures.

* Rosen, Benson, and Thomas H. Jerdee. "The Influence of

Sex-Role Stereotypes on Evaluations of Male and Female Supervisory Behavior." *Journal of Applied Psychology,* 57 (1973), 44-48. See item 450.

615. Rosenfeld, Lawrence B., and Gene D. Fowler. "Personality, Sex, and Leadership Style." *Communication Monographs,* 43 (1976), 320-324.

    A total of 178 subjects, equally divided by sex, completed various personality measures and leadership questionnaires to isolate variables by sex for autocratic and democratic leadership styles. Stepwise multiple regression analysis revealed that a democratic female leader could be characterized as open-minded, helpful, affectionate, accepting of blame, desirous of stability and unity, and not depressed when the situation was beyond her capability of handling. Democratic male leaders were characterized as mature, forceful, having superior intellect, valuing love of self and others, analytic, utilitarian, accepting of blame, and having high moral-ethical self-concept. No differences between male and female autocratic leadership characteristics appeared.

616. Ruch, Libby O., and Rae R. Newton. "Sex Characteristics, Task Clarity, and Authority." *Sex Roles,* 3 (1977), 479-494.

    To investigate the behavior of the leader in varying task and sex characteristic conditions, 234 male and female undergraduates, each designated as leader, played a card-matching game with two male or female bogus group members against an experimenter; at the completion of the task, the subjects answered a questionnaire. No significant difference was found in the degree of control over the group by male and female leaders when the task goal and role were clear to the leader. In the low task-clarity conditions male leaders exerted significantly more control than females, even in conditions where no prior relation was established between sex and the task ability. Regardless of whom they were supervising, in low task-clarity conditions females exercised significantly less control than males over their groups.

* Schein, Virginia E. "Relationships Between Sex Role Stereotypes and Requisite Management Characteristics Among Female Managers." *Journal of Applied Psycholgy,* 60 (1975), 340-344. See item 451.

617. Schneier, Craig E. "The Contingency Model of Leadership:

An Extension to Emergent Leadership and Leader's Sex." *Organizational Behavior and Human Performance*, 21 (1978), 220-239.

To extend Fiedler's contingency model (*A Theory Leadership Effectiveness*. New York: McGraw-Hill, 1967) to situations in which leaders emerged from their groups and to assess its predictability in this situation for both male and female leaders, 69 female and 138 male undergraduates engaged in a series of experiential learning exercises (self-quizzes, group reports on case studies, role plays, etc.) for a 15-week period and responded to a leader-member semantic differential. Persons who emerged as leaders had Least Preferred Coworker scores significantly lower than nonleaders; male and female leaders had similar scores. A predicted negative relationship between the Least Preferred Coworker scores and group performance was found.

618. Schneier, Craig E., and Kathryn M. Bartol. "Sex Effects in Emergent Leadership." *Journal of Applied Psychology*, 65 (1980), 314-345.

    Fifty-two task groups of from four to seven of both sexes of undergraduates (N = 176 M, 108 F) were formed at the beginning of a 15-week course and measures of leadership behaviors, perceived leader of group, and group performance were taken at the end. A similar proportion of men and women emerged as leaders, group performance was similar, and behaviors of leaders were similar to each other, but different from the behaviors of nonleaders within the groups.

619. Sharf, Barbara F. "A Rhetorical Analysis of Leadership Emergence in Small Groups." *Communication Monographs*, 45 (1978), 156-172.

    A detailed analysis of two zero history groups, one of which (all female) emerged with a leader while the other (four females, three males) did not, is given. The analysis focuses on leadership emergence, but participants' reported sex role differences and stereotyping are noted.

* Shaw, Margin E., and Blaze Harkey. "Some Effects of Congruency of Member Characteristics and Group Structure Upon Group Behavior." *Journal of Personality and Social Psychology*, 34 (1976), 412-418. See item 293.

* Sheridan, John E., and Donald J. Vredenburgh. "Predicting Leadership Behavior in a Hospital Organization." *Academy*

of Management Journal, 21 (1978), 679-689. See item 573.

* Sheridan, John E., and Donald J. Vredenburgh. "Structural Model of Leadership Influence in a Hospital Organization." *Academy of Management Journal,* 22 (1979), 6-21. See item 574.

* Sheridan, John E., and Donald J. Vredenburgh. "Usefulness of Leadership Behavior and Social Power Variables in Predicting Job Tension, Performance, and Turnover of Nursing Employees." *Journal of Applied Psychology,* 63 (1978), 89-95. See item 575.

* Silbergeld, Sam, Elizabeth S. Thune, and Ronald W. Manderscheid. "The Group Therapist Leadership Role: Assessment in Adolescent Coping Courses." *Small Group Behavior,* 10 (1979), 176-199. See item 576.

* Smith, Darrell, and Roger Miller. "Personal Growth Groups: A Comparison of the Experiences of Anglo and Mexican Americans." *Small Group Behavior,* 10 (1979), 263-270. See item 294.

620. Smith, Robert J., and Patrick E. Cook. "Leadership in Dyadic Groups as a Function of Dominance and Incentives." *Sociometry,* 36 (1973), 561-568.

    Forty-five female dyads, with one high and one low in dominance trait in each dyad, completed tasks under three conditions of incentive. High dominance subjects assumed leadership more often. Task performance was significantly affected by level of dominance of leader, but incentives did not significantly affect performance.

* Stang, David J. "Effects of Interaction Rate on Ratings of Leadership and Liking." *Journal of Personality and Social Psychology,* 27 (1973), 405-408. See item 298.

621. Stein, R. Timothy, and Tamar Heller. "An Empirical Analysis of the Correlations Between Leadership Status and Participation Rates Reported in the Literature." *Journal of Personality and Social Psychology,* 37 (1979), 1993-2002.

    Using 72 correlations from 15 previous studies, authors supported hypotheses that correlations between leadership and participation are greater for task than for maintenance functions, are directly related to skill requirements of the task, and are greater for larger groups.

In addition, a significantly higher correlation was found for mixed-sex than for same-sex groups, although there was confounding of this result with type of task. Nevertheless, males were generally permitted greater influence and higher participation rates.

622. Tindall, Jeffry H., Linda Boyler, Pat Cline, Paul Emberger, Sharon Powell, and Joseph Wions. "Perceived Leadership Rankings of Males and Females in Small Task Groups." *Journal of Psychology,* 100 (1978), 13-20.

Ten male and 14 female graduate students ranging in age from 24 to 58 completed a cognitive task in either same- or mixed-sex groups while being observed for eye and verbal patterns. Subsequently they rated each other on leadership skills. Males were ranked higher than females in all experimental conditions. Females ranked highest in leadership ranked higher than like males in same-sex groups. Females rated high in leadership showed eye and verbal patterns of talking to group, not individual, and maintained short, mutual glances. In males no discernible correlation between leadership and eye and verbal communication appeared.

* Waetjen, Walter B., James M. Schuerger, and Eleanor B. Schwartz. "Male and Female Managers: Self-Concept, Success, and Failure." *Journal of Psychology,* 103 (1979), 87-94. See item 456.

623. Welsh, M. Cay. "Attitudinal Measures and Evaluation of Males and Females in Leadership Roles." *Psychological Reports,* 45 (1979), 19-22.

Twenty-eight female and 28 male undergraduates, previously administered several attitudinal questionnaires, rated leader and group performance of a mixed-sex triad seen on videotape completing a group task. Scripts for leaders and performance of group were identical in each instance. Subjects felt that the male leader performed more successfully, but that the female leader communicated to her followers much better. Overall, male leaders were thought to affect the outcome more, though each sex rated same-sex leader high while males rated female leaders low. Author concludes that males' perception of females as leaders is more conservative than females' perceptions.

624. Wexley, Kenneth N., and Peter J. Hunt. "Male and Female Leaders: Comparison of Performance and Behavior Patterns."

Psychological Reports, 35 (1974), 867-872.

In a game situation led by 16 male and 16 female graduate students, most of whom held managerial positions as well, played by 192 undergraduates evenly divided by sex, no significant differences by sex of leader on human relations and administrative technical skills were found. Female leaders engaged in more release of tension, agreed more often, gave more opinions, and asked for more suggestions than male leaders. There were no significant sex-of-leader, sex-of-subordinate interactions relating to leadership skills, but male subordinates revealed a pattern of trying to dominate the group when working under a female leader.

625. Wood, Julia T. "Alternate Portraits of Leaders: A Contingency Approach to Perceptions of Leadership." *Western Journal of Speech Communication,* 43 (1979), 260-270.

    To investigate perceptions of appropriate leadership as contingent upon group purpose, member sex, and the interaction between purpose and sex, 217 subjects (86 F, 131 M), drawn from ongoing university and non-university groups in existence for at least a year (including sororities), answered a leadership perception questionnaire. Comparisions among groups having task or social or both task and social purposes revealed significant differences in the importance attributed by members to three factors of leadership: task guidance, interpersonal attractiveness, and team spirit. Group purpose explained the greatest amount of difference among perceptions of appropriate leadership. The sexes did not differ in the importance they attributed to task guidance and interpersonal attractiveness. They did differ in the importance attributed to team spirit, with males considering it more important in a leader than females.

* Wright, Fred. "The Effects of Style and Sex of Consultants and Sex of Members in Self-Study Groups." *Small Group Behavior,* 7 (1976), 433-456. See item 315.

626. Yerby, Janet. "Attitude, Task, and Sex Composition as Variables Affecting Leadership in Small Problem Solving Groups." *Speech Monographs,* 42 (1975), 160-168.

    From 660 undergraduates taking an attitude-toward-female leadership scale, 192 scoring in the top and bottom thirds were selected for this study of female leaders. Leaders, either given or not given helpful information leading to a task solution, attempted to persuade the others in the groups, which were varied for sex composition. Measures of group satisfaction and reaction to leader were taken. Groups with equal numbers of males and females, all with positive attitudes toward female leadership, were more satisfied both with the group and with the leader. The two groups least satisfied with their leaders were those with positive attitudes and one female, three males; and those with negative attitudes, two females, two males.

LISTENING AND FEEDBACK

* Aiello, John R. "A Further Look at Equilibrium Theory: Visual Interaction as a Function of Interpersonal Distance." *Environmental Psychology and Nonverbal Behavior*, 1, No. 1 (1977), 122-140. See item 1038.

* Archer, Richard L., and John H. Berg. "Disclosure Reciprocity and Its Limits: A Reactance Analysis." *Journal of Experimental Social Psychology*, 14 (1978), 527-540. See item 704.

* Archibald, W. Peter, and Ronald L. Cohen. "Self-Presentation, Embarrassment, and Facework as a Function of Self-Evaluation, Conditions of Self-Presentation, and Feedback from Others." *Journal of Personality and Social Psychology*, 20 (1971), 287-297. See item 3.

* Argyle, Michael, Luc Lefebvre, and Mark Cook. "The Meaning of Five Patterns of Gaze." *European Journal of Social Psychology*, 4 (1974), 125-136. See item 1042.

627. Berger, Charles R. "Proactive and Retroactive Attribution Processes in Interpersonal Communications." *Human Communication Research*, 2 (1975), 33-50.

Three experiments focused on the ways in which information disclosed early in a relationship is used to form predictions concerning the probable attitudes of the other person and to explain subsequent communication behavior as the relationship progresses. Experiment I, involving 89 male and female undergraduates, revealed that perceived background similarity led to predictions of attitude similarity. No significant sex main effect was observed, and the interaction between sex and similarity-dissimilarity variables was also nonsignificant. Experiment II (N = 64 undergraduates) and III (N = 60 high school students) found that consistency between early information and later behavior led to the utilization of early information to explain later behavior.

* Bleda, Paul R. "Conditioning and Discrimination of Affect and Attracting." *Journal of Personality and Social Psychology,* 34 (1976), 1106-13. See item 203.

628. Briggs, Gary G., and Robert D. Nebes. "The Effects of Handedness, Family History and Sex on the Performance of a Dichotic Listening Task." *Neuropsychologia,* 14 (1976), 129-133.

    Forty left-handed, 40 right-handed, and 40 mixed-handed college students of both sexes reported as many as possible of the numbers presented to them dichotically. Results showed an overall right ear superiority, implying that the left hemisphere dominance for speech is more widespread than right handedness. Females made fewer errors than males.

* Brown, Robert C., Jr., Bob Helm, and James T. Tedeschi. "Attraction and Verbal Conditioning." *The Journal of Social Psychology,* 91 (1973), 81-85. See item 102.

629. Buchli, Virginia, and W. Barnett Pearce. "Listening Behavior in Coorientational States." *Journal of Communication,* 24 (Summer 1974), 62-70.

    In a study of undergraduates (61 M, 56 F) matching judicial decisions with those of a judge, the authors found that listeners who expect to agree and who do later agree with a speaker listen less well than speakers who do not expect to agree or who expect to but do not. Authors found no significant differences by sex, as had been theorized.

630. Bush, Marshall, Sheldon J. Korchin, Lynnette Beall, and Stewart Kiritz. "Sex Differences in the Relationship Between Trait Anxiety and Auditory Selective Attention." *Journal of Auditory Research,* 14 (1974), 1-20.

    Fifteen female and 16 male college students were tested on a series of selective listening tests constructed on A.M. Treisman's hierarchical model of perceptual analyzing mechanisms ("Strategies and Models of Selective

Attention," *Psychological Review,* 76 [1969], 282-299). Trait anxiety was associated with impaired selective attention for males and with enhanced attention for females. Some significant sex differences in favor of males were found in one set of the selective listening tests and in the Embedded Figures Test. An adequate theoretical exaplanation is not yet available to explain these results.

* Cole, C.W., E.R. Oetting, and N.G. Dinges. "Effects of Verbal Interaction Conditions on Self-Concept Discrimination and Anxiety." *Journal of Counseling Psychology,* 20 (1973), 431-436. See item 12.

* Cooper, Harris M. "Controlling Personal Rewards: Professional Teachers' Differential Use of Feedback and the Effects of Feedback on the Student's Motivation to Perform." *Journal of Educational Psychology,* 69 (1977), 419-427. See item 505.

631. Cupchik, Gerald C., and Howard Leventhal. "Consistency Between Expressive Behavior and the Evaluation of Humorous Stimuli: The Role of Sex and Self-Observation." *Journal of Personality and Social Psychology,* 30 (1974), 429-442.

    In two experimental studies investigating the relationship between mirth (smiling and laughing) and evaluations of funniness of cartoons, authors found that feedback from mirth reactions influenced funniness ratings for 40 females but not for 40 males, with canned laughter increasing ratings. When subjects were made aware of mirth by requiring self-observations and ratings, females lowered their funniness ratings, and canned laughter had no effect. There were no differences for males under these conditions.

632. Currant, Elaine F., Andrew L. Dickson, Howard N. Anderson, and Patricia J. Faulkender. "Sex-Role Stereotyping and Assertive Behavior." *Journal of Psychology,* 101 (1979), 223-228.

    From a pool of 407, 40 sex-typed and 40 androgynous male and female undergraduates were selected and shown in groups of five of same sex and sex-type videotapes manipulated for sex of actors and assertive or expressive dialogue. As predicted, sex-role stereotyped males reported significantly higher probability of responding assertively in the videotape situation, and sex-role stereotyped females of responding expressively. There were no significant differences for androgynous subjects.

* Daly, John A., James C. McCroskey, and Virginia P. Richmond. "Judgments of Quality, Listening, and Understanding Based Upon Vocal Activity." *Southern Speech Communication Journal,* 41 (1976), 189-197. See item 218.

633. Dittmann, Allen T. "Developmental Factors in Conversational Behavior." *Journal of Communication,* 22 (Dec. 1972), 404-423.

    Responses of listeners ranging in age from six to 35 revealed that age is a more significant factor than sex in learning to produce responses in conversation. Various research is cited to verify that conclusion.

634. Eagly, Alice H., and George I. Whitehead, III. "Effect of Choice on Receptivity to Favorable and Unfavorable Evaluations of Oneself." *Journal of Personality and Social Psychology,* 22 (1972), 223-230.

    In this experiment to determine the effects of choice on receiving feedback, either favorable or unfavorable, on evaluations about oneself, it was found that favorable feedback raised self-evaluations and negative feedback lowered self-evaluations. Choice of feedback decreased acceptance of favorable feedback and increased acceptance of unfavorable feedback. Males changed self-ratings more toward favorable than unfavorable feedback; females changed about equally. Subjects were 78 male and 80 female undergraduates.

* Fenigstein, Allan. "Self-Consciousness, Self-Attention, and Social Interaction." *Journal of Personality and Social Psychology,* 37 (1979), 75-86. See item 225.

635. Fiedler, Decky, and Lee R. Beach. "On the Decision to be Assertive." *Journal of Consulting and Clinical Psychology,* 46 (1978), 537-546.

    Using 64 undergraduate women and 47 women in a dental hygiene program rating both consequence and risk of assertive response to nine video or written scenes, authors found subjects, irrespective of assertiveness or anxiety scores, considered consequences of being assertive when deciding how to behave. Those who chose to be assertive depended more on calculations of probabilities of good or bad consequences occurring and not on degree of how good or how bad the consequences might be.

636. Fitzpatrick, Mary Anne, and Arthur Bochner. "Beyond Ingratiation: Factors Affecting the Communication of Interpersonal Evaluations." *Communication Quarterly*, 25, No. 2 (1977), 11-17.

To examine the effects of sex of receiver, status of the communicator, and mode of communication on the exchange of evaluations, 200 undergraduates responded to an employer-employee situation by revealing how willing they were to disclose positive, negative, or neutral evaluations of a stimulus person of the same sex under conditions in which status was manipulated. Higher status persons were less likely to communicate negative evaluations indirectly. Both sexes were more willing to offer positive evaluations directly to a female or to a third party for a female than they were to a male. Females were more likely to be positively evaluated.

637. Gamble, Teri K. "Sex as a Factor Influencing Evaluation and Comprehension of 'Male' and 'Female' Monologues." *Western Journal of Speech Communication*, 41 (1977), 110-116.

Gamble investigated the effect of females interpreting male material and males interpreting female material on an audience's evaluation and comprehension of the performance. Two hundred seventy-five male and female undergraduates were randomly assigned to view and rate one of twelve videotaped performances of six monologues interpreted by a male and a female. Results indicated no main effects for the sex of the performer or the masculinity/femininity of the monologue on the evaluation of performer effectiveness.

638. Gentry, William D. "Biracial Aggression: I. Effect of Verbal Attack and Sex of Victim." *Journal of Social Psychology*, 88 (1972), 75-82.

To investigate the effects of verbal attack of a white instigator on aggression of blacks, 28 male and female black undergraduates participated in an experiment in which a white experimenter of the same sex either insulted them or not. Both blood pressure and mood and aggression questionnaire data were obtained. Insulted subjects reported more anger, more aggression, and higher diastolic blood pressure than noninsulted subjects, and insulted female subjects were more hostile in their evaluation of the experimenter than any other group, the only sex difference found.

* Giesen, Martin, and Clyde Hendrick. "Effects of Fake Positive and Negative Arousal Feedback on Persuasion." *Journal of Personality and Social Psychology,* 30 (1974), 449-457. See item 672.

* Good, Thomas L., and Jere E. Brophy. "Behavioral Expression of Teacher Attitudes." *Journal of Educational Psychology,* 63 (1972), 617-624. See item 510.

* Greenberg, Roger P. "Sexual Bias in Rorschach Administration." *Journal of Personality Assessment,* 36 (1972), 336-339. See item 536.

* Greene, Les R. "Effects of Verbal Evaluative Feedback and Interpersonal Distance on Behavioral Compliance." *Journal of Counseling Psychology,* 24 (1977), 10-14. See item 1157.

639. Gruber, Kenneth J., and Jacquelyn Gaebelein. "Sex Differences in Listening Comprehension." *Sex Roles,* 5 (1979), 299-310.

    The effect of sex of the speaker on listening comprehension in a public speaking situation was tested using the comprehension of 60 male and 60 female undergraduates who viewed either a male or female speaker talking on either a masculine (chess), feminine (interior decorating), or neutral (snow skiing) topic. The results supported the hypotheses that a male speaker is listened to more carefully than a female speaker, even when she makes the identical presentation. No differences were found when the topic was biased towards one sex; males were still recalled better than females. Sex of listener made no difference in these findings. Both male and female subjects rated male speakers equally effective, but male subjects rated the female speakers significantly more effective than they did male speakers, whereas female subjects rated male and female speakers equally.

640. Halley, Richard D. "Distractability of Males and Females in Competing Aural Message Situations: A Research Note." *Human Communication Research,* 2 (1975), 79-82.

    Sixty-three male and 83 female undergraduates, listening to a tape which played two short stories simultaneously, were to attend to one story only. Results of comprehension tests revealed that males retrieved more information.

641. Halley, Richard D. "Some Suggestions for the Teaching of Listening." *Speech Teacher*, 24 (1975), 386-389.

This essay on ideas about teaching listening includes a long paragraph on recent conflicting research findings on sex differences in listening.

* Heilman, Madeline, and Kathy E. Kram. "Self-Derogating Behavior in Women--Fixed or Flexible: The Effects of Co-Worker's Sex." *Organizational Behavior and Human Performance*, 22 (1978), 497-507. See item 583.

* Hillman, Stephen B., and G. Gregory Davenport. "Teacher-Student Interactions in Desegregated Schools." *Journal of Educational Psychology*, 70 (1978), 545-553. See item 514.

* Hoffman-Graff, Mary A. "Interviewer Use of Positive and Negative Self-Disclosure and Interviewer-Subject Sex Pairing." *Journal of Counseling Psychology*, 24 (1977), 184-190. See item 545.

642. Holzman, Philip S., and Clyde Rousey. "Disinhibition of Communicated Thought: Generality and Role of Cognitive Style." *Journal of Abnormal Psychology*, 77 (1971), 263-274.

In an extension and refinement of the authors' 1970 study (see item 643), white noise masking did not alter performance on cognitive task (reading silently) or on visual-motor test, but did decrease performance for males in oral reading test. For all 80 males and 80 females, white noise increased impulse-related themes and decreased defensive themes in the Thematic Apperception Test. Authors conclude that hearing oneself speak is necessary for modulating impulse and affect and for reality testing in general. Where vocal activity is involved, one must, apparently, hear oneself to regulate effectively the expression of thought.

643. Holzman, Philip S., and Clyde Rousey. "Monitoring, Activation, and Disinhibition: Effects of White Noise Masking on Spoken Thought." *Journal of Abnormal Psychology*, 75 (1970), 227-241.

Two experimental and two replicative studies determined the effects of not hearing oneself on the production of speech. Male and female adults (40 M and F; 10 F; 40 M and F; 40 M and F), responding to Thematic Apperception Test cards under white noise condition, produced significantly more impulse-related material and less defensive material than under normal conditions. Males contributed significantly longer stories; both sexes had longer stories in normal than in white noise conditions. Females used a higher fundamental frequency than males; in both sexes the frequency rose in white noise condition. Males had louder intensity than females; both spoke louder under white noise condition and when reading as opposed to speaking spontaneously. Females had longer phonation time than males; both sexes has longer phonation time under white noise condition and when reading rather than speaking spontaneously. In the second two experiments with the Holtzman Inkblot Test cards, women produced more color responses under noise conditions than under normal conditions; men produced the same in one experiment but declined in another.

* Jackson, David J., and Ted L. Huston. "Physical Attractiveness and Assertiveness." *The Journal of Social Psychology*, 96 (1975), 79-84. See item 1108.

* Jacobs, Alfred, Marion Jacobs, Norman Cavior, and John Burke. "Anonymous Feedback: Credibility and Desirability of Structured Emotional and Behavioral Feedback Delivered in Groups." *Journal of Counseling Psychology*, 21 (1974), 106-111. See item 248.

644. Janda, Louis H., and David C. Rimm. "Type of Situation and Sex of Counselor in Assertive Training." *Journal of Counseling Psychology*, 24 (1977), 444-447.

    Forty female undergraduates were trained by a male or a female counselor in assertiveness in making complaints, small talk, and saying *no* to unreasonable requests. Improvement occurred in all three areas, but more for making complaints than for saying *no*. Those trained by male counselor improved more than those trained by female counselor.

645. Johnson, Ronald C., and George P. Danko. "Reinforcing the Speaker: Effects of the Speech, Speaker and Listener." *Psychological Record*, 2 (1977), 489-492.

    Sixty-one college students (32 M, 29 F), almost half Japanese-Americans, indicated points at which they would reinforce what was being said on videotape by two male and two female speakers recounting either a positive or a negative emotional experience. Results of the various measures taken were that emotional content of speech, ethnicity of listener, sex of listener, and sex of speaker-sex of listener interaction did not significantly influence state of reinforcement. Extroversion was positively associated with reinforcement, however.

646. Jones, Stephen C., and J. Sidney Shrauger. "Reputation and Self-Evaluation as Determinants of Attractiveness." *Sociometry*, 33 (1970), 276-286.

    Ninety-two female undergraduates evaluated the attractiveness of an anonymous female presented systematically as of reputed high or low status and self-enhancing or self-derogating in a tape recorded talk. The high-reputation female was judged more attractive than the low, and the high self-evaluator more attractive than the low in the high reputation condition, but the low self-evaluator more attractive than the high in a low-reputation condition.

* Kleinke, Chris L. "Effects of False Feedback About Response Lengths on Subjects' Perception of an Interview." *The Journal of Social Psychology*, 95 (1975), 99-104. See item 128.

647. Lass, Norman J., and C. Elaine Prater. "A Comparative Study of Listening Rate Preferences for Oral Reading and Impromptu Speaking Tasks." *Journal of Communication*, 23 (March 1973), 95-102.

    Twenty-six college women indicated preferences of oral reading rate and impromptu speaking rate while listening to recordings in which speech rate ranged from 100 to 300 wpm. Both reading and speaking were preferred at 175 wpm; least preferred rate was 100 wpm.

648. Lass, Norman J., Margaret G. Wellford, and Debora L. Hall. "The Verbal Transformation Effect: A Comparative Study of Male and Female Listeners." *Journal of Auditory Research,* 14 (1974), 109-116.

    To determine the effect of sex in verbal transformation, seven auditory stimuli of various levels of semantic and phonetic complexity were given repeatedly to 21 female and 21 male college students. No significant sex differences were found in any measure, including the number of elicited forms, transitions, repetitions prior to first transformation, or type of transformation.

649. Mathews, Kenneth E., Jr., and Steven Cooper. "Deceit as a Function of Sex of Subject and Target Person." *Sex*

Roles, 2 (1976), 29-38.

Thirty male and 30 female undergraduates in same and opposite sex pairs were used to determine the effect of sex on various types of deceit. In role-playing situations, confronted by a confederate, subjects used "white lies" to prevent damage to self esteem more often than any other type. Males were more likely to deceive than females; females were the target of deceit more often than males, and males lied to females more than any other sex pairing.

* Mazanec, Nancy, and George J. McCall. "Sex Factors and Allocation of Attention in Observing Persons." *Journal of Psychology,* 93 (1976), 175-180. See item 139.

* Mehrabian, Albert, and Sheldon Ksionzky. "Factors of Interpersonal Behavior and Judgment in Social Groups." *Psychological Reports,* 28 (1971), 483-492. See item 271.

* Mulac, Anthony, and Torborg L. Lundell. "Differences in Perceptions Created by Syntactic-Semantic Productions of Male and Female Speakers." *Communication Monographs,* 47 (1980), 111-118. See item 874.

* Mulac, Anthony, and Mary J. Rudd. "Effects of Selected American Regional Dialects upon Regional Audience Members." *Communication Monographs,* 44 (1977), 185-195. See item 873.

* Pearce, W. Barnett, and Forrest Conklin. "Nonverbal Vocalic Communication and Perceptions of a Speaker." *Speech Monographs,* 38 (1971), 235-236. See item 1241.

650. Powell, Richard S., and Edgar C. O'Neal. "Communication Feedback and Duration as Determinants of Accuracy, Confidence, and Differentiation in Interpersonal Perception." *Journal of Personality and Social Psychology,* 34 (1976), 746-754.

Using 64 female undergraduates in conditions varied for length of either reciprocal or nonreciprocal communication, authors found support for their hypotheses that as duration increases, reciprocal communication increases accuracy in person perception and in confidence of these perceptions. Reciprocal communication produced a greater degree of differences than nonreciprocal communication did.

651. Powers, Peter A., Joyce L. Andriks, and Elizabeth F. Loftus. "Eyewitness Accounts of Females and Males." *Journal of Applied Psychology*, 64 (1979), 339-347.

Two studies used equal numbers of male and female students looking at slides of a robbery (N = 50) or of a fight (N = 150), who later recalled the incident in a multiple-choice test and in subsequent versions of the incident that contained misleading information. Females were more accurate and more resistant to false suggestion about female-oriented details, as males were about male-oriented details. Overall accuracy was unrelated to intelligence or to specific abilities such as verbal or spatial abilities.

* Reardon, Robert C. "Individual Differences and the Meanings of Vocal Emotional Expressions." *Journal of Communication*, 21 (March 1971), 72-82. See item 1244.

* Reardon, Robert, and Ellen Amatea. "The Meaning of Vocal Emotional Expressions: Sex Differences for Listeners and Speakers." *International Journal of Social Psychiatry*, 19 (1973), 214-219. See item 1245.

652. Richmond, Virginia P., and D. Lynn Robertson. "Women's Liberation in Interpersonal Relations." *Journal of Communication*, 27 (Winter 1977), 42-45.

A paper-and-pencil evaluation study of male and female bogus supporters or opponents of the Equal Rights Amendment using 229 male and 164 female undergraduates revealed that position on women's liberation had a reverse effect on perception of opposite-sex person taking a stand on liberation. Males evaluated female supporters of liberation less positively than female opponents, and females evaluated male supporters more positively than male opponents. But females did not evaluate female supporters more positively than female opponents, and males did not evaluate male supporters less positively than male opponents.

653. Rossiter, Charles M., Jr. "Sex of the Speaker, Sex of the Listener, and Listening Comprehension." *Journal of Communication*, 22 (March 1972), 64-69.

When 137 male and 225 female undergraduates responded to a measure about the message content of 14 short, informative messages, no significant differences in listening comprehension were found. The significant interaction between sex of speaker and sex of listener was considered unimportant since it accounted for less than one percent of the total variance.

* Rothbart, Myron, Susan Dalfen, and Robert Barrett. "Effects of Teacher's Expectancy on Student-Teacher Interaction." *Journal of Educational Psychology*, 62 (1971), 49-54. See item 521.

654. Savitsky, Jeffrey C., and Marguerite E. Sim. "Trading Emotions: Equity Theory of Reward and Punishment." *Journal of Communication*, 24 (Summer 1974), 140-146.

    In two experiments undergraduates (18 M, 23 F; 11 M, 29 F) read or viewed first-time juvenile male offenders played by actors revealing happy, angry, sad, distressed, or neutral emotions. The emotion of actor/criminal had a significant relationship to listeners' perceptions of severity of crime, likelihood of recurrence, and of suggested punishment for the crime. Sex of listener was insignificant except in interaction between perceived severity of crime and emotion portrayed, with females rating more harshly in both angry and happy conditions.

655. Schaible, Todd D., and Alfred Jacobs. "Feedback III: Sequence Effects: Enhancement of Feedback Acceptance and Group Attractiveness by Manipulation of the Sequence and Valence of Feedback." *Small Group Behavior*, 6 (1975), 151-173.

    Sixty female undergraduates in groups of five participated in two group consensus-seeking exercises and received either positive, negative, or no feedback. Results showed the recipients of feedback invariably rated positive feedback more credible than negative feedback, and credibility and desirability of feedback were rated higher when positive feedback preceded negative.

* Sermat, Vello, and Michael Smith. "Content Analysis of Verbal Communication in the Development of a Relationship." *Journal of Personality and Social Psychology*, 26 (1973), 332-346. See item 762.

656. Silverman, Julian. "Attentional Styles and the Study of Sex Differences." In *Attention: Contemporary Theory and Analysis*. Ed. David I. Mostofsky. New York: Appleton-Century-Crofts, 1970, pp. 61-98.

    A multidimensional model of attention is presented and prototypic attentional styles of men and women examined.

Women's style is found to be characterized by sensitivity to subtle cues, distractibility, nonanalytic attitude, receptivity, and a disposition to reduce the intensity experienced from strong stimulation. A reexamination of over 150 studies (mostly from the 1950s and 1960s) on sex differences in attention is made in light of the differing attentional styles.

* Smith, Kay H. "Changes in Group Structure through Individual and Group Feedback." *Journal of Personality and Social Psychology,* 24 (1972), 425-428. See item 297.

* Taylor, Marylee C. "Race, Sex, and the Expression of Self-Fulfilling Prophecies in a Laboratory Teaching Situation." *Journal of Personality and Social Psychology,* 37 (1979), 897-912. See item 525.

657. Timmons, Beverly A. "Sex as a Factor Influencing Sensitivity to Delayed Auditory Feedback." *Perceptual and Motor Skills,* 32 (1971), 824-826.

    Thirty men and 30 women were timed as they recorded 35-word selections under conditions of normal or delayed feedback of own voice (ranging from 0.1 to 0.5 seconds). When delayed feedback conditions were random, no significant sex differences appeared. When the conditions were ordered, women adapted significantly better than men.

658. Tognoli, Jerome, and Robert Keisner. "Gain and Loss of Esteem as Determinants of Interpersonal Attraction: A Replication and Extension." *Journal of Personality and Social Psychology,* 23 (1972), 201-204.

    Fifty female undergraduates evaluated attraction to a confederate after having various levels of positive or negative feedback from the confederate. Greatest attraction came when feedback had been consistently positive, least when consistently negative. No significant gain or loss of self esteem occurred under any set of conditions. Both findings contradict earlier ones.

* Whalen, Carol K., and John V. Flowers. "Effects of Role and Gender Mix on Verbal Communication Modes." *Journal of Counseling Psychology,* 24 (1977), 281-287. See item 177.

PERSUASION AND PERSUASIBILITY

* Adams, Gerald R. "Physical Attractiveness, Personality, and Social Reactions to Peer Pressure." *Journal of Psychology*, 96 (1977), 287-296. See item 1093.

659. Baker, Therese. "Sex Differences in Social Behavior." In *A Survey of Social Psychology*. Ed. Leonard Berkowitz. Hinsdale, Ill.: Dryden Press, 1975, pp. 535-560.

    This chapter contains a review of the various theories explaining sex differences, including psychological, anthropological, and feminist. A three-page summary of research on sex differences in persuasibility notes that studies have shown that persuasibility is allied to feelings of social inferiority for males but not for females.

* Bostrom, Robert N., John R. Basehart, and Charles M. Rossiter, Jr. "The Effects of Three Types of Profane Language in Persuasive Messages." *Journal of Communication*, 23 (Dec. 1973), 461-475. See item 803.

660. Burgoon, Judee K., Miriam Wilkinson, and Ralph Partridge. "The Relative Effectiveness of Praise and Derogation as Persuasive Strategies." *The Journal of the American Forensic Association*, 16 (1979), 10-20.

    This study was designed to assess whether praise or derogation as a debate strategy was more successful in persuading and enhancing the speaker's credibility with receivers with both traditional and nontraditional sex-role orientation. Two hundred ninety male and female undergraduates took the Bem Sex-Role Inventory and responded on a semantic differential to written persuasive messages varied by sex of the speaker and type of strategy. Speakers who praised their opponent were rated significantly more credible. A female who derogated a male was rated higher on extroversion and competence-character by non-traditional receivers, and was rated the same as males who derogated female speakers by traditional receivers.

661. Burgoon, Michael, Stephen B. Jones, and Diane Stewart. "Toward a Message-Centered Theory of Persuasion: Three Empirical Investigations of Language Intensity." *Human Communication Research*, 1 (1975), 240-256.

    Based on research on the effects of language intensity

on attitude change, a set of propositions leading to a theoretical framework of persuasion was proposed. Three separate studies were conducted to test the predictive power of the propositions. The first study was the only one controlled for sex. It used 77 female and 68 male undergraduates to test two hypotheses: that male receivers will demonstrate less attitude change than female receivers, and that an interaction between language intensity and sex of the source will be such that a female source will be more effective with low-intense language and a male will be least effective with such language. Both hypotheses were upheld.

662. Cantor, Joanne R. "Grammatical Variations in Persuasion: Effectiveness of Four Forms of Request in Door-to-Door Solicitation for Funds." *Communication Monographs,* 46 (1979), 296-305.

This empirical study of 56 undergraduates soliciting money for the American Cancer Society with four different styles of requests revealed that a polite, imperative style ("Please contribute to our fund") was significantly the best of the four styles. Female solicitors were judged more attractive and more pleasant than male solicitors, and they collected significantly more money.

663. Cantor, Joanne R., Herminia Alfonso, and Dolf Zillmann. "The Persuasive Effectiveness of the Peer Appeal and a Communicator's First-Hand Experience." *Communication Research,* 3 (1976), 293-310.

A tape-recorded interview in which a woman gave a favorable evaluation of a contraceptive device, varied in eight versions by interviewee age, first-hand experience with the device, and level of expertise, was played for 61 male and 51 female undergraduates, who responded via questionnaires to the topic and the interviewee. Same-age interviewees were more persuasive than non-peer, and first-hand experience interviewees were more persuasive than non-users. The expertise variable was not significant, nor was the sex of subject in any of the findings.

664. Carmichael, Carl W. "Frustration, Sex, and Persuasibility." *Western Speech,* 34 (1970), 300-307.

In this study of persuasibility using 193 male and female undergraduates who listened to two tape-recorded speeches, Carmichael hypothesized that a speaker would be more successful in persuading a listener who is in a state of frustration-aggression, and that male subjects would be more frustrated than female subjects and so would experience significantly more attitude change in the direction advocated by the speaker. Aggression-frustration was measured by an "Ideal Self" semantic differential scale. Males were more frustrated than females, but frustrated females changed attitudes significantly more in a negative direction than frustrated males. There were no significant sex differences for nonfrustrated subjects.

665. Chaiken, Shelly. "Communicator Physical Attractiveness and Persuasion." *Journal of Personality and Social Psychology*, 37 (1979), 1387-97.

   This field study used 68 attractive and unattractive female and male undergraduates stopping two female and two male undergraduates under specified conditions, delivering a short speech, and then obtaining questionnaire responses and signatures on a petition if possible. Attractive speakers induced more persuasion and collected more signatures. Female listeners showed greater agreement. Using pre-experiment data, however, Chaiken found attractive subjects differed from unattractive on several measures relevant to persuasive effectiveness (communication skills, educational accomplishment, etc.).

666. Chaiken, Shelly, and Alice H. Eagly. "Communication Modality as a Determinant of Message Persuasiveness and Message Comprehensibility." *Journal of Personality and Social Psychology*, 34 (1976), 605-614.

   The authors found no sex differences in persuasibility of 321 college students to easy- or difficult-to-understand messages presented in three modes. With difficult messages, greater comprehension and persuasion were found with written as opposed to audio- or videotaped material. With easy messages, videotaped material was most effective, written messages least.

667. Cooper, Harris M. "Statistically Combining Independent Studies: A Meta-Analysis of Sex Differences in Conformity Research." *Journal of Personality and Social Psychology*, 37 (1979), 131-146.

   Cooper advocates a statistical review rather than the traditional literary review of research as leading to greater theoretical progress. Using the 47 sex-differences-in-conformity studies cited by Maccoby and

Jacklin (see 1322), he demonstrates statistical analysis. The analysis leads to similar conclusions: neither sex is more susceptible to influence from peers; in face-to-face encounters women will conform more often, though there is inconsistency to this finding; and in persuasion no overall sex differences in susceptibility have been found.

668. Crano, William D. "Effects of Sex, Response Order, and Expertise in Conformity: A Dispositional Approach." *Sociometry*, 33 (1970), 239-252.

    This study used 64 male and female undergraduates in a perceptual judgment task with experimenter and confederate in systematically varied combinations and 40 control subjects. "Expertise" of confederate significantly affected responses, but sex of subject or confederate had no significant main effect, although it had interaction effects. Subjects were more influenced by same-sex confederate, and male "expert" confederates induced more conformity if they responded last, while female "experts" induced more if they responded first.

669. Dean, Robert B., John A. Austin, and William Watts. "Forewarning Effects in Persuasion: Field and Classroom Experiments." *Journal of Personality and Social Psychology*, 18 (1971), 210-221.

    In the second of two experiments, 161 male and female undergraduates were tested for persuasion relating to forewarning effects and to high or low involvement in the topics. Under low-involvement, where subjects expressed an opinion just after reading the persuasive message, forewarning seemed to facilitate opinion change for females and inhibit it for males.

* Downs, Philip E. "Intrafamily Decision Making in Family Planning." *JBR: Journal of Business Research*, 5 (1977), 63-74. See item 329.

670. Eagly, Alice H. "Sex Differences in Influenceability." *Psychological Bulletin*, 85 (1978), 86-116.

    Using over 260 references, mainly studies on persuasion and conformity research, Eagly finds no support for widely held (and published) belief that women are more influenceable than men in a variety of situations. Eagly suggests that contextual features of experimental settings may have produced sex differences (there were more studies finding female influenceability prior to 1970 than after), and that various psychological processes that may mediate persuasion and conformity (propensity to yield in female sex role, tendency to be oriented to interpersonal goals in group settings) may produce sex differences as well.

671. Eagly, Alice H., and Shelly Chaiken. "An Attribution Analysis of the Effect of Communicator Characteristics on Opinion Change: The Case of Communicator Attractiveness." *Journal of Personality and Social Psychology,* 32 (1975), 136-144.

From a total of 258 male and female undergraduates, some read a message from a source who was either attractive (praised undergraduates) or not (insulted undergraduates) and who took either a desirable or undesirable position on two topics. Other undergraduates estimated the likelihood the communicator would take either position. These estimators felt that an unattractive communicator would take an undesirable position. The attractive communicator was more persuasive than the unattractive with the reader subjects, and the desirable positions more persuasive than the undesirable ones. An attractive communicator on an undesirable topic was more persuasive than an unattractive communicator, but both were equally persuasive on the desirable topic.

* Falbo, Toni. "Relationships Between Sex, Sex Role, and Social Influence." *Psychology of Women Quarterly,* 2 (1977), 62-72. See item 224.

* Freese, Lee. "Conditions for Status Equality in Informal Task Groups." *Sociometry,* 37 (1974), 174-188. See item 232.

672. Giesen, Martin, and Clyde Hendrick. "Effects of a Fake Positive and Negative Arousal Feedback on Persuasion." *Journal of Personality and Social Psychology,* 30 (1974), 449-457.

Two experiments used 100 and 151 female undergraduates respectively in a persuasion study with high and low levels of intensity of pleasant or unpleasant feedback, all false feedback. High-arousal feedback condition resulted in more persuasion than low-arousal, regardless of emotion associated with it, including fear (second experiment).

673. Goldberg, Carlos. "Conformity to Majority Type as a Function of Task and Acceptance of Sex-Related Stereotypes." *Journal of Psychology,* 89 (1975), 25-37.

In this study, 204 female and male college students were measured on conformity, masculinity-femininity, and women's liberation instruments to determine conformity patterns of those who accept conventional sex-role stereotypes. With male-related items, feminine female and anti-liberation males and females conformed most to proported all-male majority opinion of a previous sample. Since female subjects conformed more to an all-male majority, while male subjects conformed to the same extent to all-male, all-female, and mixed groups, Goldberg suggests that the women's movement may be having a greater impact on men than on women.

674. Gordon, George N. *Persuasion: The Theory and Practice of Manipulative Communication.* New York: Hastings House, 1971.

In his chapter on "Women," Gordon traces two myths associated with women. The first, from ancient times, derived from Cassandra and Pandora, sees women as intuitive and in tune with the mystical, sometimes with evil results. The second, a modern myth, which notes the irrelevance of femininity in a world of technology and "supposed equality" with men, centers on women as second-class citizens. Because of this mythic ambiguity, women are subject to certain kinds of persuasion. Women consumers are "highly manipulable" when the appeal to them is placed in context of one of the two myths. Persuasion generally accompanies affirmations of these roles of women, the traditionally feminine one as well as the women-as-equal one. "Because ideas of feminine martyrdom are cherished by most women," persuasion is more likely when both myths are addressed.

675. Gouaux, Charles. "Induced Affective States and Interpersonal Attraction." *Journal of Personality and Social Psychology,* 20 (1971), 37-43.

Using 110 female undergraduates because "they are relatively more suggestible than males," the author tested the effect of induced mood state on attraction for a female stranger and found that elation significantly affected attraction positively and depression significantly affected it negatively.

676. Grossnickle, William F., Rosina C. Lao, C.T. Martoccia, Donna C. Range, and Frances C. Walters. "Complexity of Effects of Personal Space." *Psychological Reports*, 36 (1975), 237-238.

In two studies designed to replicate previous ones that found attitude change a function of distance, results failed to support the effect. In one with 90 undergraduates of each sex systematically arranged to hear three different topics at three different distances, only the message itself had significant impact on attitude change. In the other, the only significant difference found in perception of speaker was that close physical distance aroused negative reactions. No sex differences were found.

677. Harris, Mary B., and Hortensia Baudin. "The Language of Altruism: The Effects of Language, Dress, and Ethnic Group." *The Journal of Social Psychology*, 91 (1973), 37-41.

In a field study using 96 Spanish-and English-speaking males and females dressed alternately well or poorly seeking change from Spanish-looking males and females (N = 48) at a state fair, neither sex of requester nor of fair patron affected level of favorable response, though ethnic group and dress condition did.

678. Hollander, Steven W. "Effects of Forewarning Factors on Pre- and Postcommunication Attitude Change." *Journal of Personality and Social Psychology*, 30 (1974), 272-278.

This study used 240 male and female undergraduates in a test of change of attitude toward Peace Corps when the levels of context (open persuasion or disguised), of warning (topic information given or not), of message style (advertisement or not) and sex were manipulated. Subjects who anticipated receiving a message (warning) had precommunication attitude change in the open persuasion but not the disguised condition. Both warning and context manipulations increased postcommunication change for females but not for males.

679. Infante, Dominic A., and Robin A. Grimmett. "Attitudinal Effects of Utilizing a Critical Method of Analysis." *The Central States Speech Journal*, 22 (1971), 213-217.

Eighty-one female and 81 male undergraduates, trained to use a critical method for analyzing a controversial message, responded to a semantic differential after listening to a 12-minute tape-recorded persuasive speech. Training influenced the number of arguments discovered and increased the persuasibility of males and decreased the persuasibility of females.

680. Javornisky, Gregory. "Task Content and Sex Differences in Conformity." *The Journal of Social Psychology,* 108 (1979), 213-220.

To study the effects of sex and type of task on conformity, three-person same or mixed-sex groups of 48 naive subjects and 62 confederates, plus an additional 74 in a nongroup situation, responded to a consumer-item questionnaire. No significant main effect of sex on conformity was found, but sex-related items on the questionnaire were conformed to by the opposite sex in the triad condition.

681. Jenks, Richard J. "Effects of Sex, Locus of Control, and Issue on Attitude Change." *The Journal of Social Psychology,* 106 (1978), 283-284.

This summary of a research project on effects of internal or external locus of control and sex on persuasibility reports that externals changed their attitude more than internals and females more than males. No significant interaction between sex and issue appeared though internal and external females showed considerable differences on individual issues.

682. Juhnke, Ralph, Challenger Vought, Thomas A. Pyszczynski, Francis C. Dane, Bruce D. Losure, and Lawrence S. Wrightsman. "Effects of Presentation Mode Upon Mock Jurors' Reactions to a Trial." *Personality and Social Psychology Bulletin,* 5 (1979), 36-39.

Eighty-five female and 81 male undergraduates gave verdicts and rated the effectiveness of attorneys' presentations in a criminal trial presented by videotape, audiotape, transcript, or summary. More guilty verdicts came from the videotape mode for both sexes, who also found in the videotaped mode that the prosecutor was more conclusive. Overall, females were more influenced by the prosecutor than males were.

683. Kempe, Linda J., Patrick Maloney, and Faye H. Dambrot. "Persuasibility of Women: Conventional Wisdom Re-Examined." *Psychology of Women Quarterly,* 3 (1978), 198-202.

This study examined sex differences in persuasibility at differing levels of topic involvement. After a pilot study which showed no sex differences, 162 male and 134 female undergraduates responded to written persuasive communication on either high- or low-involvement topics, in all cases the position taken being against the opinions held by a majority. No significant sex differences on persuasibility were found, whether topics were low or high involvement ones.

684. Kohn, Paul M., and Gordon E. Barnes. "Subject Variables and Reactance to Persuasive Communications About Drugs." *European Journal of Social Psychology*, 7 (1977), 97-109.

To investigate the effects of sex, authoritarianism, rebelliousness, and suspicion in the reactance to pro- and anti-LSD messages, 80 male and 109 female undergraduates were given written persuasive messages. Responses indicated that resistance occurred with the pro-LSD message among highly suspicious male subjects only. It was suggested that resistance could have been a response to perceived threat from the experimenter rather than, or as well as, response to the communication, and that the responses reflected culturally acquired differences in sex-role behavior.

* LaCrosse, Michael B. "Nonverbal Behavior and Perceived Counselor Attractiveness and Persuasiveness." *Journal of Counseling Psychology*, 22 (1975), 563-566. See item 547.

685. Lehmann, Stanley. "Personality and Compliance: A Study of Anxiety and Self-Esteem in Opinion and Behavior Change." *Journal of Personality and Social Psychology*, 15 (1970), 76-86.

One hundred and fifty new mothers who had had normal deliveries at a hospital in an economically deprived area were tested for personality measures and opinions within two days of delivery and were interviewed two weeks later with either a threatening or a reassuring message about returning for a check-up. The threat was effective for low-anxious subjects, and reassurance was effective for high-anxious ones. High self-esteem, high-anxiety subjects were even more susceptible to reassurance, and compliance was greater for all experimental subjects than for the control group (no message).

* McGinley, Hugh, Richard LeFevre, and Pat McGinley. "The Influence of a Communicator's Body Position on Opinion Change in Others." *Journal of Personality and Social Psychology*, 31 (1975), 686-690. See item 1035.

* McGinley, Hugh, Karen Nicholas, and Patsy McGinley. "Effects of Body Position and Attitude Similarity on Interpersonal Attraction and Opinion Change." *Psychological Reports*, 42 (1978), 127-138. See item 1036.

686. Maddux, James E., and Ronald W. Rogers. "Effects of Source Expertness, Physical Attractiveness, and Supporting Arguments on Persuasion: A Case of Brains over Beauty." *Journal of Personality and Social Psychology*, 39 (1980), 235-244.

    One hundred six female college students read persuasive statements attributed to an expert or nonexpert source, either attractive or unattractive, with or without supporting arguments, and then completed a questionnaire concerning the source and the message. Agreement with source was greater for expert than for nonexpert, and for source who used supporting arguments than for source who did not, the impact of these two conditions being independent and additive. Attractiveness had no main or interaction effects on persuasion.

* Madsen, Daniel B. "Issue Importance and Group Choice Shifts: A Persuasive Arguments Approach." *Journal of Personality and Social Psychology*, 36 (1978), 1118-27. See item 264.

* Maier, Norman R.F. "Male Versus Female Discussion Leaders." *Personnel Psychology*, 23 (1970), 455-461. See item 610.

687. Mann, Leon, Kim Paleg, and Russell Hawkins. "Effectiveness of Staged Disputes in Influencing Bystander Crowds." *Journal of Personality and Social Psychology*, 36 (1978), 725-732.

    Two field experiments, one comparing a staged dispute versus a direct appeal, and the other comparing concession of one disputant to superiority of the other's argument versus no concession, revealed, in the first, that both methods resulted in persuasion of bystanders, and, in the second, that concession caused increasing persuasion. Female bystanders, however, were positively influenced with concession and negatively influenced by non-concession. Males were affected positively regardless of concession. The first experiment used 501 commuters (277 M, 224 F), the second 564 shoppers (356 F, 208 M), and both were conducted in Adelaide, Australia.

688. Montgomery, Charles L., and Michael Burgoon. "An Experimental Study of the Interactive Effects of Sex and Androgyny on Attitude Change." *Communication Monographs*, 44 (1977), 130-135.

    Probing previous findings that females are more persuasible than males, the authors tested the hypotheses that traditionally sex-typed females would change attitudes significantly more than traditionally sex-typed males, and that the difference between those two groups would be greater than the difference between androgynous females and androgynous males. Forty-two male and 42 female undergraduates, divided into groups both by gender and by sex role as determined by median split on the Bem Sex-Role Inventory, completed pre- and post-persuasive message attitude measures. Analysis of variance supported both hypotheses.

689. Morelock, Judy C. "Sex Differences in Susceptibility to Social Influence." *Sex Roles*, 6 (1980), 537-548.

    Sex differences in compliance and persuasiveness were examined while varying the sex-role relevance of the statements. One hundred thirty-six male and female undergraduates were asked to respond to opinion statements previously discussed by a bogus group. Subjects read the group's unanimous opinion accompanying each statement and were told they would participate in a discussion with this group; sex was manipulated by showing subjects all-male or all-female names of group members. Compliance was measured by the extent to which a subject's response approximated the "group's" opinion. Males were more compliant than females when the statements concerned female sex-role related activities, and females were more compliant than males when the statements concerned male sex-role related activities.

690. Newton, Rae R., and Gary I. Schulman. "Sex and Conformity: A New View." *Sex Roles*, 3 (1977), 511-521.

    This study employing 97 undergraduates tested the hypotheses that females would be more influenced by a group than males and that females would be more subject to the normative influence of the group. Neither hypothesis was supported. Sex differences found were explained in terms of direction of influence, rather than in conformity for females and independence for males.

691. Norman, Ross. "When What Is Said Is Important: A Comparison of Expert and Attractive Sources." *Journal of Experimental Social Psychology*, 12 (1976), 294-300.

A source, manipulated as physically attractive or expert, suggested that less than eight hours' sleep was needed, either as unadorned opinion or with supporting arguments. The evaluations of 98 female undergraduates revealed that the expert source was ineffective in influencing subjects unless he had arguments, while the attractive source brought about agreement whether or not arguments were included. Expert with arguments influenced agreement more than any other condition.

692. Pallak, Michael S., Margaret Mueller, Kathleen Dollar, and Judith Pallak. "Effect of Commitment on Responsiveness to an Extreme Consonant Communication." *Journal of Personality and Social Psychology*, 23 (1972), 429-436.

In the first of two studies, 104 female undergraduates received communication from a partner advocating a more or a less extreme view than the subject and were led to expect an interaction with the same or a different partner next time. Commitment to future interaction facilitated attitude change toward the partner's position, no matter which direction it took. In the second study, 102 female undergraduates wrote a personal essay consonant with their beliefs under public (to be published) or private conditions, followed by either an attack on their beliefs or agreement taking even more extreme position. Again change occurred toward the more extreme view, and public commitment led to greater resistance to changing one's position.

693. Plax, Timothy G., and Lawrence B. Rosenfeld. "Antecedents of Change in Attitudes of Males and Females." *Psychological Reports*, 41 (1977), 811-821.

Seventy-four female and 82 male college students completed personality measures and pre- and post-measures of attitudes toward a message. A multiple discriminant analysis of personality measures with level of attitude change revealed that high-changing females were obliging and changeable, while high-changing males were ordered, dependent, unstable. Low-changing females were aggressive and unchanging; low-changing males forceful, efficient, and well-informed.

694. Rosenfeld, Lawrence B., and Vickie R. Christie. "Sex and Persuasibility Revisited." *Western Speech,* 38 (1974), 244-253.

   Sixty male and female undergraduates were asked to change their neutral attitudes toward meaningless trigrams to the attitude they held for the nouns associated with the trigrams. Attitude change was measured by a semantic differential scale. Females did not show any more attitude change than males on thirteen of fifteen comparisons. Included is a detailed review of 21 studies on female persuasibility.

695. Ryckman, Richard M., and William C. Rodda. "Conformity in College Men and Women as a Function of Locus of Control and Prior Group Support." *The Journal of Social Psychology,* 86 (1972), 313-314.

   This brief summary is of an experimental study using male and female undergraduates (no N given), either internal or external in locus of control, in a task, first with reinforcement and then with criticism. Internal males conformed (to what in experiment not explained) more than external males, and external females more than internal females. External females conformed most of all.

696. Shaffer, David R., and Carole Tabor. "Salience of Own and Others' Attitudes as Determinants of Self-Persuasion." *The Journal of Social Psychology,* 111 (1980), 225-236.

   To test the competing predictions derived from self-perception theory, reinforcement theory, and dissonance theory, 60 female undergraduates wrote counterattitudinal essays under conditions of their own attitudes being made salient or not, either with or without feedback about others' opinions, and, if the former, either agreeing or disagreeing feedback. Post-attitudinal measures indicated that neither support nor non-support from others affected attitudes, but that the salience manipulation did, thus supporting the dissonance prediction.

697. Sistrunk, Frank. "Masculinity-Femininity and Conformity." *The Journal of Social Psychology,* 87 (1972), 161-162.

   As a follow-up to earlier studies that found that conformity tended to be shown by one sex on a task generally associated with the opposite sex (see item 698), Sistrunk used the 10 most masculine and 10 most feminine college undergraduates (measured on the Guilford-Zimmerman masculinity scale) from a pool of 42 in such tasks. Findings generally supported the earlier ones, with no significant differences by sex on conformity. Feminine subjects conformed more than masculine ones on masculine tasks, and masculine subjects conformed more than feminine subjects on feminine tasks.

698. Sistrunk, Frank, and John W. McDavid. "Sex Variable in Conforming Behavior." *Journal of Personality and Social Psychology*, 17 (1971), 200-207.

Four empirical studies using male and female undergraduates and high school students in experiments controlled for sex relatedness of the task items revealed that females conformed more on masculine items, males conformed more on feminine items, and generally there was no difference in conformity levels on neutral items. These findings reveal the previous generalization that females conform more than men is misleading.

699. Smith, Kay H. "Conformity as Related to Masculinity, Self, and Other Descriptions, Suspicion, and Artistic Preference by Sex Groups." *The Journal of Social Psycology*, 80 (1970), 79-88.

In this experimental study, 177 male and female subjects were tested on measures of artistic sensitivity, masculinity-femininity, and conformity, and from that group 45 females and 41 males were placed in a group-pressure situation in which they had to respond true/false when the responses of the bogus others in the group were contrasted to theirs. Females did not conform more than males, contrary to previous findings.

700. Steinbacher, Roberta, and Faith D. Gilroy. "Persuasibility and Persuasiveness as a Function of Sex." *The Journal of Social Psychology*, 100 (1976), 299-306.

In this study, 128 undergraduates, selected for sex and social attitudes, were distributed in groups of four systematically varied to have a lone disserter trying to persuade opposite-sex others or same-sex others. No significant sex differences in amount of change were found in the lone dissenters, but female dissenters were more effective than males in changing opinions of both male and female groups, significantly so for male groups.

* Wahrman, Ralph, and Meredith D. Pugh. "Sex, Nonconformity and Influence." *Sociometry*, 37 (1974), 137-147. See item 174.

701. Wheeless, Lawrence R. "The Effects of Comprehension Loss on Persuasion." *Speech Monographs*, 38 (1971), 327-330.

    This study examined the interaction of rate of speech (normal or speeded up), sex of source, and environment of receiver (alone or in group) with comprehension, persuasion, attitude toward message, and perceived source authoritativeness and character. A total of 138 undergraduates, randomly assigned to various group or individual settings, completed comprehension, persuasive, and various personality measures after hearing a normal or speeded up taped message by a male or female speaker. Significant interactions involving sex included the female source being comprehended better at normal rate and worse at compressed rate. The male source was rated higher in authoritativeness.

702. Wheeless, Lawrence R. "Some Effects of Time-Compressed Speech on Persuasion." *Journal of Broadcasting*, 15 (1971), 415-420.

    Persuasive messages delivered by a male or a female speaker were presented at various speeds to 238 male and female undergraduates, who evaluated their chances of buying the product being sold, their attitude toward the message, and the authoritativeness and character of the source of the message. Frequency of planned purchase and attitude toward a message were not affected by differences in rate conditions of recorded messages. Perceived source authoritativeness and character decreased when speech was compressed even at the relatively low level of 30%. Sex of source did not interact with rate, but the male source was perceived as more authoritative than the female source.

703. Wilder, David A. "Perception of Groups, Size of Opposition, and Social Influence." *Journal of Experimental Social Psychology*, 13 (1977), 253-268.

    Two experiments, one with 53 females, the other with 304 males and females, all undergraduates, were designed to show the interaction between social influence and the number of persons attempting to influence. These influencers were manipulated to seem like one group, like representatives of a number of groups, or like separate, unrelated individuals. Conformity to opinion increased as the number of separate groups and/or individuals increased. Varying the size of a single group had little effect. No sex differences in conformity were found.

SELF DISCLOSURE

* Annis, Lawrence V., and Donald F. Perry. "Self-disclosure Modeling in Same-sex and Mixed-sex Unsupervised Groups." *Journal of Counseling Psychology*, 24 (1977), 370-372. See item 188.

704. Archer, Richard L., and John H. Berg. "Disclosure Reciprocity and Its Limits: A Reactance Analysis." *Journal of Experimental Social Psychology*, 14 (1978), 527-540.

Sixty male and 60 female subjects were approached singly in public places by a male or a female experimenter who disclosed on low, medium, or high levels of intimacy and then either said subject's response could be on that topic (restoration of freedom condition) or not. Subjects' levels of intimacy reciprocated experimenter's levels, and the restoration of freedom condition enhanced intimacy level. The number of words of responses to female experimenters increased with intimacy level, while for male experimenters it increased between low and medium levels and decreased between medium and high levels. Female subjects responded with a greater number of words after restoration of freedom than male subjects. Discussion of implications of sex interaction with disclosure levels and societal norms is included.

705. Archer, Richard L., John H. Berg, and Thomas E. Runge. "Active and Passive Observers' Attraction to a Self-Disclosing Other." *Journal of Experimental Social Psychology*, 16 (1980), 130-145.

Eighty female undergraduates made either high or low intimacy disclosures to a confederate, who responded via videotape with either high or low intimacy, and then the undergraduates evaluated the attractiveness of the confederate. Eighty additional female undergraduates viewed an original discloser and the confederate's response and predicted the attractiveness rating. The more intimate confederate was preferred by both participants and observers, but the active participants' attraction ratings were more positive than were the observers' ratings. Methodological implications are discussed.

706. Arlett, Christine, J. Allan Best, and Brian R. Little. "The Influence of Interviewer Self-Disclosure and Verbal Reinforcement on Personality Tests." *Journal of Clinical Psychology,* 32 (1976), 770-775.

The responses of 20 undergraduates, 10 of each sex, to self-disclosure measures given under various conditions revealed that females were more self-disclosing than males. Males increased self-disclosure under a verbal reinforcement condition. Interviewer self-disclosure increased the favorable perception of both self and interviewer, especially for males, and increased social evaluation anxiety for females.

707. Bath, Kent E., and Daniel L. Daly. "Self-Disclosure: Relationships to Self-Described Personality and Sex Differences." *Psychology Reports,* 31 (1972), 623-628.

From scores on a self-report personality measure, 48 male and female undergraduates were formed into four groups and given two disclosure tests, one written and another oral, in a dyad with the experimenter. Self-descriptions of dominance and interpersonal closeness predicted high levels of written disclosure, but only the hate end of the love/hate dimension predicted high oral disclosure. Females reported more disclosure than males.

709. Bender, V. Lee, Yvonne Davis, Oliver Glover, and Joy Stapp. "Patterns of Self-Disclosure in Homosexual and Heterosexual College Students." *Sex Roles,* 2 (1976), 149-160.

To investigate patterns of self-disclosure in college students, 18 homosexual males, 21 homosexual females, 27 heterosexual males, and 26 heterosexual females responded to questionnaires on psychological masculinity and femininity and self-disclosure. Results revealed a correlation between self-disclosure and femininity, but not masculinity. Homosexual males and heterosexual females scored higher on both femininity and self-disclosure, but there was no significant difference in total disclosure between homosexual and heterosexual subjects. The conclusion was that psychological femininity and masculinity were more important than biological sex in determining self-disclosure.

709. Berger, Charles R., Royce R. Gardner, Glen W. Clatterbuck, and Linda S. Schulman. "Perceptions of Information Sequencing in Relationship Development." *Human Communication Research,* 3 (1976), 29-46.

In this study, 204 adult subjects (60% female) were asked to sort 150 statements according to their estimate of when each statement would first be made during a two-hour conversation between two strangers. Analyses were conducted on the items employing many variables, but only desired number of friends, age, sex, and education produced significant differences. No clear relationship between sex and the tendency to place items early or late in the time sequence was found, nor was there support for the proposition that females tend to be higher disclosers than males.

710. Berger, Stephen E., Jim Millham, Leonard I. Jacobson, and Kenneth N. Anchor. "Prior Self-Disclosure, Sex Differences, and Actual Confiding in an Interpersonal Encounter." *Small Group Behavior,* 9 (1978), 555-562.

The purposes of the study were to analyze the target and source of personal disclosures, to determine whether the greater openness associated with women is a self-reported tendency or an actual sex difference, and to test the hypothesis that recipients of personal disclosures must disclose themselves regardless of the behavior of others. Subjects were 28 male and 24 female undergraduates, each of whom brought a same-sex friend who served as a partner. Women disclosed and received more personal information in the dyadic situation than men did. Prior self-reports of disclosing behavior were related to actual confiding behavior, and, in order to be confided in, one had to disclose noncontingently and without regard to the disclosing behavior of others.

711. Bridges, Judith S. "Correlates of Sex Role and Attitudes toward Women." *Psychological Reports,* 43 (1978), 1279-82.

The Bem Sex-Role Inventory, the Attitudes Toward Women Scale, and either a cognitive scale or a self-disclosure scale were given to 322 male and female undergraduates. For both sexes, being sex-role traditional was correlated with high self-disclosure, although the person being interacted with made a difference to level of disclosure. Being a feminine female correlated with conservative attitudes toward women. Liberal attitudes toward women were related to high self-disclosure in males. Cognitive complexity was unrelated to sex role or to attitudes.

712. Brockner, Joel, and Walter C. Swap. "Effects of Repeated Exposure and Attitudinal Similarity on Self-Disclosure and Interpersonal Attraction." *Journal of Personality and Social Psychology,* 33 (1976), 531-540.

Using 64 college females encountering either similar or dissimilar others a systematically varied number of times, authors found subjects more attracted to a similar other, and rated the most frequently encountered other more positively and disclosed to them more.

713. Casciani, Joseph M. "Influence of Model's Race and Sex on Interviewee's Self-Disclosure." *Journal of Counseling Psychology,* 25 (1978), 435-440.

Twenty-four female and 24 male undergraduates responded to a videotape of a model for disclosure, varied by race, sex, and length of disclosure on ten topics, half favorable, half not. Neither depth of disclosure, duration, nor number of self-references of subjects was related to model's race or length of disclosure, or to subject's own scores on self-disclosure questionnaire. Subjects disclosed at greater length and depth to same-sex than to opposite-sex partner.

714. Cash, Thomas F. "Self-Disclosure in Initial Acquaintanceship: Effects of Sex, Approval Motivation, and Physical Attractiveness." *JSAS: Catalog of Selected Documents in Psychology,* 8 (1978), 11. (Ms. No. 1642).

Forty-eight male and female undergraduates in both same- and opposite-sex stranger dyads wrote and exchanged self-descriptions which were analyzed for self-disclosure. Females both gave and received more self-disclosures than males. Physically attractive partners received more disclosure in same-sex dyads. In opposite-sex dyads, subjects presented themselves in a more favorable, less critical light to physically attractive partners.

715. Certner, Barry C. "Exchange of Self-Disclosures in Same-Sexed Groups of Strangers." *Journal of Consulting and Clinical Psychology,* 40 (1973), 292-297.

Eight same-sex groups of four male or female undergraduates discussed topics scaled for intimacy. A mutual exchange of disclosures and a positive relationship between self-disclosure and liking were found. Unlike other studies, no sex differences in self-disclosure or in liking patterns were found.

716. Chelune, Gordon J. "A Multidimensional Look at Sex and Target Differences in Disclosure." *Psychological Reports,* 39 (1976), 259-263.

Twelve male and 12 female undergraduates, selected for extreme scores on a repression-sensitization scale, were interviewed by a male interviewer, a female interviewer, and taped in a self-report situation on topics pre-rated for degree of intimacy. Females verbalized significantly more, on more intimate topics, and at a higher rate per minute, but not in percent of self-references for total discourse. That is, there was no significant difference in amount of information disclosed, but females disclosed more intimate information. All subjects verbalized more in the live interviews than in self-reports, disclosed more to the male interviewer than in self-reports, and maintained affective congruence more with the male than with the female interviewer.

717. Chelune, Gordon J. "Reactions to Male and Female Disclosure at Two Levels." *Journal of Personality and Social Psychology,* 34 (1976), 1000-03.

Twenty female and 20 male undergraduates evaluated two male and two female discussants on perceived emotional health and likeability. Male speakers were rated as healthier than female speakers regardless of disclosure level. Male speakers were liked most when low disclosers; female speakers when high disclosers. Female subjects were more discriminating between conditions than male subjects.

718. Chelune, Gordon J. "Sex Differences and Relationship Between Repression-Sensitization and Self-Disclosure." *Psychological Reports,* 37 (1975), 920.

Forty-one males and 38 females completed a repression-sensitization (measuring styles of coping with threatening stimuli) and self-disclosure measures. Though no sex differences emerged on the first measure, the interaction between the two measures revealed that male sensitizers tended to be high self-disclosers. Chelune suggests that the sex difference in coping behavior may be sex-role stereotyped: females threatened in interpersonal situations can perhaps elicit help if they make themselves more vulnerable by self-disclosing; for males in the same situation, maintaining distance interpersonally is a better strategy.

719. Chelune, Gordon J. "Sex Differences, Repression-Sensitization, and Self-Disclosure: A Behavioral Look." *Psychological Reports,* 40 (1977), 667-670.

Twelve males and 12 females, all undergraduates, selected by scores on the Repression-Sensitization Scale to represent sensitizers (those who cope with conflict through rumination or intellectualization) or repressors (avoid conflict by denial or withdrawal), were interviewed by either a male or a female interviewer. Male repressors made fewer negative self-references than male sensitizers, while female repressors made more negative self-references than female sensitizers only in the opposite-sex interview condition. In same-sex interviews, both male and female subjects had significantly more negative self-references than either positive or neutral ones.

720. Chelune, Gordon J., and Associates. *Self-Disclosure: Origins, Patterns, and Implications of Openness in Interpersonal Relationships.* San Francisco: Jossey-Bass Publishers, 1979. See items 759 and 766.

721. Chelune, Gordon J., Faye E. Sultan, and Carolyn L. Williams. "Loneliness, Self-Disclosure, and Interpersonal Effectiveness." *Journal of Counseling Psychology,* 27 (1980), 462-468.

One hundred fifty undergraduate women completed self-disclosure, loneliness, and social introversion measures and an activity questionnaire, as well as role played with a male confederate. Appropriate medium disclosure across situations was related to lower levels of loneliness than either high or low disclosure. Ratings of social skills both by peers and observer were positively related to dispositional disclosure but not to flexibility of disclosure or to level of loneliness. Those whose pattern of disclosure deviated from normal expectations showed decreased levels of social activity compared to those whose pattern did not.

722. Cozby, Paul C. "Self-Disclosure: A Literature Review." *Psychological Bulletin,* 79 (1973), 73-91.

This review of the literature on self-disclosure, over 100 articles, includes self-disclosure as a personality attribute, sex differences in interpersonal relationships, including of experimenter-subject, interviewer-interviewee, and therapist-client; and nonverbal aspects of self-disclosure. Self-disclosing behavior is seen as the product of two opposing forces, one to increase disclosure, the other to inhibit it. The first, studied most extensively, is given the most positive value, but researchers are beginning to see positive values in the second.

723. Cozby, Paul C. "Self-disclosure, Reciprocity and Liking." *Sociometry*, 35 (1972), 151-160.

    Thirty female undergraduates were exposed to three levels of self-disclosure by a "bogus" female peer. Subjects reciprocated intimacy level for low and medium conditions, but not for high; subjects rated high-disclosing person as less well-adjusted. Liking and self-disclosure were related in a curvilinear way.

724. Critelli, Joseph W., and Kathleen M. Dupre. "Self-Disclosure and Romantic Attraction." *The Journal of Social Psychology*, 106 (1978), 127-128.

    This summary of a questionnaire survey of 61 dating college couples revealed that self-disclosure and loving were significantly correlated on three of the four measures taken while self-disclosure and liking had no significant correlations.

* Davis, John D. "When Boy Meets Girl: Sex Roles and the Negotiation of Intimacy in an Acquaintance Exercise." *Journal of Personality and Social Psychology*, 36 (1978), 684-692. See item 110.

* Davis, John D., and Adrian E. G. Skinner. "Reciprocity of Self-Disclosure in Interviews: Modeling or Social Exchange?" *Journal of Personality and Social Psychology*, 29 (1974), 779-784. See item 111.

725. Derlega, Valerian, and Alan L. Chaikin. "Norms Affecting Self-Disclosure in Men and Women." *Journal of Consulting and Clinical Psychology*, 44 (1976), 376-380.

    Using 128 male and female undergradautes rating fictional males and females self-disclosing to a stranger about a car accident or about their mother in a psychiatric hospital, the authors found that both sexes rated the male as better adjusted when he did not disclose than when he did. By contrast, the female subject was rated better adjusted when she did self disclose than when she did not.

726. Derlega, Valerian J., and Alan L. Chaikin. "Privacy and Self-Disclosure in Social Relationships." *Journal of Social Issues,* 33, No. 3 (1977), 102-115.

The relationship bewteen self-disclosure and privacy is developed using evidence from research. A brief discussion on the differences between disclosure patterns of women and men is included. Women disclose more and are less selective than men in choosing targets for self-disclosure. Women seem to be encouraged to disclose information which exposes their weaknesses; men seem to be encouraged to disclose information which depicts their strengths.

727. Derlega, Valerian J., Marian S. Harris, and Alan L. Chaikin. "Self-Disclosure Reciprocity, Liking and the Deviant." *Journal of Experimental Social Psychology,* 9 (1973), 277-284.

A confederate disclosed at high or low levels or at high deviant (lesbian encounter) level in a dyad with 66 female undergraduates, whose own disclosure level was analyzed. Subjects' willingness to disclose was a positive function of the amount of disclosure from the confederate, regardless of the liking of that confederate.

728. Derlega, Valerian J., Midge Wilson, and Alan L. Chaikin. "Friendship and Disclosure Reciprocity." *Journal of Personality and Social Psychology,* 34 (1976), 578-582.

This study investigated reciprocity of self-disclosure in friend or stranger dyads. Subjects, 48 female undergraduates, each of whom brought one close female friend to the experiment, were given self-disclosure messages of either high or low intimacy written by a friend or a stranger. Reciprocity of self-disclosure was more likely between stranger dyads than friend dyads. Intimacy of subjects' responses was independent of the intimacy of the initial disclosure input in friends' dyads but varied with the level of intimacy in stranger dyads.

729. Domelsmith, David E., and James T. Dietch. "Sex Differences in the Relationship Between Machiavellianism and Self-Disclosure." *Psychological Reports,* 42 (1978), 715-721.

Measures of machiavellianism and self-disclosure, given to 48 male and 77 female undergraduates, were correlated. For males, machiavellianism was significantly correlated with unwillingness to self-disclose, while for females, machiavellianism was significantly correlated with willingness. The preferred explanation was that female goals are more "social" (as opposed to males' goals), and hence those willing to use manipulative techniques to be successful could successfully use self-disclosure as a tactic.

730. Doster, Joseph A. "Sex Role Learning and Interview Communication." *Journal of Counseling Psychology*, 23 (1976), 482-485.

Thirty-two undergraduate women completed a measure of parental identification and then talked to a male interviewer on six topics designed for varying levels of difficulty of self-disclosure. Women who identified with their fathers disclosed significantly more than those who identified with their mothers and were more spontaneous and voluble. Daughters who modeled after conventional-role mothers disclosed less.

* Feldstein, JoAnn C. "Effects of Counselor Sex and Sex Role and Client Sex on Clients' Perceptions and Self-Disclosure in a Counseling Analogue Study." *Journal of Counseling Psychology*, 26 (1979), 437-443. See item 533.

731. Gelman, Richard, and Hugh McGinley. "Interpersonal Liking and Self-Disclosure." *Journal of Consulting and Clinical Psychology*, 46 (1978), 1549-51.

Brief report of a study of the interaction of 66 college females' willingness to discuss topics with a stranger seen on a videotape discussing ten social issues, and their liking and attitude similarity. Characteristic level of self-disclosure and liking for stranger were significantly positively related to level of willingness to disclose to stranger, while attitude similarity was not a significant predictor of disclosure.

732. Gilbert, Shirley J. "Self Disclosure, Intimacy and Communication in Families." *The Family Coordinator*, 25, No. 3 (1976), 221-231.

This exploratory study cites research which suggests a curvilinear relationship between self-disclosure and interpersonal satisfaction in long-term relationships. Since negative disclosers are high in rate of unhappy marriages, Gilbert suggests that self-disclosers should not be classified only by those that do and those that do not, but also by kind of disclosure. These findings are analyzed within the framework of intimacy, suggesting the need to re-think the current constructs of self-disclosure and intimacy.

733. Gilbert, Shirley J., and David Horenstein. "The Communication of Self-Disclosure: Level Versus Valence." *Human Communication Research,* 1 (1975), 316-322.

To test the hypothesis that the degree of intimacy of disclosure would be less powerful than the positiveness or negativeness of the disclosure in affecting attraction for a discloser, 80 male and female undergraduates participated in a get-acquainted dyad with a male confederate who self-disclosed at two levels and with either positive or negative information (valence). The greatest degree of attraction for the confederate came when the content was positive, regardless of the degree of intimacy of the disclosure or of sex of subject.

734. Gilbert, Shirley J., and Gale G. Whiteneck. "Toward a Multi-dimensional Approach to the Study of Self-Disclosure." *Human Communication Research,* 2 (1976), 347-355.

Toward a theory of self-disclosure, two dimensions of disclosure content, degree of personalness (intimacy) and valence (positiveness or negativeness) as well as the gender of the discloser, timing of disclosure in relationship development, and the recipient of disclosure were studied. In Study I (N = 21 M, 21 F) the personalness and valence variables were manipulated. Analysis revealed significant main effects for all three factors, personalness, valence, and gender, with males more likely to make disclosures earlier in a heterosexual relationship than females. In Study II (19 M, 19 F) personalness and valence were manipulated. Analysis again revealed significant main effects for all three factors. Males were less likely than females to disclose positive statements, although both sexes were equally likely to disclose negative statements. The likelihood of making positive rather than negative disclosures was greatest when females were disclosing to strangers and acquaintances and when males were disclosing to parents, friends, and spouses. These results, with those from Study I, may suggest that males are more candid than females in the early stages of the development of a relationship.

735. Greenblatt, Lynda, James E. Hasenauer, and Vicki S. Freimuth. "Psychological Sex Type and Androgyny in the Study of Communication Variables: Self-Disclosure and Communication Apprehension." *Human Communication Research*, 6 (1980), 117-129.

To investigate the differences between sex and sex role on self-disclosure and communication apprehension, 544 male and female undergraduates completed the Bem Sex-Role Inventory, and some a self-disclosure questionnaire and others a communication-apprehension measure. Females had higher disclosure scores than males overall, and feminine females and androgynous males and females had highest disclosure scores, while masculine males had the lowest. Females did not report more communication apprehension than males, but feminine females reported greater apprehension than masculine males, and androgynous females less than feminine females. Authors concluded that psychological sex type is superior to biological sex in identifying patterns of self-disclosure and communication apprehension.

* Greene, Les R. "Effects of Verbal Evaluative Feedback and Interpersonal Distance on Behavioral Compliance." *Journal of Counseling Psychology*, 24 (1977), 10-14. See item 1157.

* Harrell, W. Andrew. "Physical Attractiveness, Self-Disclosure, and Helping Behavior." *The Journal of Social Psychology*, 104 (1978), 15-17. See item 1107.

* Hawkins, James L., Carol Weisberg, and Dixie L. Ray. "Marital Communication Style and Social Class." *Journal of Marriage and the Family*, 39 (1977), 479-490. See item 345.

736. Heilbrun, Alfred B., Jr. "History of Self-Disclosure in Females and Early Defection from Psychotherapy." *Journal of Counseling Psychology*, 20 (1973), 250-257.

Two studies of female college students (N = 126; 58), tested for likelihood of defection from psychotherapy, showed that those likely to defect had self-reported high disclosing levels, especially with males. In a controlled laboratory situation, those likely to defect disclosed more to male counselors while those likely to continue disclosed more to female counselors.

737. Higbee, Kenneth L. "Group Influence on Self-Disclosure." *Psychological Reports*, 32 (1973), 903-909.

In the first study, 109 female undergraduates via questionnaire responses indicated they perceived themselves as more willing to disclose than their peers, particularly on low-intimacy items to strangers. In the second study, 27 female undergraduates completed the same questionnaires, then talked about them in groups of three or four, and then filled out the questionnaire anew. Group discussion had a "risky shift" effect, and subjects were more willing to disclose after discussion than before, especially to a stranger.

738. Highlen, Pamela S., and Sheila F. Gillis. "Effects of Situational Factors, Sex, and Attitude on Affective Self-disclosure and Anxiety." *Journal of Counseling Psychology*, 25 (1978), 270-276.

Twenty male and 20 female undergraduates participated in this study to determine the effects of sex of subject, subject role (initiator, responder), type of feeling (positive, negative), and sex of best friend on affective self-disclosure (audiotaped performance test) and self-reported anxiety and attitude toward self-disclosure. Female subjects disclosed significantly more feelings than males, all subjects disclosed more positive than negative feelings, and more to same-sex than to opposite-sex best friend. All subjects reported significantly more anxiety when expressing negative feelings, especially females. Females expressed greater anxiety initiating negative feelings, while males expressed greater anxiety responding to negative anxiety.

* Hoffman, Mary A., and Gregory P. Spencer. "Effect of Interviewer Self-Disclosure and Interviewer-Subject Sex Pairing on Perceived and Actual Subject Behavior." *Journal of Counseling Psychology*, 24 (1977), 383-390. See item 544.

* Hoffman-Graff, Mary A. "Interviewer Use of Positive and Negative Self-Disclosure and Interviewer-Subject Sex Pairing." *Journal of Counseling Psychology*, 24 (1977), 184-190. See item 545.

739. Horenstein, David, and Shirley J. Gilbert. "Anxiety, Likeability, and Avoidance as Responses to Self-Disclosing Communication." *Small Group Behavior*, 7 (1976), 423-432.

Forty male and 40 female undergraduates were used to determine whether self-disclosure elicited anxiety and subsequent coping attempts in interactions with direct, open, or disclosing confederates. Interactions took place in two-person stranger dyads, and subjects responded to a perception questionnaire. High levels of intimate self-disclosure did not arouse more anxiety in subjects than low levels. Some indications that the confederate's self-disclosing elicited a degree of anxiety in subjects emerged, and this anxiety produced dislike of and a desire to avoid the confederate in the future.

740. Janofsky, A. Irene. "Affective Self-Disclosure Telephone Versus Face to Face Interviews." *Journal of Humanistic Psychology*, 11 (1971), 93-103.

To investigate whether subjects would be as willing to express their feelings over the telephone as in face-toface interviews, interviews between 80 males and 80 females from a university setting (students, staff, faculty) were conducted. No significant differences between the two interview modes occurred in the mean number of self-references, affective self-references, or the ratio of affective to total self-references. Highly significant differences in ratios were found between male and female interviewees on all three variables, however. Females made more self-references, more affective self-references, and had a higher affective self-reference/total self-reference ratio than males.

741. Johnson, David L., and Larry R. Ridener. "Self-Disclosure, Participation, and Perceived Cohesiveness in Small Group Interaction." *Psychological Reports*, 35 (1974), 361-362.

Two same-sex groups of eight, heterogeneous on basis of self-disclosure scores, and one homogeneous group of seven females met four times for group discussions on issues in higher education. Self-disclosure was correlated positively to perceived group cohesiveness, but not to participation. Males' self-disclosure was associated with perceived cooperation; females' with perceived norms and influence. Participation was correlated with perceived cohesiveness only for males; for neither males nor females was there a correlation between self-disclosure and perceived liking for other members of group.

742. Jourard, Sidney, and Robert Friedman. "Experimenter-Subject 'Distance' and Self-Disclosure." *Journal of*

Personality and Social Psychology, 15 (1970), 278-282.

In one study, male and female college students self-disclosed in three groups of eight of same sex under varying conditions of distance from experimenter and eye contact with him. Males increased disclosures with experimenter present; females decreased. As distance decreased between experimenter and subjects in an interview situation in the second experiment (32 M, 32 F), disclosure increased for both sexes, including in condition of minimal physical contact. Subjects also reported increased positive feelings and impression of experimenter.

* Jourard, Sidney M., and Peggy E. Jaffe. "Influence of an Interviewer's Disclosure on the Self-Disclosing Behavior of Interviewees." *Journal of Counseling Psychology,* 17 (1970), 252-257. See item 124.

743. Jourard, Sidney M., and Jaquelyn L. Resnick. "Some Effects of Self-Disclosure Among College Women." *Journal of Humanistic Psychology,* 10 (1970), 84-93.

From 80 undergraduate women who completed a questionnaire about self disclosing, twelve high disclosers and twelve low disclosers were chosen to participate in dyads, first with one who scored at the same level, and later with an opposite-level discloser. Analyses of both weighted and unweighted scores from the participants' responses showed that high disclosers revealed more to each other than low disclosers revealed to each other and that low disclosers revealed more to high disclosers than they did to low disclosers. High disclosers revealed about the same in both conditions.

* Kelser, George J., and Irwin Altman. "Relationship of Nonverbal Behavior to the Social Penetration Process." *Human Communication Research,* 2 (1976), 147-167. See item 1285.

744. Kirshner, Barry J., Robert R. Dies, and Robert A. Brown. "Effects of Experimental Manipulation of Self-Disclosure on Group Cohesiveness." *Journal of Consulting and Clinical Psychology,* 46 (1978), 1171-77.

Eight groups of eight, four of each sex, participated in 8-hour sessions under controlled high or low levels of intimacy of self-disclosure; higher levels of intimacy produced greater group cohesiveness.

745. Kohen, Janet. "Liking and Self-Disclosure in Opposite Sex Dyads." *Psychological Reports,* 36 (1975), 695-698.

    This study of 59 same-sex dyads of both males and females revealed that only the relationship between own self-disclosure and liking was significant and only for females. No relationship was found between partner's self-disclosure and liking nor between content and similarity of amount of self-disclosure and liking.

746. Kohen, Janet A.S. "The Development of Reciprocal Self-Disclosure in Opposite-Sex Interaction." *Journal of Counseling Psychology,* 22 (1975), 404-410.

    Analyses of the disclosure level in 65 taped opposite-sex dyads revealed a moderate degree of personal consistency in disclosure and a pattern of reciprocity. No sex difference in disclosure level was found.

747. Lombardo, John P., and Michael D. Berzonsky. "Sex Differences in Self-Disclosure During an Interview." *The Journal of Social Psychology,* 107 (1979), 281-282.

    In this replication of earlier studies on self-disclosure, same-sex dyads (N not given) discussed three topics: politics, religion, and sex. Females disclosed more on the more intimate topics of religion and sex, but not on politics, on which no sex differences appeared.

748. Lord, Charles G., and Wayne F. Velicer. "Effects of Sex, Birth Order, Target's Relationship and Target's Sex on Self-Disclosure by College Students." *Psychological Reports,* 37 (1975), 1167-70.

    A questionnaire survey of 145 college students of both sexes revealed that females self-disclosed more than males, both sexes disclosed more to friends than to siblings, and sibling disclosure was preferred with same sex, while with friends no sex preference was manifested. Firstborns disclosed somewhat more to friends and a great deal less to siblings than later-borns.

749. Lynn, Steven J. "Three Theories of Self-Disclosure Exchange." *Journal of Experimental Social Psychology,* 14 (1978), 466-479.

    Using 180 female subjects in intimate vs. superficial vs. no confederate disclosure, with positive or negative evaluation by confederate, and intimate or non-intimate disclosure established as normative, Lynn tested predictions from equitable exchange, social attraction, and normative information theories of self-disclosure. Findings supported equitable exchange theory in that subjects were more willing to disclose to a high- than to a low-disclosing partner, though that finding was more a function of low disclosure in response to low disclosure than a function of high response to high disclosure. Subjects did not completely match intimacy level of confederate, however, and normative information was a potent determinant of disclosure tendency. Social attraction theory had no support.

750. MacDonald, A.P., Jr., Vicki S. Kessel, and James B. Fuller. "Self-Disclosure and Two Kinds of Trust." *Psychological Reports,* 30 (1972), 143-148.

Using 37 male and 26 female undergraduates, tested on self-disclosure and the Rotter Interpersonal Trust Scale, playing the Prisoner's Dilemma game, the authors found self-disclosure was related to trust within the game, but not with trust as measured by the Scale. The authors suggest that the game and the Rotter Scale measure two kinds of trust. No significant differences by sex on these findings emerged.

751. Morgan, Brian S. "Intimacy of Disclosure Topics and Sex Differences in Self-Disclosure." *Sex Roles,* 2 (1976), 161-166.

Thirty-two male and 32 female college students responded to a self-disclosure questionnaire. The interaction of intimacy level and level of self-disclosure revealed that while males and females disclosed about the same amount of information on low-intimacy topics, females disclosed more on high-intimacy topics.

752. Pasternack, Thomas L., and Martha Van Landingham. "A Comparison of the Self-Disclosure Behavior of Female Undergraduates and Married Women." *Journal of Psychology,* 82 (1972), 233-240.

In twenty dyads of married and unmarried undergraduate females, alternately matched or crossed for previously measured self-disclosure level, authors found, contrary to expectation, no significant difference between self-disclosure level of married and unmarried. Low disclosers significantly increased their disclosure level when paired with high disclosers.

753. Pearce, W. Barnett, Paul H. Wright, Stewart M. Sharp, and Katherine M. Slama. "Affection and Reciprocity in Self-Disclosing Communication." *Human Communication Research*, 1 (1974), 5-14.

The relationship between self-disclosing communication between friends, affection, and reciprocity of disclosure was examined using three groups of undergraduates (total N = 183) in same-sex dyads of varying degrees of acquaintance. Unlike previous results, this study found that men, not women, had a higher correlation between affection and disclosure; and women, not men, were more successful in achieving similarity in disclosure.

754. Pearson, Judy C. "Sex Roles and Self-Disclosure." *Psychological Reports*, 47 (1980), 640.

To investigate the contradictory findings on which sex self-discloses more, Pearson had 210 female and 209 male undergraduates complete the Bem Sex-Role Inventory and the Self-disclosure Situations Survey. Subjects were classified as high, moderate, or low on the masculinity-femininity scales. Regression analysis revealed no significant difference in disclosure by sex. By sex role, however, masculine women self-disclosed more than women low in masculinity, and feminine men self-disclosed more than men low in femininity.

755. Pellegrini, Robert J., Robert A. Hicks, and Susan Myers-Winton. "Effects of Simulated Approval-Seeking and Avoiding on Self-Disclosure, Self-Presentation, and Interpersonal Attraction." *Journal of Psychology*, 98 (1978), 231-240.

Observing 48 undergraduate women assigned either an approval-seeking, an approval-avoiding, or no role in interaction with a male listener, researchers found those assigned a specific role disclosed significantly more than the no-role subjects. Approval-seeking subjects presented themselves more positively and approval-avoiding subjects more negatively than control subjects. The hypothesis that simulated attraction facilitates actual attraction was supported.

756. Pellegrini, Robert J., Robert A. Hicks, Susan Meyers-Winton, and Bruce G. Antal. "Physical Attractiveness and Self-Disclosure in Mixed-Sex Dyads." *The Psychological Record*, 28 (1978), 509-516.

Twenty-four female and 24 male undergraduates, selected to be physically attractive or unattractive, were interviewed by an opposite-sex confederate manipulated to be either attractive or unattractive, and a record of their self-disclosure kept. Intimacy of self-disclosure was greater for females and for unattractive subjects of both sexes. Attractive confederates elicited more intimate disclosure than unattractive confederates.

757. Rogers, Richard, and E. Wayne Wright. "Preliminary Study of Perceived Self-Disclosure." *Psychological Reports,* 38 (1976), 1334.

A total of 120 male and female undergraduates rated people seen at various distances in an audio-slide presentation on self-disclosure and themselves completed a self-disclosure questionnaire. No significant results were found between perceived self-disclosure and distance, sex, or own level of disclosure.

758. Rosenfeld, Lawrence B. "Self-Disclosure Avoidance: Why I Am Afraid to Tell You Who I Am." *Communication Monographs,* 46 (1979), 63-74.

Though the 140 male and 220 female undergraduates of this study avoided self-disclosure for similar reasons, stepwise multiple discriminant analysis of their answers to self-disclosure and self-disclosure avoidance measures showed that males gave a complex of reasons that reveal their object in non-self-disclosure was to maintain control in relationships. Females, on the other hand, gave reasons that reveal their object was to avoid personal hurt and problems with interpersonal relationships.

759. Rosenfeld, Lawrence B., Jean M. Civikly, and Jane F. Herron. "Anatomical and Psychological Sex Differences." In *Self-Disclosure: Origins, Patterns, and Implications of Openness in Interpersonal Relationships* (item 720), pp. 80-109.

Reviewing the literature which shows that the relationship between sex and self-disclosure is a complex one, the authors report on their own research which treated separately anatomical sex, psychological sex (as measured by the Bem Sex-Role Inventory), and self-disclosure to friend and to stranger. A total of 324 male and female undergraduates completed various pertinent measures, including Jourard's Self-Disclosure Questionnaire and Chelune's Self-Disclosure Situations Survey. Results were complex, but basically males disclosed more to strangers; no overall sex differences appeared in disclosure to friends. In disclosure to friends, topic and situational factors were important. Numerous differences by psychological sex type included different psychological sex types preferring disclosure targets of other sex types.

760. Roth, Marvin, and Don Kuiken. "Communication Immediacy, Cognitive Compatibility, and Immediacy of Self-Disclosure." *Journal of Counseling Psychology*, 22 (1975), 102-107.

On the basis of pretesting, 12 conceptually simple and 12 conceptually complex subjects of each sex were assigned to a confederate described as holding attitudes indicative of either a conceptually simple or complex person and who was either immediate or not in his disclosure. Subjects were slightly more immediate ("I become angry when my parents disrespect me" rather than "It makes you kind of angry when your parents disrespect you") when confederate was immediate and conceptually complex. If confederate was conceptually simple and immediate, disclosure of subjects was less immediate. Female subjects were more immediate in similar than in dissimilar dyads; male subjects were not.

761. Rubin, Zick, Charles T. Hill, Letitia A. Peplau, and Christine Dunkel-Schetter. "Self-Disclosure in Dating Couples: Sex Roles and the Ethic of Openness." *Journal of Marriage and the Family*, 42 (1980), 305-317.

This study investigated self-disclosure patterns in dating couples. Traditional sex roles call for greater disclosure by women, but an emerging ethic of openness calls for full and equal disclosure. Questionnaires were administered to 231 male and female undergraduates who were aware of both sets of expectations. Both men and women indicated that they had disclosed their thoughts and feelings fully to their partners in most areas, but women were identified as the more highly disclosing partners. Both men and women in couples with egalitarian sex-role attitudes disclosed more than those in couples with traditional sex-role attitudes. Self-disclosure was strongly related to respondents' reported love for their partners, but not to the power structure of their relationships.

762. Sermat, Vello, and Michael Smith. "Content Analysis of Verbal Communication in the Development of a Relationship." *Journal of Personality and Social Psychology*, 26 (1973), 332-346.

Two experiments used male and female undergraduates (N = 43 M, 43 F; 12 M, 12 F) in same-sex dyads to determine the influence of various levels of feedback on self-disclosure. Confederate's statements and questions which matched or exceeded subject's level of self-disclosure increased subject's level, especially confederate's questions. Sex differences found were that female subjects tended to ask more intimate questions; and male subjects, in condition of confederate's matching his level of disclosure, disclosed less than males in statement-exceed condition and than females in either statement-match or statement-exceed conditions. The authors postulate a sex-role-stereotyping influence, with male subjects reacting to a male confederate behaving in a way not expected of males.

763. Skotko, Vincent P., and Daniel Langmeyer. "The Effects of Interaction Distance and Gender on Self-Disclosure in the Dyad." *Sociometry*, 40 (1977), 178-182.

In mixed-sex dyads, 138 male and female undergraduates talked on six topics of increasing levels of intimacy at various distances. Males increased self-disclosure dramatically as distance increased, and females increased self-disclosure slightly as distance decreased. Overall, however, females disclosed more.

764. Sote, Gbade A., and Lawrence R. Good. "Similarity of Self-Disclosure and Interpersonal Attraction." *Psychological Reports*, 34 (1974), 491-494.

One hundred thirty-two undergraduates completed questionnaires on self-disclosure and then rated a stranger presented on the basis of a bogus questionnaire as a high- or low-self-discloser. High self-disclosing females reported greater attraction for high self-disclosing stranger, but the same did not hold true for low self-disclosing females. For males, attraction was unrelated to self-disclosure similarity, but both high and low self-disclosure males desired as a work partner a high self-discloser.

765. Tobacyk, Jerome. "Sex Differences in Predictability of Self-Disclosure for Instrumental and Terminal Values." *Psychological Reports*, 44 (1979), 985-986.

A value survey and a self-disclosure questionnaire were given to 31 male and 56 female undergraduates, and a correlation matrix for each sex computed. Terminal values ("end state of existence") were better predictors of reported self-disclosure for females, and instrumental values ("mode of conduct") were better predictors for males.

766. Waterman, Jill. "Family Patterns of Self-Disclosure." In *Self-Disclosure: Origins, Patterns, and Implications of Openness in Interpersonal Relationships* (item 720), pp. 225-242.

Self-disclosure patterns in families have been conducted either in the traditional way, focusing on all possible dyads within the family, or from a family dynamics perspective, concentrating either on the structural patterns of self-disclosure or the method of self-disclosure. Waterman reviews pertinent research and points out needs for future research.

* Woods, Donald J., and James Brooks. "Nonverbal Affective Self-disclosure: Effects on Observers' Judgments." *The Journal of Social Psychology*, 105 (1978), 155-156. See item 1314.

767. Young, Jerald W. "The Subordinate's Exposure of Organizational Vulnerability to the Superior: Sex and Organizational Effects." *Academy of Management Journal*, 21 (1978), 113-122.

To examine how organizationally relevant self-disclosing behavior of a subordinate to a superior is influenced by sex of superior and subordinate and by the nature of the organizational work environment, 120 male and female undergraduates were asked to give a manager eight messages which were both important for organizational effectiveness and personally threatening to the subordinate. A questionnaire assessing the perceptions of the manager was administered after all eight messages were presented. Subordinates in the more participative-group setting were more predisposed to discuss organizationally relevant personal and work-related issues that could influence the interaction and the problem solving/decision making processes of the work group. Females tended to disclose more organizationally relevant content than males. No cross-sex disclosure or attractiveness effect was found.

MISCELLANEOUS CHARACTERISTICS

768. Andreoli, Virginia A., Stephen Worchel, and Robert Folger. "Implied Threat to Behavioral Freedom." *Journal of Personality and Social Psychology,* 30 (1974), 765-771.

    One hundred three female undergraduates rated topics for desirability for discussion and were then manipulated to expect one of three threat conditions--a threat to the freedom of another, a threat followed by retraction, or no threat. Subjects expected to interact with either the threatener or the recipient of the threat or a control subject. They then re-rated the topics. The most desired topic declined in the threat condition compared to the other conditions, regardless of expected interacter.

769. Appelbaum, Alan S. "Rathus Assertiveness Schedule: Sex Differences and Correlation with Social Desirability." *Behavior Therapy,* 7 (1976), 699.

    College undergraduates, 36 of each sex, were administered the Rathus Assertiveness Schedule and the Marlowe Crowne Social Desirability Scale to determine sex differences in social boldness and the relationship between such assertiveness and social desirability. No sex differences were found and only a negligible relationship between boldness and desirability, supporting the discriminant validity of the Rathus test.

770. Bellack, Alan S., Michel Hersen, and Danuta Lamparski. "Role-Play Tests for Assessing Social Skills: Are They Valid? Are They Useful?" *Journal of Consulting and Clinical Psychology,* 47 (1979), 335-342.

    Seventy-eight male and female undergraduates completed a heterosocial skill inventory and role played 20 scenarios developed from a 20-item heterosocial skill inventory. Each subject was videotaped with an opposite-sex experimental assistant as they followed the experimenter's intercom instructions. One week later the subjects returned and were videotaped in a waiting room in an interaction with an opposite-sex bogus subject. Videotapes of both the role-playing and the interaction were analyzed for various social skills and the results were correlated. Role-play behavior was moderately correlated with behavior in the non-role-play interaction for females, but there were few significant relationships for males.

771. Bernard, Jessie. "Where are We Now? Some Thoughts on the Current Scene." *Psychology of Women Quarterly*, 1 (1976), 21-37.

In this essay, communication techniques, networking, and interaction patterns such as the "stag effect" and "put-down" are discussed. Research is called for to document just how the self-image of women is injured by these forms of behavior, how their professional careers are prejudiced by them, and how collective coping mechanisms can help.

772. Campbell, B. Kay, and Dean C. Barnlund. "Communication Patterns and Problems of Pregnancy." *American Journal of Orthopsychiatry*, 47 (1977), 134-139.

A questionnaire survey of 28 women matched for occupation, education, ethnic identity, marital status, and age but differing in that half were effective contraceptive users (no pregnancies though sexually active) and half ineffective (two or more unplanned pregnancies) was taken to determine the role of communication in pregnancy planning. Noneffective contraceptive users were significantly lower in communication skills such as sensitivity, directness, control, empathy, and clarity. They disclosed less, were less accessible to touch, and tended to idealize interpersonal relationships and to inhibit their hostile reactions.

773. Carlson, James M. "Politics and Interpersonal Attraction." *American Politics Quarterly*, 7 (1979), 120-126.

Ninety-six undergraduates whose political attitudes were known evaluated their attraction to bogus strangers varied for sex and political attitudes. The political views of opposite-sex others had an effect on interpersonal attraction in that politically interested females rated politically interested males more attractive but political interest in males did not affect ratings for females. Political attitude similarity had little effect on politically uninterested females as well.

774. Clark, Margaret S., and Judson Mills. "Interpersonal Attraction in Exchange and Communal Relationships." *Journal of Personality and Social Psychology*, 37 (1979), 12-24.

Two experimental studies supported the idea of a distinction between communal relationships, mutual concern ones; and exchange relationships, ones in which benefits are given with expectation of return, whether economic or not. The first study, with 96 undergraduate males, showed that the receipt of a benefit after the other person benefited increased attraction in communal relationship and decreased it in exchange relationship. The second study, with 80 female undergraduates, showed that a request for a benefit after a person had been aided by another increased attraction in expected exchange relationship but decreased it in expected communal relationship. Request for a benefit when there was no prior aid decreased attraction for expected exchange relationship.

775. DePaulo, Bella M., and Robert Rosenthal. "Telling Lies." *Journal of Personality and Social Psychology*, 37 (1979), 1713-22.

Videotapes of 20 females and 20 males telling the truth or lies about their liking for others were spliced into two hour-long videotapes. One tape was judged by each subject (never the tape on which the subject appeared). Accuracy in detecting deception was far greater than accuracy in detecting true emotion. Those who were detected more readily also had their underlying emotions detected more readily. A "ham" strategy was effective in deceiving others; subjects high in machiavellian scores used the strategy more. Skill in detecting deception in women was not correlated with skill in detecting deception in men.

* Eakins, Barbsra W., and R. Gene Eakins. *Sex Differences in Human Communication*. Boston: Houghton Mifflin Co., 1978. See item 1318.

776. Eubanks, Sheryle B. "Sex-Based Language Differences: A Cultural Reflection." In *Views on Language* (item 880), pp. 109-120.

Fifteen male-female college student dyads were recorded discussing one of seven topics for from 3 to 25 minutes in various locations from dorm rooms to offices. Some dyads were friends, other strangers. Analysis of these conversations revealed that men talked more, initiated and concluded conversations more, and made more elaborated judgmental statements. Women agreed and encouraged more, made more apologies and indecisive statements. No difference in use of standard or non-standard forms was found.

777. Frodi, Ann, Jacqueline Macaulay, and Pauline R. Thome. "Are Women Always Less Aggressive than Men? A Review of the Experimental Literature." *Psychological Bulletin*, 84 (1977), 634-660.

A review of over 170 publications revealed that the common view that men are more physically aggressive and women are more likely to show indirect or displaced aggression was not supported by the evidence. When aggression is perceived as justified or prosocial, women may act as aggressively as men. Sex of investigator and/or victim of aggression, the specific variables of the situation (presence of aggression anxiety or guilt), and empathy do, however, produce sex differences in aggressive behavior.

778. Gerson, Ann C., and Daniel Perlman. "Loneliness and Expressive Communication." *Journal of Abnormal Psychology*, 88 (1979), 258-261.

From a pool of 300, 66 female undergraduates were selected to represent chronically lonely (23), situationally lonely (19), and nonlonely (24) groups. All were videotaped as they responded to and rated the pleasantness of 25 slides; the videotapes were then viewed without sound and judged as to the response and the ratings of pleasantness of the senders. Situationally lonely subjects were significantly more expressive than the other two groups, who did not differ significantly in their sending abilities. In general, highly depressed subjects were less successful communication senders, except for those in the situationally lonely group.

779. Goody, Esther, ed. *Questions and Politeness: Strategies in Social Interaction*. Cambridge: University Press, 1978.

Two comprehensive theories of universal language use, one on questions by E. Goody and the other on politeness as a verbal strategy by P. Brown and S. Levinson, both based on ethnographic studies, are presented. Explicit references to the language of women are made in both discussions. Part of the discussion on questions focuses on the use of interrogatives in mother-child communication.

780. Graney, Marshall J., and Edith E. Graney. "Communications Activity Substitutions in Aging." *Journal of Communication*, 24 (Autumn 1974), 88-96.

A follow-up interview survey of 60 women, aged 62 to 89 at initial interview and 66 to 92 four years later (N =

46) and their use of various communications activities, from visiting neighbors to being members of an organization, revealed that as one kind of activity decreased in frequency, another kind increased often in matched pairs (for example, between visiting neighbors and organizational membership).

781. Grush, Joseph E., and Janet G. Yehl. "Marital Roles, Sex Differences, and Interpersonal Attraction." *Journal of Personality and Social Psychology,* 37 (1979), 116-123.

One hundred twenty-eight college students, half of each sex, with traditional or nontraditional attitudes toward sex roles and marriage, rated similar or dissimilar opposite-sex strangers on three attraction measures. Nontraditional women and traditional men preferred similar others in personal relationships (dating, work, marriage), while traditional women and nontraditional men were attracted equally to similar and dissimilar others. All subjects rated all others as equally suited for functional relationships (debaters, discussants, and panelists).

782. Hartsook, Judith, Doris R. Olch, and Virginia A. deWolf. "Personality Characteristics of Women's Assertiveness Training Group Participants." *Journal of Counseling Psychology,* 23 (1976), 322-326.

Compared to a control group of vocational counselees and a norm group on the Edwards Personal Preference Schedule, the 25 female undergraduate and graduate students in an assertiveness program were more concerned with the approval of others and somewhat inhibited in expressing their feelings, although otherwise they were autonomous and integrated.

783. Henley, Nancy, and Jo Freeman. "The Sexual Politics of Interpersonal Behavior." In *Female Psychology: The Emerging Self.* Ed. Sue Cox. Chicago: Science Research Associates, 1976. pp. 171-179.

The authors analyze briefly such topics as address forms, posture and dress, language (including swearing), gaze, touch, and use of space, all as they reveal asymmetrical status or power.

784. Hoffman, Martin L. "Sex Differences in Empathy and Related Behaviors." *Psychological Bulletin,* 84 (1977), 712-722.

Reviewing over 70 sources, Hoffman concludes that females are more empathetic than males from infancy on, but are not more able to assess another's affective, cognitive, or spatial perspective than males are. Evidence suggests that female empathy is related to prosocial affective orientation which includes feeling guilty at harming others, while males may be socialized more to act and not to feel.

785. Hollandsworth, James G., Jr., and Kathleen E. Wall. "Sex Differences in Assertive Behavior: An Empirical Investigation." *Journal of Counseling Psychology,* 24 (1977), 217-222.

A review of the literature on assertive behavior (only 7 out of 108 articles gave sex-identified data) revealed that males report higher frequencies of assertive behavior than females, although the means are significantly different in only 29% of the samples reviewed. Responses from 294 males and 408 females to the Adult Self Expression Scale revealed males reporting more assertion with supervisors, stating opinions, and in taking initiative in meeting opposite sex. Females reported themselves as more assertive in expressing love, affection, and compliments, and in anger toward parents.

786. Johnson, Miriam, Jean Stockard, Joan Ackers, and Claudeen Naffziger. "Expressiveness Re-evaluated." *School Review,* 83 (1975), 617-644.

A brief review of theories of "masculinity" and "femininity" leads to a more complete analysis of the T. Parson, R. Bales, and E. Shils theory of an instrumental-expressive distinction (*Working Papers in the Theory of Action.* Glencoe, Ill.: Free Press, 1954). The authors' own research with over 400 male and female undergraduates led to a list of adjectives divisible into six categories: positive and negative expressive, positive and negative instrumental, active or passive and/or independent, plus a residual category for words that did not fit one of the other categories. Both factor analysis and cluster analysis of the results basically supported the groupings of the adjectives based on the theory. Female subjects saw themselves as more positively expressive than males, and those traits correlated with positive instrumentality and independence as well. Male subjects, however, did not associate expressiveness with independence and instrumentality, supporting the hypothesis that the development of masculinity involves a rejection of femininity. Such a rejection could explain the devaluation of women generally found in society.

787. McCroskey, James C., Virginia P. Richmond, John A. Daly, and Barbara G. Cox. "The Effects of Communication Apprehension on Interpersonal Attraction." *Human Communication Research,* 2 (1975), 51-65.

Two studies, one using 341 female and 310 male undergraduates, the other 104 female and 108 male undergraduates, tested the hypotheses that in cross-sex dyads the low communication apprehensives would be perceived as more socially attractive, more task attractive, more desirable as potential communication partners, more desirable as potential sexual partners, and that these effects would apply at all levels of apprehension but would be greater for low apprehensives. All the hypotheses but the last received support in one or both of the studies.

788. Miller, Gerald, ed. *Annual Review of Communication Research, Vol. 5: Explorations in Interpersonal Communication.* Beverly Hills: Sage Press, 1976.

789. Murray, David C. "Talk, Silence, and Anxiety." *Psychological Bulletin,* 75 (1971), 244-260.

In this review of over 60 studies relating to anxiety and verbal production, most of them from the 1960s, only a few used female subjects, and none, apparently, tested for sex differences. The studies about women revealed that female undergraduates high in fear of public speaking spoke slower and had more silences than those low in fear of speaking. For married women, the least stressful topic to discuss was husbands; the most stressful, illness. For nursing students a stressful topic led to lower verbal productivity (not significant), and shorter silence quotients (significant). Nursing students also responded with fewer words to a cold interviewer.

790. Patton, Bobby R., and Bonnie R. Patton. *Living Together: Female/Male Communication.* Columbus, Ohio: Charles E. Merrill Publishing Co., 1976.

Topics covered in this book include the socialization process, nonverbal and verbal communication between men and women, relationship patterns and styles, conflict and its resolution, and the actualizing relationship.

791. Powell, Larry, Mark L. Hickson, III, and Sidney R. Hill, Jr. "Canonical Relationships between Prestige and Interpersonal Attraction." *Perceptual and Motor Skills,* 44 (1977), 23-29.

One hundred twenty-six male and 159 female undergraduates were used to test the hypothesis that judgments about the prestige of a speaker would serve as a basis for judgments about interpersonal attraction of that speaker. Subjects evaluated either a male or female speaker on five dimensions of prestige and three of interpersonal attraction. Males based their judgments about speakers on task attraction characteristics, namely extroversion for male speakers and character, competence, and composure for female speakers. Females based their judgments on multiple dimensions besides task attraction. Differences by sex of speaker were that composure and character were considered for the male speaker but not for the female, and judgments of female speakers used social and physical dimensions as well as competence and sociability.

792. Soltz, Donald F. "On Sex and the Psychology of 'Playing Dumb': A Reevaluation." *Psychological Reports,* 43 (1978), 111-114.

A brief questionnaire of "playing dumb" was administered over a five-year period to 142 males and 260 females of various ages (range from 17-67) and education attainment (8th grade to graduate degree). The same proportion of males and females reported "playing dumb" at times (82.4% and 83.7%) and believed that women play dumb more than men (61.7%, 62.5%). No differences by age, religious background, or level of schooling emerged.

793. Talley, Mary A., and Virginia P. Richmond. "The Relationship between Psychological Gender Orientation and Communicator Style." *Human Communication Research,* 6 (1980), 326-339.

To determine whether sex-role orientation has effects on communicator style, 156 males and 117 females completed the Bem Sex-Role Inventory, a shyness scale, and a communicator style measure, interacted in at least five dyadic exercises, and 11 weeks later re-rated themselves and their partner's communication style. Sex role had no effects on perceived communicator style.

794. Wedel, Janet M. "Ladies, We've Been Framed! Observations on Erving Goffman's 'The Arrangement between the Sexes'." *Theory and Society,* 5 (1978), 113-125.

This analysis of Erving Goffman's "The Arrangement Between the Sexes" (*Theory and Society,* 4 [1977], 301-331) criticizes his stereotypes of male-female interaction and his failure to include the politics of sexual interaction. Wedel rejects his view that men and women are equally but differentially defined by sex-class assignment.

795. Wheeler, Ladd, and John Nezlek. "Sex Differences in Social Participation." *Journal of Personality and Social Psychology,* 35 (1977), 742-754.

    Analysis of the diaries of social interactions for two weeks early in the fall and another two weeks late in the spring of 20 female and 38 male first-year college students revealed that females decreased time per day in interaction more than males, including with three same-sex best friends. The authors theorized females socialize more intensely in a new environment than males. By spring, differences were minimal.

796. Zammuto, Raymond F., Manual London, and Kendrith M. Rowland. "Effects of Sex on Commitment and Conflict Resolution." *Journal of Applied Psychology,* 64 (1979), 227-231.

    This survey of 106 (56 M, 50 F) college resident advisers and their male or female resident supervisors queried the advisers on commitment to their position and to their supervisor, and queried the supervisors on the advisers' strategies for resolving conflicts between them. The interaction between commitment and conflict strategy depended on the sex composition of supervisor-subordinate. Males reporting to female supervisors used smoothing, compromise, and confrontation strategies when they felt committed to a position; females did not. Females were more likely to use confrontation when reporting to females. Males with male supervisors were more likely to withdraw from conflict than either males or females with female supervisors.

PART THREE
MEANS OF COMMUNICATION

VERBAL

LANGUAGE USED BY WOMEN

797. Bailey, Lee A., and Lenora A. Timm. "More on Women's--and Men's--*Expletives*." *Anthropological Linguistics*, 18 (1976), 438-449.

   A questionnaire survey was taken of fourteen women (ages 19-56) and fifteen men (ages 19-61) on what type of expletive they would use in situations ranging from mildly annoying to serious. Women aged 31-34 had the highest incidence of strong expletives; men had a far wider range of strong expletives. Both sexes reported self-censorship in use of expletives depending on social context, most noticeably in presence of strangers or people much older than themselves.

* Barber, Sharla, Brenda Hancock, and Bonnie Spillman. "Rhetoric of Feminism." *Female Studies*, 7 (1973), 109-110. See item 458.

798. Barron, Nancy. "Sex-Typed Language: The Production of Grammatical Cases." *Acta Sociologica*, 14 (1971), 24-42.

   The hypotheses, based on evidence of sex differences in cognitive and interactional styles, that men would favor agentive, instrumental, locative, and objective cases while women would prefer participative, manner, and purposive cases, were partially substantiated by an analysis of transcripts of the videotaped classroom speech of male and female social studies teachers teaching in both ghetto and suburban schools. Significant differences in usage between the sexes were found in men's use of instrumental and objective cases and women's use of participative cases.

799. Baumann, Marie. "Two Features of 'Women's Speech?'" In *The Sociology of the Languages of American Women* (item 1003), pp. 38-40.

An examination of the use of tag questions and statements prefaced by a doubt phrase or clause ("I may be wrong, but..."), features which Lakoff (see item 858) attributed to female speech, was conducted in graduate linguistics classes, a women's discussion group, and an office staff meeting. No differences by gender of speaker were found.

* Blass, Thomas, and Aron W. Siegman. "A Psycholinguistic Comparison of Speech, Dictation and Writing." *Language and Speech,* 18 (1975), 20-34. See item 1223.

800. Beck, Kay. "Sex Differentiated Speech Codes." *International Journal of Women's Studies,* 1 (1978), 566-572.

To test the hypothesis that males use an elaborated speech code and females a restricted speech code, 24 male and female undergraduates' oral responses to slides were taperecorded and analyzed for sentence length, number of subordinate clauses, conjunctions, prepositions, and by adjective and adverb range. Males used longer sentences, including clauses within clauses, and had an ordered selection of adverbs, adjectives, and prepositions. Females' speech was characterized by coordination; one sentence was added to another "haphazardly." Beck concludes that females' speech displays an inferior verbal code.

801. Borker, Ruth. "Anthropology: Social and Cultural Perspectives." In *Women and Language in Literature and Society* (item 1014), pp. 26-44.

This anthropological look at language and women reviews research relating to how women's social power determines their speech, how their speech is used to cope with their social position, and how the different social experiences of men and women lead them to use language in different ways. Specific topics discussed include at-home talk, gossip, the speech of black American women, and the relationship between power and language. Studies cited include many from cultures other than American.

802. Bornstein, Diane. "As Meek as a Maid: A Historical Perspective on Language for Women in Courtesy Books from the Middle Ages to *Seventeen Magazine*." In *Women's Language and Style* (item 808), pp. 132-138.

This review of books setting up standards of speech behavior for women finds that the ideal of meekness and politeness pervades from the fourteenth century to the 1970s.

803. Bostrom, Robert N., John R. Basehart, and Charles M. Rossiter, Jr. "The Effects of Three Types of Profane Language in Persuasive Messages." *Journal of Communication,* 23 (Dec. 1973), 461-475.

One hundred twenty-eight undergraduates heard a speech either by a male or a female with either religious, excretory, or sexual profanity, and 32 more the same speech with no profanity. Results of attitude change and speaker credibility measures revealed that profanity did not increase the persuasiveness of the message over nonprofanity, and profanity use decreased credibility. Female speakers using profanity affected greater attitude change than male speakers, with increasing effectiveness from religious to excretory to sexual profanity.

804. Bradshaw, John L., and E. Anne Gates. "Visual Field Differences in Verbal Tasks: Effects of Task Familiarity and Sex of Subject." *Brain and Language,* 5 (Dec. 1978), 166-187.

Four experiments dealt with the right hemisphere's contribution to speech. The 24 college students of both sexes in each experiment were required either to distinguish manually between words and nonwords or to repeat nonwords presented tachistoscopically. Results led to the conclusion that the left hemisphere had greater superiority for overt naming rather than for manual response to naming. The authors suggest a verbal mechanism in the right hemisphere, more strongly developed in females, that is involved in mediating lexical or phonological decisions, but not directly with letter or word recognition.

805. Brotherton, P.L., and R.A. Penman. "A Comparison of Some Characteristics of Male and Female Speech." *Journal of Social Psychology,* 103 (1977), 161-162.

This brief summary of research with fifteen male and fifteen female Australian undergraduates revealed that, contrary to stereotype, no differences by sex emerged in the production of speech, the rate of speech, the number of sentences left unfinished, or the conceptual level contained in the speech.

806. Brouwer, Dédé, Marinel Gerritsen, and Dorian De Hann. "Speech Differences Between Men and Women: On the Wrong Track?" *Language in Society*, 8 (1979), 33-50.

Following a brief discussion of methods of investigating linguistic differences between men and women, the authors report their analysis of the speech communication of 309 females and 278 males buying tickets from a male or female ticket seller in Amsterdam, The Netherlands. They found no significant relation between sex of speaker and number of words used, politeness, use of diminutives, or other features regularly associated with sex of speaker. Sex of addressee, however, did produce significant differences, with both males and females using speech characteristics indicating insecurity and politeness with the male ticket seller significantly more frequently than with the female ticket seller.

807. Brown, Penelope. "Women and Politeness: A New Perspective on Language and Society." *Reviews in Anthropology*, 3 (1976), 240-249.

* Bryant, Jennings, Paul Cominsky, and Dolf Zillmann. "Teachers' Humor in the College Classroom." *Communication Education*, 28 (1979), 110-118. See item 503.

* Burgoon, Michael, Stephen B. Jones, and Diane Stewart. "Toward a Message-Centered Theory of Persuasion: Three Empirical Investigations of Language Intensity." *Human Communication Research*, 1 (1975), 240-256. See item 661.

808. Butturff, Douglas, and Edmund L. Epstein, eds. *Women's Language and Style: Studies in Contemporary Language #1*. Akron, Ohio: University of Akron, 1978.

This compendium contains thirteen essays ranging in topic from samples of women's language to analyses of the literary styles of various women writers. References are included for each essay. See items 333, 802, 822, 860, and 866.

809. Cohen, Marshall M., and Thomas J. Saine. "The Role of Profanity and Sex Variables in Interpersonal Impression Formation." *Journal of Applied Communications Research*, 5 (1977), 45-51.

This study of the role of profanity and sex in forming impressions used 35 male and 39 female undergraduates responding to written hypothetical conversations with the sex of speakers and use of profanity systematically manipulated. The use of profanity resulted in significantly more negative impressions. Males formed more positive impressions of females using profanity than they did of males using profanity, while females formed more positive impressions of males than of other females.

810. Conklin, Nancy F. "Toward a Feminist Analysis of Linguistic Behavior." *Michigan Papers in Women's Studies,* 1, No. 1 (1974), 51-73.

811. Crosby, Faye, and Linda Nyquist. "The Female Register: An Empirical Study of Lakoff's Hypotheses." *Language in Society,* 6 (1977), 313-322.

In one laboratory and two field studies designed to test the validity of the six characteristics Lakoff (see items 858 and 1012) designated for women's speech--greater vocabulary for color and adjectives, use of tag questions or question intonation with declaratives, use of modifiers or hedges, use of *so,* and hypercorrectness and politeness--Crosby and Nyquist found two of the studies supporting the use of the female register (the six characteristics), and the third tending in that direction but without a significant difference by sex.

812. De Stefano, Johanna. "Women's Language--By & About." In *Views on Language* (item 880), pp. 66-76.

This brief review of research covers the phonology, syntax, and lexicon of women's language, attitudes toward women's language, discourse analysis, power, and conversation modes.

813. Dubois, Betty L., and Isabel Crouch. "The Question of Tag Questions in Women's Speech: They Don't Really Use More of Them, Do They?" *Language in Society,* 4 (1975), 289-294.

This criticism of a Lakoff article on women's speech (item 858) focuses primarily on the use of tag questions. Examining the conversational give-and-take following lectures at a professional meeting attended by both men and women (varying in number from 15 to 25), the authors found 17 formal tag questions ("weren't you?") and 16 informal ones ("right?"), all of them spoken by men.

* Eakins, Barbara, and Gene Eakins. "Verbal Turn-Taking and Exchanges in Faculty Dialogue." In *The Sociology of the Languages of American Women.* Eds. Betty L. Dubois

and Isabel Crouch. San Antonio, Texas: Trinity University, 1976, pp. 53-62. See item 506.

814. Eble, Connie C. "Etiquette Books as Linguistic Authority." In *The Second LACUS Forum, 1975*. Ed. Peter A. Reich. Papers from the Linguistic Association of Canada and the United States Forum, University of Toronto, August 3-7, 1975. Columbia, S.C.: Hornbeam, 1976, pp. 468-475.

This historical review of American courtesy and etiquette books from colonial days to the 1923 Emily Post *Etiquette* focuses on linguistic admonitions to women.

815. Eble, Connie C. "Girl Talk: A Bicentennial Perspective." In *Views on Language* (item 880), pp. 77-86.

A review of courtesy and etiquette book admonitions to young women from the colonial period to the 1970s reveals them generally reflecting and abetting women's passive role. Historical material on the first female public speakers in America is included, the very first being a free-born black, Frances Maria W. Stewart, in winter 1832-33, speaking out against slavery.

816. Eble, Connie C. "If Ladies Weren't Present, I'd Tell You What I Really Think." In *Papers in Language Variation: SAMLA-ADS Collection*. Eds. David L. Shores and Carole P. Hines. University: University of Alabama Press, 1977, pp. 295-301.

This discussion of different standards of appropriateness for males and females focuses on subject matter for conversation and the use of abusive language.

817. Edelsky, Carole. "The Acquisition of Communicative Competence: Recognition of Linguistic Correlates of Sex Roles." *Merrill-Palmer Quarterly*, 22 (1976), 47-59. Rpt. in *Child Discourse*. Eds. Susan Ervin-Tripp and Claudia Mitchell-Kernan. New York: Academic, 1977, pp. 225-243.

To determine adult norms of the ability to interpret language as sex "appropriate," written statements (*oh dear, damn,* tag questions) were presented to 122 white middle-class adults (70 female and 52 male) and to 122 white middle-class first, third, and sixth graders, all of whom were asked to specify which sex would more likely make those statements. From all groups ten subjects were selected to be interviewed for explaining their choices. Results indicated a linguistic sex-role stereotype by adults. With children, the stereotype increased with age, moving from stereotype based on topic (first grade) to one based on form, with, for example, tag questions being increasingly stereotyped as feminine with increasing grade level. Two patterns of acquisition of adult norms are posited.

818. Edelsky, Carole. "Subjective Reactions to Sex-Linked Language." *The Journal of Social Psychology*, 99 (1976), 97-104.

    Forty-one female and 21 male PTA attenders responded to a questionnaire on sex-linked language on an adjective scale with male and female poles. Sex of responder was not significant in the finding that all lexical items were rated stereotypically male or female and were significantly related to the adjective attributes also stereotypically male or female on all attributes but logicality. Thus *oh dear* was judged "female" language, and was perceived not only as gentle and less aggressive but also as neater, more dependent, more easily influenced, less decisive, more submissive, less confident, and more passive.

819. Elyan, Olwen, Philip Smith, Howard Giles, and Richard Bourhis. "RP-Accented Female Speech: The Voice of Perceived Androgyny?" In *Sociolinguistic Patterns in British English*. Ed. Peter Trudgill. Baltimore: University Park Press, 1978, pp. 122-131.

    A passage was read in prestige dialect (Received Pronunciation--RP) and in a northern dialect (Lancashire) by two females, and the spoken passages were rated by 38 male and 38 female undergraduates on various measures of intelligence, self-confidence, sociability, etc. Analysis of variance revealed that the listeners perceived the RP speaker to be higher in 18 of the 25 items rated, including self-esteem, fluency, intelligence, self-confidence, independence, and femininity than the Northern dialect speaker. Female listeners polarized their ratings more than male listeners on six of these 18 scales. The Northern dialect speaker was found more likeable and sincere and less aggressive and egotistic. The authors discuss the contradiction of masculine traits and perceived femininity of the RP speaker in light of the theory of androgyny.

820. Erickson, Bonnie, E. Allen Lind, Bruce C. Johnson, and William M. O'Barr. "Speech Style and Impression Formation in a Court Setting: The Effects of 'Powerful' and 'Powerless' Speech." *Journal of Experimental Social Psychology*, 14 (1978), 266-279.

The same substantive evidence delivered by male and female actors either on audiotape or in written transcript was manipulated to be "powerless" style (intensifiers, hedges, hesitations, questioning intonation [all stereotypical features of female speech]) or "powerful" (absence of those markers). Seventy-three male and 79 female undergraduate subjects rated the powerful-style witness as more attractive regardless of sex of subject or of witness or mode of communication. They also rated the powerful-style witness more credible, especially when sex of subject matched sex of witness. Moreover, in all but male-witness/written presentation condition, the powerful style produced more acceptance of the position advocated in the testimony. See also items 561 and 1013.

* Eubanks, Sheryle B. "Sex-Based Language Differences: A Cultural Reflection." In *Views on Language*. Eds. Reza Orboubadian and Walburga von Raffler-Engel. Murfreesboro, Tenn.: Inter-University Publishing, 1975, pp. 109-120. See item 776.

* Farrell, Thomas J. "The Female and Male Modes of Rhetoric." *College English*, 40 (1979), 909-921. See item 396.

821. Ferguson, Nicola. "Simultaneous Speech, Interruptions and Dominance." *British Journal of Social and Clinical Psychology*, 16 (1977), 295-302.

To explore the assumption that simultaneous speech and interruptions are measures of dominance, 16 female undergraduate friends completed a personality questionnaire and ranked each other according to dominance. Each of the 15 participated in a half-hour tape-recorded unstructured conversation with the sixteenth, a confederate. The four types of interruptions analyzed, simple interruptions, overlaps, butting-in, and silent interruptions, revealed that only overlaps and silent interruptions were significantly correlated with dominance.

* Fishman, Pamela. "Interaction: The Work Women Do." *Social Problems*, 25 (1978), 397-406. See item 332.

* Fishman, Pamela M. "What Do Couples Talk About When They're Alone?" In *Women's Language and Style*. Eds. Douglas Buttruff and Edmund Epstein. Akron, Ohio: University of Akron Press, 1978, pp. 11-22. See item 333.

822. Frank, Francine W. "Women's Language in America: Myth and Reality." In *Women's Language and Style* (item 808), pp. 47-61.

Frank's review of the literature on women's language in America begins with Jespersen's *Language* (1922) and covers topics such as vocabulary, semantics, syntax, voice, paralinguistic elements, and language ability. Specific attention is paid to separating myth about women's language from reality based on empirical evidence. References are given in the 74 footnotes.

823. French, Marilyn. "Women in Language." *Soundings*, 59 (1976), 329-344.

This essay begins with the Whorf belief that language reflects and perpetuates attitudes and then examines research substantiating the belief concerning both the language used by women and the language used about women. The context, semantics, and grammar of language about women are examined, and, using examples from public statements, laws, and literature, four areas of stereotyping are enumerated: men are the standard, women the deviates; women are seen not as autonomous but in relationship to men; women are invisible (example, "generic" *he*); and women are associated with the subhuman or subadult.

824. Gal, Susan. "Peasant Men Can't Get Wives: Language Change and Sex Roles in a Bilingual Community." *Language in Society*, 7 (1978), 1-16.

This examination of the bilingual culture of Oberwart, Austria, revealed women's speech choices were explained by their social position, by their life choices, and by the symbolic values of their linguistic alternatives. For both men and women, whether Hungarian or German or both were spoken depended on the age of the speaker and the "peasantness" of the social network. For women age was more closely correlated with language spoken, with the youngest generation using more German regardless of peasantness of social network. The explanation was that they preceived a harder life (borne out by evidence) as a peasant farmer's wife than as a town worker's wife, and so eschewed not only the language of the peasant, but, as marriage records reveal, the peasant himself, who must find monolingual peasant girls from other villages.

825. Garcia, Gilbert N., and Susan F. Frosch. "Sex, Color and Money: Who's Perceiving What? or Men and Women: Where Did All the Differences Go (To?)?" In *The Sociology of the Languages of American Women* (item 1003), pp. 63-71. Rpt. in *International Journal of the Sociology of Language*, 17 (1978), 65-72.

Forty men and women, ages 18 to 65, black, white, and Spanish-surnamed, were asked to describe what they saw in both a "feminine" picture (ruffle-decorated bedroom) and a "masculine" one (landscape scene with rifle). No significant differences were found in the descriptions by ethnic background or by education level. Sex differences found were that males described more in terms of spatial relationships while females tended to describe in terms of patterns or colors. Further, each sex for its "appropriate" picture began descriptions with details and moved on to generalizations, while for the "opposite-sex" picture each sex began with generalizations and moved on to details.

826. Giles, Howard et al. "Women's Speech: The Voice of Feminism." In *Women and Language in Literature and Society* (item 1014), pp. 150-156.

A series of studies by the authors and others on the perception from women's voices of their personality and how those perceptions differentiated between profeminists and nonfeminists is presented. Thirty-second excerpts from the spontaneous conversation of 16 nonfeminists, 8 feminists (both determined on the basis of scores on the Attitudes Toward Women Scale), and 8 feminists active in a feminist organization were rated by 16 female and male students. Feminist speakers were rated statistically more intelligent, sincere, profeminist, and as having higher lucidity of argument. Nonfeminists were perceived as more frivolous, superficial, and as using more standard accents. Another study used 10 female students (5 profeminists, 5 nonfeminists) reading the same 40-second passage. The 16 raters judged the feminist speakers as less fluent, using less standard dialect, lower pitched, less careful in articulation, more masculine and, unlike the first study, less intelligent. A third study found that women scoring higher on the ATW scale talked longer and faster than women who scored lower on the ATW. The results of the study are interpreted as showing the adoption by profeminist women of a male style of speech. All subjects and raters were British.

827. Gilley, Hoyt M., and Collier S. Summers. "Sex Differences in the Use of Hostile Verbs." *Journal of Psychology,* 76 (1970), 33-37.

Fifty female and fifty male undergraduates chose between a hostile verb ("stabbed") or a neutral one ("began") in a sentence completion task when pronoun subject was either first person ("I," "we") or third ("He," "They"). Female subjects chose significantly fewer hostile verbs than male subjects; pronouns made no difference.

* Gleason, Jean B. "Sex Differences in the Language of Children and Parents." In *Language, Children and Society: The Effect of Social Factors in Children Learning to Communicate.* Eds. Olga Garnica and Martha L. King. Oxford: Pergamon, 1979, pp. 149-157. See item 339.

828. Golden, Charles J. "Sex Differences in Performance on the Stroop Color and Word Test." *Perceptual and Motor Skills,* 39 (1974), 1067-70.

Two hundred nineteen college students (117 F, 102 M) took a group form of the Stroop Color and Word Test. Women performed significantly better on the color-word task basically because of their faster color-naming ability rather than their ability to overcome the interference embedded in Stroop cards.

829. Gorcyca, Diane A., William R. Kennan, and Marianne G. Stich. "Discrimination of the Language Behavior of College- and Middle-Aged Encoders." *Communication Quarterly,* 27, No. 1 (1979), 38-43.

Language samples from 22 male and female college students and 22 middle-aged employed adults taking continuing education courses were analyzed in order to determine if the use of college students is appropriate for generalizations to other elements of the population. A multiple discriminant analysis revealed fundamental differences in language behavior between the college population and the adult population, some differences by occupation of adults, and some sex differences. Females used more words implying feelings, emotions, or motivation, while males used more words implying time, space, and quantity. The results question the validity of studying the verbal behavior of college students as indicative of larger population groups.

* Grantham, Robert J. "Effects of Counselor Sex, Race, and Language Style on Black Students in Initial Interviews." *Journal of Counseling Psychology,* 20 (1973), 553-559. See item 535.

830. Gregersen, Edgar A. "Sexual Linguistics." In *Language, Sex, and Gender* (item 1017), pp. 3-19.

    This overview of the topics covered in the 1979 Academy of Sciences conference on "Language, Sex, and Gender" contains a summary of the results of research on cross-cultural swearing patterns. A sampling of cases shows that women's status and the structural features of a language co-vary independently. The relevance of such matters to political issues raised by the women's movement is emphasized.

831. Haas, Adelaide. "Male and Female Spoken Language Differences: Stereotypes and Evidence." *Psychological Bulletin,* 86 (1979), 616-626.

    A review of 60 empirical findings about the form, topic, content and use of language revealed that men may be more loquacious and directive, use more nonstandard forms, and talk more about sports, money, and business. Women seem to be more supportive, polite, and expressive, and talk more about home and family. Women use more emotional language (feeling, evaluation, interpretation), and men use language focused on perceptual attributes. Men use speech more assertively, issuing more directives; women are more tentative and supportive. A brief discussion of the validity and verifiability of different speech styles by gender is included, including the use of expletives. For a rebuttal, see item 841.

832. Halaby, Raouf, and Carolyn Long. "Future Shout: Name-Calling in the Future." *Maledicta,* 3 (1979), 61-68.

    Seventy-one college freshmen and sophomores (40 M, 31 F) responded to a survey in attitudes toward name-calling and the use of four-letter words. Almost all felt such words could not be eliminated, and 96% were not shocked by the use of profanity in movies and novels. Almost 40% objected to profanity in newspapers, however. Only about a third objected to using profanity in front of the opposite sex, and each sex reported using more such words with their own sex.

833. Harris, Lauren J. "Sex Differences in the Growth and Use of Language." In *Women: A Psychological Perspective*. Eds. Elaine Donelson, and Jeanne E. Gullahorn. New York: John Wiley & Sons, 1977, pp. 79-94.

Although Harris focuses on sex differences in the development of language, she also addresses the issue of sex superiority in language biologically (hemispheric dominance), psychologically, and sociologically.

834. Hartford, Beverly S. "Phonological Differences in the English of Adolescent Chicanas and Chicanos." In *The Sociology of the Languages of American Women* (item 1003), pp. 73-80.

Language samples from 15 female and 15 male first-generation Chicano adolescents (ages not given) were analyzed for phonological variation, specifically for which sex would use more prestige forms and how use of these forms correlated with attitudes toward own and dominant cultures, upward mobility, etc. Females had a higher proportion of prestige forms of the variables studied and these forms did not accompany rejection of either own or dominant cultures. It appears that female peer pressure, not family or teachers, is most influential in acquiring prestige forms.

835. Hartman, Maryann. "A Descriptive Study of the Language of Men and Women Born in Maine around 1900 as It Reflects the Lakoff Hypotheses in 'Language and Women's Place.'" In *The Sociology of the Languages of American Women* (item 1003), pp. 81-91. Rpt. in *International Journal of the Sociology of Language*, 17 (1978), 55-64.

Interviews held separately with 15 male and 16 female Maine respondents aged 70 or above to test Lakoff's hypotheses (item 858) revealed that the females used more qualifiers and tag questions and that females' speech was more hesitant.

836. Henley, Nancy, and Barrie Thorne. "Womanspeak and Manspeak: Sex Differences and Sexism in Communication, Verbal and Nonverbal." In *Beyond Sex Roles*. Ed. Alice Sargent. St. Paul, Minn.: West Publishing, 1977, pp. 201-218.

This survey of the nature of white, middle class male and female verbal and nonverbal communication examines how the sexes use language differently, sexism in the English language, and myths of sex differences in speech. Henley and Thorne recommend that females retain the positive qualities of their communication, such as avoiding a competitive and aggressive conversational style, and that males adopt some female patterns, such as supportive listening and a considerate conversational style. In examining differences in demeanor, use of space, eye contact, smiling, touching, and gestures, they conclude that women can change nonverbal patterns more easily than verbal. Specifically, they recommend that women should stop smiling unless happy, stop lowering their eyes, stop getting out of men's way on the street, and stop letting themselves be interrupted. Thirty-seven references are given.

837. Hensley, Anne. "Black High School Students' Reactions to Black Speakers on Standard and Black English." *Language Learning*, 22 (1972), 253-259.

One hundred and twenty black high school students of both sexes evaluated by semantic differential black male and female speakers reading an identical passage in both Standard English and Black English. Standard English was rated significantly higher than Black English in all traits but one, "Knows what's happening." Women speaking Black English were given the least favorable ratings on seven of eight traits where a significant difference by sex and dialect occurred.

838. Higgins, E. Tory. "Social Class Differences in Verbal Communicative Accuracy: A Question of 'Which Question?'" *Psychological Bulletin*, 83 (1976), 695-714.

In this review of research articles pertaining to communication accuracy and social class, social class differences were found to be greater than sex differences, for which no significant or consistent pattern of differences has been found despite the fact that there is "a general belief that females have better verbal skills." Over 100 references are included.

839. Holzman, Mathilda. "The Use of Interrogative Forms in the Verbal Interaction of Three Mothers and Their Children." *Journal of Psycholinguistic Research*, 1 (1972), 311-336.

Four 100-word samples of verbal communication between three mothers and their children when children had mean utterance length of two and four morphemes were analyzed by a classification-of-interrogatives scheme. Interrogatives comprised from 15-33% of the mothers' talk; all three mothers used questions not only to ask questions but to make suggestions and to evaluate negatively the child's behavior.

840. Hopper, Robert, Larry G. Coleman, and John A. Daly. "Expletives and Androgyny." *Anthropological Linguistics*, 22 (1980), 131-137.

    In order to determine the relationship between sex, sex role, and the use of strong or weak expletives, the authors had 118 undergraduate students (85 F, 33 M) complete the Bem Sex Role Inventory and an expletive-use questionnaire. Males reported using more strong expletives, females weak ones, both differences significant. Although both sexes agreed that most of the words were appropriate for either sex, both also agreed that males generally use more strong expletives. By sex role, masculine and feminine subjects of both sexes duplicated the results by biological sex. Androgyns showed a preference for weak expletives.

841. Jay, Timothy B. "Sex Roles and Dirty Word Usage: A Review of the Literature and a Reply to Haas." *Psychological Bulletin*, 88 (1980), 614-621.

    Citing studies from 1935 to 1978, Jay refutes Haas' claim (item 831) that there are "no empirical studies" on the use of expletives by men and women and argues that laboratory study is possible for this topic. All of the studies reveal some sex differences, generally with men recognizing and recalling more taboo words, using more such language in jokes and stories, and having a wider command of the sexual vernacular.

842. Jesser, Clinton J. "Male Responses to Direct Verbal Sexual Initiatives of Females." *The Journal of Sex Research*, 14 (1978), 118-128.

    A questionnaire administered to 50 male and 75 female coitally experienced university students dealt with various aspects of sexual experiences, attitudes, and behavior relating to initiating sexual relationships. Over half of the females reported asking for sex directly. They were no more likely than those using less direct means to be rejected by their male partners. Women asking for sex directly were less conventional, more assertive, and more likely to be involved with males who also used direct means of asking for sex and whom they regarded as able to cope with direct female requests.

843. John-Steiner, Vera, and Patricia Irvine. "Women's Verbal Images and Associations." In *The Sociology of the Languages of American Women* (item 1003), pp. 91-101. Rpt. in *International Journal of the Sociology of Language*, 17 (1978), 103-114.

Word association and imagery data were collected from 20 English-speaking Navajo women, 20 university women enrolled and 20 not enrolled in a women's studies course, and 20 university men. Stimulus words were *sky, house, library, fantasy, teacher, man* and *marriage*. The Navajo group had the largest percentage of visual imagery responses, and the women's studies women the largest percentage of combined visual-verbal responses. Verbal response percentages were about the same for all three sets of university subjects. Cultural themes and attitudinal and thematic differences are discussed, with examples, including the strong tendency for Navajo women to respond in interpersonal terms while non-Indian women responded in intrapersonal terms.

844. Johnson, Robbie D. "Folklore and Women: A Social Interactional Analysis of the Folklore of a Texas Madam." *Journal of American Folklore*, 86 (1973), 211-224.

This report of a field study of a Texas madam focuses on her role as a joke teller to dominate men and applies Erving Goffman's facework concept (*Interaction Ritual: Essays on Face-to-Face Behavior*. Chicago: Aldine Publishers, 1967) to the social interaction within the brothel.

845. Jonas, Doris F., and A. David Jonas. "Gender Differences in Mental Function: A Clue to the Origin of Language." *Current Anthropology*, 16 (1975), 626-630.

Citing research concerning the bond between mother and infant during the babbling stage of development and citing references to the greater aptitude for language skills among females, the authors propose a theory that language originated in the human female response to infant babble. Responses to the theory, often followed by replies, appeared in subsequent issues: H.K.J. Cowan, "On Gender Differences and the Origin of Language," 17 (1976), 521-526; Harold H. Dibble, Jon D. Schwartz,

James N. Olsen, Jan Wind, Doris F. Jonas, and A. David Jonas, "More on Gender Differences and Language," 17 (1976), 744-749; and Stevan R. Harnad, "On Gender Differences and Language," 17 (1976), 327-329.

846. Jones, Deborah. "Gossip: Notes on Women's Oral Culture." *Women's Studies International Quarterly,* 3 (1980), 193-198.

    This study of women's oral culture uses sociolinguistic features of setting, participants, topic, form, and functions to analyze gossip. The four categories of gossip discussed are house-talk, scandal, bitching, and chatting.

847. Kalčik, Susan. "'... Like Ann's Gynecologist or the Time I Was Almost Raped': Personal Narratives in Women's Rap Groups." *Journal of American Folklore,* 88 (January-March 1975), 3-11.

848. Key, Mary R. "Linguistic Behavior of Male and Female." *Female Studies,* 2 (1970), 118-120.

    The outline and bibliography for a course on the linguistic behavior of men and women is presented.

849. Key, Mary R. "Linguistic Behavior of Male and Female." *Linguistics,* 88 (1972), 15-31.

    Key reviews and comments on research revealing differences in the phonological, grammatical, and, more in detail, the semantic components of male and female speech. Examples to illustrate the features (for example, gender pronouns) are from contemporary sources (texts, public statements) as well as historical ones.

850. Key, Mary R. *Male/Female Language.* Metuchen, N.J.: Scarecrow Press, 1975.

    Key cites and discusses social, cultural, linguistic, extra-linguistic, and literary features of language that differ by sex. A 21-page critically annotated bibliography is included.

 * Kolin, Philip C. "The Language of Nursing." *American Speech,* 48 (1973), 192-210. See item 570.

851. Kramarae, Cheris. "Proprietors of Language." In *Women and Language in Literature and Society* (item 1014), 58-68.

Drawing on numerous studies for support, Kramarae argues that the social dominance of men is allied to their control over language. This linguistic "proprietorship" means that women's and men's language use will be judged differently and not to women's benefit. Moreover, it means that women lack the language necessary to talk about their own perceptions of their experiences. The feminist challenge is to destroy the myths of linguistic proprietorship.

852. Kramer, Cheris. "Perceptions of Female and Male Speech." *Language and Speech,* 20 (1977), 151-161.

Using free responses, 466 white parochial and public high school students and university students, equally divided by sex, listed speech characteristics of males and females. Of the 51 traits most frequently mentioned, 36 yielded significant differences, so that the speech characteristics were sex stereotyped; however, on about one-third of these the male and female subjects differed. Female subjects perceived differences between the sexes significantly more often than male subjects. Stereotyped male speech characteristics included demanding voice, deep voice, boastful dominating speech, loud speech, use of swear words and slang, and sense of humor in speech. Female speech was characterized by clear enunciation, high pitch, gentleness, speed, self-revelation, politeness, and gibberish.

853. Kramer, Cheris. "Sex-Related Differences in Address Systems." *Anthropological Linguistics,* 17 (1975), 198-210.

The influence of sex of speaker and sex of addressee in determining appropriate address forms is examined by reviewing data from *New Yorker* cartoons and fiction, from a collection of 500 actual address forms given by male and female salesclerks to 14 female and male customers, and from a questionnaire survey of 28 women and 19 men (age range 18-69). Sex of both speaker and addressee was important, but women's variety of forms to choose from was more restricted than men's. Both women and young males, noted as those with relatively low status, are more concerned than older men about "correct" terms of address. Inferences which can be made about an individual from his or her address choices and about the social rights in society are discussed.

854. Kramer, Cheris. "Women's Speech: Separate but Unequal?" *Quarterly Journal of Communication,* 60 (1974), 14-24.

Rpt. in *Language and Sex: Difference and Dominance* (item 1326), pp. 43-56.

Kramer surveys both past research and "folk" sources (etiquette books, cartoons, novels, etc.) on women's speech, showing both the strength of sex stereotypes and the weakness of the evidence to support them. Areas mentioned include lexicon, articulation, subjective reactions to speech of others, pathology (stuttering), syntax, and amount of talking.

855. Kutner, Nancy G., and Donna Brogan. "An Investigation of Sex-Related Slang Vocabulary and Sex-Role Orientation Among Male and Female University Students." *Journal of Marriage and the Family,* 36 (1974), 474-484.

Thirty-seven female graduate nursing students and 56 female and 73 male undergraduates, all measured for sex-role orientation, listed all the slang expressions they knew for 17 sex-related stimulus words. Males listed a significantly larger total number of words than either female group. Other variables showed no relationship to extent of slang vocabularies except that, for females, religious involvement and traditional sex-role orientation were inversely related to extensiveness of vocabulary. A content analysis of the expressions listed for three stimulus words (*woman, man,* and *coitus*) revealed much exploitative imagery in male's slang vocabulary.

856. Labov, William. *Sociolinguistic Patterns*. Philadelphia: University of Pennsylvania Press, 1972.

Labov presents evidence from his own and other research that reveals that women are in the forefront of linguistic change (all changes cited are phonological). On the basis of all of the studies, however, Labov asserts that the "correct" generalization is that "sexual differentiation of speech often plays a major role in the mechanism of linguistic evolution."

857. Lakoff, Robin T. "Language and Sexual Identity." *Semiotica,* 19, 1/2 (1977), 119-130.

In this review article of M. Key's *Male/Female Language* (item 850), Lakoff points out that some men of power (academics, artists) also use features of Key's female language of "powerlessness," and that the difference is that women use this language "from denial of responsibility, itself arising from a lack of self-confidence." Lakoff doubts the practicality of Key's "androgynous" speech (without gender markings) or its desirability. All modes of speech should be equally commendable so long as they are appropriate to context, clear, and noninjurious.

858. Lakoff, Robin T. "Language and Woman's Place." *Language in Society*, 2 (1973), 45-80. Rpt. as Part I in R. Lakoff, *Language and Woman's Place* (item 1012).

    Arguing that the "marginality and powerlessness of women" are mirrored both in the way women speak and the way they are spoken of, Lakoff examines lexicon (color terms, particles, evaluative adjectives such as *divine*) and syntax (tag-questions and intonation with requests or orders and their responses) as well as various terms used to refer to women, especially in contrast to the companion terms for men (*master, mistress*). Conclusions and suggestions are offered, including about the gender pronoun controversy, which, Lakoff suggests, is "misguided." For a rebuttal, see item 813.

859. Lakoff, Robin T. "Stylistic Strategies within a Grammar of Style." In *Language, Sex, and Gender* (item 1017), pp. 53-78.

    This extension of a model of transformational grammar to women's and men's language styles indicates that as males and females differ in their surface styles, so they do in their transformational strategies. The styles, based on the degree of relatedness between speaker and hearer, are clarity (the impersonal language adopted by newscasters), distance (the language of professionals in scientific journals), deference (the language which reflects sensitivity to the needs of the listener), and camaraderie (language which relies heavily on shared knowledge). Lakoff suggests that the stereotypical American male style lies between clarity and distance, while the stereotypical female style is deference. The gap between the two appears to be narrowing, with males moving toward comaraderie and females toward distance.

860. Lakoff, Robin T. "Women's Language." *Language and Style*, 10 (1977), 222-247. Rpt. in *Women's Language and Style* (item 808), pp. 139-158.

    An examination of the style of women's speech is used to begin a consideration of a theory of style. Specifically, lexical (for example, intensifiers), phonological (for example, precise articulation), and syntactic-pragmatic (for example, hedging) components of style are analyzed to reveal an underlying unity of a feminine deferential style, which Lakoff interprets as an attempt to achieve or maintain non-responsibility. Using that analysis, Lakoff proposes a "grammar" of style with rules relating levels of style much like rules relating levels of syntax.

861. Lakoff, Robin T. "You Say What You Are: Acceptability and Gender-Related Language." In *Acceptability in Language*. Ed. Sidney Greenbaum. The Hague: Mouton, 1977, pp. 73-86.

    This essay establishes women's language as deviating from a "standard" in nondirectness, emotional expression, and conservation. Lakoff argues that the social/psychological context, being different for men and women, leads to different interpretations and so different requirements for acceptability. She sees danger in opposing women's language to a "standard" and a lack of certainty in whether to perpetuate dual standards of acceptability or to merge them.

862. Lapadat, Judy, and Maureen Seesahai. "Male versus Female Codes in Informal Contexts." *Sociolinguistics Newsletter*, 8, No. 3 (1977), 7-8.

    The informal conversations of all-male and all-female groups of three or more University of British Columbia students (N = 1200) were recorded without the prior knowledge of the participants. Linguistic analysis showed that women used more intensifiers and exaggerations than males, who used more direct imperatives and tag questions. Twelve expressions "heavily marked" by sex were given to 50 female and 50 male undergraduates to identify sex of speaker. Though some were recognized correctly, there were more "neutral" responses than "masculine" or "feminine" ones. Neither style of speech emerged as standard or superior.

863. Levine, Joan B. "The Feminine Routine." *Journal of Communication*, 26 (Summer 1976), 173-175.

    To determine whether the routines of male and female stand-up comics differed, an analysis was made of the routines of George Carlin, Robert Klein, Bill Cosby, David Steinberg, Totie Fields, Moms Mably, Phyllis Diller, and Lily Tomlin. The principal finding was that female comics used self-deprecatory humor 64% of the time; males, 12% of the time.

864. McConnell-Ginet, Sally. "Address Forms in Sexual Politics." In *Women's Language and Style* (item 808), pp. 23-25.

This examination of the address forms used by and to men and women begins with a review of research in cultures with a formal-informal pronoun distinction (*vous, tu*) and then examines the inventories, semantic systems, and developmental cycles of address usage in America. The thesis is that gender is "a central dimension" in the address system and that, since address forms reveal power and status in asymmetrical relationships, address forms are part of sexual politics.

865. McConnell-Ginet, Sally. "Linguistics and the Feminist Challenge." In *Woman and Language in Literature and Society* (item 1014), pp. 3-25.

This essay presents material on the social and cultural meanings of sexist language and on feminists' proposals to eliminate the sexism. Specific examples of sexist language are given. A brief review of research of sex-differentiated language is included, as well as a discussion on sex differences in speech styles and strategies.

866. McConnell-Ginet, Sally. "Our Father Tongue: Essays in Linguistic Politics." *Diacritics*, 5 (Winter 1975), 44-50.

This essay-review of Lakoff's *Language and Woman's Place* (item 1012) criticizes many of Lakoff's assertions and conclusions, including a point-by-point analysis of Lakoff's six features of women's language. Emphasis is placed on the context of speaking, not just the speech itself.

* McDowell, Margaret B. "The New Rhetoric of Woman Power." *The Midwest Quarterly*, 12 (1971), 187-198. See item 470.

867. McMillan, Julie R., A. Kay Clifton, Diane McGrath, and Wanda S. Gale. "Women's Language: Uncertainty or Interpersonal Sensitivity and Emotionality?" *Sex Roles*, 3 (1977), 545-559.

The linguistic behavior observed in interactions in classrooms and committee meetings of same-sex and mixed-sex problem-solving groups of graduates (61 F and 37 M) was content analyzed. Females more frequently than males used intensifiers, modal constructions, tag questions, and imperative constructions in question form, the latter three more in the presence of men than women. Males interrupted females more than other males.

868. Majeres, Raymond L. "Sex Differences in Clerical Speed: Perceptual Encoding vs. Verbal Encoding." *Memory & Cognition,* 5 (1977), 468-476.

A series of four experiments (three with 24 of each sex; one with 30 of each sex) tested the successful identification by college students of listed stimulus items by tapping matching items on response cards. Females were significantly faster than males in responding to words, colors, and directional symbols, but no sex difference was found in responding to shapes. The results are interpreted with reference to verbal encoding, memory, and evaluation processes.

869. Martin, Christopher M. "Verbal and Spatial Encoding of Visual Stimuli: The Effects of Sex, Hemisphere, and Yes-No Judgements." *Cortex,* 14 (1978), 227-233.

Six male and six female subjects were given 112 trials on each of two tasks requiring a yes-no comparison of pairs of letters presented to the right or left hemispheres. One task was predominantly visual and the other was predominantly verbal. For the "yes" decision, females were faster in the right hemisphere than in the left, while the males were faster in the left hemisphere. For females, "no" decisions were faster than "yes" decisions in the left hemisphere but not as fast as the right-hemisphere "yes" decisions.

870. Masling, Joseph, Cynthia Johnson, and Carol Saturansky. "Oral Imagery, Accuracy of Perceiving Others, and Performance in Peace Corps Training." *Journal of Personality and Social Psychology,* 30 (1974), 414-419.

Two experiments obtaining identical results used unacquainted males (32) and females (34) in one, and, in the other, well-acquainted Peace Corps trainees (33 M, 14 F). Subjects took Rorschach tests, then completed a questionnaire for both self and a partner (in the unacquainted experiment, pairs had a 15-minute get-acquainted session). Orality, the number of oral images reported in the Rorschach test, was significantly related to accurate interpersonal perceptions by males for males only.

871. Mitchell, Carol. "Hostility and Aggression Toward Males in Female Joke Telling." *Frontiers: A Journal of Women's Studies*, 3, No. 3 (1978), 19-23.

This account of female jokes and joke telling focuses on jokes with a female protagonist and a male butt, a type analyzed as an example of hostility to males.

872. Mulac, Anthony. "Effects of Obscene Language upon Three Dimensions of Listener Attitudes." *Communication Monographs*, 43 (1976), 300-307.

Twenty-six male and female undergraduates and 21 community adults (11 M, 10 F, mean age of 43.6) rated male and female speakers taking pro and con stances on an environmental issue and using obscene language or not. Speakers using obscenity, whether male or female, were rated lower by both sexes on socio-intellectual status and on aesthetic quality, but not on dogmatism. Female users of obscenity were not downgraded more than male users, and female listeners did not downgrade obscenity-using speakers more than male listeners.

873. Mulac, Anthony, and Mary J. Rudd. "Effects of Selected American Regional Dialects upon Regional Audience Members." *Communication Monographs*, 44 (1977), 185-195.

Although peripheral to its central research, this study found that female speakers were rated significantly higher on Aesthetic Quality and male speakers on Dynamism by 49 readers of the transcripts of the spontaneous speech of General American, Appalachian, and Bostonian dialect speakers, but not among the 106 listeners to the tapes of the same set of speakers.

874. Mulac, Anthony, and Torborg L. Lundell. "Differences in Perceptions Created by Syntactic-Semantic Productions of Male and Female Speakers." *Communication Monographs*, 47 (1980), 111-118.

Audiotaped language samples from 63 male and female volunteers (neither ethnics nor foreign-born were included), representing sixth graders, university undergraduates, and adults in their 50s and 60s, were evaluated by 85 male and 81 female undergraduates on the Speech Dialect Attitudinal Scale. Comparison revealed no sex differences on socio-intellectual status. Female speakers rated higher on aesthetic quality, and male speakers rated higher on dynamism.

875. Newcombe, Nora, and Diane B. Arnkoff. "Effects of Speech Styles and Sex of Speaker on Person Perception." *Journal of Personality and Social Psychology,* 37 (1979), 1293-1303.

Rating male and female speakers in conversational segments in which they used or did not use three linguistic variables which R. Lakoff (item 858) attributed to women, 138 male and female undergraduates found speeches with tag questions, qualifiers, and compound requests less assertive, though the latter two were also found warmer, regardless of sex of speaker. Study was replicated using 32 female secretaries, age range 18-58, with similar results.

876. Nichols, Patricia. "Black Women in the Rural South." In *The Sociology of the Languages of American Women* (item 1003), pp. 103-114. Rpt. in *International Journal of the Sociology of Language,* 17 (1978), 45-54.

After discussion of the methodological problems associated with the investigation of women's language use, Nichols reports her study of sex differences in the use of those morphological and syntactic variables in the speech of three sociologically different groups of blacks in Georgetown County, South Carolina, where Gullah (Geechee) is a dominant language variety. Individual interview data revealed that women in the lower socio-economic group of the mainland were more conservative linguistically than men in that group while women in the more socially mobile island community were more innovative than the island men. The interaction of language and social life is stressed. See also item 877.

877. Nichols, Patricia C. "Women in Their Speech Communities." In *Women and Language in Literature and Society* (item 1014), pp. 140-149.

After briefly reviewing research about women's speech in their communities, research which combines sociolinguistic and ethnographic features of investigation, Nichols presents evidence from her own research on black women of two communities in rural South Carolina. In one, with more educational and occupational opportunities, the women are abandoning creole forms for standard ones more than men are. In the other, a community with restricted opportunities, older women retain the old forms more than any other group of speakers. See also item 876.

878. O'Barr, William M., and Bowman K. Atkins. "'Women's Language' or 'Powerless Language'?" In *Women and Language in Literature and Society* (item 1014), pp. 93-110.

Examining over 150 hours of taped criminal court trials, the authors conclude that the features of women's speech that Lakoff proposed (see item 858) are really features of the speech of those not in power, female or male. Illustrative excerpts from court testimony as well as excerpts on handling women from trial practice manuals for lawyers are included.

879. Oliver, Marion M., and Joan Rubin. "The Use of Expletives by Some American Women." *Anthropological Linguistics*, 17 (1975), 191-197.

A questionnaire of the use of six expletives in various situations was given to 14 married and 14 single white, upper-class, college-educated women between 40-55. A clear-cut difference between "strong" and "weak" expletives emerged with usage varied depending on the formality of the situation, the degree of intimacy, and the need to assert identity. Single women tended to use expletives more frequently, and women who reported that they were working on being liberated used expletives more than either those not liberated or those completely liberated.

880. Ordoubadian, Reza, and Walburga von Raffler-Engel, eds. *Views on Language*. Murfreesboro, Tenn.: Inter-University Publishing, 1975.

This collection of some of the papers presented at the Thirteenth Southeastern Conference on Linguistics, 1975, includes a section of five articles on Women's Language. See items 776, 812, 815, 991, and 997.

* Parlee, Mary B. "Psychology and Women." *Signs: Journal of Women in Culture and Society*, 5 (1979), 121-133. See item 612.

881. Patrick, Jane A. "Male/Female Differences in Narrative Style." *The SECOL Bulletin*, 4 (1980), 91-106.

Analyzing the speech style of ten male and ten female narratives given in response to a film with no dialogue, Patrick found that males (no age given) produced shorter narratives in a streamlined style as contrasted to the elaborated style given by females. Males were interested more in the activities that occurred in the movie; females in the characters. Females used more "empty" language, that is, hedges, hesitations, intensifiers, and qualifiers, and males used repetition extensively and virtually exclusively.

882. Redlinger, Wendy. "Mothers' Speech to Children in Bilingual Mexican-American Homes." In *The Sociology of the Languages of American Women* (item 1003), pp. 119-130. Rpt. in *International Journal of the Sociology of Language,* 17 (1978), 73-82.

Twenty-five bilingual Mexican-American mothers were interviewed for their language attitudes and behavior. Most reported being comfortable in either language (64%), but more (40%) used Spanish with their children at home than English (28%; the rest used both equally). Overwhelmingly the mothers scolded in Spanish (80%), but tended to praise (68%) and console (56%) in English. Emphasis is made of the importance of language use of mother, of her attitudes toward both languages, and of the context of language use of bilingual families when their language is studied.

883. Rich, Elaine. "Sex-Related Differences in Colour Vocabulary." *Language and Speech,* 20 (1977), 404-409.

Five groups of subjects--male graduate students or technical workers (ages 20-35), professional males (ages 45-60), technical or well-educated females (ages 20-35), middle-aged women (ages 45-60), and Catholic nuns--named the color on 25 cards. Their responses indicated that women have larger color vocabularies than men, including the nuns who had the lowest score among the women. Younger males had larger color vocabularies than older males, while age made no difference for women's vocabularies.

884. Rieber, Robert W., Carl Wiedemann, and Jeanette D'Amato. "Obscenity: Its Frequency and Context of Usage as Compared in Males, Nonfeminist Females, and Feminist Females." *Journal of Psycholinguistic Research,* 8 (1979), 201-223.

A semantic differential to determine attitude toward three obscene words (*shit, fuck,* and *bastard*) was given to 29 males, 29 nonfeminist females, all of whom were college students; and 29 feminists, all active members of a feminist organization, some of whom were college students. Women reacted more strongly than men to these obscenities, though feminists rated them as less potent than the other two groups. Feminists also reported greater use of the words. *Fuck* was rated highest in activity, potency, and evaluation, and *bastard* least potent, especially so for feminists.

885. Samovar, Larry, and Fred Sanders. "Language Patterns of the Prostitute: Some Insights into a Deviant Subculture." *ETC.*, 35 (1978), 30-36.

    This examination of the language of a subculture focuses on how prostitutes use language to manipulate the situation and client to enhance group solidarity and cohesiveness. Data were collected primarily from field studies. Prostitutes engage in verbal game playing to make a client feel at ease while they size up the situation. They must be able to converse on a variety of topics at various intellectual levels and must keep the conversation moving toward a desired negotiation of the terms of the encounter. The rules for verbally manipulating the client and the situation are transmitted orally within the subculture.

886. Sanders, Janet S., and William L. Robison. "Talking and Not Talking About Sex: Male and Female Vocabularies." *Journal of Communication*, 29 (Spring 1979), 22-30.

    A questionnaire survey of 197 college students from four different universities (84 M, 113 F) on their use of terms for male and female genitalia and for the act of copulation and the context of their use revealed differences between the sexes in all contexts except "talking with parent/guardian." Females revealed greater difficulty finding a term for their own genitals than for male genitals and revealed more difficulty and less flexibility than males in finding a response in all contexts except in "spouse/lover."

887. Scherer, Klaus R., and Howard Giles, eds. *Social Markers in Speech*. Cambridge: Cambridge University Press, 1979.

    This collection of essays, mostly by psychologists and sociologists, on markers of speech includes references to sex differences in the chapter on phonetic and linguistic markers and social markers, and one chapter solely on sex markers. See also item 896.

888. Schneider, Michael and Karen A. Foss. "Thought, Sex, and Language: The Sapir-Whorf Hypothesis in the American Women's Movement." *Bulletin: Women's Studies in Communication*, 1, No. 1 (1977), 1-8.

889. Scott, Kathryn P. "Perceptions of Communication Competence: What's Good for the Goose Is Not Good for the Gander." *Women's Studies International Quarterly*, 3 (1980), 199-208.

In these studies about communication competence, a language stereotype questionnaire consisting of 36 bipolar items linked stereotypically to either female or male speech was used to elicit college students' perceptions of socially desirable or effective speech. In Experiment 1, 44 female and 50 male undergraduates gave ratings for socially desirable language traits and indicated that female-linked traits were seen as more desirable than male-linked traits. In Experiment 2, 47 female and 49 male undergraduates gave ratings for either an effective female, male, or sex-unspecified adult speaker. Perceptions of communication competence for a sex-unspecified adult more closely resembled that for a female than for a male speaker, and stereotypic female language characteristics were preferred over stereotypic male characteristics for competent female and adult speakers.

890. Shimanoff, Susan B. "Investigating Politeness." In *Discourse Across Time and Space*. Eds. Elinor Keenan and Tina L. Bennett. Los Angeles: Southern California Occasional Papers in Linguistics No. 5, 1977. Pp. 213-241.

891. Shuy, Roger W. "Sex as a Factor in Sociolinguistic Research." In *Language in its Social Setting*. Ed. William W. Gage. Washington, D.C.: Anthropological Society of Washington, 1974, pp. 74-83.

Although not published until 1974, this paper was delivered in 1969 and covers early research on sex differences in language. Studies in Detroit of both black and white male and female speakers revealed that female speakers of lower social classes more nearly approached the prestige forms in phonology than male speakers of lower social classes. A further study revealed that black adult females successfully identified white speakers heard on tape slightly more often than males did.

892. Shuy, Roger W. "Sociolinguistic Research at the Center for Applied Linguistics: The Correlation of Language and Sex." *Giornata Internazional di Sociolinguistica*. Roma: Palazzo Baldasini, 1970, pp. 849-857.

893. Siegler, David M., and Robert S. Siegler. "Stereotypes of Males' and Females' Speech." *Psychological Reports*, 39 (1976), 167-170.

Forty-eight female and 48 male undergraduates read statements with strong assertion, modified assertion with tag question attached, and neutral-control statements and were asked either to judge the sex of the speaker or the intelligence of the speaker. Tag questions were more often attributed to females and to be thought from unintelligent speakers; strong assertions were often attributed to males and to be thought from "bright" speakers. The authors suggest recent tests showing less prejudice toward women may be more a function of change in social desirability of expressing prejudice than of actual change in attitude.

* Silverman, Ellen-Marie, and Catherine H. Zimmer. "The Fluency of Women's Speech." In *The Sociology of the Languages of American Women*. Eds. Betty L. Dubois and Isabel Crouch. San Antonio, Texas: Trinity University, 1976, pp. 131-136. See item 1248.

894. Singer, Dorothy, Jill Avedon, Robin Hering, Annie McCann, and Cindi Sacks. "Sex Differences in the Vocabulary of College Students." *Journal of Sex Research*, 13 (1977), 267-273.

    This study replicated an 1891 one concerning differences between male and female vocabularies. Forty male and female undergraduates had 15 minutes in which to write down 100 nouns that came to mind. Analysis by category revealed that males used significantly more body-part words than females, who used significantly more clothing words and who produced more different words.

* Smith, Darrell, and Roger Miller. "Personal Growth Groups: A Comparison of the Experiences of Anglo and Mexican Americans." *Small Group Behavior*, 10 (1979), 263-270. See item 294.

895. Smith, J. Jerome. "Male and Female Ways of Speaking: Elaborately Restricted Codes in a CB Speech Community." *Papers in Linguistics*, 12 (Spring/Summer 1979), 163-184.

    An examination of how speech coding found in citizens band radio conversations in neighborhood networks is affected by gender and sex-role behavior revealed four distinct ways of speaking: talking skip, emergency reporting, mobiling, and ratchetjawing. In this last, although it is a restricted code in Basil Bernstein's terms ("Social Class, Language, and Socialization." In *The Psycho-Sociology of Language*. Ed. S. Moscovici. Chicago: Markham Publishing, 1972, pp. 222-242), individuality in expression is found. Although gender identity is clear because of self-selected nicknames and voice quality, both sexes seem to have equal access to all coding strategies and to all the roles played in the CB community.

896. Smith, Philip M. "Sex Markers in Speech." In *Social Markers in Speech* (item 887), pp. 109-146.

    This review of research covers sex differences in speech, in dialect, nonsequential features, and content; and the social significance of these differences, including stereotyped female speech attributes. The bibliography includes studies earlier than 1970 and non-English studies.

897. Solé, Yolanda R. "Sociocultural and Sociopsychological Factors in Differential Language Retentiveness by Sex." In *The Sociology of the Languages of American Women* (item 1003), pp. 137-153. Rpt. in *International Journal of the Sociology of Language,* 17 (1978), 29-44.

    Questionnaire data from 164 male and female university students of Mexican descent on language usage in and with various groups revealed that the generation of the person being interacted with was more influential than the sociocultural context of the situation, with Spanish being used almost exclusively with grandparents and English or code-switching with peers. Females claimed only English usage in far more contexts, including intrapersonal, than males, who favored code-switching. These findings are explored in light of such factors as the congruence between value orientation and role expectation of subculture versus dominant culture for each sex, the barriers each sex faces, the predispositions of each sex toward language learning, and the possible rewards for assimilation into mainstream society.

* Spradley, James P., and Brenda Mann. *The Cocktail Waitress: Woman's Work in a Man's World*. New York: John Wiley & Sons, 1975. See item 1325.

898. Staley, Constance M. "Male-Female Use of Expletives: A Heck of a Difference in Expectations." *Anthropological Linguistics,* 20 (1978), 367-380.

    A questionnaire survey was taken of 55 college students (25 F, 30 M) on their use of expletives as responses to 20 social situations with or without the presence of others and their prediction of what the opposite sex would say in response. Both sexes reported using about the same number of strong expletives, although men thought women would use fewer and women thought men would use more. Women used fewer excretory, sexual, and mixed strong expletives than men, which agreed with men's predictions. Current religious practice correlated with less strong expletive use for Protestants but not for Catholics. Both sexes reported most frequent use alone and less frequent use when in the presence of someone of higher social status.

899. Steckler, Nicole A., and William E. Cooper. "Sex Differences in Color Naming of Unisex Apparel." *Anthropological Linguistics,* 22 (1980), 373-381.

Eighteen male and 18 female Harvard-Radcliffe first-year students named as quickly and briefly as possible the colors of sweaters modeled by two other students, a male and a female. Females described most colors more specifically than males, generally using specific color terms (aquamarine) while males used basic color plus adjective (light blue). Females were more specific for colors like pink, dark red, yellow, and medium blue; males were equal or slightly more specific on colors like grey, brown, and green. These findings may reflect a developmental difference in acquisition of color terms.

900. Steingart, Irving, Norbert Freedman, Stanley Grand, and Charles Buchwald. "Personality Organization and Language Behavior: The Imprint of Psychological Differentiation on Language Behavior in Varying Communication Conditions." *Journal of Psycholinguistic Research,* 4 (1975), 241-255.

Twelve field-independent and twelve field-dependent college women, selected from a pool of 134 on their extreme scores on field dependence, were recorded in a dialogue with a woman interviewer and then were invited to talk (monologue) under warm or cold conditions (based on behavior of experimenter). Analysis of the verbal responses revealed that field-dependent subjects talked less in monologue conditions, but produced more grammatically elaborate language than in their dialogue condition. Field-independent subjects talked more, but their pattern of language behavior was similar in both monologue and dialogue conditions; that is, they continued to talk in monologue as if still in a dialogue condition.

901. Stitzel, Judith. "Unlearning to Not Speak: Feminism in the Classroom." *Frontiers*, 4, No. 1 (1979), 47-49.

   Stitzel presents an exercise in which students analyze the dialogue of a mixed-sex dyad for stereotyping and discusses the kinds of responses students make.

902. Swacker, Marjorie. "The Sex of the Speaker as a Sociolinguistic Variable." In *Language and Sex: Differences and Dominance* (item 1326), pp. 76-83.

   After reviewing five of the few linguistic studies (from 1944-1972) which use sex as a variable, Swacker reports the results of her own investigation. Seventeen male and 17 female students (ages 20-28) responded spontaneously to directions to describe pictures. Males talked significantly more than females (a mean of 13 minutes vs. 3.17 minutes). They used specific numbers (not necessarily accurately) where females used qualifiers such as *about* or *around*. In pauses between shifts in topic, males used interjections (*ok*, *oh*, *well*) where females used significantly more conjunctions.

903. Swacker, Marjorie. "Women's Verbal Behavior at Learned and Professional Conferences." In *The Sociology of the Languages of American Women* (item 1003), pp. 155-160.

   Analysis of the responses of men and women to papers given at three conferences of academic professional organizations revealed that males spoke more often and longer than females, used prequestion prediction (references to other studies) far more, and asked more questions per comment. Women more often couched their questions in polite form, often with personal pronouns ("I would like to ask...") or with modals ("Mightn't it be the case that..."). Implications for professional advancement are made.

904. Tixier y Vigil, Yvonne, and Nan Elasser. "The Effects of the Ethnicity of the Interviewer on Conversation: A Study of Chicana Women." In *The Sociology of the Languages of American Women* (item 1003), pp. 161-170. Rpt. in *International Journal of the Sociology of Language*, 17 (1978), 91-102.

   Fifteen Chicana women of three different age groups were interviewed informally both by an Anglo and a Chicana on topics covering home, family, sexual values, and discrimination. As predicted, the women talked more and more openly to the Anglo than to the Chicana about sexual matters (since Chicana culture does not condone open discussion), younger more than older. They talked more to the Chicana about discrimination. Frequencies, examples, and implications are included.

905. Trudgill, Peter. "Sex, Covert Prestige, and Linguistic Change in the Urban British English of Norwich." *Language in Society*, 1 (1972), 179-195. Rpt. in *Language and Sex: Difference and Dominance* (item 1326), pp. 88-104.

Based on evidence from American studies in the 1950s and 1960s showing women using prestige standard linguistic forms more than men, Trudgill investigated the use of prestige and working-class linguistic forms among both sexes and five classes of Norwich, England, respondents. Women used prestige standard forms more frequently than men. Trudgill speculates on two possible reasons for this finding: that women, less secure and subordinate to men in society, must signal social status in linguistic ways, that is, that they must be rated by how they appear whereas men are rated more on what they do; and that working-class culture, including its language, is viewed positively by men as masculine and therefore not only are working class linguistic forms retained but the prestige forms are actively rejected.

906. Walsh, Robert H., and Wilbert M. Leonard, II. "Usage of Terms for Sexual Intercourse by Men and Women." *Archives of Sexual Behavior*, 3 (1974), 373-376.

In this study 248 male and female undergraduates listed synonyms for sexual intercourse and indicated whether they would use such terms in same-sex or mixed-sex groups. Males listed more synonyms (total N = 160) than females (N = 130). Males approved of the use of both *fuck* and *screw* in either same-sex or mixed-sex groups.

907. Warshay, Diana W. "Sex Differences in Language Style." In *Toward a Sociology of Women*. Ed. Constantina Safilios-Rothschild. New York: John Wiley & Sons, 1972, pp. 3-9.

Sex differences in language style were studied by having 171 female and 92 male undergraduates write down all the important past events of their lives. Females were more fluent, referred to events more in noun phrases (males in verb phrases), were less time-oriented and less involved in the events than males, located the event within the community (males within personal sphere), and referred more to others. Warshay analyzes the data as showing that the female exhibits concern with "being" and seeks satisfaction in primary relationships and the community, while males are more active, ego-involved, and less concerned about others.

908. Weigle, Marta. "Women as Verbal Artists: Reclaiming the Sisters of Enheduanna." *Frontiers: A Journal of Women's Studies,* 3, No. 3 (1978), 1-9.

    This overview of a group of articles about women as verbal artists suggests that research on this topic has been neglected in favor of similar investigations of men and verbal arts. She urges research on women in the areas of gossip, conversation, collaborative lore, verbal aggression, humor, and audience-performer relationships.

909. Weisman, Martha. "Rhetoric of Women Activists in the United States." *Female Studies,* 7 (1973), 111-112.

    The syllabus and bibliography for a course in feminist rhetoric are presented.

910. Wells, Theodora. "Handling Sexism at Work: Nondefensive Communication." In *New Life Options: The Working Woman's Resource Book.* Eds. Rosalind K. Loring and Herbert A. Otto. New York: McGraw-Hill Book Co., 1976. Pp. 119-138.

    After defining sexism, Wells examines sexist put-downs and double messages, and analyzes the ways that verbal and nonverbal communication are used to keep women on the defensive at work.

911. West, Candace. "Against Our Will: Male Interruptions of Females in Cross-Sex Conversation." In *Language, Sex, and Gender* (item 1017), pp. 81-97.

    In a previous study of naturally occurring conversations, West observed that men interrupt women more often than women interrupt men or than either sex interrupts in same-sex conversations. This study focused on deep interruptions, "those that occur more than two syllables away from a terminal boundary of a possibly complete utterance," which may be considered attempts to take control of the conversation. Responses to deep intrusions of five male and five female speakers in cross-sex conversations among previously unacquainted college students were examined to determine submission patterns; a hierarchy of responses varying from submissiveness to assertiveness was developed. Males interrupted females three times more often than females interrupted males. However, females were as likely as males to respond assertively to deep interruptions.

912. Zimmerman, Mary. "Alignment Strategies in Verbal Accounts of Problematic Conduct: The Case of Abortion." In *The Sociology of the Languages of American Women* (item 1003), pp. 171-183.

The strategies of alignment, those techniques used by persons to reconcile their actions which go against acceptable cultural standards, usually either justifications (reducing the negative aspects of the action) or excuses (rejecting personal responsibility for the action), were examined through analysis of interviews with 40 women (ages 14-39) who had had abortions. Most (53%) held themselves accountable for becoming pregnant, some (32%) ignored accountability, and a few (15%) tried to excuse their pregnancy. Most (65%) felt they had only this way (abortion) out of their predicament, so it was a decision forced on them, and others (35%) took responsibility for the action but said they did not want the child. Thus only a small group (15%) used alignment strategies for becoming pregnant, but a large group (80%) used these strategies for the abortion.

LANGUAGE USED ABOUT WOMEN

913. American Psychological Association. "Guidelines for Nonsexist Language in APA Journals: Publication Manual Change Sheet 2." *American Psychologist,* 32 (1977), 487-494.

914. American Psychological Association. Task Force on Issues of Sexual Bias in Graduate Education. "Guidelines for Nonsexist Use of Language." *American Psychologist,* 30 (1975), 682-684.

915. American Psychological Association. Task Force on Issues of Sexual Bias in Graduate Education. "Guidelines for Nonsexist Use of Language." *The School Counselor,* 23 (1976), 271-274.

916. American Speech-Language-Hearing Association. "Guidelines for Nonsexist Language in Journals of ASHA." *ASHA,* 21, No. 11 (1979), 973-977.

917. Baker, Robert. "'Pricks' and 'Chicks': A Plea for 'Persons.'" In *Philosophy and Sex* (item 918), pp. 45-64.

    The dehumanizing concepts underlying words used to identify women and copulation are analyzed in this essay.

918. Baker, Robert, and Frederick Elliston, eds. *Philosophy and Sex.* Buffalo, N.Y.: Prometheus Books, 1975.

    Of the four topics covered in this collection of essays, the section on the semantics of sex contains three essays on language used about women. See items 917, 932, and 939.

919. Bate, Barbara. "Nonsexist Language Use in Transition." *Journal of Communication,* 28 (Winter 1978), 139-149.

    In this report of interviews with ten male and ten femmale university faculty members on their degree of comfortableness with certain sexist terms and their substitutes, *lady poet* was discredited by most. *Girl* tended to be acceptable for a female in college, *boy* tended to be for a male; and generic *he, they, he and she,* and *s/he* had some supporters of each sex. Theoretical questions about language change are included.

920. Beardsley, Elizabeth L. "Traits and Genderization." In *Feminism and Philosophy* (item 1024), pp. 117-123.

    Beardsley notes the linguistic practice of making a sex distinction in language about humans (genderization) more frequently affects personality traits than character traits. For example, *aggressive* shows male genderization since the word for the same personality trait in women is *pushy.* She hypothesizes the reason for the personality/character distinctions is that females have not been accorded full status as persons and thus are not considered for character genderization but are for personality.

921. Berger, Gertrude, and Beatrice Kachuck. *Sexism, Language and Social Change.* U.S. Department of HEW, National Institute of Education, 1976.

    This 16-page publication contains the argument that language can and will change because of its structure, its regular process of change, and the relationship between thought and language.

922. Berryman, Cynthia L., and James R. Wilcox. "Attitudes Toward Male and Female Speech: Experiments on the Effects of Sex-Typical Language." *The Western Journal of Speech Communication,* 44 (1980), 50-59.

Two experiments were conducted to test the effects of messages containing sex-based language distinctions on evaluations of the speaker, attitudes toward the message, and sex-role stereotype of the speaker. Experiment I had 108 female undergraduates and Experiment II, 59 female and 42 male undergraduates; all responded to a bogus transcript of a group discussion manipulated for male and female linguistic code features. In Experiment I, evaluation of the female linguistic code differed significantly from evaluation of the male linguistic code on the dimensions of command, self-orientation, and compliance. Results of Experiment II indicated that sex of subject did not affect the findings of Experiment I; both sexes perceived the male linguistic code speaker as more masculine, more commanding, and less accommodating, and the female linguistic code speaker just the opposite.

923. Blakar, Rolv M. "How Sex Roles are Represented, Reflected and Conserved in the Norwegian Language." *Acta Sociologica,* 18 (1975), 162-173.

An analysis of the relationship between social reality and language by examining the realities implied by *mann* (man) and *kvinne* (woman) revealed that there is a two-way interaction between social reality and language and that, whenever rival or divergent interests can be expressed, the interests or perspectives of the one in power (man) will dominate at the expense of the other (woman). Strategies for the woman's liberation movement are suggested. Written in English.

924. Blaubergs, Maija S. "Changing the Sexist Language: The Theory Behind the Practice." *Psychology of Women Quarterly,* 2 (1978), 224-261.

A discussion of the literature on sexist language (57 references) leads Blaubergs to conclude that the three major approaches to sexism in the language are to do nothing since the language reflects the actuality which must change first; to change irrelevant masculine references to neutral terminology; or to emphasize feminine terms to enhance female self-concept. Blaubergs suggests guidelines and research needs for the second two approaches.

925. Bliese, Nancy W. "Sex-Role Stereotyping of Adjectives: A Hopeful Report." *Bulletin: Women's Studies in Communication,* 1, No. 2 (1977), 27-32.

926. Bosmajian, Haig A. *The Language of Oppression.* Washington, D.C.: Public Affairs Press, 1974.

    This book contains a chapter on "The Language of Sexism" and sexism in the language of the law. A shorter version of this essay appears in *ETC.* (item 927). The expansion includes material on sexism in legal language, in marriage and name change, and the sexism inherent in protecting women from vulgar language.

927. Bosmajian, Haig A. "The Language of Sexism." *ETC.,* 29 (1972), 305-313.

    An essay delineating through examples the manner in which women have been linguistically subordinated and suppressed, made not only inferior but invisible, and calling for correction of the abuses.

* Bridges, Judith S. "Correlates of Sex Role and Attitudes toward Women." *Psychological Reports,* 43 (1978), 1279-82. See item 711.

928. Burr, Elizabeth, Susan Dunn, and Norma Farquhar. "The Language of Inequality." *ETC.,* 29 (1972), 414-416.

    The authors suggest changes in language use to eliminate phrases that reflect "outdated" assumptions about women.

929. Burr, Elizabeth, Susan Dunn, and Norma Farquhar. "Women and the Language of Inequality." *Social Education,* 36 (1972), 841-845.

    This article argues that sexism in language, especially in textbooks, must be eliminated.

930. Coyne, James C., Richard C. Sherman, and Karen O'Brien. "Expletives and Woman's Place." *Sex Roles,* 4 (1978), 827-835.

    In this examination of the relationship between the expletives *bitch* and *bastard* and sex-role stereotyping, 136 undergraduates rated 80 trait adjectives as to how typical or characteristic each was of the expletives. For male subjects the most distinguishing feature between the two expletives was the inclusion of the stereotypically masculine trait dominant in their characterization of *bitch*. Female subjects did not ascribe such opposite sex-role stereotypic traits to *bitch*, but emphasized stereotypically masculine traits in their characterization of *bastard*.

931. Crowley, Sharon. "The Semantics of Sexism." *ETC.*, 4 (1973), 407-411.

    This essay examines the miscommunication involved in three reactions to women's liberation: refusal to believe women are equal to men in capabilities (and that they are discriminated against), fears concerning changes in society if liberation goals are achieved, and the ethos of women in the movement. The last reaction is based on extrinsic ethos, the image that exists before the message, and intrinsic ethos, the image projected by the message itself, dress, appearance, and delivery. Crowley notes that the extrinsic ethos has proved "nearly insurmountable because of our polarized notions of male/female, masculinity/femininity and the consequent assumption that anything not feminine wants to be masculine."

* French, Marilyn. "Women in Language." *Soundings*, 59 (1976), 329-344. See item 823.

932. Frye, Marilyn. "Male Chauvinism: A Conceptual Analysis." In *Philosophy and Sex* (item 918), pp. 65-79.

    In a philosophic-semantic essay, Frye argues that sexism stems from a belief that excludes women from the conceptual community and that "chauvinism" is a misleading term for it.

933. Garnica, Olga K. "The Boys Have the Muscles and the Girls Have the Sexy Legs: Adult-Child Speech and the Use of Generic Person Labels." In *Language, Children and Society: The Effect of Social Factors on Children Learning to Communicate*. Eds. Olga K. Garnica and Martha L. King. Oxford: Pergamon, 1979, pp. 135-148.

    A study of the use of generic person words (*boy, girl, baby, man, woman,* etc.) by adult daycare staff members in dyadic interaction with six girls ages eleven months to two years revealed that elaborated sequences were partly a source of learning social categories, and that *girl* was used in more elaborated sequences than *boy*, perhaps partly because of the gender of the children.

934. Gershuny, H. Lee. "Sexist Semantics in the Dictionary." *ETC.*, 31 (1974), 159-169.

A study of the number of sentences using masculine or feminine words and the context of their use as illustrative sentences of the *Random House Dictionary of the English Language* (1966) revealed that, of the 2028 sentences, those with only masculine gender words outnumbered sentences with only feminine gender words three to one. Both male and female sex roles were stereotyped significantly more than chance. Implications and recommendations are included.

935. Goffman, Erving. "Footing." *Semiotica*, 25, 1/2 (1979), 1-29.

This article laying the theoretical groundwork for a description of changing the frame of events in a conversation, which Goffman calls footing, begins and ends with an anecdote after a bill-signing ceremony involving President Nixon's bandiage with reporter Helen Thomas about her style of dressing. Not only footing but sexism and power forces were evident in the exchange.

936. Graham, Alma. "The Making of a Nonsexist Dictionary." *ETC.*, 31 (1974), 57-64. Rpt. in *Language and Sex: Difference and Dominance* (item 1326), pp. 57-63.

This essay by the Executive Editor of the Dictionary Division of American Heritage Publishing Company details the editing and compiling of *The School Dictionary* (1972). An analysis of five million words used in school textbooks revealed overwhelming male supremacy in both number of mentions and positive attributes.

937. Grim, Patrick. "Sexism and Semantics." In *Feminism and Philosophy* (item 1024), pp. 109-116.

Noting that sexism is more than just semantics, Grim analyzes the semantics of sexist statements to show that, although not all sexist statements are false, they all carry implications that are false.

938. Heilman, Madeline E. "Miss, Mrs., Ms., or None of the Above." *American Psychologist*, 30 (1975), 516-518.

To determine the effect of title on ratings of the potential enjoyableness and intellectual stimulation of a course, 90 undergraduates (88 M, 2 F) evaluated 2 courses, one more technical than the other, presented as being taught by a Miss, Mrs., Ms., or Mr. J.R. Erwin or by J.R. Erwin (no title). Subjects rated the less technical course less enjoyable and less intellectually stimulating if it were to be taught by a Miss or Mrs. than by a Ms., Mr., or no title. The experiment was replicated with 160 high school seniors with the same results.

* Lakoff, Robin T. "Language and Woman's Place." *Language in Society,* 2 (1973), 45-80. Rpt. as Part I in R. Lakoff, *Language and Woman's Place.* New York: Harper and Row, 1975. See item 858.

939. Lawrence, Barbara. "Four-Letter Words Can Hurt You." In *Philosophy and Sex* (item 918), pp. 31-33.

This essay is on the sexism of taboo sex references.

940. Legman, G. "A Word for It." *Maledicta,* 1 (1977), 9-18.

This inventory of dirty words and expressive remarks currently in use in the United States contains many relating to women, including all-purpose insults that relate to illegitimate parentage and to relationships with whores as well as insulting expressions that describe women as either sexually attractive and desirable (or just the reverse) or as money- (or success-) minded in sexual relationships.

941. Lerner, Harriet E. "Girls, Ladies, or Women? The Unconscious Dynamics of Language Choice." *Comprehensive Psychiatry,* 17 (1976), 295-299.

Lerner, staff psychologist at the Menninger Foundation, analyzes the assumptions underlying her colleagues' preferred use of the terms *girl* and *lady* rather than *woman,* exploring why these choices arose and why they are maintained. The significance the language choice may have in treating patients is also examined.

942. McGraw-Hill Book Company. *Guidelines for Equal Treatment of the Sexes.* McGraw-Hill Book Company Publications. New York: McGraw-Hill Book Company, 1974.

943. Miller, Casey, and Kate Swift. *The Handbook of Nonsexist Writing.* New York: Lippincott and Crowell, 1980.

This handbook contains chapters on masculine generics, on examples of their use and the use of miscellaneous gender terms (*coed, maiden/master,* etc.), alternatives to them, and on the belittling of women, their role, and their titles. References are included.

944. Miller, Casey, and Kate Swift. *Words and Women: New Language in New Times.* Garden City, N.Y.: Anchor Press/ Doubleday, 1976.

Using historical accounts and observing the current scene, Miller and Swift present their case for a nonsexist use of language that stresses the includion of women in the meaning of words referring to humans of either sex.

945. Murray, Jessica. "Male Perspective in Language." *Women: A Journal of Liberation,* 3, No. 2 (1972), 46-50.

Murray argues that the male bias in language indicates a male outlook that pervades human culture and is based on the archetypal assumption that *human* means *male.* She cites examples from literature, art, and language usage to prove her point.

946. National Council of Teachers of English. *Guidelines for Nonsexist Use of Language in NCTE Publications.* Urbana, Ill.: NCTE, 1975.

947. Nilsen, Alleen P. "Sexism in English: A Feminist View." *Female Studies,* 6 (1972), 102-109.

An examination of the contents of a standard desk dictionary revealed many sex biases, including that our culture considers important a woman's body but a man's mind. The dictionary compilations had many positive connotations with "masculine" concepts, but negative or trivial ones with "feminine" concepts.

948. Nilsen, Alleen P., Haig Bosmajian, H. Lee Gershuny, and Julia P. Stanley. *Sexism and Language.* Urbana, Ill.: National Council of Teachers of English, 1977.

This collection of eight essays covers sexism in the language of legislatures, courts, literature, and marirage, plus gender marking in American English usage. References are included.

949. O'Donnell, Holly S. "Sexism in Language." *Elementary English,* 50 (1973), 1067-72.

This is a general report with annotated references to five documents which discuss sexism in the language.

950. Purnell, Sandra E. "Politically Speaking, Do Women Exist?" *Journal of Communication,* 28 (Winter 1978), 150-155.

An examination of the representation of women in speeches of both parties' candidates for the presidency in 1968, 1972, and 1976 revealed the use of both generic masculine terms and nonsexist terms, very few (7% of total) references to women, and sex-role stereotyping by occupation.

951. Rysman, Alexander. "How the 'Gossip' Became a Woman." *Journal of Communication*, 27 (Winter 1977), 176-180.

    Noting that the word *gossip* acquired its derogatory connotations only after it began to be applied to women, Rysman conjectures that because it retains its implications of solidarity, it is derided since solidarity can lead to social ties outside areas of male dominance.

952. Safilios-Rothschild, Constantina. *Women and Social Policy*. Englewood Cliffs, N.J.: Prentice-Hall, 1974.

    Research, theories, and a description of social actions and policies that should occur are given on a wide range of issues relating to women. Topics discussed include sexist language and sexism in the legal system, in politics, and in counseling and therapy.

953. Saporta, Sol. "Language in a Sexist Society." In *Studies in Descriptive and Historical Linguistics: Festschrift for Winfred P. Lehmann*. Ed. Paul J. Hopper. Amsterdam: John Benjamins, 1977, pp. 209-216.

    Noting the absence of theory relevant to language and sexism, Saporta discusses facts of the language that such a theory will have to take into account, illustrating each with many examples. He notes that the masculine is an unmarked form, the feminine marked (*prince, princess; waiter, waitress*), although sometimes the unmarked form is used neutrally (the generic use of the masculine). Also, there is asymmetry in syntax (for example, with verbs for sexual intercourse--*He screws her*, but not *She screws him*) and in lexicon (*guy* seems to have no female equivalent; *housewife* no male). Metaphoric terms, euphemisms, and epithets are frequently asymmetrical (*chick, piece* seem to apply only to females), while some words are symmetrical by form but not in meaning (*governor, governess*). Some vocabulary seems symmetrical but ultimately is not. *He is an old maid* means he has some undesirable qualities usually associated with a female; *she is a ballsy feminist*, also perjorative, means she has desirable qualities usually associated with a male.

954. Schultz, Muriel R. "The Semantic Derogation of Woman."
In *Language and Sex: Difference and Dominance* (item 1326), pp. 64-75.

Tracing the semantic changes in terms designating the sexes, Schultz finds systematic perjoration, that is, debasing or obscene changes, for terms for women but not for men. *Lady* has been debased, *lord* has not; *governess* has, *governor* has not; *mistress* has, *master* has not; etc. Three causes of such degeneration, prejudice, euphemism, and association with a contaminating concept, are discussed.

955. Schultz, Muriel R. "How Serious Is Sex Bias in Language?" *College Composition and Communication*, 26 (1975), 163-167.

Noting that the English language reflects the dominance of males in our society as well as some of the proposals to eradicate this masculine bias (use of *Ms, person,* and new generic pronouns), Schultz finds many of the suggestions unworkable and recommends using plural pronouns, with or without a singular antecedent, or accepting *he* as a true generic.

956. Scott, Foresman, and Company. Sexism in Testbooks Committee of Women at Scott, Foresman. *Guidelines for Improving the Image of Women in Textbooks.* Glenview, Ill.: Scott, Foresman and Company, 1972.

957. Stanley, Julia P. "Paradigmatic Women: The Prostitute." In *Papers in Language Variation: SAMLA-ADS Collection.* Eds. David L. Shores and Carole P. Hines. University: University of Alabama Press, 1977, pp. 303-321.

Stanley identifies semantic features of sexual terms applied to prostitutes and creates a visual representation, a parametric grid, of the semantic field relationships among these terms. The semantic features are denotative or connotative, dysphemistic or euphemistic, metonymic, and metaphoric.

958. Stanley, Julia P., and Cynthia McGowan. "Woman and Wife: Social and Semantic Shifts in English." *Papers in Linguistics,* 12 (1979), 491-502.

This essay esamines the history of the word *woman* in the context of related vocabulary changes in Old English, such as with *wer, man, wīf,* and *hūsbōnd,* and the social conditions of the time. Stanley concludes that the compound *wifman,* eventually *woman,* was but one of a series of terms shifting semantically. A reexamination of contemporary interpretations of the linguistic changes of that period is called for.

959. Stanley, Julia P., and Susan W. Robbins. "Sex-Marked Predicates in English." *Papers in Linguistics,* 11 (1978), 487-516.

An analysis of sex-marked predicates in English reveals that some (for example, "menstruate," "castrate") are based on biological functions, but others (for example, terms for copulation) continue to proliferate but reflect only the male version of reality. Both the asymmetrical relationships between *to mother* and *to father* and the assigning of predicates not biologically sex-marked to one sex with assumed positive or negative connotations are seen as evidence of sex-role stereotyping.

960. Stephenson, Harriet B. "De-Stereotyping Personnel Language." *Personnel Journal,* 54 (1975), 334-355.

Stephenson suggests seven guidelines (mostly dealing with the "generic" nouns and pronouns) for removing sexism in language. She includes examples from management and personnel texts and journals to reveal what needs to be rewritten and gives possible rewordings.

961. Stevens, Betsy. "Improving Communication With Clerical Workers: The Non-Sexist Directive." *Personnel Journal,* 56 (1977), 170-172.

Offending remarks heard by clerical workers at a university were collected via a questionnaire and categorized. Almost 50% returned the questionnaires, and, of these, over 73% listed remarks ranging from "After all, you're not here to make a career of it" to being called an "office girl."

962. Strainchamps, Ethel. "Our Sexist Language." In *Woman in Sexist Society.* Eds. Vivian Gornick and Barbara K. Moran. New York: Basic Books, 1971, pp. 240-250.

Strainchamps argues that English is a male-dominated language, supporting her position by an examination of sexual words and words denoting gender.

963. Swatos, William H., Jr., and Judith A. Kline. "The Lady is Not a Whore: Labeling the Promiscuous Woman." *International Journal of Women's Studies,* 1 (1978), 159-166.

Interviews with 250 undergraduates revealed their perception of a prostitute was "better" than their perception of a whore.

964. Teidt, Iris M. "Sexism in Language: An Editor's Plague." *Elementary English,* 50, No. 7 (1973), 1073-74.

965. Toth, Emily. "How Can a Woman MAN the Barricades? Or Linguistic Sexism Up Against the Wall." *Women: A Journal of Liberation,* 2, No. 1 (1970), 57.

   Toth discusses the use of masculine gender words such as *man* and *he* to refer to women. She advocates changing our vocabularies to rid them of chauvinistic language.

966. Weiher, Carol. "Sexism in Language and Sex Differences in Language Usage: Which Is More Important?" *College Composition and Communication,* 27 (1976), 240-243.

   This essay notes the attention to sex bias in the language but the lack of attention to differences in the way the two sexes use the language. Descriptive studies on such differences are referred to, and a call made to wipe out the myths and folk beliefs that prevail.

967. Williams. Juanita H. "Woman: Myth and Stereotype." *International Journal of Women's Studies,* 1 (1978), 221-247.

   In this historic review of the myth and stereotyped image of women, Williams discusses the myth-image-stereotype of woman through the ages. Some attention is given to the language used to describe women.

968. Wolfson, Nessa, and Joan Manes. "'Don't "Dear" Me!'" in *Women and Language in Literature and Society* (item 1014), pp. 79-92.

   An analysis of over 800 interactions between service people (gas station attendants, waitresses, etc.) and the researchers revealed that address terms could be either polite (*ma'am*), terms of endearment (*dear, hon*), or absent. A polite term was used more in the South than in the Northeast, and used more with men (*sir*) than with women. In general, endearment terms were used more for people in a position of helplessness or for people without power, namely women.

GENERIC NOUN AND PRONOUN

* Bate, Barbara. "Nonsexist Language Use in Transition." *Journal of Communication,* 28 (Winter,1978), 139-149. See item 919.

969. Baron, Naomi. "A Reanalysis of English Grammatical Gender." *Lingua,* 27 (August 1971), 113-140.

    This reinterpretation of the data on the development of the English gender system notes discrete stages in the development, not the gradual evolution from grammatical gender to a natural gender system that traditional grammar purports.

970. Beardsley, Elizabeth L. "Referential Genderization." *Philosophical Forum,* 5 (1973-74), 285-293.

    In this essay Beardsley examines linguistic genderization, specifically the attribution of sex in words to refer to human beings, the use of one set of these sex-distinguishing words for sex-neutral referents (*Each one* had *his* passport ready), and the ethical implications of such referential genderization.

971. Bendix. Edward H. "Linguistic Models as Political Symbols: Gender and the Generic 'He' in English." In *Language, Sex, and Gender* (item 1017), pp. 23-39.

    Reviewing three theories concerning the meaning of *he,* Bendix shows that a neutral *he* may connote maleness even when applied to females. Considering whether changing a generic *he* would change social behavior, Bendix states that when people already have sex role and status beliefs/ knowledge, language usage may only be a symptom and a reminder. Language can influence behavior, however, particularly in children in the enculturation process. Adults seem influenced by language reform not as a carrier of information but as a political symbol.

972. Blaubergs, Maija S. "An Analysis of Classic Arguments Against Changing Sexist Language." *Women's Studies International Quarterly,* 3 (1980), 135-147.

    Blaubergs analyzes the arguments for retaining masculine generic usage, from the cross-cultural arguments, to word-etymology arguments to appeal-to-authority arguments, and concludes that nonsexist language forms and usage patterns now coexist with earlier forms and that resistance to the new usage will continue. Study of such resistance may add to the understanding of the social nature of language and to the bases of antifeminism.

* Blaubergs, Maija S. "On 'The Nurse Was a Doctor.'" In *Views on Language*. Eds. Reta Ordoubadian and Walburga von Raffler-Engel. Murfreesboro, Tenn.: University Publishing, 1975, pp. 87-95. See item 997.

973. Bodine, Ann. "Androcentrism in Prescriptive Grammar's Singular 'They,' Sex-Indefinite 'He,' and 'He or She.'" *Language in Society*, 4 (1975), 129-146.

This historical account of the prescriptive grammarian's advocacy of *he* rather than *they* or *he or she* reveals its social motivation, an androcentric motivation still used in the 33 current school grammars examined. Since changes are occurring in second person pronouns in other languages, and since the "singular" use of *they* has survived in spoken English despite the prescriptive grammarian's ban ("Anyone can do it if they try hard enough"), and since feminists oppose *he* as a sex-indefinite pronoun, Bodine expects change to occur.

974. Cohen, Philip M. "He, She, It, They." *Word Ways*, 10 (1977), 157-162.

After a review of twenty-five proposals during the past century to modify personal pronoun structure, Cohen concludes that the use of *he* to refer to an antecedent of unspecified sex appears impervious to change. Other, more successful adaptations, including occupational titles and the use of *they*, are also discussed.

* Garnica, Olga K. "The Boys Have the Muscles and the Girls Have the Sexy Legs: Adult-Child Speech and the Use of Generic Person Labels." In *Language, Children and Society: The Effect of Social Factors on Children Learning to Communicate*. Eds. Olga K. Garnica and Martha L. King. Oxford: Pergamon, 1979, pp. 135-148. See item 933.

975. Green, William H. "Singular Pronouns and Sexual Politics." *College Composition and Communication*, 28 (1977), 150-153.

A survey of pronoun use from 184 junior college students revealed more errors in singular-common gender sentences than in singular-specific gender sentences, with *they*, *them*, and *their* often functioning as singular pronouns. Green suggests that this usage is more likely to prevail than introducing a new, singular generic pronoun.

976. Huber, Joan. "On the Generic Use of Male Pronouns." *The American Sociologist*, 11 (1976), 89.

977. Johnson, Carole S., and Inga K. Kelly. "'He' and 'She': Changing Language to Fit a Changing World." *Educational Leadership*, 32 (1975), 527-530.

Reviewing previous research on the images produced by the generic *he*, the authors conclude that its continued use is unwarranted and that educators, as facilitators of individual development, should adopt inclusionary language.

978. Korsmeyer, Carolyn. "The Hidden Joke: Generic Uses of Masculine Terminology." In *Feminism and Philosophy* (item 1024), pp. 138-153.

This philosophic look at sexism in language notes that terms used with males are often neutral as well (*driver, traffic cop*) while their equivalent for females often carry humorous overtones (*woman driver, meter maid*). Reviewing Bergson's ideas about humor, Korsmeyer concludes that such usages reveal that the concept of woman itself is limited to particular physical features while the concept of *man* can also refer to *person*, free from particular physical features. Using neutral generic terms like *person*, therefore, should help to free the rigidity in the concept of *woman*.

* Lakoff, Robin T. "Language and Woman's Place." *Language in Society*, 2 (1973), 45-80. Rpt. as Part I in R. Lakoff, *Language and Woman's Place*. New York: Harper and Row, 1975. See item 858.

979. Luepton, Lloyd B. "Gender Wording, Sex, and Response to Items on Achievement Value." *Psychological Reports*, 46 (1980), 140-142.

The responses of 437 male and female college students to items from two achievement value scales worded with the original generic *man* and masculine pronouns, with neutral *person* and *one*, or with *woman* and feminine pronouns were analyzed. The response pattern indicated no significant differences for females by style of wording.

980. MacKay, Donald G. "On the Goals, Principles, and Procedures for Prescriptive Grammar: Singular They." *Language in Society*, 9 (1980), 349-367.

In this essay reviewing the rift between prescriptive and theoretical linguists, MacKay focuses on the suggested use of *they* as a substitute for the prescriptive *he*. An examination of 108 articles, both scientific and popular, and of textbooks yielded no occurrences of *they* and less than 1% of generic *she*, *it*, or *he and she*. Substituting *they* in sample sentences, however, resulted in ambiguities, loss of precision, distancing, and other problems. MacKay discusses the costs and benefits of such changes, with a glance at the possibility of a neologism substitute for *he*.

981. MacKay, Donald G. "Psychology, Prescriptive Grammar, and the Pronoun Problem." *American Psychologist,* 35 (1980), 444-449.

Forty undergraduates read either silently or aloud in groups of ten (5 M, 5 F) paragraphs containing *he*, *E*, *e*, or *tey*, all used generically to refer to a noun either male or female. Those reading *he* misunderstood the antecedent as solely male 40% more than those reading identical passages but with a neologism substituted for *he*.

982. Martyna, Wendy. "Beyond the 'He/Man' Approach: The Case for Nonsexist Language." *Signs: Journal of Women in Culture and Society,* 5 (1980), 482-493.

Martyna reviews and refutes trivialization of the sexist language controversy, particularly the "generic" masculine nouns and pronouns, and argues for adopting nonsexist language.

983. Martyna, Wendy. "The Psychology of the Generic Masculine." In *Women and Language in Literature and Society* (item 1014), pp. 69-78.

In a series of experiments involving the use of *he* as a generic, Martyna found that women used *he* less than men, regardless of the antecedent, and used other alternatives (*they*, *he and she*) more than men. Although women report less imagery than men when neutral subjects are used, the imagery is male when it occurs. Women explain their generic use in terms of standards of grammar. The psychological consequences of the use of a generic masculine are discussed.

984. Martyna, Wendy. "What Does 'He' Mean?" *Journal of Communication,* 28 (Winter 1978), 131-138.

Twenty male and 20 female college students completed sentence fragments requiring pronouns. Pronouns reflecting traditional roles by sex were used by both males and females, and "neutral" nouns ("student," "person," etc.) elicited generic *he*, generic *she*, *they*, or *he and she*. Females were significantly less likely than males to use generic *he*. In a follow-up questionnaire on which they reported the image that went along with their pronoun choice, males reported sex-specific imagery for generic *he*; females did not but used generic *he* because it is grammatically sanctioned.

* Miller, Casey, and Kate Swift. *The Handbook of Nonsexist Writing*. New York: Lippincott and Crowell, 1980. See item 943.

985. Moulton, Janice. "The Myth of the Neutral 'Man.'" In *Feminism and Philosophy* (item 1024), pp. 124-137.

Moulton argues that a neutral use of *man* and masculine pronouns is virtually impossible. Like other unmarked terms, the masculine terms have positive associations (as with unmarked terms like *tall* as opposed to the marked term *short*). Their ambiguity also interferes with their neutral use, since they can be used generically and sex-specifically in consecutive sentences. Also, because of the higher status of men, the generic term persists even though a true neutral (*person*) is available.

986. Moulton, Janice, George M. Robinson, and Cherin Elias. "Sex Bias in Language Use: 'Neutral' Pronouns That Aren't." *American Psychologist*, 33 (1978), 1032-36.

Writing stories with theme sentences in which *his, his or her,* or *their* pronouns were used alternately, 226 male and 264 female college students used significantly increasing numbers of females in the stories as the pronouns shifted from *his* to *their*. The authors conclude that "gender-neutral" *his*, and by extension *he* and *man*, can hardly be considered to be "neutral."

987. Nilsen, Aileen P. "You'll Never Be the Man Your Mother Was, and Other Truisms." *ETC.*, 36 (1979), 365-370.

This essay presents examples from jokes to politics of the confusion caused by the generic use of *man* and masculine pronouns. Nilsen feels coined pronouns stand no chance but that there will be increasing use of the plural pronouns, including when the antecedent is singular. ("Someone left their car in the driveway, didn't they?")

* Nilsen, Alleen P., Haig Bosmajian, H. Lee Gershuny, and Julia P. Stanley. *Sexism and Language.* Urbana, Ill.: National Council of Teachers of English, 1977. See item 948.

* Purnell, Sandra E. "Politically Speaking, Do Women Exist?" *Journal of Communication,* 28 (Winter 1978), 150-155. See item 950.

988. Schneider, Joseph W., and Sally L. Hacker. "Sex Role Imagery and the Use of the Generic 'Man' in Introductory Tests: A Case of the Sociology of Sociology." *American Sociologist,* 8 (1973), 12-18.

    In order to test how *man* used generically in introductory sociology textbooks would be interpreted, 306 male and female undergraduates were asked to supply pictures, cartoons, illustrations, advertisements, and photographs to illustrate topics discussed in sociology textbooks. Overwhelmingly, the sex composition of the selected pictures was male. The authors conclude that generic *man* in introductory sociology textbooks is not interpreted to mean *people* or *human beings,* but *male.*

* Schultz, Muriel R. "How Serious Is Sex Bias in Language?" *College Composition and Communication,* 26 (1975), 163-167. See item 955.

* Sherman, Julia A., and Florence L. Denmark, eds. *The Psychology of Women: Future Directions in Research.* New York: Psychological Dimensions, 1978. See item 1323.

989. Silveira, Jeanette. "Generic Masculine Words and Thinking." *Women's Studies International Quarterly,* 3 (1980), 165-178.

    A review of the research on and the arguments for the elimination of the generic use of *man* and *he* leads Silveira to conclude provisionally that a reduction in the generic use of *man* and *he* would result in a long-term reduction in sexist thinking. The implication that women experience more alienation than men in the presence of the generic *man* and *he* is explored. Thirty-five references are included.

990. Spencer, N.J. "Can 'She' and 'He' Coexist?" *American Psychologist,* 33 (1978), 782-783.

Alternatives to the use of the generic use of masculine pronouns are examined and found wanting. Suggested is the creation of *co, co's,* and *coself* to replace *he, his,* and *himself* as generics, since the neologisms are already familiar as prefixes and come from an Indo-European form.

991. Stanley, Julia P. "Prescribed Passivity: The Language of Sexism." In *Views on Language* (item 880), pp. 96-108.

In this argumentative essay Stanley contends that the reasons used to support the masculine generics are political, not substantive, ones. Examples of the semantic exclusion of women from sources as diverse as *Star Trek* and Ervin Goffman's *Encounters* are included.

992. Stanley, Julia P. "Sexist Grammar." *College English,* 39 (1978), 800-811.

In this essay the history of the generics *he, man,* and *mankind* is traced from their prescription by eighteenth-century grammarians, contrary to the usage current at the time, through the binary analysis of semantic features of present-day transformationalists. Stanley cites the continued use of stereotypic examples in grammar textbooks as a means by which males maintain control of media and academia. She calls for both a rewriting of the textbooks and a change in the usage.

993. Timm, Lenora A. "Not Mere Tongue-in-Cheek: The Case for a Common Gender Pronoun in English." *International Journal of Women's Studies,* 1 (1978), 555-565.

After discussing seven proposals to replace masculine generic pronouns, Timm proposes her own: *heesh, hiser, hisrs, herm,* and *hermself.*

994. Wilson, LaVisa C. "Teachers' Inclusion of Males and Females in Generic Nouns." *Research in the Teaching of English,* 12 (1978), 155-161.

Twenty-one secondary teachers and 104 elementary teachers were given a word-picture association test with either masculine-generic key words (*caveman*) or neutral-generic ones (*cavepeople*). On the masculine generic test, 15% of the teachers associated no females with the items; hence some terms were limited to masculine gender, though others, such as salesman, were seen as generic. On the neutral-generic test, most items were seen as generic rather than as sex-specific. Female teachers interpreted key terms more generically than male teachers, and elementary teachers more than secondary ones.

GENERAL REFERENCES

995. Beatty, John. "Sex, Role, and Sex Role." In *Language, Sex, and Gender*. Eds. Judith Orasanu, Marian K. Slater, and Lenore L. Adler. New York: New York Academy of Sciences, 1979, pp. 43-49.

The interrelationships among the biological status of male/female, the social roles defined culturally as masculine/feminine, the influence of sex roles, and the linguistic expression of these variables is examined through the use of the male-female pronouns in Mohawk, a branch of Iroquois. Implications of the interrelationships for other language speakers are given.

996. Blakar, R.M. "Language as a Means of Social Power: Theoretical-Empirical Explorations of Language and Language Uses as Embedded in a Social Matrix." In *Studies of Language, Thought and Verbal Communication*. Eds. Ragnar Rommetveit and R.M. Blakar. London: Academic, 1979, pp. 109-145.

997. Blaubergs, Maija S. "On 'The Nurse Was a Doctor.'" In *Views on Language* (item 880), pp. 87-95.

Using empirical support, Blaubergs argues that the structure and usage of language are socializing agents influencing sex-role learning, that language is used deliberately to socialize children, including into sex-roles, and that the so-called "generic" pronouns also reflect and reinforce sex-role stereotyping.

998. Bodine, Ann. "Sex Differentiation in Language." In *Language and Sex: Difference and Dominance* (item 1326), pp. 130-151.

An analysis of research on sex differences in language from the beginning of the twentieth century to the current interest leads Bodine to categorize such studies as representing the sex of speaker, one spoken to, both, or one spoken about. Examples from studies in various languages are discussed, and a Cross-Cultural Summary of Sex Differentiation in Language table is included.

999. Bugental, Daphne, Jacques W. Kaswan, Leonore R. Love, and Michael N. Fox. "Child versus Adult Perception of Evaluative Messages in Verbal, Vocal, and Visual Channels." *Developmental Psychology*, 2 (1970), 367-375.

One hundred and twenty white, middle-class children, aged 5-18, and 80 parents rated friendly, neutral, or unfriendly videotaped messages presented either in verbal channel, vocal channel, or in the visual channel (facial expression). The major finding was that for younger children the auditory channel had more importance than the visual channel, reaching significance for perception of women's smiles. Younger children (5-8 years) found such smiles less positive than older (13 years and above) ones did.

1000. Cox, Sue, ed. *Female Psychology: The Emerging Self*. Chicago: Science Research Associates, 1976.

This collection of wide-ranging articles on the psychology of women covers biological perspectives as well as ethnic and cultural variations. Three articles are pertinent to the speech communication of women: Nancy Henley and Jo Freeman, "The Sexual Politics of Interpersonal Behavior," 171-179; Sandra L. and Daryl J. Bem, "Case Study of a Nonconscious Ideology: Training the Woman to Know Her Place," 180-191; and Dair L. Gillespie, "Who Has the Power? The Marital Struggle," 192-210.

1001. Daly, Mary. *Beyond God the Father: Toward a Philosophy of Women's Liberation*. Boston: Beacon, 1973.

A basic premise of this feminist argument is that the instruments for communication, both symbolic and linguistic, have been made by males. "We have not been free to use our own power to name ourselves, the world, or God." Liberation, therefore, will require a new reality characterized by new words or new meanings for old words.

1002. Davis, Alan E., and Juhn A. Wada. "Speech Dominance and Handedness in the Normal Human." *Brain and Language*, 5 (1978), 42-55.

Spectral analysis was used on the responses to flash and click stimuli of sixteen left- and six right-speech dominant adults and twelve right- and twelve left-handed adults, both sexes in each group, to determine coherence (similarity of form). Both right- and left-handed subjects had greater coherence in the right hemisphere for flash stimuli, as was true of left-speech dominant subjects as well. However, within the framework of spatial analysis occurring primarily in the right hemisphere and temporal analysis in the left, the handling of auditory and visual information depended on sex and handedness. Males and right-handers tended to place greater emphasis on the verbal and temporal nature of auditory input and on the spatial or nonverbal aspect of visual input. Females and left-handers tended to do the opposite.

1003. Dubois, Betty L., and Isabel Crouch, eds. *The Sociology of the Languages of American Women*. San Antonio, Texas: Trinity University, 1976. See also "American Minority Women in Sociolinguistic Perspective." *International Journal of the Sociology of Language*, 17 (1978), entire issue, for many of these papers.

This collection of the 15 papers read at the Conference on the Sociology of the Languages of American Women held at New Mexico State University in 1976 plus two invited papers includes summaries of workshops on intonation, the masculine generic, and male/female interaction. Topics range from conversational interaction to intonation patterns to fluency to the generic pronouns. See items 112, 506, 799, 825, 834, 835, 843, 876, 882, 897, 903, 904, 912, 1009, 1243, and 1248.

1004. Eakins, Barbara, Gene Eakins, and Barbara Lieb-Brilhart, eds. *SISCOM '75: Women's (and Men's) Communication*. Falls Church, Va.: Speech Communication Association, 1976.

This transcript of the papers and workshops of Summer Conference XI (1975) of the Speech Communication Association includes sections on research and resources in male/female interaction, nonverbal communication, language, and stereotyping and on nonprint media sources.

1005. Fairweather, Hugh. "Sex Differences in Cognition." *Cognition*, 4 (1976), 231-280.

In this review of research on sex differences in motor, spatial, and linguistic skills (development, reading, laterality), Fairweather concludes that there are "very few" sex differences in cognition. Over 300 references are cited.

1006. Hiller, Dana V., and Robin A. Sheets, eds. *Women & Men: The Consequences of Power: A Collection of New Essays*.

Cincinnati, Ohio: Office of Women's Studies, University of Cincinnati, 1977.

Thirty-six papers from the National Bicentennial Conference, Pioneers for Century III, April 1976, on the topic of power are collected. Topics covered include restraints on women's power in language, in society, and in confrontation and change.

1007. Jacobson, Marsha B. "A Rose by Any Other Name: Attitudes Toward Feminism as a Function of Its Label." *Sex Roles*, 5 (1979), 365-371.

Sixty-four males and 64 female undergraduates rated one of the following labels on a variety of dimensions: "equal rights for women," "feminism," "women's liberation," and "women's lib." "Equal rights for women" was the most positively evaluated, and "women's liberation" the most negatively evaluated. While sex differences were not as consistent as label differences, females had more positive attitudes toward all four concepts than males.

1008. Kramarae, Cheris, ed. "The Voices and Words of Women and Men." *Women's Studies International Quarterly*, 2/3 (1980).

This special issue of 16 essays, devoted to the speech communication of women and men, covers the social meaning of language structure, evaluation of voices and writing, methodology in language and sex research, and language in the home and classroom. See items 341, 846, 889, 972, 989, and 1015.

1009. Kramer, Cheris. "The Problem of Orientation in Sex/Language Research." In *The Sociology of the Languages of American Women* (item 1003), pp. 17-27.

This essay outlines the problem of orientation in researching the sex variable in speech communication, including the agentic, male-oriented research tradition and cultural stereotypes. Directions for research in the future are given.

1010. Kramer, Cheris, Barrie Thorne, and Nancy Henley. "Perspectives on Language and Communication." *Signs: Journal of Women in Culture and Society*, 3 (1978), 638-651.

This review essay assesses sex differences and similarities in speech and in nonverbal communication and examines sexism in language, the relationship between language structure and language use, and the efforts and prospects for change in the language.

1011. Kuykendall, Eleanor. "Breaking the Double Binds." *Language and Style*, 13 (1980), 81-93.

Kuykendall points out the confusion of R. Lakoff (item 858) in her concepts of language, knowledge of language, and social situations. Lakoff had concluded that women's speech was nonserious and nonassertive. Using examples from academic, diplomatic, and women's writing, Kuykendall shows that assertiveness in language is not reserved for males, that seriousness is not invariably associated with assertiveness, and that the ability to assert is not a matter of a formal language structure at all. Yet women can assert and not be taken seriously, a double bind. Along with other ideas, she concludes about women's assertive powerlessness that women lose control over their audience's response by calling attention to their low status ("I'm only a secretary, but..."), and that a reflexive speaker can learn to avoid the indirect constructions that make nonserious, nonassertive, or deferent speech and so break the double bind.

1012. Lakoff, Robin. *Language and Woman's Place*. New York: Harper & Row, 1975.

Lakoff examines sexism in the English language and argues that women are discriminated against by the way language is taught to them and by the way language in general treats them. Her observations are based on an analysis of her own speech and that of her acquaintances. For rebuttal reviews see items 866 and 1023.

1013. Lind, E. Allan, John Conley, Bonnie E. Erickson, and William M. O'Barr. "Social Attributions and Conversational Style in Trial Testimony." *Journal of Personality and Social Psychology*, 36 (1978), 1558-67.

A taped reenactment of criminal trial testimony, either in fragmented, short-answer style or in narrative style by either a male or a female witness, was judged by 82 undergraduates and 43 law students, both sexes in both groups, as they thought a lawyer would respond. Undergraduates attributed favorable evaluation by a lawyer to the female witness-narrative style. Law students attributed unfavorable evaluation by a lawyer to a male witness using fragmented style. Subjects' own evaluations showed the same pattern. See also items 561 and 820.

1014. McConnell-Ginet, Sally, Ruth Borker, and Nelly Furman. *Women and Language in Literature and Society*. New York: Praeger Publishers, 1980. See items 801, 826, 851, 865, 877, 878, 968, and 983.

1015. Martyna, Wendy. "Teaching About Language and the Sexes." *Women's Studies International Quarterly*, 3 (1980), 295-303.

A description of the syllabus, reading list, assignments, and examinations for a course on language and the sexes is given.

1016. Mazanec, Nancy, and George J. McCall. "Sex, Cognitive Categories, and Observational Accuracy." *Psychological Reports*, 37 (1975), 987-990.

A questionnaire designed to measure individual's cognitive categories needed for observing others was administered to 82 male and female undergraduates previously tested on observational accuracy. Females, who had better overall observational accuracy, scored significantly higher than males in verbal style observation. Within same-sex observation, each sex scored significantly higher on overall accuracy, on verbal content, and in verbal style.

1017. Orasanu, Judith, Mariam K. Slater, and Lenore L. Adler, eds. *Language, Sex, and Gender*. New York: New York Academy of Sciences, 1979.

This collection of papers from a 1977 workshop entitled "Language, Sex, and Gender: Does 'la Différence' Make a Difference?" sponsored by the Anthropology, Linguistics, and Psychology Sections of the New York Academy of Sciences, contains seven essays discussing the designation of sex and gender in a language, the speech of males and females, and the acquisition of linguistic differences. See also items 830, 859, 911, 971, and 995.

1018. Saint-Jacques, Bernard. "Sex, Dependency and Language." *La Linguistique*, 9, No. 1 (1973), 89-96.

Using Japanese examples as the starting point to show sex distinctions in language which emphasize the view of women as dependent, Saint-Jacques goes on to show the same underlying dependency concept in the English and French languages as well. Written in English.

1019. Silberstein, Sandra. *Bibliography: Women and Language*. Michigan Occasional Papers in Women's Studies, No. XII, Winter, 1980.

1020. Spender, Dale. *Man Made Language*. Boston: Routledge & Kegan Paul, 1980.

   This feminist study of language posits the argument that it is through patriarchal language that women's subordination is structured. Language is man-made in that it reflects men's definitions of the world from their positions of power and dominance; for women these positions are false. Topics covered include sexism in language, sex differences in language use, female silence and male dominance, and women's writing. A ten-page bibliography is included.

* Stead, Bette A., ed. *Women in Management*. Englewood Cliffs, N.J.: Prentice-Hall, 1978. See item 454.

1021. Thorne, Barrie, and Nancy Henley. "Difference and Dominance: An Overview of Language, Gender, and Society." In *Language and Sex: Difference and Dominance* (item 1326), pp. 5-42.

   This introductory chapter on the difference in language use by sex and male dominance of language use includes a brief history of the research in sexual differentiation of language, a framework for its study within sociolinguistics, an examination of the social context of the differentiation, and commentary on change and speculations and remaining questions.

1022. Trudgill, Peter. *Sociolinguistics: An Introduction*. Baltimore, Md.: Penguin, 1974.

   This general introduction to the social function of language includes an overview chapter on language and sex. References are included.

1023. Valian, Virginia. "Linguistics and Feminism." In *Feminism and Philosophy* (item 1024), pp. 154-156.

   This critique of sections of R. Lakoff's *Language and Woman's Place* (see item 1012) concludes that the differences between men's and women's speech sometimes show the superiority of women's speech (not its triviality), that men and women use different speech but not different languages, and that linguistic oppression is not a symptom that will disappear when fundamental inequalities are corrected.

1024. Vetterling-Braggin, Mary, Frederick A. Elliston, and Jane English. *Feminism and Philosophy.* Totowa, N.J.: Littlefield, Adams and Company, 1977.

This collection of articles includes a section on language. See items 920, 937, 978, 985, and 1023.

1025. Weitz, Shirley. *Sex Roles: Biological, Psychological, and Social Foundations.* New York: Oxford University Press, 1977.

This work contains a brief section on sex differences in verbal ability and a section on language as a symbol system perpetuating sex role differences.

1026. Wilson, Wayne. "Sex Differences in Response to Obscenities and Bawdy Humor." *Psychological Reports,* 37 (1975), 1074.

Two questionnaire studies, the first using 41 male and 75 female undergraduates rating use and reaction to obscenities, and the second using a total of 57 undergraduates responding to ten bawdy stories using obscenities, revealed that males were more familiar with and used more obscenities than females. Both sexes responded more angrily to opposite sex using obscenities. Females censored the bawdy stories more; males found them more humorous.

1027. Wright, Thomas L., and Edwin G. Sharp. "Content and Grammatical Sex Bias on the Interpersonal Trust Scale and Differential Trust toward Women and Men." *Journal of Consulting and Clinical Psychology,* 47 (1979), 72-85.

Using results of 513 female and 341 male undergraduates taking the Standard Interpersonal Trust Scale or one modified to refer only to female or to male referents, authors found clear evidence of both masculine content sex bias and grammatical sex bias (unspecified sex of referent thought of as male by subjects). Both male and female subjects indicated greater trust toward women than toward men or non-sex-specified referents, with female subjects trusting women referents more than male subjects did.

1028. Zillman, Dolf, and S. Holly Stocking. "Putdown Humor." *Journal of Communication,* 26 (Summer 1976), 154-163.

Equal numbers of males and females (no numbers or source of population given) heard audiotapes of a male comedian disparaging himself, disparaging a well-liked friend, or disparaging a detested roommate. Males found the routine disparaging an enemy funnier than the self-disparaging routine; females rated the two routines in the opposite way. To test that sex difference in appreciation of humor, a second study was done with both male- and female-initiated humor (columns and cartoons) being rated. Females rated the self-disparaging humor of both sexes about equally, and they rated the female self-disparager significantly funnier than males did, who found the male self-disparager funnier. Ratings of the intelligence, confidence, and wittiness of the sources of the humor also differed by sex.

NONVERBAL

BODY MOVEMENT

* Borden, Richard J., and Gorden M. Homleid. "Handedness and Lateral Positioning in Heterosexual Couples: Are Men Still Strong-Arming Women?" *Sex Roles,* 4 (1978), 67-73. See item 1261.

1029. Bull, Peter. "The Interpretation of Posture Through an Alternative Methodology to Role Play." *British Journal of Social and Clinical Psychology,* 17 (1978), 1-6.

    A methodology to investigate the postural expression of different emotions and attitudes using a technique which avoided role play was designed. Twelve female undergraduates were secretly videotaped as they, in an interview, categorized tape-recorded extracts of role plays as either funny, sad, interesting, or boring. The videotapes showed distinctive postures while perceiving all four emotions, such as dropping the head while perceiving sadness and leaning the head on one hand while perceiving boredom. Results provided empirical support for the utility of the method.

* Campbell, Anne, and J. Philippe Rushton. "Bodily Communication and Personality." *The British Journal of Social and Clinical Psychology,* 17 (1978), 31-36. See item 1263.

* Cary, Mark S. "Does Civil Inattention Exist in Pedestrian Passing?" *Journal of Personality and Social Psychology,* 36 (1978), 1185-93. See item 1044.

1030. Collett, Peter, and Peter Marsh. "Patterns of Public Behavior: Collision Avoidance on a Pedestrian Crossing." *Semiotica*, 12, No. 4 (1974), 281-299.

From four hours of videotape of pedestrians crossing at Oxford Circus in London, 94 "passes" between single individuals were analyzed. The "most striking" sex difference was that men oriented themselves (shoulder, line of approach, direction of pass) to face the person to be passed, the "open" pass, while women did the opposite, turning from the person to be passed, the "closed" pass, even when that maneuver required more difficult avoidance movements. Women also significantly more often than men drew one or both arms across their bodies when passing, whether while carrying packages or not and whether in an open or closed pass. Authors speculate that both the arm cross and closed pass are breast-protection techniques.

1031. Ekman, Paul, Wallace V. Friesen, and Klaus R. Scherer. "Body Movement and Voice Pitch in Deceptive Interaction." *Semiotica*, 16, No. 1 (1976), 23-27.

Sixteen student nurses were videotaped in interviews that permitted honest behavior or that called for deceptive behavior and their hand movements and pitch analyzed. In deception condition, use of illustrator hand movement significantly decreased, shrugs (symbolic gestures transmitting uncertainty) increased to near-significant level, and pitch increased significantly.

1032. Freedman, Norbert, Thomas Blass, Arthur Rifkin, and Frederick Quitkin. "Body Movements and the Verbal Encoding of Aggressive Affect." *Journal of Personality and Social Psychology*, 26 (1973), 72-85.

Using videotapes of 24 female college students, the authors analyzed the relationship between kinetic behavior and verbal aggression and found correlations between object-focused movement (kinetic behavior linked to rhythm or content of speech) and overt hostility, and between body-focused movements (unrelated to rhythm or content) and covert hostility.

1033. Freedman, Norbert, James O'Hanlon, Philip Oltman, and Herman A. Witkin. "The Imprint of Psychological Differentiation on Kinetic Behavior in Varying Communicative Contexts." *Journal of Abnormal Psychology*, 79 (1972), 239-258.

Twenty-four undergraduate females, 12 field independent, 12 field dependent, were videotaped in an interview situation with both cold and warm interviewers, in a 5-minute monologue, and with the warm interviewer in an interpersonal exchange. Gestural behavior distinguished the two groups: the field dependents had more hand-to-hand body-focused movements during cold and warm interview conditions and more object-focused motor-primary gestures during interpersonal exchange. Authors conclude that some gestures are governed by cognitive style and others, perhaps, by unverbalized experiences of the dyadic relationship.

1034. Johnson, Kenneth R. "Black Kinesics--Some Nonverbal Communication Patterns in the Black Culture." In *Messages: A Reader in Human Communication*. Ed. Jean M. Civikly. New York: Random House, 1974, pp. 103-115.

Explaining differences between the nonverbal communication of black Americans and other Americans by focusing on kinesics, Johnson concentrates almost entirely on black males. About black females he explains the hand-on-hip stance, eye rolling, and nose twitching.

1035. McGinley, Hugh, Richard LeFevre, and Pat McGinley. "The Influence of a Communicator's Body Position on Opinion Change in Others." *Journal of Personality and Social Psychology,* 31 (1975), 686-690.

Ninety-six female undergraduates, pretested on attitude toward 24 items, saw the attitude questionnaire of a bogus female, which was manipulated for agreement level with a subject, and pictures of a bogus female talking on a topic displaying either open or closed body positions. Retesting subjects showed significant change toward other's viewpoint for those who saw open body position pictures.

1036. McGinley, Hugh, Karen Nicholas, and Patsy McGinley. "Effects of Body Position and Attitude Similarity on Interpersonal Attraction and Opinion Change." *Psychological Reports,* 42 (1978), 127-138.

One hundred and sixty-four female college students viewed slides of a female communicator either similar or dissimilar to them in attitude and displaying either open or closed body positions. Subjects similar in attitude to the communicator on the slide evaluated her more positively than dissimilar subjects, and evaluated more positively this communicator in open rather than in closed positions. The position of the communicator had no effect on evaluation of those dissimilar in attitudes. For subjects given a retest on the attitude questionnaire, changes were positively correlated with evaluation of the communicator, but not with body position.

* Poling, Tommy H. "Sex Differences, Dominance, and Physical Attractiveness in the Use of Nonverbal Emblems." *Psychological Reports*, 43 (1978), 1087-92. See item 1122.

1037. Russell, J. Curtis, David O. Wilson, and John F. Jenkins. "Informational Properties of Jaywalking Models as Determinants of Imitated Jaywalking: An Extension to Model Sex, Race and Number." *Sociometry*, 39 (1976), 270-273.

This field experiment tested the hypotheses that high status black and white female and black male and female jaywalking models would be as effective as white high status males in inducing jaywalking and that two models would be more effective than one in inducing jaywalking. Both hypotheses were supported.

EYE CONTACT/GAZE

1038. Aiello, John R. "A Further Look at Equilibrium Theory: Visual Interaction as a Function of Interpersonal Distance." *Environmental Psychology and Nonverbal Behavior*, 1, No. 1 (1977), 122-140.

To examine the relationship between visual interaction and interpersonal distance as it relates to an equilibrium theory of social interaction, 66 male and 65 female undergraduates were interviewed by two male undergraduates. Males looked more as distance increased, and females looked less after an intermediate distance of 6.5 feet and more when the interviewer's direct gaze increased over the course of an interview. Subjects of both sexes looked into the region of their partners' eyes a greater percentage of the time while listening than while speaking. At distances typically used during seated interaction, males looked into their partners' eyes about 40% of the time and females about 50% while speaking; in the listening situation, males looked about 60% of the time and females about 75%.

1039. Aiello, John R. "A Test of Equilibrium Theory: Visual Interaction in Relation to Orientation, Distance and Sex of Interactants." *Psychonomic Science*, 27 (1972), 335-336.

To test an equilibrium theory of social interaction by examining the effects of physical distance, body orientation, and sex of interactants on visual interaction, 51 male and 54 female undergraduates were interviewed by either a male or female confederate. Females engaged in more visual interactions than males; males looked more at male confederates, and females looked more at female confederates. The amount of looking and length of glance increased linearly with distance for males in a face-to-face orientation. For females, the amount of looking and length of glances was curvilinear (increased between two feet and six feet but decreased between six feet and ten feet). Subjects, especially females, maintained longer glances when face to face.

1040. Argyle, Michael, and Mark Cook. *Gaze and Mutual Gaze*. Cambridge: Cambridge Univ. Press, 1976.

In this detailed review of gaze, a section on sex differences notes that females look more than males perhaps because of an innate sex difference since differences in gaze occur as early as six months. Greater need for affiliation and less association of mutual gaze with threat may be other causes. A 22-page bibliography is included.

1041. Argyle, Michael, and Roger Ingham. "Gaze, Mutual Gaze, and Proximity." *Semiotica*, 6 (1972), 32-49.

The relationship between gazing, mutual dyadic gazing, and distance was established in two experiments (N = 48 in first, N = 34 in second). Distance had a great effect on gaze, mutual gaze, and length of mutual and individual glances, increasing with distance. Sex differences found were that females looked at a partner more when speaking, males when listening, and, in a oneway glass condition, females gazed more than males did. Same-sex dyads had more gaze than mixed sex dyads.

1042. Argyle, Michael, Luc Lefebvre, and Mark Cook. "The Meaning of Five Patterns of Gaze." *European Journal of Social Psychology*, 4 (1974), 125-136.

Twenty male and 20 female subjects engaged in a get-acquainted or evaluative interview with a same-sex confederate who displayed one of five patterns of gaze, from none to continuous. A principal components analysis of the ratings of the confederates by the subjects yielded five main components. The first two, liking/ evaluation and activity/potency, were both affected by the amount of gaze. Subjects responded to amount of gaze, not to its relation to speaker or to listener role. The only sex difference found was that females gazed more at those they liked while talking and males gazed less at those they disliked while listening.

* Buchanan, Douglas R., Morton Goldman, and Ralph Juhnke. "Eye Contact, Sex, and the Violation of Personal Space." *The Journal of Social Psychology,* 103 (1977), 19-25. See item 1142.

* Bugental, Daphne E., Leonore R. Love, and Robert M. Gianetto. "Perfidious Feminine Faces." *Journal of Personality and Social Psychology,* 17 (1971), 314-318. See item 321.

* Burroughs, W., W. Schultz, and S. Autrey. "Quality of Argument, Leadership Votes, and Eye Contact in Three-Person Leaderless Groups." *The Journal of Social Psychology,* 90 (1973), 89-93. See item 212.

* Campbell, Anne, and J. Philippe Rushton. "Bodily Communication and Personality." *The British Journal of Social and Clinical Psychology,* 17 (1978), 31-36. See item 1263.

1043. Caproni, Valerie, Douglas Levine, Edgar O'Neal, Peter McDonald, and Gray Garwood. "Seating Position, Instructor's Eye Contact Availability, and Student Participation in a Small Seminar." *The Journal of Social Psychology,* 103 (1977), 315-316.

    This summary of a study in which an instructor shifted his seat at a table from class to class indicates that only eye contact availability, not sex of student or position taken by instructor, related to rate of participation by the students.

* Carr, Suzanne J., and James M. Dabbs, Jr. "The Effects of Lighting, Distance and Intimacy of Topic on Verbal and Visual Behavior." *Sociometry,* 37 (1974), 592-600. See item 1264.

1044. Cary, Mark S. "Does Civil Inattention Exist in Pedestrian Passing?" *Journal of Personality and Social Psychology*, 36 (1978), 1185-93.

Four studies, both laboratory and field, found no support for the rule of civil inattention in pedestrian passing, which states that pedestrians look at each other at a distance as if to recognize mutual legitimacy, and then look away. Cary found in one study a continuous stare followed by no looking followed by a sudden look at close distance as most friendly, polite, and natural. Sex differences found included persons look more at others of opposite sex and that females drop gaze and lower heads when male stares at them. Looking responses of male and female subjects to staring are mirror opposites; staring at a male increases directness of his gaze but decreases it for a female.

1045. Cary, Mark S. "Gaze and Facial Display in Pedestrian Passing." *Semiotica*, 28 (1979), 323-326.

Analysis of the gaze and facial display of 60 singles and of 60 pairs of four combinations of sexes passing each other and of another set of 40 singles and 40 pairs, also balanced by sex, revealed no differences due to sex except in passing pairs. Same-sex pairs gazed at each other significantly less often than opposite pairs.

1046. Cary, Mark S. "The Role of Gaze in the Initiation of Conversation." *Social Psychology*, 41 (1978), 269-271.

In this experimental study using 40 opposite-sex and 40 same-sex dyads, when one person entered a room where the other was sitting, both initial looking (more for enterer than for sittee) and verbal greetings were common; both predicted conversation to follow. Person to speak first was evenly divided between enterer and sitter, though in opposite-sex pairs the initiator was significantly more often the male.

1047. Cegala, Donald J., Sydel Sokuvitz, and Alison F. Alexander. "An Investigation of Eye Gaze and Its Relation to Selected Verbal Behavior." *Human Communication Research*, 5 (1979), 99-108.

This study examined eye gaze avoidance in relation to turn-taking, vocalized pauses, sentence changes, repetitions, "you know," "like," sentence fragments, simple sentences, and complex sentences. Subjects were 22 female undergraduates in dyads in free discussion. Analysis of the videotapes supported the hypothesis that subjects would avoid eye gaze when experiencing difficulty in encoding.

* Cherulnik, Paul D., William T. Neely, Martha Flanagan, and Max Zachau. "Social Skill and Visual Interaction." *The Journal of Social Psychology,* 104 (1978), 263-270. See item 105.

1048. Cook, Mark. "Gaze and Mutual Gaze in Social Encounters." *American Scientist,* 65 (1977), 328-333.

    Gaze, a primary nonverbal indicator of communicative intent, occurs about 60% of interaction time generally, more continuously during listening and in a series of short glances during speaking. Mutual gaze may be one-third of speaking time, though each contact may be brief. Women gaze more than men, especially when conversing with other women. These and other findings as well as the role of gaze in social relationships are presented.

* Coutts, Larry M., and Maribeth Ledden. "Nonverbal Compensatory Reactions to Changes in Interpersonal Proximity." *The Journal of Social Psychology,* 102 (1977), 283-290. See item 1149.

1049. Coutts, Larry M., and Frank W. Schneider. "Affiliative Conflict Theory: An Investigation of the Intimacy, Equilibrium and Compensation Hypothesis." *Journal of Personality and Social Psychology,* 34 (1976), 1135-42.

    Forty dyads of friend or stranger females were observed in three discussions: in the third discussion, one member was instructed to avoid looking at the other. Friends smiled more and had more individual and mutual gaze than strangers. Reduction in gaze, however, did not increase immediacy behavior in the other (distance, body orientation, etc.), leading authors to question the validity of a compensation hypothesis.

1050. Coutts, Larry M., and Frank W. Schneider. "Visual Behavior in an Unfocused Interaction as a Function of Sex and Distance." *Journal of Experimental Social Psychology,* 11 (1975), 64-77.

    Ten female, 10 male, and 20 mixed-sex undergraduate dyads were observed interacting in a waiting room in distances manipulated from 2 to 7 feet. Gazing decreased over time and with increasing proximity. Females received more glances than males, although sex of gazer was not significantly different. Female dyads had more gazing than the other two types, but amount of mutual gaze was insignificant, 1% compared to 10-30% found in usual social interactions.

1051. Ellsworth, Phoebe C., J. Merrill Carlsmith, and Alexander Henson. "The Stare as a Simulus to Flight in Human Subjects." *Journal of Personality and Social Psychology,* 21 (1972), 302-311.

A series of five field studies showed that staring at others at an intersection increased the rate of moving of pedestrians when the light turned green. Although some sex differences occurred in first studies, when controlled for in later experiments, no significant sex differences were found.

1052. Ellsworth, Phoebe C., Howard S. Friedman, Deborah Perlick, and Michael E. Hoyt. "Some Effects of Gaze on Subjects Motivated to Seek or to Avoid Social Comparison." *Journal of Experimental and Social Psychology,* 14 (1978), 69-87.

In this study, 86 female undergraduates were placed in a condition either of being motivated to seek social comparison (fear condition--presence of snake) or to avoid it (embarrassment condition--required to disclose intimate information). Through plausible manipulation, each subject was left with a confederate either in the same state or a neutral state, who either gazed at or avoided gazing at the subject. Fear subjects liked gazing confederate and felt less tense then, while embarrassed subjects preferred non-gazing confederate, both findings holding when subjects believed confederate was in the same state as themselves. The authors conclude that people's responses to social comparison are affected by their motivation for comparison and by the behavior of the reference person.

1053. Ellsworth, Phoebe C., and Linda M. Ludwig. "Visual Behavior in Social Interaction." *Journal of Communication,* 22 (Dec. 1972), 375-403.

A review of research (55 articles and books, mainly from the 1960s) contains a section on sex differences in visual behavior in social interaction and mentions of sex differences in other sections. Sex differences "are the rule, rather than the exception."

1054. Ellsworth, Phoebe, and Lee Ross. "Intimacy in Response to Direct Gaze." *Journal of Experimental Social Psychology,* 11 (1975), 592-613.

Subjects in 50 male and 60 female dyads in which the designated listener was instructed to observe one of four conditions of gazing (from constant to avoidance) and the designated speaker was encouraged to deliver a personally revealing monologue were analyzed. Direct gaze, whether constant or contingent on intimate statements, promoted intimacy between females but reticence between males. Gaze avoidance had the opposite effect. Male speakers, however, rated themselves most intimate in the direct gaze conditions. Personal liking as well as other positive feelings and task satisfaction correlated positively with direct gaze for females only.

1055. Ellyson, Steve L., John F. Dovidio, Randi L. Corson, and Debbie L. Vinicur. "Visual Dominance Behavior in Female Dyads: Situational and Personality Factors." *Social Psychology Quarterly,* 43 (1980), 328-336.

Two experiments investigated visual behavior patterns in women. In the first, 24 from a pool of 200 female undergraduates, all of whom scored at the median on Schultz's Fundamental Interpersonal Relations Orientation (FIRO) Inventory, interacted with a confederate presented as either higher or lower in status. Those subjects higher in status than their confederate had nearly equivalent look-speak and look-listen behavior, while those lower in status had more look-listen than look-speak behavior. In the second experiment, 32 female undergraduates who scored either high or low on the Expressed Control subscale of the FIRO-B Personality Inventory revealed a similar pattern in similar dyads.

1056. Exline, R.V. "Visual Interaction: The Glances of Power and Preference." In *Nebraska Symposium on Motivation.* Ed. James K. Cole. Lincoln: University of Nebraska Press, 1971, pp. 163-206.

This review of over 50 studies on gaze and mutual gaze notes the relationship of gaze to power and to preference. There are many references to sex differences.

1057. Greenbaum, Paul, and Howard M. Rosenfeld. "Patterns of Avoidance in Response to Interpersonal Staring and Proximity: Effects of Bystanders on Drivers at Traffic Intersection." *Journal of Personality and Social Psychology*, 36 (1978), 575-587.

In this field study of the interrelationship of staring by male confederates, distance, and other variables on the behavior of 846 drivers stopped at traffic intersection, female drivers avoided both verbal and nonverbal (gazing) interaction more than males did.

* Griffitt, William, James May, and Russell Veitch. "Sexual Stimulation and Interpersonal Behavior: Heterosexual Evaluative Responses, Visual Behavior, and Physical Proximity." *Journal of Personality and Social Psychology*, 30 (1974), 367-377. See item 1158.

1058. Hedge, B.J., B.S. Everitt, and C.D. Frith. "The Role of Gaze in Dialogue." *Acta Psychologica*, 42 (1978), 453-475.

In a study designed primarily to investigate the use of Markov chains in analyzing dialogue, the authors found that gaze behavior was not independent of speech behavior. For stranger dyads of either sex, the speech state of the 3 seconds preceding determined the current state of the dialogue. But for friends dyads of either sex, both the speech and the gaze states of the preceding 3 seconds must be taken into account. That is, decisions to speak are made independent of gaze in stranger dyads, but are based on combined speech-gaze behavior in friends dyads. Data was derived from 32 pairs of male friends, 32 pairs of female friends, 16 pairs of male strangers, and 16 pairs of female strangers (presumably British college students, but unspecified).

1059. Kleinke, Chris L. "Compliance to Requests Made by Gazing and Touching Experimenters in Field Settings." *Journal of Experimental Social Psychology*, 13 (1977), 218-223.

Two experiments, one at an airport and another at a shopping mall, used female experimenters either retrieving a dime (53 male subjects) or requesting one (90 male, 88 female subjects), under varying conditions of gaze, touch, and proximity. Both touching and gaze increased positive responses in subjects. Female subjects complied less than male subjects in the second experiment.

1060. Kleinke, Chris L., Armando A. Bustos, Frederick B. Meeker, and Richard A. Staneski. "Effects of Self-

Attributed and Other-Attributed Gaze on Interpersonal Evaluations Between Males and Females." *Journal of Experimental Social Psychology*, 9 (1973), 154-163.

Thirty female-male dyads who had become acquainted in 10-minute sessions were told they gazed at the other either higher than usual, average, or less than usual during the dyad. In subsequent evaluations, high-gaze females rated their male partners more favorably, while low-gaze males rated their female partners more favorably. Males rated low-gazing females least attractive while females rated high-gazing males as least attractive.

1061. Kleinke, Chris L., Frederick B. Meeker, and Carl LaFong. "Effects of Gaze, Touch, and Use of Name on Evaluation of Engaged Couples." *Journal of Research in Personality*, 7 (1974), 368-373.

Six actors playing roles of three engaged couples either gazing at each other or not, touching or not, and using the other's name or not were evaluated on a bipolar adjective scale by 57 male and 32 female undergraduates. Gaze was the most important variable, with gazing couples rated more favorably than nongazing ones. Touching couples were rated more favorably than nontouching, but name-using couples were rated less favorably than non-name-using couples.

1062. Kleinke, Chris L., Richard A. Staneski, and Dale E. Berger. "Evaluation of an Interviewer as a Function of Interviewer Gaze, Reinforcement of Subject Gaze, and Interviewer Attractiveness." *Journal of Personality and Social Psychology*, 31 (1975), 115-122.

Fifty-four male undergraduates were interviewed by female confederates using various levels of gazing. Gaze of the subjects increased as level of gazing by the interviewer increased, but attitudes toward interviewers remained the same. Subjects disliked nongazing interviewers, liked high rates of talking in interviewers, and did not discriminate between attractive and unattractive interviewers.

1063. Kleinke, Chris L., Richard A. Staneski, and Sandra L. Pipp. "Effects of Gaze, Distance, and Attractiveness on Males' First Impressions of Females." *Representative Research in Social Psychology*, 6 (1975), 7-12.

Forty-eight male undergraduates interacted with six female confederates, either attractive or not, who gazed at their partner either 10% or 90% of the interaction time, and who moved either closer or farther from their partners during the interaction. Those who gazed 90% of the time were seen as more attentive than those who gazed 10% of the time, and attractive confederates were preferred to unattractive ones. Attractive confederates were rated somewhat more favorably at the 10% gaze level. Distance shifts did not affect ratings.

* Lesko, Wayne A. "Psychological Distance, Mutual Gaze, and the Affiliative-Conflict Theory." *The Journal of Social Psychology*, 103 (1977), 311-312. See item 1171.

1064. Levine, Marion H., and Brian Sutton-Smith. "Effects of Age, Sex, and Task on Visual Behavior during Dyadic Interaction." *Developmental Psychology*, 9 (1973), 400-405.

A total of 96 subjects of four age groups (4-5-6, 7-8-9, 10-11-12, adult) were observed in same-sex dyads for gaze behavior during "free" conversation and during a construction task. Analysis of variance revealed significant increase in gazing with increasing age except for the 10-11-12 group, and significantly more gaze by females than males in conversation condition, which had more gaze than the task condition.

1065. Libby, William L., Jr., and Donna Yaklevich. "Personality Determinants of Eye Contact and Direction of Gaze Aversion." *Journal of Personality and Social Psychology*, 27 (1973), 197-206.

The eye responses of 35 male and 35 female undergraduates during a structured interview with a female were observed and related to personality needs. Females maintained eye contact more than males. Subjects high in need for abasement looked away to left more than low abasement-need subjects, and subjects high in need for nurturance maintained more eye contact than those low in nurturance need. No sex differences in these two results were found.

1066. Muirhead, Rosalind D., and Morton Goldman. "Mutual Eye Contact as Affected by Seating Position, Sex, and Age." *Journal of Social Psychology*, 109 (1979), 201-206.

In four shopping centers, 216 pairs of same- or mixed-sex adults, young, middle, or senior in age, were observed for mutual gaze and seating position. Opposite-seat pairs had significantly more mutual gaze than adjacent-seat pairs, and young and senior pairs had significantly more mutual gaze than middle-aged adults. Young female dyads had more mutual gaze than males, but senior male dyads had more than senior female, while middle-aged males and females had similar mutual gaze. The lowest level of gaze was for male-female, middle-aged dyads seated beside each other and for the other two age groups of mixed-sex dyads when seated opposite each other.

* Murray, Robert P., and Hugh McGinley. "Looking as a Measure of Attraction." *Journal of Applied Social Psychology*, 2 (1972), 267-274. See item 146.

1067. Neville, Dorothy. "Experimental Manipulation of Dependency Motivation and Its Effect on Eye Contact and Measures of Field Dependency." *Journal of Personality and Social Psychology*, 29 (1974), 72-79.

In an experimental study with 40 female and 40 male undergraduates in either helping or dependency situation (help withdrawn), significantly greater amounts of eye contact occurred under dependency conditions. Females had somewhat higher eye contact duration scores than males.

1068. Scherwitz, Larry, and Robert Helmreich. "Interactive Effects of Eye Contact and Verbal Content on Interpersonal Attraction in Dyads." *Journal of Personality and Social Psychology*, 25 (1973), 6-14.

A report of several experimental studies, one of which used sex as a variable along with personal or impersonal positive evaluation and low or high eye contact, found no sex differences among 95 undergraduates on liking for confederate. With personal evaluation condition, the confederate was better liked with low eye contact; with impersonal evaluation, the confederate was better liked with high eye contact.

1069. Schneider, Frank W., and Christine L. Hansvick. "Gaze and Distance as a Function of Change in Interpersonal Gaze." *Social Behavior and Personality*, 5 (1977), 49-53.

In 20 mixed-sex dyads of undergraduates, half were instructed to gaze at, then away from their partner's eyes while the others were given just the opposite instruction. Videotapes of the interviews revealed that distance was unaffected by gaze pattern, that partners began to reciprocate the gaze instigator's behavior, and that females gazed more and were more responsive to a change in their partner's gaze behavior.

1070. Smith, Brenda J., Fonda Sanford, and Morton Goldman. "Norm Violations, Sex, and the 'Blank Stare.'" *The Journal of Social Psychology*, 103 (1977), 49-55.

Two males and three females stared at 16 females and 16 males for 15 minutes in a library setting. Female subjects left sooner and with greater frequency than males, especially if the starer was male. Males returned the stare more frequently, especially when the starer was female.

1071. Thayer, Stephen, and William Schiff. "Eye Contact, Facial Expression, and the Experience of Time." *The Journal of Social Psychology*, 95 (1975), 117-124.

Forty-eight undergraduate females judged the length of time with either a male or a female who had either a friendly or a scowling face, either with eye-contact or not. Time was perceived as passing more slowly under scowling-face condition, especially so in female-female dyads.

1072. Thayer, Stephen, and William Schiff. "Gazing Patterns and Attribution of Sexual Involvement." *The Journal of Social Psychology*, 101 (1977), 235-246.

This study asked 171 undergraduates to evaluate the degree of sexual involvement from filmed clips of mixed-sex or same-sex pairs using various lengths and types of gaze, either reciprocated or not. Duration and reciprocity of gaze and same-sex pairs all resulted in more attributions of involvement. Female judges made significantly greater sexual involvement attributions to mixed-sex pairs under all conditions, suggesting females were relatively more discriminating.

* Tindall, Jeffry H., Linda Boyler, Pat Cline, Paul Emberger, Sharon Powell, and Joseph Wions. "Perceived Leadership Rankings of Males and Females in Small Task Groups." *Journal of Psychology*, 100 (1978), 13-20. See item 622.

1073. Valentine, Mary E. "The Attenuating Influence of Gaze upon the Bystander Intervention Effect." *The Journal of Social Psychology*, 111 (1980), 197-203.

In a helping situation (dropped coins at bus stop, arm in sling), a confederate needing assistance either gazed or did not at an adult, white woman waiting at a bus stop (total N = 150) and was either accompanied or not by a confederate who remained aloof. Gaze increased helping behavior whether victim was alone or not. In the no-gaze condition, significantly more subjects helped the victim when alone than with confederate, while in the gaze condition, significantly more helped when the victim had the confederate than when he was alone.

1074. Valentine, Mary E., and Howard Ehrlichman. "Interpersonal Gaze and Helping Behavior." *The Journal of Social Psychology*, 107 (1979), 193-198.

Male and female confederates, each with an arm in a sling, sought help, either with or without a look, from individual men and women at bus stops (320 in all). Helping behavior between mixed-sex dyads was not affected by gaze, but an all-female dyad had 40% increased rate of help with gaze and an all-male dyad a 28% decrease.

1075. Wahlers, Kathy J., and Larry L. Barker. "Bralessness and Nonverbal Communication." *The Central States Speech Journal*, 24 (1973), 222-226.

Observation of the nonverbal responses of 329 male and female undergraduates to 42 braless females revealed that males looked more at the breast area than the eyes of the braless females and females attempted to avoid looking at the breast area.

* Walsh, Nancy A., Lynn A. Meister, and Chris L. Kleinke. "Interpersonal Attraction and Visual Behavior as a Function of Perceived Arousal and Evaluation by an Opposite Sex Person." *The Journal of Social Psychology*, 103 (1977), 65-74. See item 175.

FACIAL EXPRESSION

1076. Buck, Ross. A Test of Nonverbal Receiving Ability: Preliminary Studies." *Human Communication Research*, 2 (1976), 162-171.

The development of a test of the ability to decode emotion in others is described as well as a preliminary study using 100 undergraduates, high school teachers, and high school students. Subjects matched spontaneous unposed facial expressions and gestures of college student encoders to emotionally loaded color slides. Females were slightly better decoders than males, and business and fine arts majors were relatively good decoders while science majors were relatively poor.

1077. Buck, Ross, Reuben Baron, Nancy Goodman, and Beth Shapiro. "Unitization of Spontaneous Nonverbal Behavior in the Study of Emotion Communication." *Journal of Personality and Social Psychology,* 39 (1980), 522-529.

In Experiment I, 46 female and 35 male undergraduates viewed videotapes of spontaneous facial and gestural responses to emotion-inducing slides of adults and children and marked off each meaningful segment or unit of behavior. Subjects could segment the behaviors; female senders elicited more breakpoints than male senders, especially on unpleasant slides. Female senders were more accurately decoded on unpleasant slides; male senders on sexual slides. With children, however, boys were more accurately decoded than girls and elicited more breakpoints as well. Sex of receiver was not significantly related to any variable. In Experiment II, 50 male undergraduates found expressive female sender easier to decode than expressive male sender, and nonexpressive male sender easier than nonexpressive female sender. The expressive female sender elicited more breakpoints than the nonexpressive female sender, whereas the nonexpressive male sender elicited more breakpoints than the expressive male sender.

* Buck, Ross, Robert E. Miller, and William F. Caul. "Sex, Personality, and Physiological Variables in the Communication of Affect via Facial Expression." *Journal of Personality and Social Psychology,* 30 (1974), 587-596. See item 103.

1078. Buck, Ross W., Robert E. Miller, Virginia J. Savin, and William F. Caul. "Communication of Affect through Facial Expressions in Humans." *Journal of Personality and Social Psychology,* 23 (1972), 362-371.

Using 21 female and 17 male college students responding to slides while being monitored physiologically and each observed unknowingly by a same-sex observer, the authors found female pairs more effective than male pairs both in transmitting and in receiving nonverbal emotional cues. Physiological responses were negatively related to accuracy of observers' evaluations of the nonverbal communication.

* Bugental, Daphne, Jacques W. Kaswan, Leonore R. Love, and Michael N. Fox. "Child versus Adult Perception of Evaluative Messages in Verbal, Vocal, and Visual Channels." *Developmental Psychology*, 2 (1970), 367-375. See item 999.

* Cary, Mark S. "Gaze and Facial Display in Pedestrian Passing." *Semiotica*, 28 (1979), 323-326. See item 1045.

1079. Cherulnik, Paul D. "Sex Differences in the Expression of Emotion in a Structured Social Encounter." *Sex Roles*, 5 (1979), 413-424.

Eighteen female and 18 male undergraduates were videotaped in a mock interview situation and their facial activity, speech, and gaze analyzed for expressing emotion. Women were more expressive of emotion in facial activity, but no sex difference in speech and gaze expressive behavior was found.

* Cupchik, Gerald C., and Howard Leventhal. "Consistency Between Expressive Behavior and the Evaluation of Humorous Stimuli: The Role of Sex and Self-Observation." *Journal of Personality and Social Psychology*, 30 (1974), 429-442. See item 631.

1080. Eiland, Rebecca, and Don Richardson. "The Influence of Race, Sex, and Age on Judgments of Emotion Portrayed in Photographs." *Communication Monographs*, 43 (1976), 167-175.

An analysis of variance of the judgments of 40 black and white second-graders and 40 black and white college students, equally distributed by race and sex, of 40 photographs of similar people depicting emotions, revealed no significant differences between race, sex, or age of subjects in perceiving emotions (accuracy was not a factor). All subjects, however, judged female faces differently from male faces, young faces differently from older, and black faces differently from white.

1081. Ekman, Paul, and Wallace V. Friesen. "Detecting Deception from the Body or Face." *Journal of Personality and Social Psychology*, 29 (1974), 288-298.

Twenty-two student nurses, all female, honestly described their feelings about a pleasant film and dishonestly described them about an unpleasant film, reporting later on what part of their bodies they tried to control most for the deception. Videotapes of their descriptions of the films were evaluated by a separate group. Face was mentioned more often as the part of the body controlled. In others' evaluation, judgments were more accurate from body than from face if others saw the normal behavior of the subject first.

1082. Gitter, A. George, Harvey Black, and David Mostofsky. "Race and Sex in the Communication of Emotion." *Journal of Social Psychology*, 88 (1972), 273-276.

Twenty professional actors, 10 white (5 M, 5 F) and 10 black (5 M, 5 F) expressed 7 emotions for a series of 120 photographs. As perceivers, 24 white and 24 black undergraduates (equally divided by sex) identified the emotions in 35 pictures. Race of perceiver, nature of emotion, and sex of one photographed influenced perceptions. Black perceivers were superior in accuracy overall. Female pictures were associated with a higher incidence of correct perceptions of surprise and fear, and a higher incidence compared to male pictures of erroneous perceptions of fear and pain, and a lower incidence of correct perceptions of anger and disgust.

1083. Gitter, A. George, Harvey Black, and David Mostofsky. "Race and Sex in the Perception of Emotion." *Journal of Social Issues*, 28, No. 4 (1972), 63-78.

This study using 20 facial photographs and 160 undergraduate perceivers investigated the effects of race and sex on the perception of black and white male and female students. Overall results indicated significant main effects for race (whites were more accurately perceived), for sex (females were more accurately perceived), for race of perceiver (blacks perceived more accurately), but not for sex of perceiver. The nature of the emotion had an influence on its perception; happiness and pain had the highest rate of accurate perception; fear and sadness the lowest.

1084. Hackney, Harold. "Facial Gestures and Subject Expression of Feelings." *Journal of Counseling Psychology*, 21 (1974), 173-178.

To investigate the effects of nonverbal facial gestures on client verbal behavior in a quasi-interview setting,

72 female undergraduates in an interview responded to head nod, smile, and head nod/smile combination, or no such behavior by a male and female graduate student experimenter. Subjects produced progressively and significantly greater amounts of feeling and self-reference feeling statements for head nod, smile, and head nod/smile combination when stimuli were presented by the female experimenter, but produced just the opposite for the male experimenter.

1085. Hirschberg, Nancy, Lawrence E. Jones, and Michael Haggerty. "What's in a Face: Individual Differences in Face Perception." *Journal of Research in Personality,* 12 (1978), 488-499.

Thirty black and 33 white female undergraduates judged the similarity of pairs of white or black male faces seen in photographs and completed a number of measures of personality, attitude, and adjective scales in relation to the pictures. An individual difference multidimensional scaling analysis revealed that most of the variables underlying perception of the faces involved affective characteristics (honest, tense, attractive) rather than physical features (eye width, mouth, height). The major physical dimension was face shape (long vs. wide). Both black and white subjects employed similar dimensions.

1086. Kendon, Adam. "Some Functions of the Face in a Kissing Round." *Semiotica,* 15, No. 4 (1975), 299-334.

In a detailed analysis of the facial behavior of a couple videotaped as they were observed on a park bench, Kendon found that, while the male's face showed little change, the female's face was highly variable and apparently functioned to regulate the male's behavior. For example, the female's "teeth smile" as she turned to the male was an initiation of intimacy involvement; if the male sat turned away from her, she kissed his neck or leaned on him; if he turned toward her, they mutually moved together and touched foreheads or noses, but did not kiss. Kissing occurred only when the male turned to her, and she remained still and switched from "teeth smile" to "closed smile." Then the male approached for the kissing contact.

1087. Mackey, Wade C. "Parameters of the Smile as a Social Signal." *Journal of Genetic Psychology,* 129 (1976), 125-130.

A total of 733 adults of both sexes were observed in laboratory (university students) and field (adults from rural and urban Southern communities) settings for smiling behavior. In the laboratory setting, females smiled more often than males and increased the number of smiles when introduced into a social milieu, especially when paired with another female. Milieu had no effect on the incidence of male's smiling. In the field setting, verbal greetings with a smile elicited more smile responses than verbal greetings alone. Females smiled more than males, and males smiled more greeting females than greeting males. Results were interpreted as supporting the hypothesis that the smile is an appeasing device used to prevent or ameliorate aggression.

1088. Milord, James T. "Aesthetic Aspects of Faces: A (Somewhat) Phenomenological Analysis Using Multidimensional Scaling Methods." *Journal of Personality and Social Psychology*, 36 (1978), 205-216.

In a series of experiments with various numbers of males and females, measures were taken of their viewing time and their rating of pairs of 16 photographs of faces. Though both age and race correlated with factors emerging from factor analysis, sex did not. Sex differences were that male subjects weighted smiling more heavily and that young female faces were preferred, including being looked at longer.

* Thayer, Stephen, and William Schiff. "Eye Contact, Facial Expression, and the Experience of Time." *The Journal of Social Psychology*, 95 (1975), 117-124. See item 1071.

1089. Woodall, W. Gill, Judee K. Burgoon, and Norman N. Markel. "The Effects of Facial-Head Cue Combinations on Interpersonal Evaluations." *Communication Quarterly*, 28 (Summer, 1980), 47-55.

Two studies were conducted to examine the role of visual cues in interpersonal attraction and credibility. In one study, 128 male and female undergraduates looked at videotapes of trained male actors presenting a short speech accompanied by head nods, eyebrow raises, smiles, and combinations or absence of those cues, and rated the speakers on task and social attraction. The presence of any facial or head cues produced more attraction. The smiles/head nod combination produced the greatest social attraction, and the head nod only produced the greatest task attraction. Females expressed highest attraction when the speakers used the combination of eyebrow raises, smiles, and head nods. In the second study, an interview situation, data by sex was not reported.

1090. Zuckerman, Miron, Richard Frank, Judith A. Hall, and Robert Rosenthal. "Encoding and Decoding of Spontaneous and Posed Facial Expressions." *Journal of Personality and Social Psychology,* 34 (1976), 966-977.

Thirty female and 30 male undergraduates were videotaped viewing pleasant and unpleasant scenes (spontaneous encoding), when talking about the scenes (talking encoding), and when posing to express the emotions of the four scenes (posed encoding). These videotapes were then presented for decoding. Accuracy of communication varied according to the mode of encoding, the scene, and the mode-by-scene interaction, with the highest mode for accuracy the posed encoding. Although there were no sex differences in encoding, females decoded significantly more accurately than males.

1091. Zuckerman, Miron, Marsha S. Lipets, Judith H. Koivumaki, and Robert Rosenthal. "Encoding and Decoding Nonverbal Cues of Emotion." *Journal of Personality and Social Psychology,* 32 (1975), 1068-76.

Forty males and females encoded six emotions twice, via facial expressions and via tone of voice, all of which were decoded by 102 males and females, all participants being undergraduates. The ability to encode and decode both sets of cues was significantly related, but the relationship between encoding and decoding cues of the same emotion was negative. Females were slightly better encoders and significantly better decoders than males. Acquaintance between encoder and decoder improved scores for males but not for females. Auditory decoding scores were high if both communicators were of the same sex, but visual decoding scores were high if the two were of the opposite sex.

PHYSICAL ATTRACTIVENESS

1092. Adams, Gerald R. "Physical Attractiveness Research: Toward a Developmental Social Psychology of Beauty." *Human Development,* 20 (1977), 217-239.

This review of physical attractiveness research leads to a proposed relation between outer appearance and inner psychological characteristics. The studies show a relationship between attractiveness and social stereotyping, social exchange, internalized personality patterns, and social behavior. Conclusions are that an individual's external appearance over the life cycle will intermittently become asychronized with inner perceptions as physical features change. It is during normal "crisis periods" that an individual will be most susceptible to the consequences of a physical attractiveness stereotype. Of the approximately 130 studies in this review, over 20 include females.

1093. Adams, Gerald R. "Physical Attractiveness, Personality, and Social Reactions to Peer Pressure." *Journal of Psychology*, 96 (1977), 287-296.

Personality measures, a peer pressure measure, peer ratings, and ratings of self-perceptions of attractiveness were gathered from 181 female and male undergraduates to determine the relationship between physical attributes, personality development, and susceptibility to peer pressure. Physically attractive undergraduates were more likely to have internalized socially desirable personality characteristics and to resist peer pressure influences. For males in this group the association was related to a sense of responsibility for their own behavior; for females, it was related to a sense of self-confidence. For males thinness and physical angularity were related to unfavorable personality characteristics, while for females tallness was related to those characteristics.

* Altemeyer, Robert A., and Keith Jones. "Sexual Identity, Physical Attractiveness and Seating Position as Determinants of Influence in Discussion Groups." *Canadian Journal of Behavioural Science*, 6 (1974), 357-375. See item 186.

1094. Anderson, Rosemarie, and Steve A. Nida. "Effect of Physical Attractiveness on Opposite- and Same-Sex Evaluations." *Journal of Personality*, 46 (1978), 401-413.

Male and female undergraduates (144 of each) evaluated a freshman essay attributed by picture to a male or female of three levels of attractiveness. The essay's quality also had three levels. Analysis of variance revealed that highly attractive writers received the highest evaluation from opposite-sex evaluators while medium attractive writers received the highest evaluation from same-sex evaluators. Some "traditional" sex differences were not found: male writers did not receive higher ratings than female writers, and women did not evaluate higher than men.

1095. Banziger, George, and Lynn Hooker. "The Effects of Attitudes Toward Feminism and Perceived Feminism on Physical Attractiveness Ratings." Sex Roles, 5 (1979), 437-442.

Seventy-six male undergraduates, pretested to include both profeminists and antifeminists, rated six photographs of women, either attractive or not, presented as feminists or not. No difference in ratings of attractiveness for feminism level of women was found, but profeminist males rated profeminist women as more attractive than nonfeminist women, and nonfeminist males rated nonfeminist women more attractive.

1096. Bar-Tal, Daniel, and Leonard Saxe. "Perceptions of Similarly and Dissimilarly Attractive Couples and Individuals." Journal of Personality and Social Psychology, 33 (1976), 772-781.

In experiments on physical attractiveness the existence of an attractiveness stereotype was confirmed. In one experiment, 64 female and 64 male college students evaluated the characteristics of persons in photographs of purportedly married couples, varied for physical attractiveness. "Wives" were evaluated independently of "husband's" physical attractiveness, but not vice versa. In all cases, the attractive female was evaluated higher than the unattractive, including inducing higher scores for her "husband" on certain measures.

1097. Bar-Tal, Daniel, and Leonard Saxe. "Physical Attractiveness and Its Relationship to Sex-Role Stereotyping." Sex Roles, 2 (1976), 123-133.

This review of the literature on physical attractiveness indicates that as a cue in person perception, attractiveness is a more important factor in the evaluation of females than in the evaluation of males. Physical attractiveness functions as an indicator of the degree of successful role fulfillment for women but not for men. Thirty-nine references are listed.

1098. Benson, Peter L., Stuart A. Karabenick, and Richard M. Lerner. "Pretty Pleases: The Effects of Physical Attractiveness, Race, and Sex on Receiving Help." *Journal of Experimental Social Psychology*, 12 (1976), 409-415.

In this field study, a completed graduate school application form, including a picture of a male or a female, black or white, attractive or unattractive, and a stamped, addressed envelope were left in a telephone booth where the behavior of 442 males and 162 females, all white, between about 18 and 70, was observed. The attractive stimulus person's application was mailed or turned in significantly more often than the unattractive stimulus person's, and white stimulus person's more than black's. Both sexes gave help and received help in almost equal proportions.

* Cash, Thomas F. "Self-Disclosure in Initial Acquaintanceship: Effects of Sex, Approval Motivation, and Physical Attractiveness." *JSAS: Catalog of Selected Documents in Psychology*, 8 (1978), 11. (Ms. No. 1642). See item 714.

1099. Cash, Thomas F., Barry Gillen, and D. Steven Burns. "Sexism and 'Beautyism' in Personnel Consultant Decision Making." *Journal of Applied Psychology*, 62 (1977), 301-310.

Professional personnel consultants, 36 male, 36 female, rated the suitability of bogus applicants for jobs and for alternative employment. The resumes were identical except for sex and inclusion of a photograph, either attractive or unattractive. Males were preferred for traditionally masculine or "neuter" jobs, females for traditionally "feminine" ones. For both sexes of applicants, the physically attractive were perceived of as more desirable.

* Cash, Thomas F., and Jo Anne Kehr. "Influence of Nonprofessional Counselors' Physical Attractiveness and Sex on Perceptions of Counselor Behavior." *Journal of Counseling Psychology*, 25 (1978), 336-342. See item 532.

* Chaiken, Shelly. "Communicator Physical Attractiveness and Persuasion." *Journal of Personality and Social Psychology*, 37 (1979), 1387-97. See item 665.

* Dabbs, James M., and Neil A. Stokes. "Beauty is Power: The Use of Space on the Sidewalk." *Sociometry*, 38 (1975), 551-557. See item 1150.

1100. Dermer, Marshall, and Darrel L. Thiel. "When Beauty May Fail." *Journal of Personality and Social Psychology*, 31 (1975), 1168-76.

Forty females, preassessed for high, mid, and low levels of attractiveness, judged the personality of pictures of females of varying attractiveness levels. Unattractive subjects did not judge attractive females as having the most desirable personality, as mid and high subjects did. Attractive females were expected to be more vain, egotistical, unsympathetic with oppressed, and so forth. Authors conclude that the "beautiful is good" thesis needs to be modified. See also item 1101.

1101. Dion, Karen, Ellen Berscheid, and Elaine Walster. "What Is Beautiful Is Good." *Journal of Personality and Social Psychology*, 24 (1972), 285-290.

Thirty male and 30 female undergraduates judged personality and future lives of males or females from photographs selected for degrees of physical attractiveness. The stereotype of beautiful being good regardless of sex of subject or sex of person in photograph was found.

1102. Dipboye, Robert L., Richard D. Arvey, and David E. Terpstra. "Sex and Physical Attractiveness of Raters and Applicants as Determinants of Resumé Evaluations." *Journal of Applied Psychology*, 62 (1977), 288-294.

One hundred and ten male and female undergraduates evaluated twelve bogus job applicants of both sexes and of varying qualifications and physical attractiveness. Regardless of interviewer's sex or physical attractiveness, highly qualified applicants were preferred over poorly qualified ones, males over females, and attractive over unattractive ones.

1103. Efran, Michael G. "The Effect of Physical Appearance on the Judgment of Guilt, Interpersonal Attraction, and Severity of Recommended Punishment in a Simulated Jury Task." *Journal of Research in Personality*, 8 (1974), 45-54.

A questionnaire survey of 55 male and 53 female students revealed that they believed defendant's character and previous history should influence juror's decisions and that defendant's attractiveness should not. Subsequently, 33 male and 33 female students participated in a single-sex mock jury with either an attractive or unattractive opposite-sex defendant. Attractive defendants were evaluated with less certainty of guilt and with less recommended punishment than unattractive defendants, especially by male subjects.

1104. Goldberg, Philip A., Marc Gottesdiener, and Paul R. Abramson. "Another Put-Down of Women?: Perceived Attractiveness as a Function of Support for the Feminist Movement." *Journal of Personality and Social Psychology*, 32 (1975), 113-115.

Twenty-nine females and 40 males rated photographs of 30 women whose position on the feminist movement was known. Asked to pick out photographs of supporters, subjects significantly more often chose less attractive women regardless of sex of subject or own attitudes toward the movement.

1105. Goldman, William, and Philip Lewis. "Beautiful Is Good: Evidence that the Physically Attractive Are More Socially Skillful." *Journal of Experimental Social Psychology*, 13 (1977), 125-130.

Using 60 male undergraduates talking on a telephone with 60 female undergraduates and rating their telephone partners on social skills and other measures, the authors found that female subjects independently rated attractive by observers were judged by their telephone partners as more socially skillful and more likeable than those subjects rated less attractive.

1106. Gross, Alan E., and Christine Crofton. "What is Good is Beautiful." *Sociometry*, 40 (1977), 85-90.

One hundred and twenty-five male and female undergraduates picked which of three pictures of females (prejudged in a previous experiment as attractive, average, or unattractive) matched a printed personality description, favorable, average, or unfavorable. Subjects matched the more favorable personality descriptions with the more attractive photographs.

1107. Harrell, W. Andrew. "Physical Attractiveness, Self-Disclosure, and Helping Behavior." *The Journal of Social Psychology*, 104 (1978), 15-17.

An attractive and an unattractive female, either giving name or not, requested directions from 216 males. The greatest amount of help was given to the attractive self-disclosers, the least amount to the unattractive self-disclosers.

* Heilman, Madeline E., and Lois R. Saruwatari. "When Beauty is Beastly: The Effects of Appearance and Sex on Evaluations of Job Applicants for Managerial and Nonmanagerial Jobs." *Organizational Behavior and Human Performance*, 23 (1979), 360-372. See item 432.

1108. Jackson, David J., and Ted L. Huston. "Physical Attractiveness and Assertiveness." *The Journal of Social Psychology*, 96 (1975), 79-84.

Five very attractive and five very unattractive (experimenter selected) female undergraduates responded to impoliteness of the experimenter (male in one experiment, female in the other). Both studies revealed that physically attractive females asserted themselves significantly more quickly than unattractive females.

1109. Jacobson, Marsha B., and Walter Koch. "Attributed Reasons for Support of the Feminist Movement as a Function of Attractiveness." *Sex Roles*, 4 (1978), 169-174.

Thirty-two undergraduates made judgments from photographs to test the hypothesis that people attribute a different set of reasons for being a feminist to attractive and unattractive women. Subjects attributed more positive, flattering reasons to the attractive women than to the unattractive women. The results were interpreted as a put-down not only of unattractive women but of feminism because they imply that feminism is an ideology that is more appealing to and more needed by people who are undervalued in society.

1110. Johnson, Ronald W., Denyse Doiron, Garland P. Brooks, and John Dickson. "Perceiving Attractiveness as a Function of Support for the Feminist Movement: Not Necessarily a Put-Down of Women." *Canadian Journal of Behavioral Science*, 10 (1978), 214-221.

Two investigations of perceptions of attractiveness and feminists used, in one study, 30 non-student and 30 student females, and in the other, 40 non-student and 40 student males. Photographs of female subjects identified as either supporters or non-supporters of the feminist movement were shown to the subjects to identify the pro-feminists. Undergraduate male subjects chose photographs of less attractive women, and female undergraduates chose photographs of more attractive women. The choices of the non-student subjects, both male and female, were not significantly different.

1111. Kaplan, Robert M. "Is Beauty Talent? Sex Interaction in the Attractiveness Halo Effect." *Sex Roles*, 4 (1978), 195-204.

Two experiments were performed to replicate and extend previous findings of judgmental bias which favors physically attractive people. Subjects were 140 undergraduates who judged an essay purportedly written by attractive or unattractive female authors, or, in the second experiment, male authors. Males rated the essay more favorably when the female author was attractive; female judges tended not to be significantly affected by the attractiveness of a female author. In the second experiment, neither sex of subject, attractiveness of author, nor their interaction had significant effects upon judgments of the essay and its author. Female judges tended to give more favorable evaluations in general.

* Kleck, Robert E., and Angelo Strenta. "Perceptions of the Impact of Negatively Valued Physical Characteristics on Social Interaction." *Journal of Personality and Social Psychology*, 39 (1980), 861-873. See item 127.

1112. Kleinke, Chris L., and Richard A. Staneski. "First Impressions of Female Bust Size." *The Journal of Social Psychology*, 110 (1980), 123-134.

In four experiments, female stimulus persons with small, medium, or large bust sizes were rated on various personal and interpersonal measures. In Experiment 1, using written descriptions only, 135 male and 135 female undergraduates rated the medium-bust stimulus person higher on liking and personal appeal. In the other experiments (N = 108, 92, 88, all male and female undergraduates), using photographs, subjects did not evaluate differentially on bust size. In all four experiments, large-bust females were evaluated as less intelligent, competent, moral, and modest, while small-bust females were evaluated higher in all four categories.

* Kleinke, Chris L., Richard A. Staneski, and Sandra L. Pipp. "Effects of Gaze, Distance, and Attractiveness

on Males' First Impressions of Females." *Representative Research in Social Psychology*, 6 (1975), 7-12. See item 1063.

1113. Krebs, Dennis, and Allen A. Adinolfi. "Physical Attractiveness, Social Relations, and Personality Style." *Journal of Personality and Social Psychology*, 31 (1975), 245-253.

Analysis of the relationship between scores on personality measures and ratings of physical attractiveness of 60 males and 60 females grouped by peer sociometric ratings into those accepted, those rejected, and those isolated (nobody mentioned them) revealed that peer-rejected subjects were rated most attractive. Physical attractiveness was related positively to dating for females, but not for males. Peer-rejected subjects of both sexes were independent, achieving, ambitious; accepted subjects were affiliative and affectionate; and isolated subjects were emotionally constricted, defensive, and withdrawn.

1114. LaVoie, Joseph C., and Gerald R. Adams. "Physical and Interpersonal Attractiveness of the Model and Imitation in Adults." *The Journal of Social Psychology*, 106 (1978), 191-202.

This experimental study used 52 male and 56 female undergraduates in a task situation where they could both evaluate and imitate a model, a male or female confederate, who had systematically varied behavior. Warmth of model was more influential on imitation, on personality rating, and on experience than attractiveness of model. The female model was more imitated than the male.

* Lerner, Richard M., Stuart A. Karabenick, and Joyce L. Stuart. "Relations Among Physical Attractiveness, Body Attitudes, and Self-Concept in Male and Female College Students." *Journal of Psychology*, 85 (1973), 119-129. See item 36.

* Lewis, Kathleen N., and W. Bruce Walsh. "Physical Attractiveness: Its Impact on the Perception of a Female Counselor." *Journal of Counseling Psychology*, 25 (1978), 210-216. See item 548.

* Maddux, James E., and Ronald W. Rogers. "Effects of Source Expertness, Physical Attractiveness, and Supporting Arguments on Persuasion: A Case of Brains over Beau-

ty." *Journal of Personality and Social Psychology*, 39 (1980), 235-244. See item 686.

* Mahoney, E.R., and M.D. Finch. "Body-Cathexis and Self-Esteem: A Reanalysis of the Differential Contribution of Specific Body Aspects." *The Journal of Social Psychology*, 99 (1976), 251-258. See item 40.

1115. Mashman, Robert C. "The Effect of Physical Attractiveness on the Perception of Attitude Similarity." *The Journal of Social Psychology*, 106 (1978), 103-110.

A questionnaire survey of 220 male and female undergraduates about their perceptions of attitude similarity with the opposite sex of varying levels of attractiveness revealed that the more attractive the other, the greater the perceived similarity in attitudes, with females showing more influence of attractiveness.

1116. Mathes, Eugene W., and Linda L. Edwards. "Physical Attractiveness as an Input in Social Exchanges." *Journal of Psychology*, 98 (1978), 267-275.

In a first experiment, 72 male and female undergraduates had a chance to reward attractive and unattractive others of the same and opposite sex. Attractive males and females obtained greater rewards in the opposite-sex condition but not in the same-sex condition. A second experiment was designed to see if reward to attractive people related to their providing more erotic pleasure. Twenty-eight male and female undergraduates rated how erotically arousing ten slides of each sex were; attractive persons in slides were rated more erotic than unattractive persons by members of the opposite sex.

1117. Miller, Arthur G. "Role of Physical Attractiveness in Impression Formation." *Psychonomic Science*, 19 (1970), 241-243.

Photographs of males and females, previously rated as high, moderate, or low in physical attractiveness, were evaluated on the Adjective Preference Scale by 360 female and 360 male undergraduates. High attractiveness was associated with positive traits and low attractiveness with undesirable traits. Some sex differences emerged both for sex of photographed person and for sex of subjects, some of them sex-role stereotyped (female subjects seeing female in photograph as passive, reserved, for example).

1118. Miller, Howard L., and W.H. Rivenbark, III. "Sexual Differences in Physical Attractiveness as a Determinant of Heterosexual Liking." *Psychological Reports,* 27 (1970), 701-702.

 A questionnaire of attitudes of 177 male and 177 female undergraduates was used to determine the importance of physical attractiveness in eight interpersonal situations from first impression through marriage. Males revealed greater interest in attractiveness than females in all eight situations. Both sexes rated attractiveness least important for friendship situation and most important for infrequent, important social functions such as proms.

1119. Murstein, Bernard I., and Patricia Choisty. "Physical Attractiveness and Marriage Adjustment in Middle-Aged Couples." *Journal of Personality and Social Psychology,* 34 (1976), 537-542.

 Twenty-two married couples ranging in age from 28 to 59 evaluated self and other for attractiveness and took a test for marriage adjustment. Couples matched each other on physical attractiveness evaluations, but no correlation between attractiveness and marital adjustment emerged except that perception of spouse as attractive by either husband or wife was related to husband's marital adjustment.

1120. Nida, Steve A., and John E. Williams. "Sex-Stereotyped Traits, Physical Attractiveness, and Interpersonal Attraction." *Psychological Reports,* 41 (1977), 1311-22.

 In two experiments, college students of both sexes (N = 132, 184) responded to the desirability as work partner or marital partner of opposite-sex hypothetical stimulus persons manipulated for degree of attractiveness and for degree of sex-stereotyping of personality traits. Subjects strongly preferred attractive simulus persons for marriage partners and tended to prefer hypothetical persons with "feminine" traits.

1121. Owens, Gayle, and J. Guthrie Ford. "Further Consideration of the 'What is Good is Beautiful' Finding." *Social Psychology,* 41 (1978), 73-75.

 To test the "good is beautiful" finding (see item 1101), authors used both male and female pictures of varying levels of attractiveness to be matched with paragraphs describing personalities of varying levels of attractiveness. The results from 60 male and 60 female undergraduates confirmed the earlier finding that the more attractive pictures were matched with the more attractive paragraph descriptions for females. No difference, however, appeared with male pictures and descriptions.

* Pellegrini, Robert J., Robert A. Hicks, Susan Meyers-Winton, and Bruce G. Antal. "Physical Attractiveness and Self-Disclosure in Mixed-Sex Dyads." *The Psychological Record*, 28 (1978), 509-516. See item 756.

1122. Poling, Tommy H. "Sex Differences, Dominance, and Physical Attractiveness in the Use of Nonverbal Emblems." *Psychological Reports*, 43 (1978), 1087-92.

Forty female and forty male undergraduates selected to represent high and low physical attractiveness and high and low levels of dominance were interviewed by a male or female and their nonverbal emblems (head nods, shoulder shrugs, etc.) counted. Females used more emblems than males, and high dominant subjects used more than low dominants. High attractive females used more than low attractive females or males, though no such correspondence was found for males. In cross-sex dyads, high dominant subjects used more than low dominant ones; no such correspondence was found in same-sex dyads.

* Powell, Patricia H., and James M. Dabbs. Jr. "Physical Attractiveness and Personal Space." *The Journal of Social Psychology*, 100 (1976), 59-64. See item 1185.

* Rosen, Sidney, Robert D. Johnson, Martha J. Johnson, and Abraham Tesser. "Interactive Effects of News Valence and Attraction on Communicator Behavior." *Journal of Personality and Social Psychology*, 28 (1973), 298-300. See item 159.

1123. Shea, Judy, Sharyn M. Crossman, and Gerald R. Adams. "Physical Attractiveness and Personality Development." *Journal of Psychology*, 99 (1978), 59-62.

Through interviews and personality measures assessing identity formation, locus of control, and ego functioning of 294 male and female undergraduates, researchers found no significant difference between attractiveness and personality measures, thus providing no support for the "beauty is good" hypothesis (see item 1101).

1124. Sigall, Harold, and John Michela. "I'll Bet You Say That to All The Girls: Physical Attractiveness and Reactions to Praise." *Journal of Personality,* 44 (1976), 611-626.

Forty female undergraduates, made to feel physically attractive or not, each wrote an essay and received praise from a male evaluator who had or had not seen them. In rating the evaluator's credibility, attractive subjects found the evaluator more credible when they were not seen by him than when they were; unattractive subjects, on the other hand, rated him more credible when they had been seen. The findings were discussed in terms of the relationship between attractiveness and self-esteem.

1125. Sigall, Harold, and Nancy Ostrove. "Beautiful But Dangerous: Effects of Offender Attractiveness and Nature of the Crime on Juridic Judgment." *Journal of Personality and Social Psychology,* 31 (1975), 410-414.

Sixty male and 60 female undergraduates sentenced attractive, unattractive or unspecified attractiveness female defendants for crimes either unrelated to attractiveness (burglary) or related (swindle). More lenient sentences were given to attractive defendants for unrelated-to-attractiveness crime, and harsher sentences for the related crime.

1126. Smith, Edward D., and Anita Hed. "Effects of Offenders' Age and Attractiveness on Sentencing by Mock Juries." *Psychological Reports,* 44 (1979), 691-694.

A total of 120 female college students in groups of three acted as juries to assign a sentence to an attractive or unattractive defendant, young or old, accused either of swindle or a burglary. Older defendants were sentenced more harshly than young, and, for burglary only, the attractive defendant was sentenced less harshly than the unattractive.

1127. Snyder, Mark, Elizabeth D. Tanke, and Ellen Berscheid. "Social Perception and Interpersonal Behavior: On the Self-Fulfilling Nature of Social Stereotypes." *Journal of Personality and Social Psychology,* 35 (1977), 656-666.

Fifty-one male undergraduates interacted with 51 unseen males who, they were led to believe, were either attractive or unattractive. Analysis of tape recordings revealed that females perceived as attractive by males came to behave in a more friendly, likeable, and sociable manner, all stereotypic attributes of attractiveness, more than females perceived as unattractive.

1128. Touhey, John C. "Sex-Role Stereotyping and Individual Differences in Liking for the Physically Attractive." *Social Psychology Quarterly*, 42 (1979), 285-289.

Sixty male and 60 female undergraduates, either high or low scorers on the Macho Scale, estimated liking for an opposite-sex person either attractive or not. High scorers, whether male or female, reported greater liking for an attractive person than for unattractive one; low scorers were unaffected by the attractiveness variable.

1129. Turkat, David, and Joseph Dawson. "Attributions of Responsibility for a Chance Event as a Function of Sex and Physical Attractiveness of Target Individual." *Psychological Reports*, 39 (1976), 275-279.

Twenty-four female and 24 male undergraduates rated responsibility of a male or female, attractive or not, in a story with a chance event with negative or nonnegative outcome. Attractive target persons were attributed greater responsibility for chance events with nonnegative outcomes; unattractive target persons were attributed greater responsibility for chance events with negative outcomes. The hypothesis that these findings would be stronger for female target persons was not clearly supported, although a tendency in that direction emerged.

1130. Widgery, Robin N. "Sex of Receiver and Physical Attractiveness of Source as Determinants of Initial Credibility Perception." *Western Speech*, 38 (1974), 13-17.

To examine how sex of receiver and physical attractiveness of source affect perceptions of source credibility, 45 male and 30 female undergraduates viewed photographs of an unattractive and an attractive male and female and recorded their reactions to the photograph on a 7-point semantic differential. Females made higher evaluations of both male and female sources' credibility than males on the variables of safety, qualification, and dynamism.

1131. Wilson, David W. "Helping Behavior and Physical Attractiveness." *The Journal of Social Psychology*, 104 (1978), 313-314.

Attractive or unattractive female confederates asked thirty male undergraduates for directions, and forty more to mail a letter for them. In both studies, responses to the attractive female were significantly more helpful.

1132. Wilson, Glenn D., David K.B. Nias, and Anthony H. Brazendale. "Vital Statistics, Perceived Sexual Attractiveness, and Response to Risqué Humor." *The Journal of Social Psychology*, 95 (1975), 201-205.

Correlations of the ratings of "funniness" of four risqué cartoons and self-perceived physical attractiveness of 190 female student teachers and bust-waist measurements of a subgroup of 62 revealed that the self-perceived physically attractive viewed the cartoons as less funny than the unattractive and that the "shaplier" viewed cartoons as more funny than the less shapely.

SPACE/DISTANCE

1133. Ahmed, S.M.S. "Reactions to Crowding in Different Settings." *Psychological Reports*, 46 (1980), 1279-84.

To examine how subjects would respond to personal space invasions, a male or a female confederate, either with or without a question, approached undergraduates in a laboratory (N = 108) or adults in a shopping center (N = 120). In the shopping center setting, subjects asked a question walked faster than those not asked a question, and male subjects faster than female. In the laboratory setting, a dyadic situaution, subjects waited less long when invaded with a question and showed greater frustrative tension and a higher lack of self-sentiment score. Invaded male subjects showed an increase in guilt proneness more than females did.

* Aiello, John R. "A Further Look at Equilibrium Theory: Visual Interaction as a Function of Interpersonal Distance." *Environmental Psychology and Nonverbal Behavior*, 1, No. 1 (1977), 122-140. See item 1038.

1134. Allgeier, A.R., and Donn Byrne. "Attraction toward the Opposite Sex as a Determinant of Physical Proximity." *The Journal of Social Psychology*, 90 (1973), 213-219.

Ten male and 10 female undergraduates, meeting opposite-sex person unknown to them except by attitude scores, which were manipulated to match or diverge from their own, took seats closer to liked (closer in attitude) than to a disliked member of the opposite sex.

* Altemeyer, Robert A., and Keith Jones. "Sexual Identity, Physical Attractiveness and Seating Position as Determinants of Influence in Discussion Groups." *Canadian Journal of Behavioural Science,* 6 (1974), 357-375. See item 186.

* Argyle, Michael, and Roger Ingham. "Gaze, Mutual Gaze, and Proximity. *Semiotica,* 6 (1972), 32-49. See item 1041.

1135. Bailey, Kent G., John J. Hartnett, and Frank W. Gibson, Jr. "Implied Threat and the Territorial Factor in Personal Space." *Psychological Reports,* 30 (1972), 263-270.

   Forty male and 40 female undergraduates, already measured on anxiety and heterosexuality scales, either approached or were approached by a male or female experimenter-confederate. Subjects allowed greater distance to the male than female experimenter, with least distance being male subjects to the female experimenter. All subjects allowed the experimenter-confederate to approach closer than they themselves approached the confederates. Female subjects were more influenced by anxiety, males by degree of heterosexuality.

1136. Baron, Robert A. "Invasions of Personal Space and Helping: Mediating Effects of Invader's Apparent Need." *Journal of Experimental Social Psychology,* 14 (1978), 304-312.

   Male or female confederates approached 40 female and 41 male undergraduates either at close (1 to 1-1/2 feet) or far (3-4 feet) distances from the seated subjects and requested help either greatly needed or not. Helping behavior was lower when personal space was invaded and need for assistance low, but was facilitated by personal space invasions when need for assistance was high. Neither sex-of-subject nor sex of confederate significantly influenced helping behavior.

* Barrios, Billy, and Martin Giesen. "Getting What You Expect: Effects of Expectation on Intragroup Attraction and Interpersonal Distance." *Personality and Social Psychology Bulletin,* 3 (1977), 87-90. See item 196.

1137. Bauer, Ernest A., "Personal Space: A Study of Blacks and Whites." *Sociometry*, 36 (1973), 402-408.

Equal numbers (15 of each) male and female and black and white undergraduates approached a peer-stranger of same sex and race "as close as comfortable"; distances chosen, in increasing order, were to black females, black males, white females, and white males. Sex, however, did not have a significant main effect.

1138. Baum, Andrew, and Stuart Koman. "Differential Response to Anticipated Crowding: Psychological Effects of Social and Spatial Density." *Journal of Personality and Social Psychology*, 34 (1976), 526-536.

Thirty-two female and 32 male undergraduates filled out questionnaires about their anticipated participation in groups of 5 or 10, in a large or small room, in either a structured or unstructured discussion, then participated, and responded to another qeustionnaire. Those who expected large-group, unstructured discussions felt more crowded than those expecting large-group, structured discussions, regardless of room size. Males reported feeling more crowded than females in small-group, small-room condition.

1139. Baxter, James C. "Interpersonal Spacing in Natural Settings." *Sociometry*, 33 (1970), 444-456.

This cross-cultural (Anglo-, Black-, or Mexican-American), cross-age, cross-sex study of use of space by 859 subject pairs observed in indoor and outdoor settings at a zoo found closer distance for mixed-sex dyads, farthest distance for male/male dyads. Mexican female/female dyads were closest.

1140. Bleda, Paul R., and Sharon E. Bleda. "Effects of Sex and Smoking on Reactions to Spatial Invasion at a Shopping Mall." *Journal of Social Psychology*, 104 (1978), 311-312.

One by one, a male or female smoking or non-smoking confederate sat 6, 18, or 30 inches away from 54 males and 54 females on a bench at a shopping center. The greatest effect, at 6 inches, found subjects fleeing male invaders more often and more quickly than they fled female invaders. If the invaders were smoking, the likelihood of subjects' leaving was greater.

1141. Brady, Adele T., and Michael B. Walker. "Interpersonal Distance as a Function of Situationally Induced Anxiety." *British Journal of Social and Clinical Psychology,* 17 (1978), 127-133.

Two experiments with undergraduates (I, 32 M, 32 F; II, 24 M, 24 F) were conducted to investigate the effects of situationally induced anxiety on interpersonal distance in a dyad of same or mixed sexes. In the anxiety-arousing situation subjects were asked to discuss an interesting incident while their social competence was assessed from behind a one-way screen. Speech disturbance rates showed that the anxiety manipulation was successful. A significant increase in interpersonal distance was found in the anxiety-inducing situation relative to the low-stress situation for both sexes. Male pairs appeared to maintain greater interpersonal distance than mixed pairs, and female pairs maintained the closest, both in the non-anxious and anxious conditions.

1142. Buchanan, Douglas R., Morton Goldman, and Ralph Juhnke. "Eye Contact, Sex, and the Violation of Personal Space." *The Journal of Social Psychology,* 103 (1977), 19-25.

Three field experiments (N = 147; 112; 46) involving different gazing behavior of a male or female confederate in an elevator and the spatial responses of people on entering revealed that, in general, direct gazing lessened likelihood of spatial invasion. Between diverting gaze and avoiding gaze altogether, subjects chose to violate space of avoider, with no sex differences found. In direct gaze condition by male and female confederates, male subjects showed no sex preferences while female subjects moved into space of female confederate more often.

1143. Buchanan, Douglas, Ralph Juhnke, and Morton Goldman. "Violation of Personal Space as a Function of Sex." *The Journal of Social Psychology,* 99 (1976), 187-192.

In field experimental studies using 215 males and females positioning themselves in an elevator already occupied by a male or female confederate (Experiment 1) or both (Experiment 2), all subjects tried to avoid moving into personal space, with female subjects being somewhat less reluctant to move in on female confederate's space. In the second experiment male subjects violated the female confederate's space significantly more often than the male confederate's space. Female subjects showed no significant sex preference.

1144. Burgoon, Judee K., and Stephen B. Hines. "Toward a Theory of Personal Space Expectations and Their Violations." *Human Communication Research,* 2 (1976), 131-146.

Eighty-five articles on proxemics are synthesized and placed in a theoretical framwork based on norms and expectations. Male-female differences are discussed in the section on social norms, as are race, culture, age, and status. Whether sitting or standing, a greater distance was maintained in male than in female dyads. In general, closer proximity was found in opposite-sex pairs. Black females sat closer to an interviewer, followed by white females, white males, and then black males. All white subjects sat further from black interviewers than from white interviewers, while black subjects maintained approximately the same distance from both black and white interviewers. Some studies have found more intimate distancing among blacks than whites.

1145. Byrne, Donn, Glen D. Baskett, and Louis Hodges. "Behavioral Indicators of Interpersonal Attraction." *Journal of Applied Social Psychology,* 1 (1971), 137-149.

In two studies, using 40 and 60 undergraduates, evenly divided by sex, one confederate overwhelmingly agreed with the subject's views and another confederate overwhelming disagreed, with both confederates the same sex as the subject. In a subsequent free-choice seating arrangement, males were more attracted to and sat opposite the agreeing confederate and females were more attracted to and sat beside the agreeing confederate. Both sexes preferred the agreeing confederates.

1146. Calsyn, Robert J. "Group Responses to Territorial Intrusion." *The Journal of Social Psychology,* 100 (1976), 51-58.

In this field study, 116 attempts by undergraduate groups varied in size from one to five to intrude on dining hall tables habitually used by male groups (8 tables) or female groups (3 tables) resulted in the intruders being ignored 68% of the time and 9% being greeted in a friendly fashion. Female groups directed communication to intruders more often than male groups, and significantly more often it was friendly communication.

* Caproni, Valerie, Douglas Levine, Edgar O'Neal, Peter McDonald, and Gray Garwood. "Seating Position, Instructor's Eye Contact Availability, and Student Parti-

cipation in a Small Seminar." *The Journal of Social Psychology,* 103 (1977), 315-316. See item 1043.

1147. Carducci, Bernardo J., and Arthur W. Webber. "Shyness as a Determinant of Interpersonal Distance." *Psychological Reports,* 44 (1979), 1075-78.

A total of 73 undergraduates, both male and female and both shy and not shy, approached and were approached by a male or female experimenter and the distances recorded. Shy subjects maintained significantly greater distance than not-shy subjects, especially with the opposite sex.

* Carr, Suzanne J., and James M. Dabbs, Jr. "The Effects of Lighting, Distance and Intimacy of Topic on Verbal and Visual Behavior." *Sociometry,* 37 (1974), 592-600. See item 1264.

1148. Cheyne, James A., and Michael G. Efran. "The Effect of Spatial and Interpersonal Variables on the Invasion of Group Controlled Territories." *Sociometry,* 35 (1972), 477-489.

In these experimental studies, one with a university locale and the other in a shopping center, using single-sex or mixed-sex dyads with the two at various distances from each other, passers-by were most likely to go through a male/male dyad, least likely a male/female. The difference was significant, however, only at forty inches.

1149. Coutts, Larry M., and Maribeth Ledden. "Nonverbal Compensatory Reactions to Changes in Interpersonal Proximity." *The Journal of Social Psychology,* 102 (1977), 283-290.

In individual interviews with forty female undergraduates, the female interviewer shifted positions to be either closer or farther away between sessions of the interview. When she moved closer, the subjects had less eye contact and smiled less. When she moved farther away, the subjects looked at her more, smiled more, and placed their bodies in a more direct orientation.

* Coutts, Larry M., and Frank W. Schneider. "Visual Behavior in an Unfocused Interaction as a Function of Sex and Distance." *Journal of Experimental Social Psychology,* 11 (1975), 64-77. See item 1050.

1150. Dabbs, James M., and Neil A. Stokes. "Beauty is Power: The Use of Space on the Sidewalk." *Sociometry*, 38 (1975), 551-557.

Using a movie camera to record 470 pedestrians passing by confederates standing at the edge of a sidewalk, the authors found wider paths of deviation for males than for females, for two people than for one person, and for attractive than for unattractive female. They interpret sex, number, and attractiveness in terms of social power.

1151. Edney, Julian J., and Nancy L. Jordan-Edney. "Territorial Spacing on a Beach." *Sociometry*, 37 (1974), 92-104.

This field study, on a beach, of the territorial "claims" of various sized groups with differing sex compositions revealed that females claimed less space than males, whether alone or in groups. Female groups had higher densities and used less space than either all-male or mixed groups; single-sex groups expanded territory over time, but mixed groups did not.

1152. Edwards, David J.A. "Perception of Crowding and Personal Space as a Function of Locus of Control, Arousal Seeking, Sex of Experimenter, and Sex of Subject." *Journal of Psychology*, 95 (1977), 223-229.

Twelve male and 12 female experimenters gave four tests relating to arousal-seeking, locus of control, crowding, and confortable interpersonal distance to 72 male and female undergraduates. Contrary to predictions, arousal-seeking scores did not correlate with crowding scores and locus of control did not correlate with comfortable interpersonal distance with strangers. Distances were larger for female experimenters than for male, arousal-seeking scores were larger for female subjects than male subjects, and male experimenters elicited greater arousal-seeking levels.

1153. Evans, Gary W., and Roger B. Howard. "Personal Space." *Psychological Bulletin*, 80 (1973), 334-344.

Major findings of 110 articles on personal-space are reported, including research on sex, age, and cross-cultural differences. The inconsistent findings are attributed to the lack of experimental controls in most of the personal-space research.

1154. Fisher, Jeffrey D., and Donn Byrne. "Too Close for Comfort: Sex Differences in Response to Invasions of Personal Space." *Journal of Personality and Social Psychology*, 32 (1975), 15-21.

    Two studies of the effects of invasion of personal space revealed that males had negative affect, attraction, and attributions of intent when a stranger sat across from them, while females had negative emotions when a stranger sat next to them. In the second study of 66 students in a library, males erected barriers against face-to-face invasion, and females erected barriers against an invasion at their side.

1155. Freedman, Jonathan L., Alan S. Levy, Roberta W. Buchanan, and Judy Price. "Crowding and Human Aggressiveness." *Journal of Experimental Social Psychology*, 8 (1972), 528-548.

    To determine the effects of crowding on aggression, two experiments were run. The first used 136 high school students and the second 191 volunteers recruited through an advertisement in the *New York Times*, a heterogeneous group of both sexes, black, white, employed, unemployed, and retired, ranging in age from 18 to 80. In Experiment II, the subjects determined sentences in a mock-jury situation under either crowded or non-crowded conditions (large or small room). All-male groups gave more severe sentences in a small room than a large; all-female groups did the opposite, and mixed-sex groups were unaffected by room size. Females were positive about each other in the small room, males in the large room.

*   Giesen, Martin, and Clyde Hendrick. "Physical Distance and Sex in Moderated Groups: Neglected Factors in Small Group Interaction." *Memory and Cognition*, 5 (1977), 79-83. See item 237.

*   Giesen, Martin, and Harry A. McClaren. "Discussion, Distance and Sex: Changes in Impressions and Attraction During Small Group Interaction." *Sociometry*, 39 (1976), 60-70. See item 238.

1156. Greene, Les R. "Effects of Field Dependence on Affective Reactions and Compliance in Dyadic Interactions." *Journal of Personality and Social Psychology*, 34 (1976), 569-577.

A male interviewer meeting 40 field independent and 40 field dependent women interested in dieting varied his levels of verbal feedback in an interview in which distances were measured. Field independent women maintained more distancing from the interviewer, and field dependent expressed more willingness to comply with dieting directions. Five weeks later, however, field independents were more successful in losing weight.

1157. Greene, Les R. "Effects of Verbal Evaluative Feedback and Interpersonal Distance on Behavioral Compliance." *Journal of Counseling Psychology*, 24 (1977), 10-14.

Eighty women in a weight-reduction clinic were interviewed by male counselors who gave either accepting or neutral verbal feedback to clients' self-disclosures and who sat at either "personal" or "social" distance from the client. Results of both a questionnaire and behavioral measures indicated that physical proximity strengthened adherence to diet recommendations under accepting feedback condition, but lowered it under neutral feedback condition.

1158. Griffitt, William, James May, and Russell Veitch. "Sexual Stimulation and Interpersonal Behavior: Heterosexual Evaluative Responses, Visual Behavior, and Physical Proximity." *Journal of Personality and Social Psychology*, 30 (1974), 367-377.

The first study on the effect of sexual stimulation on interpersonal behavior, using 160 female and male undergraduates, either sexually aroused or not, found that aroused females evaluated likeability of symbolic male more favorably than symbolic female, although no such sex difference was found for males. In the second study, 27 males and 25 females under same conditions looked at the opposite sex more than the same sex. Those who responded negatively to sexual arousal avoided proximity to the opposite sex compared to those whose responses were positive or indifferent.

* Grossnickle, William F., Rosina C. Lao, C.T. Martoccia, Donna C. Range, and Frances C. Walters. "Complexity of Effects of Personal Space." *Psychological Reports*, 36 (1975), 237-238. See item 676.

1159. Haase, Richard F. "The Relationship of Sex and Instructional Set to the Regulation of Interpersonal Interaction Distance in a Counseling Analogue." *Journal of Counseling Psychology*, 17 (1970), 233-236.

One hundred male and 100 female undergraduates responded on a semantic differential scale to slides showing a male and a female seated at varying distances from each other in a counseling situation, either for a personal psychological problem or for an academic problem. An analysis of variance indicated no significant differences by sex of either subject or stimulus person, or by type of problem. Distance, however, did produce significant differences, with the closest distance (30 inches) being preferred to all the others.

1160. Harris, Bruce, James E.R. Luginbuhl, and Jill E. Fishbein. "Density and Personal Space in a Field Setting." *Social Psychology,* 41 (1978), 350-353.

In a shopping center, two male and two female confederates violated the personal space (18 inches) of 189 male and female shoppers under low or high density conditions. Male shoppers were more likely to react to the intruder under low crowding if the intruder was male. Male shoppers glanced over their shoulder, moved, or left more than females did in low crowded conditions.

1161. Hartnett, John J., Kent G. Bailey, and Frank W. Gibson, Jr. "Personal Space as Influenced by Sex and Type of Movement." *Journal of Psychology,* 76 (1970), 139-144.

Using sex of experimenter and sex of 64 undergraduates and approaching or being approached as variables in an experiment on space, authors found sex of subject significant but sex of experimenter not. Females allowed greater personal space invasion by experimenter than males did, although both male and female subjects allowed experimenter to approach closer than they approached experimenter. High heterosexual males allowed female experimenter closer than low heterosexual males. No significant differences by heterosexual level in females appeared.

1162. Hartnett, John J., Kent G. Bailey, and Craig S. Hartley. "Body Height, Position, and Sex as Determinants of Personal Space." *Journal of Psychology,* 87 (1974), 129-136.

Using 41 male and 43 female undergraduates approaching a standing or seated short or tall person, investigators found that subjects maintained greater distance from the taller person and from the standing person. Sex of subject was not significant, but height appeared to have more effect on females than males.

1163. Hendricks, Michael, and Richard Bootzin. "Race and Sex as Stimuli for Negative Affect and Physical Avoidance." *The Journal of Social Psychology,* 98 (1976), 111-120.

In a study to test the physical distancing behavior and self-report level of discomfort, 80 white female undergraduates were confronted by male or female and black or white confederates of the experimenter. More subjects reported discomfort with males than with females and maintained greater distance from blacks than from whites.

1164. Heshka, Stanley, and Yona Nelson. "Interpersonal Speaking Distance as a Function of Age, Sex, and Relationship." *Sociometry,* 35 (1972), 491-498.

This field study in London, England, of dyads in outdoor public settings revealed that female dyads had closest distance with friends and relatives, then male-female dyads, and furthest, male dyads. With strangers, however, male dyads were closer than female dyads, although neither distance was as great as that which the male/female dyad maintained.

1165. Kahn, Arnold, and Timothy A. McGaughey. "Distance and Liking: When Moving Close Produces Increased Liking." *Sociometry,* 40 (1977), 138-144.

Forty-four male and 44 female undergraduates evaluated male and female confederates systematically varied by sitting distance, friendliness, and by sex. Significantly more liking of the closer-distance confederate occurred when sex of subject and confederate was opposite. Female confederates were liked significantly more than male confederates. The authors suggest that males and females interpret proximity differently since males show most liking for near female (out of four conditions), and females show least liking for far male; perhaps males see acceptance in proximity and females rejection in distance.

* Kleinke, Chris L. "Compliance to Requests Made by Gazing and Touching Experimenters in Field Settings." *Journal of Experimental Social Psychology,* 13 (1977), 218-223. See item 1059.

* Kleinke, Chris L., Richard A. Staneski, and Sandra L. Pipp. "Effects of Gaze, Distance, and Attractiveness on Males' First Impressions of Females." *Representative Research in Social Psychology,* 6 (1975), 7-12. See item 1063.

1166. Knowles, Eric S., and Rodney L. Bassett. "Groups and Crowds as Social Entities: Effects of Activity, Size, and Member Similarity on Nonmenbers." *Journal of Personality and Social Psychology,* 34 (1976), 837-845.

   This field study used two, four, or six confederates in a group in varied activities but the same positions at the entrance to a library to study the effects on 309 people entering the library. The activity of the group affected the distance subjects maintained, with males responding more strongly than females.

1167. Krail, Kristina, and Gloria Leventhal. "The Sex Variable in the Intrusion of Personal Space." *Sociometry,* 39 (1976), 170-173.

   Male and female experimenters intruded at varying distances on 36 male and 36 female undergraduates seated alone at a library table. Closer distances resulted in quicker responses; the same-sex experimenter/subject condition resulted in quicker responses; and the male subject/female experimenter dyad had the longest period before response. No significant difference between male and female subjects in time for response was found, but in all cases the male invader elicited a response more quickly than the female invader.

1168. Krivonos, Paul D. "The Effects of Attitude Similarity, Spatial Relationship, and Task Difficulty on Interpersonal Attraction." *Southern Speech Communication Journal,* 45 (1980), 240-248.

   This study investigated the invasion of personal space and attitude of the person whose space was being invaded. Eighty undergraduate females had their personal space occupied by a female confederate who was either similar or dissimilar in attitude to the subject, while the subject was involved in either a difficult or a leisure task. Regardless of task or spatial position, attraction responses were more positive toward similar than toward dissimilar confederates. Regardless of task or proportion of similar attitudes, attraction responses were more positive toward confederate who sat close to the subject than toward those who sat one seat away. No attraction differences were found for the effect of the difficulty of the task.

1169. Leginski, Walter, and Richard R. Izzett. "Linguistic Styles as Indices for Interpersonal Distance." *The Journal of Social Psychology,* 91 (1973), 291-304.

In two studies two sets of equal numbers of males and females (N = 20 and 24) estimated the distance between communicators in various situations. No significant sex differences in estimation of distance for a particular communication style (intimate, public, business, etc.) appeared.

1170. Leginski, Walter, and Richard R. Izzett. "The Selection and Evaluation of Interpersonal Distances as a Function of Linguistic Styles." *The Journal of Social Psychology*, 99 (1976), 125-137.

An equal number of male and female undergraduates, after listening to intimate, friendly, business-like, or public-address recorded talks by males and females, judged the distance they would take from that person. In the first experiment (N = 80), distances were significantly closer for female speakers than for male speakers, and in same-sex dyads, males tended to judge a farther distance than females in both intimate and personal styles. Distances chosen generally supported the Hall model of interpersonal distances from intimate through public, as they did in Experiment II (N = 26), in which sex differences did not materialize.

1171. Lesko, Wayne A. "Psychological Distance, Mutual Gaze, and the Affiliative-Conflict Theory." *The Journal of Social Psychology*, 103 (1977), 311-312.

In this brief report Lesko cites his research manipulating psychological distance (a glass partition) between 20 pairs of female undergraduates. As psychological distance increased, so did mutual gaze.

1172. Leventhal, Gloria, Marsha Lipshultz, and Anthony Chiodo. "Sex and Setting Effects on Seating Arrangement." *Journal of Psychology*, 100 (1978), 21-26.

In this field study the seating arrangements of males and females seated three or more at one of 176 tables in social settings and 150 tables in nonsocial settings were observed. In social settings, opposite-sex pairs selected a side-by-side seating pattern while same-sex male pairs sat opposite each other, and same-sex female pairs chose either arrangement. In nonsocial settings, subjects sat side by side, regardless of sex.

1173. Leventhal, Gloria, Michelle Matturro, and Joel Schanerman. "Effects of Attitude, Sex, and Approach on Nonverbal, Verbal and Projective Measures of Personal Space." *Perceptual and Motor Skills*, 47 (1978), 107-118.

Ten male and ten female undergraduates were approached from the front and side by either a male or a female friend or by a stranger approaching in either an affable, a neutral, or a hostile manner and then completed a questionnaire on distances they would permit various people. Males allowed the affable male friend closer than the hostile person of either sex or either sex stranger. They allowed the female stranger to come closer than the hostile female. Females allowed a closer approach by a hostile male than a hostile female.

1174. Liebman, Miriam. "The Effects of Sex and Race Norms on Personal Space." *Environment and Behavior*, 2 (1970), 208-246.

Working women between the ages of 17 and 59, 98 white and 18 black, were observed choosing a seat on a park bench already occupied by a black or white male or female confederate under various conditions of length and number of benches. Intrusion was avoided where possible, females were intruded upon significantly more often than males, and subjects sat closer to a female than a male already seated on the bench. White subjects were not influenced by the race of the confederate in intrusion likelihood or in distance. Female black subjects preferred to intrude on a black male. Black subjects sat significantly further from the white confederates when they intruded upon them than upon black confederates, whom they chose most frequently. They sat closer to the black female than to the white female, to whom they sat closer than to the black or white males. Discussion of the salience of these norms and a lengthy list of references are included.

1175. Long, Gary T., James W. Selby, and Lawrence G. Calhoun. "Effects of Situational Stress and Sex on Interpersonal Distance Preference." *Journal of Personality*, 105 (1980), 231-238.

To test the prediction that people would prefer greater distance from others when they anticipate a stressful situation, 65 male and 52 female undergraduates completed a seating preference questionnaire, which consisted of 10 descriptions of campus situations, 5 of them stressful, and a drawing in which a seat could be selected. Both sexes chose more distant seats in

1176. Mahoney, E.R. "Compensatory Reactions to Spatial Immediacy." *Sociometry*, 37 (1974), 423-431.

This field study of 10 male and 10 female undergraduates' reactions when a female "intruded" into their space by taking one of four positions at their library table found that two of those positions (2 and 3 seats adjacent to subject) did not affect behavior. Females tended to lean away more than males and to block more; but, in across-the-table invasions, they decreased both leaning and blocking. This finding is consistent with a previous one that females prefer side-by-side positioning, males face-to-face.

* Markel, Norman N., Joseph F. Long, and Thomas J. Saine. "Sex Effects in Conversational Interaction: Another Look at Male Dominance." *Human Communication Research*, 2 (1976), 356-364. See item 136.

* Marshall, Joan E., and Richard Heslin. "Boys and Girls Together: Sexual Composition and the Effect of Density and Group Size on Cohesiveness." *Journal of Personality and Social Psychology*, 31 (1975), 952-961. See item 268.

1177. Mehrabian, Albert, and Shirley G. Diamond. "Seating Arrangement and Conversation." *Sociometry*, 34 (1971), 281-289.

In same-sex groups of four, 124 male and 120 female undergraduates entered, one by one, a room arranged with eight arm chairs in one of four different positions. Measures of the seats chosen, the conversation, affiliative and sensitivity and rejection measures, and a post test for recall of the room were taken. Females and affiliative subjects sat closer, and more conversation occurred between people who took immediate positions, i.e., either directly oriented to each other, or, for those sensitive to rejection, closer to another. Males were more accurate in the room recall test.

* Muirhead, Rosalind D., and Morton Goldman. "Mutual Eye Contact as Affected by Seating Position, Sex, and Age." *Journal of Social Psychology*, 109 (1979), 201-206. See item 1066.

1178. Nesbitt, Paul D., and Girard Steven. "Personal Space and Stimulus Intensity at a Southern California Amusement Park." *Sociometry,* 37 (1974), 105-115.

In field studies using males and females (numbers not given) standing in line behind a cohort, either conservatively or flashily dressed and either with or without perfume or shaving lotion, the flashy clothing and scent increased distance between cohort and subjects. Male subjects tended to stand closer to a female cohort than females to a male cohort.

* Patterson, Miles L., and Lee B. Sechrest. "Interpersonal Distance and Impression Formation." *Journal of Personality,* 38 (1970), 161-166. See item 151.

1179. Patterson, Miles L., Carl E. Kelly, Bruce A. Kondracki, and Linda J. Wulf. "Effects of Seating Arrangement on Small-Group Behavior." *Social Psychology Quarterly,* 42 (1979), 180-185.

In this experimental study of the behavior of 32 four-person, single-sex groups seated at an L-shaped or a circular table, the circular table enhanced behaviors associated with positive interaction, and the L-shaped table enhanced self-manipulative and anxiety behaviors. No distance or sex differences were found.

1180. Patterson, Miles L., Sherry Mullens, and Jeanne Romano. "Compensatory Reactions to Spatial Intrusion." *Sociometry,* 34 (1971), 114-121.

Females took a seat at a library table already occupied by a lone male or female undergraduate (40 of each sex) to determine their reaction. Males were more likely to leave than females except when the intruder took the furthest seat. Females were more likely to block (with books or body shift) at closest side distance while males blocked more when an intruder took opposite-seat position.

* Patterson, Miles L., and Russell E. Schaeffer. "Effects of Size and Sex Composition on Interaction Distance Participation, and Satisfaction in Small Groups." *Small Group Behavior,* 8 (1977), 433-442. See item 281.

1181. Paulus, Paul B., Angela B. Annis, John J. Seta, Janette K. Schkade, and Robert W. Matthews. "Density Does Affect Task Performance." *Journal of Personality and Social Psychology,* 34 (1976), 248-253.

In three different experiments, the effects of manipulating group size, room size, and interpersonal proximity on the task preference of male and female undergraduates (N = 27, 60, 56) were determined. In a short-term situation, increased group size decreased interpersonal distance, and decreased room size led to lower task scores, although the room-size effect was found for males only.

1182. Pedersen, Darhl M. "Factors Affecting Personal Space Toward a Group." *Perceptual and Motor Skills,* 45 (1977), 735-743.

To explore the effects of a number of group characteristics on spacing within a group, 160 male and 160 female undergraduates completed a paper-and-pencil simulated task which measured personal space in a group containing various combinations of an adult man, adult woman, boy or girl figures, varied in size and direction of orientation. Personal space was smaller toward groups not containing a man; for groups of children, not adults, when approaching face-to-face; for groups of females, not males, when approaching from behind; for groups facing away, not facing at right angles or facing forward. Sex of subject was not significant, and no significant differences were found for group size.

1183. Pedersen, Darhl M., and Anne B. Heaston. "The Effects of Sex of Subject, Sex of Approaching Person, and Angle of Approach Upon Personal Space." *Journal of Psychology,* 82 (1972), 277-286.

In a simulated condition, females were allowed to approach more closely than males to the 20 male and 20 female undergraduates tested. All permitted closer approach on the sides than at the front, and males permitted closer frontal approaches than females. In a real measure, a closer side than frontal approach was also found, and again males permitted closer frontal approaches. Males approaching from left off-center were permitted to approach closer than females coming from the same angle.

1184. Polit, Denise, and Marianne La France. "Sex Differences in Reaction to Spatial Invasion." *The Journal of Social Psychology,* 102 (1977), 59-60.

A confederate joined 60 male and 60 female undergraduates seated alone at a library table either with or without asking. Females left the table sooner than males, especially in the asking condition, although neither males nor females left immediately.

1185. Powell, Patricia H., and James M. Dabbs, Jr. "Physical Attractiveness and Personal Space." *The Journal of Social Psychology,* 100 (1976), 59-64.

To test distances male and female subjects would maintain in an encounter with an attractive or unattractive male or female, both laboratory and field experiments were devised. In the lab setting, attractive targets were approached more closely, with the 15 female subjects approaching both male and female attractive targets and the 15 male subjects the female targets only. In the field setting, however, no differences by sex or distance were observed in male and female pedestrians (N = 102) stopped by an attractive or unattractive male or female interviewer.

1186. Powers, William G., and Delana Guess. "Research Note on 'Invasion of Males' Personal Space by Feminists and Non-Feminists.'" *Psychological Reports,* 38 (1976), 1300.

From a pool of 200 female undergraduates taking a test which included feminist/nonfeminist items, 15 feminists and 15 nonfeminists were selected. Each entered a room with a male confederate for an interview; distances at initial entry point and ultimate invasion were recorded. No significant differences between feminists and nonfeminists were found.

* Roger, D.B. "Personal Space, Body Image, and Leadership: An Exploratory Study." *Perceptual and Motor Skills,* 43 (1976), 25-26. See item 614.

* Rogers, Richard, and E. Wayne Wright. "Preliminary Study of Perceived Self-Disclosure." *Psychological Reports,* 38 (1976), 1334. See item 757.

1187. Rosegrant, Teresa J., and James C. McCroskey. "The Effect of Race and Sex on Proxemic Behavior in an Interview Setting." *Southern Speech Communication Journal,* 40 (1975), 408-420.

This empirical study, involving 240 undergraduates (60 white and 60 black females, 60 white and 60 black males), investigated the effects of sex and race on interpersonal spacing in a dyadic interview setting with a stranger.

Interviewees in male-male dyads established greater interpersonal distance than interviewees in any dyad including a female. White interviewees established greater interpersonal distance from black interviewers than any other racial combination. Female black interviewees established closer interpersonal distance to all interviewers than any other sex-race combination.

1188. Sanders, Jeffrey L. "Relation of Personal Space to the Human Menstrual Cycle." *Journal of Psychology*, 100 (1978), 275-278.

Using menstrual cycle information of each of 84 female undergraduates and the distance they maintained in relation to a male confederate, Sanders determined that the personal space zone became larger during menstruation.

* Schneider, Frank W., and Christine L. Hansvick. "Gaze and Distance as a Function of Change in Interpersonal Gaze." *Social Behavior and Personality*, 5 (1977), 49-53. See item 1069.

1189. Schwarzwald, Joseph, Naomi Kavish, Monica Shoham, and Mark Waysman. "Fear and Sex-Similarity as Determinants of Personal Space." *Journal of Psychology*, 96 (1977), 55-61.

Forty male and forty female undergraduates, anticipating either electric shocks or nonthreatening physiological measurements, placed their chair in relation to an already seated male or female confederate. In the fear condition, subjects sat closer to same-sex confederates than to opposite-sex ones. In the non-fear condition, male subjects sat closer to the female confederate than to the male confederate.

1190. Shaffer, David R., and Cyril Sadowski. "This Table is Mine: Respect for Marked Barroom Tables as a Function of Gender of Spatial Marker and Desirability of Locale." *Sociometry*, 38 (1975), 408-419.

This field study in a college bar investigated the invasion of a table marked with male (jacket, briefcase) or female (lacy sweater, flowered bookbag) items. The spatial markers, whether masculine or feminine, delayed invasion, but masculine markers were more effective, especially with female invaders. Single invaders and groups (two or more) occupied unmarked or feminine-marked tables, but only groups occupied masculine marked tables.

* Skotko, Vincent P., and Daniel Langmeyer. "The Effects of Interaction Distance and Gender on Self-Disclosure in the Dyad." *Sociometry*, 40 (1977), 178-182. See item 763.

1191. Sobel, Robert S., and Nancy Lillith. "Determinants of Nonstationary Personal Space Invasion." *The Journal of Social Psychology*, 97 (1975), 39-45.

   The responses of 116 male and female adults walking in New York City when either a male or a female experimenter made a straight-line approach to them showed that subjects deflected from the female experimenter at a greater distance than from the male experimenter. The male experimenter was brushed significantly more often. No significant main effect differences by sex of pedestrians appeared.

1192. Stratton, Lois O., Dennis J. Tekippe, and Grad L. Flick. "Personal Space and Self-Concept." *Sociometry*, 36 (1973), 424-429.

   Nineteen male and 14 female first-year college students, divided into low, mid, and high self-concept groups, established their closest comfortable distance to a dummy, to a male undergraduate experimenter, and to silhouette figures. High self-concept males and females approached closer to the dummy and the male than low self-concept subjects, with low self-concept females approaching less closely than low self-concept males. Silhouette placement showed an opposite trend in the distance, with high self-concepts using the greatest distance, low self-concepts the closest distance.

1193. Sussman, Nan M., and Howard M. Rosenfeld. "Touch, Justification, and Sex: Influences on the Aversiveness of Spatial Violations." *The Journal of Social Psychology*, 106 (1978), 215-225.

   In two experiments, a female (in the first) or a male (in the second) confederate invaded the intimate space of 21 males and 23 females (40 of each sex in the second experiment), either with or without justification and with or without touching. Males were more adverse to invasion and to touching. Neither distance nor touching affected females, who reported increased liking for the intruders, while the males reported decreased liking.

1194. Tennis, Gay H., and James M. Dabbs, Jr. "Sex, Setting and Personal Space: First Grade Through College." *Sociometry*, 38 (1975), 385-394.

This experimental test of distance established by 20 males and 20 females in same-sex dyads in corner and center settings used first, fifth, ninth, and twelfth graders, and college sophomores. Distances were found to be greater for older than for younger students, for males than for females, and in a corner rather than in a center setting. Greater sex differences occurred among the older students.

1195. Tesch, Frederick E. "Interpersonal Proximity and Impression Formation: A Partial Examination of Hall's Proxemic Model." *The Journal of Social Psychology*, 107 (1979), 43-55.

Forty-eight male and 48 female undergraduates evaluated a male or female confederate-interviewer when the distance between them was systematically varied. Distance did not directly affect impressions, but sex did. Males attributed more inclusion and affection, both wanted and expressed, to the interviewer, regardless of sex. In same-sex dyads, evaluations of expressed control increased as distance between the two decreased (except for the greatest distance). In opposite-sex dyads, evaluations of expressed control were greater at extreme distances than at moderate distances. The hypothesis that proximity was a significant cue in impression formation was not supported.

* Tesch, Frederick E., Ted L. Huston, and Eugene A. Indenbaum. "Attitude Similarity, Attraction, and Physical Proximity in a Dynamic Space." *Journal of Applied Social Psychology*, 3 (1973), 63-72. See item 167.

1196. Tipton, Robert M., Kent G. Bailey, and Janet P. Obenchain. "Invasion of Males' Personal Space by Feminists and Nonfeminists." *Psychological Reports*, 37 (1975), 99-102.

A group of 72 female undergraduates selected by scores on the Attitudes Toward Women Scale to be feminists or nonfeminists approached and then were approached by a male or female. Distance to the female was about the same for each group, but feminists approached the male significantly closer than nonfeminists. No other significant differences emerged.

1197. Tognoli, Jerome. "Differences in Women's and Men's Responses to Domestic Space." *Sex Roles,* 6 (1980), 833-842.

To examine differences in feelings toward rooms in their homes, 26 adult Scottish men and women responded to two items: "Describe all the things that the room has been used for within the last week" and "Describe any feelings that come to you regarding the room." In general, women recalled more activities occurring in the rooms than men did. Both sexes were sensitive to and aware of their living space.

1198. Tyler, Ann I., Wayne L. Waag, and Clay E. George. "Determinants of the Ecology of the Dyad: The Effects of Age and Sex." *Journal of Psychology,* 81 (1972), 117-120.

A field study of seating arrangements of 1,073 dyads in a university cafeteria analyzed by sex and age revealed that, under age 30, participants in male-male and male-female dyads preferred diagonal seating while female-female dyads preferred face-to-face seating. Over 30, no differences by sex were observed; all preferred face-to-face seating.

1199. Watson, O. Michael. "Conflicts and Directions in Proximic Research." *Journal of Communication,* 22 (Dec. 1972), 443-459.

This summary and commentary of the author's research in proximics includes one- or two-sentence summaries of preliminary findings of interactions between black and white males and females.

1200. Weiskott, Gerald N., and Charles C. Cleland. "Assertiveness, Territoriality, and Personal Space Behavior as a Function of Group Assertion Training." *Journal of Counseling Psychology,* 24 (1977), 111-117.

Changes in the assertiveness, territoriality, and personal space of 42 women who volunteered for an assertion training program were evaluated by questionnaire and behavioral measures. Subjects showed significantly more assertive behavior after treatment than a control group (waiting list), and used more space on a drawing task. The prediction that treatment subjects would have smaller personal space zones had only partial support.

1201. Wellens, A. Rodney, and Myron L. Goldberg. "The Effects of Interpersonal Distance and Orientation upon the Perception of Social Relationships." *Journal of Psychology*, 99 (1978), 39-47.

In this study, 240 male and female undergraduates evaluated via an adjective scale and open questions the psychological relationships of silhouetted dyads varied by sex composition, by body orientations, and by distance between silhouettes. Body orientation affected ratings more than distance. Sex differences included female dyads being evaluated more positively than male dyads, and each sex evaluating same-sex dyad at six inches more positively than like dyad at back-oblique orientation.

1202. White, Michael J. "Interpersonal Distance as Affected by Room Size, Status, and Sex." *The Journal of Social Psychology*, 95 (1975), 241-249.

Forty male and 40 female undergraduates individually selected seats in a small (9' x 15') or large (9' x 30') room with a peer or a professor already seated. An inverse relationship between size of room and seating distance occurred so that the larger the room, the smaller the distance between the two, while the smaller the room the larger the distance. Female subjects sat closer than males and all subjects sat farther away from the female professor than they did from the female peer.

1203. Willis, Frank N., Jr., Joseph A. Gier, and David E. Smith. "Stepping Aside: Correlates of Displacement in Pedestrians." *Journal of Communication*, 29 (Autumn 1979), 34-39.

Although theory has it that human power relationships affect displacement (who steps aside for whom in a head-on encounter), this study of 1,038 displacements by 3,141 males and females, black, white, Chicano, or Oriental, revealed that gallantry is also a factor. Females displaced males, blacks displaced whites, larger groups displaced smaller, those with vehicles (stroller, wheeler) displaced others, and those with an obvious handicap displaced others, all significantly so.

1204. Wittig, Michele A., and Paul Skolnick. "Status Versus Warmth as Determinants of Sex Differences in Personal Space." *Sex Roles*, 4 (1978), 493-503.

This study investigated differences in personal space when the status, warmth level, extroversion, and self-esteem of the person being interacted with were manipulated. Videotapes of 80 male and female undergraduates interacting with either a warm or cold male or female professor or student revealed that males were given more space than females. Both status and sociability influenced the amount of space. Cold, low-status males were allowed the most space. High-status females were allowed more space than the low-status ones, but warmth bore no relation to distance to the low-status female. Personality measures of extroversion and self-esteem failed to correlate with interpersonal distance.

TOUCH

* Alagna, Frank J., Sheryle J. Whitcher, Jeffrey D. Fisher, and Edward A. Wicas. "Evaluative Reaction to Interpersonal Touch in a Counseling Interview." *Journal of Counseling Psychology*, 26 (1979), 465-472. See item 528.

1205. Boderman, Alvin, Douglas W. Freed, and Mark T. Kinnucan. "'Touch Me Like Me': Testing an Encounter Group Assumption." *Journal of Applied Behavioral Science*, 8 (1972), 527-533.

Twenty-one college women completed bogus ESP tasks with a female confederate in either a touch or no-touch (face and head) condition. Post-experimental evaluations of the confederate showed that those in the touch condition gave a significantly higher total score to the confederate, although only one of the subsets of scores, "How responsive is partner?", achieved significance.

1206. deWever, Margaret K. "Nursing Home Patients' Perception of Nurses' Affective Touching." *Journal of Psychology*, 96 (1977), 163-171.

Ninety-nine nursing home patients (81 F, 18 M), ranging in age from 62-94, responded to an inventory measuring comfort when touched by nurses varied for age and sex. Patients perceived discomfort if touched by older male nurse or if either male or female nurse put arms around the patient's shoulders. The majority of patients, however, perceived they would feel comfortable with all of the 28 specific touching behaviors investigated.

1207. Fisher, Jeffrey D., Marvin Rylting, and Richard Heslin. "Hands Touching Hands: Affective and Evaluative Effects of an Interpersonal Touch." *Sociometry,* 39 (1976), 416-421.

In this experimental study in a field setting, 101 undergraduates at a library check-out counter were either touched or not by the male or female library clerk. Female subjects responded more favorably to touch than to no-touch, whether they were aware of the touch or not, on both affective and evaluative dimensions. The sex of the clerk made no significant difference. Male subjects' responses to touch were more ambivalent.

1208. Henley, Nancy. "Body Politics: Power, Sex, and Nonverbal Communication." *Liberation,* 20, No. 2 (1977), 3-10. Excerpt from *Body Politics* (item 1277).

1209. Henley, Nancy. "The Politics of Touch." *Women: A Journal of Liberation,* 3, No. 1 (1972), 7-8. Rpt. in *Radical Psychology.* Ed. Phil Brown. New York: Harper & Row, 1973, pp. 421-433.

With both anecdotal and research material, Henley argues that touch is allied to status such that the one higher in status can initiate touching; the lower cannot. Thus males can initiate touch with females. When females initiate touch with males, however, it is interpreted not as friendliness, as his touch is interpreted, but as sexual advancement. Henley's interpretation is that touch is an indication of power, and so is acceptable for men; since women are perceived as powerless, their initiation of touching must be explained as sexual.

1210. Henley, Nancy M. "Status and Sex: Some Touching Observations." *Bulletin of the Psychonomic Society,* 2 (1973), 91-93.

Observing touching behavior in various settings and paying attention to the variables of sex, race, age, and socioeconomic status, Henley found touching behavior used, like terms of address, in an asymmetrical pattern revealing the higher status of the one who does the touching.

* Kleinke, Chris L. "Compliance to Requests Made by Gazing and Touching Experimenters in Field Settings." *Journal of Experimental Social Psychology,* 13 (1977), 218-223. See item 1059.

* Kleinke, Chris L., Frederick B., Meeker, and Carl LaFong. "Effects of Gaze, Touch, and Use of Name on Evaluation of Engaged Couples." *Journal of Research in Personality,* 7 (1974), 368-373. See item 1061.

* Lamb, Michael E. "Father-Infant and Mother-Infant Interaction in the First Year of Life." *Child Development,* 48 (1977), 167-181. See item 352.

1211. Montagu, Ashley. *Touching: The Human Significance of the Skin.* New York: Columbia University Press, 2nd ed. 1978.

    In his examination of the way in which tactile experience (or its absence) affects behavior, Montague includes a chapter on sex and sex differences in tactile experience and development, Chapter Five, "Skin and Sex."

1212. Nguyen, Tuan, Richard Heslin, and Michele L. Nguyen. "The Meanings of Touch: Sex Differences." *Journal of Communication,* 25 (Summer 1975), 92-103.

    In a questionnaire survey of 41 male and 40 female undergraduates on the meanings of tactile modalities (pat, squeeze, brush, or stoke) when applied to various body areas by a person of the opposite sex, the sexes disagreed on which modes meant playfulness, warmth/love, or friendship, but not on which modes meant pleasantness and sexual desire. Touch was perceived as highly pleasant and expressive of warmth/love, but different criteria were used to decode the meaning of touch. Playfulness and warmth were determined more by mode of touch, but sexuality and friendliness more by body area touched. For females, the more a touch was associated with sexual desire, the less playful, warm, and pleasant it was considered. Males considered pleasantness, sexual desire, and warmth to go together.

1213. Rinck, Christine M., Frank N. Willis, Jr., and Larry M. Dean. "Interpersonal Touch Among Residents of Homes for the Elderly." *Journal of Communication,* 30 (Spring 1980), 44-47.

    From observations of the touching behavior of 490 residents of homes for the elderly (385 white, 104 black; 109 male, 381 female) in their social activities, the authors found that females initiated touch significantly more often than males, and more to other females than to males. No difference by sex in body area touched occurred, but blacks were more likely than whites to be touched in personal area (hand) than in impersonal (upper arm, shoulder, back). No other significant difference by race appeared.

1214. Rosenfeld, Lawrence B., Sallie Kartus, and Chett Ray. "Body Accessibility Revisited." *Journal of Communication,* 26 (Summer 1976), 27-30.

To replicate an earlier study on touch, 98 female and 103 male undergraduates completed a questionnaire on touching behavior. Results indicated very little change in areas of the body touched by mothers, fathers, and same-sex friends. Female friends touched male's chest, stomach, and hip regions with greater frequency, and male friends touched the entire torso of females with greater frequency.

* Silverman, Alan F., Mark E. Pressman, and Helmut W. Bartel. "Self-Esteem and Tactile Communication." *Journal of Humanistic Psychology,* 13, No. 2 (1973), 73-77. See item 58.

1215. Silverthorne, Colin, John Micklewright, Marie O'Donnell, and Richard Gibson. "Attribution of Personal Characteristics as a Function of the Degree of Touch on Initial Contact and Sex." *Sex Roles,* 2 (1976), 185-193.

To evaluate factors attributed to the individuals who touch others on initial contact, 60 male and 60 female undergraduate students were introduced to a confederate who touched or did not touch the subjects in greeting them. The subjects then evaluted the confederate. Same-sex greeters were judged more favorably the more contact they used. In general, the person who shook hands and clasped the arm was seen as better adjusted, more likeable, and more suitable as a person with whom to spend time in the future. When the female shook hands, however, she was seen by male subjects as less knowledgeable of current events and less well adjusted than the woman who nodded. Findings would indicate that males are best served by using as much socially accepted touch as possible upon initial contact and females as little touch as possible, particularly if her encounter is with a male.

1216. Stolte, Karen M., and Paul G. Friedman. "Patients' Perceptions of Touch During Labor." *Journal of Applied Communications Research,* 8 (1980), 10-21.

This study investigated perceptions about being touched during labor of 150 women. Overall, the women perceived the touch that they received during labor as positive. Doctors were responsible for most of the negatively perceived touch and husbands the positively perceived touch.

1217. Summerhayes, Diana L., and Robert W. Suchner. "Power Implications of Touch in Male-Female Relationships." *Sex Roles,* 4 (1978), 103-110.

To examine the Henley theory (item 1212) that nonreciprocal touch in male-female relations is used by men as a status reminder to keep women in their places, 60 undergraduates rated dominance in photographs of male-female interactions. Nonreciprocal touch reduced the perceived power of the person being touched regardless of status or gender. Thus, non-reciprocal touch was used by high-status men to remind lower-status women of their subordinate positions. Touch was also used by lower status women, however, to undermine the status claims of higher status men. In conditions of equal perceived status, touch was not sufficient to alter power perceptions. These findings suggest that without other status cues evident in the relationship, touch alone is insufficient to establish a power advantage for either party.

* Sussman, Nan M., and Howard M. Rosenfeld. "Touch, Justification, and Sex: Influences on the Aversiveness of Spatial Violations." *The Journal of Social Psychology,* 106 (1978), 215-225. See item 1193.

1218. Walker, David N. "A Dyadic Interaction Model for Nonverbal Touching Behavior in Encounter Groups." *Small Group Behavior,* 6 (1975), 308-324.

The nonverbal touching behavior of strangers in a dyadic interaction was assessed using 180 unmarried male and female undergraduates. Personality characteristics were important in determining the nature of subjects' responses to the touching interaction. Touching may be used most appropriately with persons who are not guilty concerning sex, who are not sexually calloused toward females, and who have a strong need for affection. These results implied that trainers for encounter groups need to know something about the personality characteristics of the participants before they use touching techniques.

1219. Watson, Wilbur H. "The Meanings of Touch: Geriatric Nursing." *Journal of Communication,* 25 (Summer, 1975), 104-112.

The touching behavior of geriatric nursing personnel with the elderly was analyzed for kinds, instances, and rules of propriety. Factors which influenced touching behavior were distance of body area from genital zones, the sex of the dyad pair, the social status of the initiator, and the degree of patient impairment. Women were touched more frequently than men by the virtually all-female staff. Shoulder touchers occurred more frequently and female-female dyads had more touching. The higher the status of the staff person, the more likely touching was initiated. Mildly impaired patients were touched more than severely impaired.

1220. Whitcher, Sheryle J., and Jeffrey D. Fisher. "Multidimensional Reaction to Therapeutic Touch in a Hospital Setting." *Journal of Personality and Social Psychology,* 37 (1979), 87-96.

This field study of the effects of touching or no touching on 48 male and female patients in a hospital revealed the female subjects' in the touch condition experienced more favorable emotional, behavioral, and physiological (blood pressure and pulse) responses than no-touch groups. Males in the touch condition, however responded more negatively than in the no-touch condition.

* Young, David M., Kim M. Korner, J.D. Gill, and Ernst G. Beier. "'Beneficial' Aggression." *Journal of Communication,* 27 (Summer 1977), 100-103. See item 383.

VOCAL CHARACTERISTICS

1221. Addington, David W. "The Effect of Vocal Variations on Ratings of Source Credibility." *Speech Monographs,* 28 (1971), 242-247.

Fifteen recordings of vocal variations from monotone to orotund were made of a single passage by five male and five female speakers, and were evaluated for credibility on a semantic differential by 180 undergraduates. Though there were significant interactions between vocal characteristic and evaluation, no differences by sex were found.

1222. Aronovitch, Charles D. "The Voice of Personality: Stereotyped Judgments and Their Relation to Voice Quality and Sex of Speaker." *The Journal of Social Psychology,* 99 (1976), 207-220.

This questionnaire survey of 100 male and female undergraduates rating taped voices of 25 male and 32 female undergraduates on ten personality traits revealed that judgments of speaker personality for males related to speech rate and variation in loudness and pitch while for females it related to speech rate, time, and average volume and pitch. Sex of rater made no difference.

1223. Blass, Thomas, and Aron W. Siegman. " A Psycholinguistic Comparison of Speech, Dictation and Writing." *Language and Speech,* 18 (1975), 20-34.

In an interview setting, 18 female nursing students responded to personal and impersonal questions by speaking, dictating, and writing in a systematically varied procedure. Analysis of various extralinguistic, syntactic, and content measures indicated the speaking condition, in contrast to the writing, produced significantly faster reaction time, production rate, greater verbal productivity, higher silence quotients, and lower passive voice verb ratings. Dictation scores were intermediate between speaking and writing except for the silence quotient. Impersonal questions, contrasted to personal, produced greater productivity, faster reaction time, a lower silence quotient and silent pause ratio, higher filled pause ratio, and longer and more superficial sentences. The data confirmed the hypothesis that decreasing the amount of visual contact would lead to decreasing psychological pressure and hence to increased control of the situation by the interviewee.

1224. Brend, Ruth M. "Male-Female Intonation Patterns in American English." In *Language and Sex: Difference and Dominance* (item 1326), pp. 84-87. Rpt. from "Male-Female Differences in American English Intonation." *7th International Congress of Phonetic Sciences,* Canada, 1971, 866-869.

Noting eleven intonation patterns used differently by the sexes, Brend summarizes that men have only three contrastive levels of intonation, while women have at least four. Men avoid certain intonation patterns and always terminate at their lowest pitch level except for certain special effects, incomplete sentences, and interrogative sentences. Sex differences in intonation patterns may be present in all languages.

1225. Brown, W.S., Jr., and S.H. Feinstein "Speaker Sex Identification Utilizing a Constant Laryngeal Source." *Folia Phoniatrica*, 29 (1977), 240-248.

Six males and six females recorded a sentence using a closed glottis and an electronic artificial larynx (fundamental frequency of 120 hertz). The recordings were played to 30 listeners who were to identify the speaker's sex. Males whose speech spectra shifted toward lower frequencies were identified correctly more than chance, as were females whose spectra shifted toward higher frequencies. The results were seen as confirming the hypothesis that supraglottal vocal tract characteristics (vocal tract size and shape) play a major role in sex identification of speaker and not just fundamental frequency.

1226. Coleman, Ralph O. "Male and Female Voice Quality and Its Relationship to Vowel Formant Frequencies." *Journal of Speech and Hearing Research*, 14 (1971), 565-577.

In order to ascertain if it would be possible to distinguish male and female voices when fundamental frequency variations between them were eliminated, ten male and ten female adults recorded a passage while they articulated a tone produced by a single-frequency electrolarynx. Fifteen university students correctly identified the sex of the speaker 88% of the time. Formant frequencies for two vowels, /i/ and /u/, produced in isolation by the 20 speakers, were obtained by spectrographic analysis, and their averages were closely associated with the degree of "maleness" or "femaleness" in the voices recorded. A distinct cue to speaker sex, therefore, may be in the individual vocal tract resonances, a cue relied on when the sex variations in laryngical fundamentals are absent.

1227. Dale, Philip S. "Hesitations in Maternal Speech." *Language and Speech*, 17 (1974), 174-181.

Six mothers, each with one child between 2 and 3-1/2 and another between 5 and 8, were recorded in their normal interactions with the children, and their sentences analyzed for various hesitations. Results indicated a shift in hesitation to sentence boundaries for younger children, but no consistent pattern of hesitations at phrase boundaries within sentences for the older children.

1228. Edelsky, Carole. "Question Intonation and Sex Roles." *Language in Society,* 8 (1979), 15-32.

   Edelsky investigated into R. Lakoff's contention (item 858) that women use rising intonation for responses to questions for which only they have the answers. Using the responses of 154 male and 165 female adults entering a student union building on a college campus, she found no sex differences by intonation pattern except that more women used rise-fall-rise pattern with the female investigator. When 9 male and 21 female college juniors rated matched-guise "interviews" of male or female using various intonations, sex differences were found. The falling contour was rated more stereotypically masculine on a semantic differential scale, the simple rise more stereotypically feminine. Female voices, regardless of intonation pattern, were judged less confident, competent, dominant, objective, and more influenceable. A speaker, whether male or female, who used straight rise intonation was rated more stereotypically feminine.

* Ekman, Paul, Wallace V. Friesen, and Klaus R. Scherer. "Body Movement and Voice Pitch in Deceptive Interaction." *Semiotica,* 16, No. 1 (1976), 23-27. See item 1031.

1229. Geiselman, Ralph E., and Francis S. Bellezza. "Incidental Retention of Speaker's Voice." *Memory and Cognition,* 5 (1977), 658-665.

   A series of four experiments was devised to test whether memory retention of sex of speaker of verbal material, previously found to be automatic, is a function of voice-connotation or of dual-hemisphere parallel processing. Number of subjects, always equally divided by sex, ranged from 24 to 128. Two experiments supported the voice-connotation hypothesis, a third replicated that support, and the fourth found that sentences spoken by males were rated more "potent" than the same sentences spoken by females, also supporting the connotation hypothesis.

1230. Geiselman, Ralph E., and Janet Glenny. "Effects of Imagining Speakers' Voices on the Retention of Words Presented Visually." *Memory and Cognition,* 5 (1977), 499-504.

   Fifteen female and fifteen male college students listened to a tape recording of a male or female voice,

then used either one of those voices or their own to
repeat eighteen word pairs presented to them. In a
subsequent word recognition test, words were more likely to be recognized if they were spoken in the same
voice as in the repetition task. In a second experiment, thirty subjects repeated the procedure, this time
with different male or female voices available for the
repetition part of the experiment. Though scores were
generally lower, again there was a significant interaction between sex of voice at encoding and at test.
Conclusion was that a speaker's voice forms part of the
verbal memory code.

1231. Gilbert, Harvey R., and Gary G. Weismer. "The Effects
of Smoking on the Speaking Fundamental Frequency of
Adult Women." *Journal of Psycholinguistic Research,* 3
(1974), 225-231.

Fifteen nonsmoking and fifteen smoking (pack a day for
fifteen years) women ranging in age from 30 to 54 recorded a set passage and had a laryngeal examination.
Analysis of the recordings revealed the smoking group
had a lower fundamental frequency value than the norm
for adult females, perhaps explained by the pathological condition found in 87% of the smokers (versus 7% of
the nonsmokers), whose fundamental frequency value was
also lower than the norm. Since post-menopausal women
were part of the sample studied, authors suggest the
lower fundamental frequencies may, in part, be attributed to menopause.

1232. Hart, Roland J., and Bruce L. Brown. "Interpersonal
Information Conveyed by the Content and Vocal Aspects
of Speech." *Speech Monographs,* 41 (1974), 371-380.

In a replication of an earlier experiment with male
subjects, three speech samples were created for twelve
female speakers, a "vocal" one in which vocal characteristics varied while content was held constant; a "content" one, in which content varied and vocal characteristics were removed; and the third that included both
vocal and content messages. A total of 84 female undergraduates rated the speakers via an adjectives pairs
list. Factor analysis revealed that most of the information for the "benevolence" attribute was conveyed by
content, while information for "social attractiveness"
was conveyed by vocal characteristics.

1233. Horowitz, Leonard M., David Weckler, Amanda Saxon, Julie D. Livaudais, and Lana I. Boutacoff. "Discomforting Talk and Speech Disruptions." *Journal of Consulting and Clinical Psychology,* 45 (1977), 1036-42.

An analysis of latency, duration, and disruptions in tales reflecting four levels of sensitivity told in dyads by 31 male and 31 female undergraduates revealed that the more sensitive the tale, the longer latency and duration and the more numerous disruptions. Females had fewer disruptions than males.

1234. Johnson, Lawrence. "Voiced *t* in Post-Voiceless Contexts." *Lingua,* 44 (1978), 379-387.

Both wide and narrow band spectograms of the speech of 25 female and 25 male native (or nearly so) West Los Angeles inhabitants representing three age groups and three social classes were made. In addition, ten black informants from South Central Los Angeles were recorded. Analysis revealed that /t/ is not invariably voiced intervocalically, and phonetic constraints were found more significant than social constraints on /t/ voicing in postvoiceless consonant environments. Males showed more /t/ voicing than females in intervocalic contexts among the white subjects.

1235. Lalljee, Mansur, and Mark Cook. "Uncertainty in First Encounters." *Journal of Personality and Social Psychology,* 26 (1973), 137-141.

The filled-pause rate and speech rate of five male and five female undergraduates at their first interview with an experimenter revealed that males had a higher filled pause ratio, but there were no sex differences in non-*ah* speech disturbances or in speech rate.

1236. Lass, Norman J., Karen R. Hughes, Melanie D. Bowyer, Lucille T. Waters, and Victoria T. Bourne. "Speaker Sex Identification from Voiced, Whispered and Filtered Isolated Vowels." *Journal of the Acoustical Society of America,* 59 (1976), 675-678.

Ten male and ten female speakers recorded six vowels in normal and whispered voices. These tapes plus a filtered tape made from the voiced one (passed through a 225-H_2 low-pass filter) were played to 15 listeners who were asked to identify the sex and their confidence in their identification. Results of the judgments were 96% correct from the voiced tape, 91% from the filtered tape, and 75% from the whispered tape, with confidence ratings following the same pattern. Findings indicated that the fundamental frequency of the larynx is a more important cue in speaker sex identification than the resonance characteristics of the speaker.

1237. Lass, Norman J., Pamela J. Mertz, and Karen L. Kimmel. "The Effect of Temporal Speech Alterations on Speaker Race and Sex Identifications." *Language and Speech*, 21 (1978), 279-290.

Ten black males and females and ten white males and females recorded four sentences, which were placed on master tapes either in forward-play, backward-play, or time-compressed conditions. Thirty white female undergraduates judged sex and race of speakers under all conditions. Temporal alterations affected race identification but not sex identifications, sex judgments were more accurate than race judgments under all three conditions, and accuracy for both sex and race under all three conditions was better than that expected by chance.

1238. McConnell-Ginet, Sally. "Intonation in a Man's World." *Signs: Journal of Women in Culture and Society*, 3 (1978), 541-559.

McConnell-Ginet outlines a preliminary theoretical perspective on sex differences in intonation based on speech melodies as the primary cues of the speaker's sex. Some intonational patterns are explicitly associated with the speech of women. In addition to the overt stereotypes, our culture predisposes us to believe that learned behavior is androgynous and that actual sex differences in behavior must be due to biological rather than to social and cultural factors. The feminine habit of keeping pitch and changing loudness may serve to attract and hold listener's attention. Because the primary linguistic function of intonation is to indicate how an utterance fits in a discourse, women and men will typically use different patterns for equivalent situations because they have different strategies for speech action.

1239. Markel, Norman N., Layne D. Prebor, and John F. Brandt. "Biosocial Factors in Dyadic Communication: Sex and Speaking Intensity." *Journal of Personality and Social Psychology*, 23 (1972), 11-13.

Measuring the intensity of voice of 36 male and 36 female undergraduates speaking to a male or female investigator at near or far distances, the authors found all subjects used greater intensity at far distance, with males using more. Both males and females showed decreased intensity with same-sex investigator.

1240. Page, Richard A., and Joseph L. Balloun. "The Effect of Voice Volume on the Perception of Personality." *The Journal of Social Psychology,* 105 (1978), 65-72.

Twenty-seven male and 36 female undergraduates evaluated the personality of a female interviewer whose taped voice was manipulated for volume. The high-volume voice was judged most aggressive, the low-volume one most mature, sincere, and desirable to work with. Overall, males rated the interviewer higher on interestingness, attractiveness, sociability, and likeability than females did.

1241. Pearce, W. Barnett, and Forrest Conklin. "Nonverbal Vocalic Communication and Perceptions of a Speaker." *Speech Monographs,* 38 (1971), 235-236.

Two tapes of a speech, one delivered dynamically and the other in a conversational mode, were made for each of four topics and played to 160 undergraduates through a filter to remove verbal intelligibility. Results of their assessments for personality, demographic, and credibility characteristics included some sex differences. Male listeners rated the speaker wealthier in conversational style; females rated the speaker taller in conversational styles. All found the conversational delivery to be from an honest and person-oriented speaker and the dynamic delivery to be from someone toughminded, task-oriented, self-assured, and assertive.

1242. Ragsdale, J. Donald. "Relationships Between Hesitation Phenomena, Anxiety, and Self-Control in a Normal Communication Situation." *Language and Speech,* 19 (1976), 257-265.

Fifteen male and fifteen female undergraduates, in three groups of ten, discussed spontaneously a case problem, and a sample of each participant's talk was coded for three hesitations phenomena, *ah*, non-*ah*, and silent pauses. Correlations between these kinds of hesitations and measures of anxiety and self-control revealed a significant positive correlation between non-*ah* hesitations and anxiety, as predicted, and between non-*ah* hesitations and self-control, not predicted. Contrary to an earlier study with a clinical population, men as well as women showed the non-*ah*/anxiety correlation.

1243. Raffler-Engel, Walburga von, and Janis Buckner. "A Difference Beyond Inherent Pitch." In *The Sociology of the Languages of American Women* (item 1003), pp. 115-118.

Five female and five male undergraduates recorded the same passage under normal, white noise, and rock music conditions in this investigation of how noise affects the volume of speech by sex. Females increased their volume as noise increased and their pitch level as well. Males increased far less, and almost not at all from white to rock music. Peer groups of the same sex ratio perceived the female voices as less pleasant and overwhelmingly preferred the male voices in noise conditions.

1244. Reardon, Robert C. "Individual Differences and the Meanings of Vocal Emotional Expressions." *Journal of Communication,* 21 (March 1971), 72-82.

Ninety-six undergraduates of both sexes, divided into three groups by levels of self-concept scores, rated six audiotaped emotional expressions on a semantic differential. The sex of both the listener and the speaker interacted significantly with ratings of emotional expression, with female speakers rated more positively than male, and female listeners with high and low self-concepts rating speakers more positively than male listeners in those self-concept groups. Moreover, female listeners rated positive emotions (love, happiness) significantly more positive and negative ones (sadness, anger, fear) more negative than males.

1245. Reardon, Robert, and Ellen Amatea. "The Meaning of Vocal Emotional Expressions: Sex Differences for Listeners and Speakers." *International Journal of Social Psychiatry,* 19 (1973), 214-219.

In an investigation of the effect of sex on the connotative meaning of six vocal emotional expressions, 39 men and 39 women rated audiotaped emotional expressions recorded by six male and six female undergraduates. Significant differences for speaker sex and the speaker sex-emotion interaction occurred on all factors. Female listeners' ratings were significantly lower for all six emotions. Only one significant listener sex difference was revealed, on social control. Females viewed emotional speech as socially appropriate, but were repulsed by the expression of anger. Across all emotions, male speakers' emotional expressions were viewed as more socially controlled and less active.

1246. Sachs, Jacqueline. "Cues to the Identification of Sex in Children's Speech." In *Language and Sex: Difference and Dominance* (item 1326), pp. 152-169.

In two experiments, the sex of 18 boys and girls matched for size ranging in age from five to twelve was judged by university students. Correct judgments based on three isolated vowels were significantly better than chance, but not as great as for whole sentences. Correct judgments based on backwards sentences were not significantly better than chance. A third experiment used a semantic differential to find characteristics of the children's voices, then presented those characteristics to another group to judge voices unlabeled as to sex. Overwhelmingly, the "appropriate" characteristic was assigned to the right sex voice. Boys' voices were judged "rough, unsure, masculine, and high"; the girls' voices as "feminine, meek, delicate, high, and smooth."

1247. Schwartz, Martin F. "Intensities of /s/ and /ʃ/ in Oral and Whispered Vowel Environments." *Speech Monographs*, 38 (1971), 146-147.

Using electronic means, Schwartz found that two voiceless sounds, /s/ and /ʃ/, were reduced in intensity when whispered, but that the relative intensity reduction between oral and whispered was greater for females than for males.

1248. Silverman, Ellen-Marie, and Catherine H. Zimmer. "The Fluency of Women's Speech." In *The Sociology of the Languages of American Women* (item 1003), pp. 131-136.

An analysis of the speech fluency of ten female and ten male university students matched for age and socioeconomic level (parents' occupations) was conducted. Three-minute tape-recorded responses for a request to describe a memorable life experience revealed no significant difference by sex in fluency, in vocabulary, or in readiness of speech. These findings do not support the behaviors O. Jespersen hypothesized in *Language: Its Nature, Development, and Origin* (1922).

1249. Silverman, Ellen-Marie, and Catherine H. Zimmer. "Speech Fluency Fluctuations During the Menstrual Cycle." *Journal of Speech and Hearing Research,* 18 (1975), 202-206.

   Twelve university women between 17 and 22 years gave four three-minute speeches, one at ovulation and one at premenstruation for two consecutive months. Significantly more speech disfluencies were produced at premenstruation than at ovulation (generally the period of highest self-esteem and self-confidence). The most frequently produced disfluencies were interjection and revision-incomplete phrase, the latter being produced significantly more often at premenstruation.

1250. Steer, Angela B. "Sex Differences, Extraversion and Neuroticism in Relation to Speech Rate during the Expression of Emotion." *Language and Speech,* 17 (1974), 80-86.

   Twenty-four females and 24 males recorded a counting task in neutral, angry, and pleased conditions and completed the Eysenck Personality Inventory and a personal questionnaire. Extraversion and neuroticism did not significantly affect speech rate, and males had a significantly lower rate of change in expressing anger than females did.

* Zuckerman, Miron, Marsha S. Lipets, Judith H. Koivumaki, and Robert Rosenthal. "Encoding and Decoding Nonverbal Cues of Emotion." *Journal of Personality and Social Psychology,* 32 (1975), 1068-76. See item 1091.

GENERAL REFERENCES

1251. Andersen, Peter A., John P. Garrison, and Janis F. Andersen. "Implications of a Neurophysiological Approach for the Study of a Nonverbal Communication." *Human Communication Research,* 6 (1979), 74-89.

   This review of the neurological research on nonverbal communication includes material on the differences in hemisphere functions for males and females, among many other topics, and a 122-item bibliography.

1252. Archer, Dave, and Robin M. Akert. "Words and Everything Else: Verbal and Nonverbal Cues in Social Interpretation." *Journal of Personality and Social Psychology*, 35 (1977), 443-449.

For twenty brief videotapes of spontaneous social interaction, 76 male and female undergraduates received a verbal transcript only and 370 received a full-channel videotape; all were to interpret specific and verifiable information about the stimuli. Those with verbal transcripts only did worse than chance; those with full-channel did significantly better. No sex differences were reported.

1253. Argyle, Michael, Florisse Alkema, and Robin Gilmour. "The Communication of Friendly and Hostile Attitudes by Verbal and Nonverbal Signals." *European Journal of Social Psychology*, 1 (1971), 385-402.

In two experiments, 30 female and 30 male undergraduates rated videotapes of a female performer reading friendly, neutral, or hostile messages in a friendly, hostile, or neutral nonverbal style. Both experiments revealed that nonverbal cues had a greater effect on ratings than verbal cues. When verbal and nonverbal signals were inconsistent, the performance was rated as insincere, unstable, and confusing. In one experiment, females attributed a lesser degree of "liking me" to the performer than males did and found the neutral nonverbal condition less friendly than males did. In the other experiment, females did not find the performer as confusing as males did, and, in the nonverbal hostile conditions, found the female performer more sincere and thought she liked them more than males did.

1254. Argyle, Michael, Veronica Salter, Hilary Nicholson, Marylin Williams, and Philip Burgess. "The Communication of Inferior and Superior Attitudes by Verbal and Nonverbal Signals." *British Journal of Social and Clinical Psychology*, 9 (1970), 222-231.

The hypotheses that nonverbal cues would have a greater effect than equal verbal cues in communicating interpersonal attitudes and that conflicting verbal and nonverbal cues would create double-bind effects and be experienced as unpleasant and insincere were investigated. The first experiment was carried out twice with 40 male and 40 female undergraduates who rated via semantic differential two videotaped female performers communicating messages verbally and nonverbally, with three levels of cues for both the verbal and nonverbal channels. Nonverbal cues proved more effective than verbal cues in communicating interpersonal attitudes. Little evidence of a double-bind effect was detected. Females were relatively more responsive to nonverbal compared to verbal dues; the more neurotic subjects found the combination of superior nonverbal cues with inferior verbal cues unpleasant and responded more to the verbal cues.

1255. Ayres, Joe. "Observers' Judgments of Audience Members' Attitudes." *Western Speech,* 39 (1975), 40-50.

To assess the ability to judge an audience's attitudes, 31 male and 31 female undergraduates evaluated via a semantic differential the attitudes and ego involvement of members of an audience who were themselves watching a videotape of someone giving a speech. By comparing the observers' judgments with audience members' statements, a measure of accuracy was obtained. Observers assessed females' attitudes more accurately than males' attitudes. High ego-involved audience members' attitudes were more accurately assessed than low ego-involved members' attitudes.

1256. Balswick, Jack, and Christine P. Avertt. "Difference in Expressiveness: Gender, Interpersonal Orientation, and Perceived Parental Expressiveness as Contributing Factors." *Journal of Marriage and the Family,* 39 (1977), 121-127.

Two hundred and sixty-three male and 260 female undergraduates were used to test the hypothesis that greater female expressiveness could be explained by interpersonal orientation and by perceived parental expressiveness. Questionnaire results indicated greater female expressiveness of love, happiness, and sadness (but no difference in expressiveness of anger), but the relationship with interpersonal orientation and perceived parental expressiveness was spurious.

1257. Beier, Ernst G., et al. "Marital Communication." *Journal of Communication,* 27 (Summer, 1977), 92-103. Special section of this issue on communication within the marriage. See items 375, 383, and 1258.

1258. Beier, Ernst G., and Daniel Sternberg. "Subtle Cues Between Newlyweds." *Journal of Communication,* 27 (Summer, 1977), 92-97.

Fifty-one couples married from three to six months were videotaped as they conversed on a topic and then made up a story relating to three Thematic Appercetion Test cards. Their nonverbal behavior was analyzed and correlated, and all subjects completed a marital disagreement measure. Eye contact was correlated with open posture of arms, with other-touching, with talking time, and with laughing. Husbands sat in open position longer and talked longer, wives laughed more, and each had about the same amount of touching. Couples reporting least discord in the family displayed more eye contact, other touching, and open arm- and leg-position and had the least smiling. For a follow-up study, see item 375.

1259. Benjamin, Gail R., and Chet A. Creider. "Social Distinctions in Non-Verbal Behavior." *Semiotica*, 14, No. 1 (1975), 52-60.

Two men and two women, each about 25, and two boys and two girls, each nine years old, were videotaped as they conversed in all possible pairings. A test tape of 30-second vignettes of speaker only, with no audio, was shown to 20 adults, aged 18-30, and 40 boys, aged 8 or 9, who were asked to identify the person being talked to by sex, age, and degree of familiarity. All viewers were able to identify better than chance the sex and acquaintance level, and the older ones also identified the age better than by chance. In analyzing the tape for interpretable behavior that could have led to such results, it was found that adults behaved differently with children (less facial muscle tonus, for example), and that stereotypical "flirting" behavior, whether by male or female, occurred with others besides the same age partners.

1260. Benoist, Irving R., and James N. Butcher. "Nonverbal Cues to Sex-Role Attitudes." *Journal of Research in Personality*, 11 (1977), 431-442.

From a pool of 192 college undergraduates taking the Minnesota Attitude Survey, 15 high-feminine females, 15 low-feminine females, 16 low-feminine males, and 16 high-feminine males were interviewed and videotaped while performing standard tasks. One hundred eighty-seven undergraduates (sex not specified) viewed the tapes without sound and rated the taped performers on 170 adjectives. Although many adjectives distinguished the groups, in general women were seen as warm, affable, over-socialized, emotional, and unstable; men as forceful, dominant, and detached. High feminine women were seen as submissive, low-feminine ones as dominant. High feminine men were seen as impulsive, dominant, and socially uneasy, while low-feminine men were seen as oversocialized and conventional.

* Bloom, Larry J., Richard G. Weigel, and Gregory M. Trautt. "'Therapeugenic' Factors in Psychotherapy: Effects of Office Decor and Subject-Therapist Sex Pairing on the Perception of Credibility." *Journal of Consulting and Clinical Psychology*, 45 (1977), 867-873. See item 530.

1261. Borden, Richard J., and Gorden M. Homleid. "Handedness and Lateral Positioning in Heterosexual Couples: Are Men Still Strong-Arming Women?" *Sex Roles*, 4 (1978), 67-73.

    The way in which 199 male-female couples arranged themselves while walking together was examined. In same-handed couples, significantly more females were on the males' preferred (dominant) side, especially when the partners were touching. In opposite-handed couples, males and females put their dominant sides together, especially when touching. The conclusion was that handedness and lateral positioning were usually combined to reflect male dominance.

* Brooks, Douglas M., and Barry J. Wilson. "Teacher Verbal and Nonverbal Behavior Expression Toward Selected Pupils." *Journal of Educational Psychology*, 70 (1978), 147-153. See item 501.

1262. Bugental, Daphne, Jaques W. Kaswan, and Leonore R. Love. "Perception of Contradictory Meanings Conveyed by Verbal and Nonverbal Channels." *Journal of Personality and Social Psychology*, 16 (1970), 647-655.

    Ratings of videotaped messages systematically varied by conflicting tone (friendly or unfriendly) in verbal, vocal, and visual channels were made by 80 children (Boy and Girl Scouts) and their parents. Joking messages were judged more negatively by children than by adults, especially if speaker were female. Female speakers generally were rated more negatively than male, even when message was positive, and strongly so if messages in channels conflicted. The visual channel was found dominant in interpreting conflicting messages.

* Bugental, Daphne E., Leonore R. Love, Jaques W. Kaswan, and Carol April. "Verbal-Nonverbal Conflict in Parental Messages for Normal and Disturbed Children." *Journal of Abnormal Psychology,* 77 (1971), 6-10. See item 322.

1263. Campbell, Anne, and J. Philippe Rushton. "Bodily Communication and Personality." *The British Journal of Social and Clinical Psychology,* 17 (1978), 31-36.

    Fifteen measures of nonverbal communication were coded from videotaped social interactions between a female confederate and 46 female undergraduates who had previously completed measures of personality, including extroversion and neuroticism measures and intelligence tests. Extroversion was strongly associated with speaking more. Instructors' ratings of neuroticism were associated with touching the self, pausing during conversations, and limited expressive gestures, while self-report neuroticism was associated with gaze aversion. Lower intelligence was associate with smiling while listening.

1264. Carr, Suzanne J., and James M. Dabbs, Jr. "The Effects of Lighting, Distance and Intimacy of Topic on Verbal and Visual Behavior." *Sociometry,* 37 (1974), 592-600.

    Forty female undergraduates were intervewed with a female experimenter about intimate and non-intimate topics under two conditions of lighting and two of distance. Subjects reduced verbal production (longer pauses, fewer words) and eye contact during intimate interview, especially under dim light conditions. Distance had no significant effect on either verbal or visual behavior.

1265. Cary Mark S., and David Rudick-Davis. "Judging the Sex of an Unseen Person from Nonverbal Cues." *Sex Roles,* 5 (1979), 355-361.

    In this two-part study, videotapes of eight male and eight female undergraduate actors interacting in dyads were played to 40 male and female undergraduates in such a manner as to exclude one member of the dyad; subjects were asked to determine the sex of the unseen partner. The first study revealed that observers could judge the sex of the unseen member by watching the male's but not the female's nonverbal behaviors in the situation where the actors had been requested to produce sex-stereotyped behavior. Under these conditions, females were better judges of the sex of the unseen person than males. In the second study, where the actors were not asked to produce stereotyped behaviors, raters were less able to judge the sex of the unseen person and females were not better judges than males.

1266. Chaikin, Alan L., Edward Sigler, and Valerian J. Derlega. "Nonverbal Mediators of Teacher Expectancy Effects." *Journal of Personality and Social Psychology*, 30 (1974), 144-149.

In a study using 42 undergraduates (half female) videotaped while tutoring a 12-year old boy presented to them as bright, dull, or with no information, subjects in the interaction with the "bright" boy smiled more, had more direct eye gaze, leaned forward more, and nodded more than subjects with the "dull" or no-information boy.

1267. Clore, Gerald L., Nancy H. Wiggins, and Stuart Itkin. "Gain and Loss in Attraction: Attributions from Nonverbal Behavior." *Journal of Personality and Social Psychology*, 31 (1975), 706-712.

Over 300 male and female undergraduates rated the attraction of a mixed-sex dyad for each other and their own attraction to the female in the dyad, whose nonverbal behavior was manipulated to show various levels of warmth. Significant gain/loss effects were found only in ratings of the male's attraction to the female, not in the subjects' attraction nor in the female's attraction to the male.

1268. Darden, Ellington. "Masculinity-Femininity Body Rankings by Males and Females." *Journal of Psychology*, 80 (1972), 205-212.

One hundred and one male and 133 female college students ranked twelve whole-body outlines on most masculine to least masculine or most feminine to least feminine scales. Sex differences in evaluating femininity emerged, but for males the masculinity evaluation reversed the femininity one and for females it did not. Darden speculates that "cultural lag" plays a role in retention of the rural society notion of masculinity and that females are better able than males to adjust to the changing roles.

1269. Deaux, Kay. "Honking at the Intersection: A Replication and Extension." *Journal of Social Psychology*, 84 (1971), 159-160.

In this replication of an earlier study in which a car obstructed traffic, Deaux added the sex and status of the car driver as variables. She found that a significantly greater percentage of the 90 male and 33 female car drivers honked at a female driver than at a male driver.

1270. DePaulo, Bella M., Robert Rosenthal, Russell A. Eisenstat, Peter L. Rogers, and Susan Finkelstein. "Decoding Discrepant Nonverbal Cues." *Journal of Personality and Social Psychology*, 36 (1978), 313-323.

In a first study, a videotaped test of decoding accuracy was given to 18 male and 24 female undergraduates, some getting audio only, some video only, and some both, of tapes in which the video and the audio emotional messages were discrepant. Subjects were more influenced by video than by audio cues. In a second study, males and females from junior high (73), high school (150), and college (95) received the audiovisual tape. All those groups showed video primacy. Sex differences found were that high school females showed more video primacy than high school males, and that females showed more facial primacy than males. In judging highly discrepant messages, the subjects attended more to audio than to video cues.

1271. Duckworth, Douglas H. "Personality, Emotional State, and Perception of Nonverbal Communication." *Perceptual and Motor Skills*, 40 (1975), 325-326.

Thirty-six married couples participated in a study which hypothesized a change in the perceptual ability of one partner in identifying the other's feeling from tone of voice following emotionally provoking disagreements. In the experimental group, the partners made joint decisions on the emotion, arranged in such a manner that the partners would disagree. The hypothesis was not supported. Only the males experienced annoyance. Further analysis by scores on the Eyseneck Personality Inventory showed a change in perceptual ability of males only.

* Eakins, Barbara W., and R. Gene Eakins. *Sex Differences in Human Communication*. Boston: Houghton Mifflin Co., 1978. See item 1318.

* Feldman, Robert S., and Lawrence F. Donohoe. "Nonverbal Communication of Affect in Interracial Dyads." *Journal of Educational Psychology,* 70 (1978), 979-987. See item 508.

1272. Frances, Susan J. "Sex Differences in Nonverbal Behavior." *Sex Roles,* 5 (1979), 519-535.

    This study involving 88 professional school students investigated, via videotaped dyadic same-sex and cross-sex conversations, the effects of sex on the use of a number of nonverbal variables, including speaking turns, response behaviors, filled pauses, laughing and smiling behaviors, gazing behaviors, postural shifts, hand movement, and foot movement. The subjects' scores on the behavioral measures were correlated with their scores on several personality measures and on pre- and post-conversation questionnaires. The sex of the subject but not the sex of the partner had a significant effect on many of the nonverbal behaviors. Females smiled more, laughed more, and paid more visual attention to their partners than males did. Males tended to talk longer and use more filled pauses.

* Fretz, Bruce R., Roger Corn, Janet M. Tuemmler, and William Bellet. "Counselor Nonverbal Behaviors and Client Evaluations." *Journal of Counseling Psychology,* 26 (1979), 304-311. See item 534.

1273. Frieze, Irene H., and Shelia J. Ramsey. "Nonverbal Maintenance of Traditional Sex Roles." *Journal of Social Issues,* 32, No. 3 (1976), 133-141.

    A review of nonverbal communication literature on dominance and high status and warmth and expressiveness was used to support the thesis that sex differences in nonverbal communication perpetuate sex-role stereotypes, are resistant to change, and serve to maintain traditional sex roles.

* Gitter, A. George, Harvey Black, and John Walkley. "Nonverbal Communication and the Judgment of Leadership." *Psychological Reports,* 39 (1976), 1117-18. See item 605.

* Givens, David B. "Contrasting Nonverbal Styles in Mother-Child Interaction: Examples from a Study of Child Abuse." *Semiotica,* 24, No. 1/2 (1978), 33-47. See item 338.

1274. Hall, Judith A. "Gender Effects in Decoding Nonverbal Cues." *Psychological Bulletin,* 85 (1978), 845-857.

   This review of 75 studies on decoding nonverbal cues reveals that more studies found a female advantage in decoding nonverbal communication than would occur by chance, especially in visual-plus-auditory studies as opposed to one-channel-only ones. The size of the sex difference did not vary reliably with sample size, sex of stimulus person, or age of either stimulus person or judges.

* Harris, Mary B., and Hortensia Baudin. "The Language of Altruism: The Effects of Language, Dress, and Ethnic Group." *The Journal of Social Psychology,* 91 (1973), 37-41. See item 677.

1275. Harris, Mary B., and Gail Bays. "Altruism and Sex Roles." *Psychological Reports,* 32 (1973), 1002.

   In this brief report of a study of the effects of sex-role stereotyping on altruism, two women dressed in either masculine style (shirt, jeans, straight hair) or feminine style (ruffled blouse, high heels, curly hair) requested help from 80 male and 80 female shoppers in a large store. The feminine style dressers were helped significantly more, and the dress-style effect on males was greater than it was on females. Helping was not significantly related to the specific woman seeking help, to the type of request, or to the sex of the helper.

1276. Haviland, Jeannette M. "Sex-Related Pragmatics in Infants' Nonverbal Communication." *Journal of Communication,* 27 (Spring 1977), 80-84.

   Sixty undergraduates rated the emotion expressed in ten-second videotapes of a male or female infant, either with sex specified or not. Those infants either specified as a girl or guessed to be a girl were found more often to express "joy" and "interest," whereas those specified or guessed as boy were found more often to express "fear," "anger," and "distress." Sex labeling appears, therefore, to influence adults' interpretations of infants' nonverbal communication.

1277. Henley, Nancy M. *Body Politics: Power, Sex, and Nonverbal Communication*. Englewood Cliffs, N.J.: Prentice Hall, 1977.

Henley analyzes how females and males differ in their use of space, time, environment, language, demeanor, touch, body movement, eye contact, and facial expression. She concludes that these means of communicating reveal the relative powerlessness of women. Many citations are included, but there is no bibliography.

1278. Henley, Nancy M. "Power, Sex, and Nonverbal Communication." *Berkeley Journal of Sociology*, 18 (1973-74), 1-26. Rpt. in *Language and Sex: Difference and Dominance* (item 1326), pp. 184-203, and in *Doing unto Others: Joining, Molding, Conforming, Helping, Loving*. Ed. Zick Rubin. Englewood Cliffs, N.J.: Prentice-Hall, 1974, pp. 48-60.

  A review of research in nonverbal and some verbal behavior leads Henley to conclude that both types of behavior maintain the social structure and the power dominance over women. Women's verbal disadvantages can be found in areas such as grammar, vocabulary, vocal quality, and intonation patterns. Women's inferior position in society is maintained by terms of address, conversational patterns, self-disclosure, and nonverbally in the use of touch, demeanor, space, and eye contact. The accessibility of information about women is used to subordinate and subdue them. Manipulating these status cues will not change the fundamental power relationships in society, but knowledge of them will raise consciousness and enable people to detect the subtle ways in which women are inhibited, coerced, and controlled. Fifty-six references are given.

1279. Henley, Nancy, and Jo Freeman. "The Sexual Politics of Interpersonal Behavior." In *Women: A Feminist Perspective*. Ed. Jo Freeman. Palo Alto, Cal.: Mayfield, 1975, pp. 391-401.

  This discussion of evidences of power in interpersonal behavior includes material on such nonverbal indicators as demeanor, clothing, posture, use of space, touch, gaze, and gestures.

  * Heppner, Paul, and Steve Pew. "Effects of Diplomas, Awards, and Counselor Sex on Perceived Expertness." *Journal of Counseling Psychology*, 24 (1977), 147-149. See item 541.

1280. Holman, Rebecca H. "A Transcription and Analysis System for the Study of Women's Clothing Behavior." *Semiotics*, 32 (1980), 11-34.

The rationale and the development of a system to transcribe women's clothing basically on form (not color, texture, pattern) are preseted.

1281. Holstein, Carolyn M., Joel W. Goldstein, and Daryl J. Bem. "The Importance of Expressive Behavior, Involvement, Sex, and Need Approval in Induced Liking." *Journal of Experimental Social Psychology,* 7 (1971), 534-544.

Using 142 male and female undergraduates interviewing with and then evaluating a male interviewer, who either used expressive nonverbal behavior or not, the authors found subjects liked better those interviewers who used expressive nonverbal behavior. Males high in need for approval expressed more liking than males low in need, while females high in need for approval expressed less liking than females low in need.

* Ickes, William, Brian Schermer, and Jeff Steeno. "Sex and Sex-Role Influences in Same-Sex Dyads." *Social Psychology Quarterly,* 42 (1979), 373-385. See item 122.

1282. Isenhart, Myra W. "An Investigation of the Relationship of Sex and Sex Role to the Ability to Decode Nonverbal Cues." *Human Communication Research,* 6 (1980), 309-318.

To investigate the relationship of sex, sex role, and nonverbal sensitivity, the Bem Sex-Role Inventory and the PONS test of nonverbal decoding ability were administered to 51 female and 55 male undergraduates. As had been found before, females were better decoders than males, but female sex role and the ability to decode nonverbal cues were not related.

1283. Jorgenson, Dale O. "Nonverbal Assessment of Attitudinal Affect with the Smile-Return Technique." *The Journal of Social Psychology,* 106 (1978), 173-179.

In two studies Jorgenson noted the number of smile-returns of male and female undergraduates when the initiator gave evidence of a similar attitude through wearing a Ford or Carter campaign button or a woman-power T-shirt. Significantly more smile returns were made for the Ford button than for the **Carter button**, reflecting campus voter preference (N = 200), and, for the T-shirt, from the 25 women leaving classrooms where women's studies were held than from the 20 women leaving home economics classrooms.

* Jourard, Sidney, and Robert Friedman. "Experimenter-Subject 'Distance' and Self-Disclosure." *Journal of Personality and Social Psychology,* 15 (1970), 278-282. See item 742.

1284. Jurich, Anthony P., and Julie A. Jurich. "Correlations Among Nonverbal Expressions of Anxiety." *Psychological Reports,* 34 (1974), 199-204.

    Of the twelve nonverbal ratings of anxiety, a finger sweat index, and a subjective evaluation of anxiety made by each of the 40 undergraduate and graduate females being interviewed on increasingly intimate questions, there were high correlations among finger sweat index, independent rater's global rating, immediacy, tone, postural relaxation, speech errors, filled pauses, editorial errors, and eye contact. Subjects' subjective rating, self head touching, and articulation errors yielded low correlations.

1285. Kelser, George J., and Irwin Altman. "Relationship of Nonverbal Behavior to the Social Penetration Process." *Human Communication Research,* 2 (1976), 147-167.

    Two college student actresses, interacting in 12 dyads, were videotaped playing good friends or casual acquaintances and disclosing intimate or nonintimate topics. An analysis of their nonverbal behavior revealed patterns that could be predicted, namely that the good-friend, nonintimate condition had relaxed nonverbal behaviors and the casual acquaintance, intimate condition had tense behaviors.

1286. Key, Mary R. *Paralanguage and Kinesics (Nonverbal Communication).* Metuchen, N.J.: The Scarecrow Press, 1975.

    This account of vocal, kinetic, and sensory communication includes chapters on silence, context, and the dialects of nonverbal behaviors, the last of which includes a section on sex differences. A 59-page bibliography is included.

1287. Kleinke, Chris L. "Effects of Dress on Compliance to Requests in a Field Setting." *The Journal of Social Psychology,* 101 (1977), 223-224.

    When either neatly or sloppily dressed females approached 62 males and 62 females at an airport and asked for a dime, the neatly dressed received significantly more dimes. Significantly more males than females gave them dimes.

1288. Kleinke, Chris L. *First Impressions: The Psychology of Encountering Others*. Englewood Cliffs, N.J.: Prentice-Hall, 1975.

   The influence of attractiveness, gaze, distance, body language, facial expression, and voice on interpersonal communication is examined, with many references to sex differences and a specific section on differences in gaze behavior. References at ends of chapters, but no bibliography.

* Kramer, Cheris, Barrie Thorne, and Nancy Henley. "Perspectives on Language and Communication." *Signs: Journal of Women in Culture and Society*, 3 (1978), 638-651. See item 1010.

* LaCrosse, Michael B. "Nonverbal Behavior and Perceived Counselor Attractiveness and Persuasiveness." *Journal of Counseling Psychology*, 22 (1975), 563-566. See item 547.

1289. LaFrance, Marianne, and Clara Mayo. *Moving Bodies: Nonverbal Communication in Social Relationships*. Monterey, Cal.: Brooks/Cole Publishing Co., 1978.

   One chapter in this book synthesizes research on differences in male and female nonverbal communication, specifically facial expression, vocal expression, nonverbal decoding abilities, smiling, personal space, touch, and talk. The authors conclude that a woman's face reflects not only her own inner state but that of those with whom she communicates and that women are reactive and responsive, especially with men. Women vary their nonverbal behavior to complement what is needed by others by being good listeners, by giving way to others, and by being available when others want to get close to them or touch them.

1290. LaFrance, Marianne, and Clara Mayo. "A Review of Nonverbal Behaviors of Women and Men." *Western Journal of Speech Communication*, 43 (1979), 96-107.

   This review of gender differences in nonverbal communication (over 50 references) reveals that differences reflect societal expectations that men be proactive and women reactive. Women demonstrate their reactivity by being more sensitive to others' expressivity and more nonverbally variable in order to complement their partner's behavior. Men demonstrate their proactivity by talking more, interrupting more, and in general being nonverbally dominant, particularly with women.

* Lerner, Richard M., and Barbara E. Brackney. "The Importance of Inner and Outer Body Parts Attitudes in the Self-Concept of Late Adolescents." *Sex Roles,* 4 (1978), 225-238. See item 35.

1291. Lewis, Benjamin F. "Group Silences." *Small Group Behavior,* 8 (1977), 109-120.

 This article enumerated a number of types of silence, each a discrete and significant communication related to the state of group development, the state of interpersonal relations, and the dynamics of leadership. Attention is also called to the life-space of a silence and its implications for purposeful intervention in small group situations. Many excerpts from case studies are about females.

* McClintock, Charles C., and Raymond G. Hunt. "Nonverbal Indicators of Affect and Deception in an Interview Setting." *Journal of Applied Social Psychology,* 5 (1975), 54-67. See item 132.

* Maslach, Christina. "Social and Personal Bases of Individuation." *Journal of Personality and Social Psychology,* 29 (1974), 411-425. See item 269.

1292. Mathes, Eugene W., and Sherry B. Kempher. "Clothing as a Nonverbal Communicator of Sexual Attitudes and Behavior." *Perceptual and Motor Skills,* 43 (1976), 495-498.

 In this study to determine if clothing is a valid clue to sexual attitudes and behaviors or if clothing is just believed to be such an indicator, 82 male and 177 female undergraduates from two universities responded to questionnaires about the frequency of wearing various types of clothing, their sexual attitudes, the frequency of sexual relations, etc., and their beliefs about the relationship between clothing and sex attitudes. Correlation analysis revealed that males did not perceive clothing as a valid cue to sexual attitudes and/or reported behavior. For females, clothing and styles (cut-offs, tops exposing midriff, work shirts, and going braless) indicated liberal attitudes and/or reported behavior.

1293. Mehrabian, Albert. *Nonverbal Communication.* Chicago: Aldine-Atherton, 1972.

   Over thirty references to sex differences in nonverbal communication are reported in this general survey of the field. Bibliography is included.

* Mehrabian, Albert. "Verbal and Nonverbal Interaction of Strangers in a Waiting Situation." *Journal of Experimental Research in Personality,* 5 (1971), 127-138. See item 142.

1294. Miller, Franklin G., and Kathleen L. Rowold. "Attire, Sex-Roles, and Responses to Requests for Directions." *Psychological Reports,* 47 (1980), 661-662.

   A female experimenter attired braless in tube top (perceived as sensuous), braless in tailored blouse (perceived as feminist), or in feminine blouse with bra asked 90 middle-aged men for directions. A significant difference by attire revealed that 70% of the men gave detailed directions to the experimenter in the tube-top attire, 50% to the one in the tailored blouse, and 40% to the one in the feminine blouse attire.

* Noller, Patricia. "Misunderstandings in Marital Communication: A Study of Couples' Nonverbal Communication." *Journal of Personality and Social Psychology,* 39 (1980), 1135-48. See item 360.

1295. Putnam, Linda L., and Linda McCallister. "Situational Effects of Task and Gender on Nonverbal Display." In *Communication Yearbook 4.* Ed. Dan Nimmo. New Brunswick, N.J.: Transaction Books, 1980, pp. 679-697.

   From a pool of 423 undergraduates who completed the Bem Sex-Role Inventory, 12 androgynous males and females and 12 sex-typed males and females were assigned to same-sex or mixed-sex dyads to solve a masculine task (rescue mission for a military brigade) and a feminine one (emotionally charged, moralistic situation). Analysis of interruptions, back channels, turn time, postural shifts, body orientation, gesticulations, head nods, smiling, laughing, and eye gaze indicated that androgynous males were more nonverbally adaptive to the task (dominant in masculine, warm/expressive in feminine). Androgynous females used consistent frequency of nonverbal behavior, but were selective in the behavior used (less smiling and laughing, more head nods and longer gaze, especially in the feminine task). Sex-typed subjects generally displayed more sex-typed nonverbal behavior.

1296. Renne, Karen S., and Paul C. Allen. "Gender and the Ritual of the Door." *Sex Roles*, 2 (1976), 167-174.

Analysis of 396 observations of opening a door for another revealed that tradition still is observed; men were twice as likely as women to hold a door open for a stranger, and both men and women were more likely to ignore a man. Women were four times as likely as men to have the door held open for them; six times if their attire was "feminine." If their arms were full carrying books or papers, men and women were twice as likely to have the door held for them, provided, however, that the potential holder was of the opposite sex.

1297. Robert, M. Evans, Paul D. Cherulnik, et al. "Sex Composition and Intimacy in Dyads: A Field Study." *Journal of Social Psychology*, 110 (1980), 139-140.

Fifty female, 51 male, and 50 female-male dyads on park benches or tables in a cafeteria-style restaurant were observed for distance, gaze, and body orientation. Male dyads sat farther apart on benches than female or mixed-sex dyads. In all three dyad types at the restaurant, partners sat opposite each other. Females and mixed-sex dyads had more body orientation toward each other, and male dyads tended to be less intimate in distance and orientation.

1298. Rosenfeld, Lawrence B., and Timothy G. Plax. "Clothing as Communication." *Journal of Communication*, 27 (Spring 1977), 24-31.

Seven personality measures and a clothing questionnaire were completed by 240 male and female undergraduates in a study of the relationship between dress and personality. In general, personalities of both sexes were similar if they scored either high or low on clothing consiousness, with high scorers compliant and anxious and low scorers independent and aggressive. Differences by sex were found on the dimension of exhibitionism, designer, and practicality, though males who scored high and females who scored low on this last dimension had similar personalities.

1299. Rosenthal, Robert, and Bella M. DePaulo. "Expectancies, Discrepancies, and Courtesies in Nonverbal Communication." *Western Journal of Speech Communication*, 43 (1979), 76-95.

This review of nonverbal behavior research of the past decade (45 footnotes) gives special attention to sex differences in encoding and decoding nonverbal cues.

1300. Rosenthal, Robert, and Bella M. DePaulo. "Sex Differences in Eavesdropping on Nonverbal Cues." *Journal of Personality and Social Psychology*, 37 (1979), 273-285.

This series of studies investigated the hypothesis that, nonverbally, females are more interpersonally accommodating than men. The first series showed that women of three different age groups lost much of their decoding advantage over men in high-speed (250 msec.) display conditions. The second series showed a decreasing advantage in decoding nonverbal cues the less intended (leakier) they became, with a tendency for females to use visual cues rather than voice tone cues. A trend was noticed for women with skill at decoding nonverbal cues under these conditions to have less successful interpersonal relationships. The third series showed women more "polite" in ascribing characteristics to others, i.e., more accurate in decoding deceptive behavior but more likely to interpret it as the deceiver wanted it to be interpreted. The politeness result was interpreted as traditional sex-role behavior.

1301. Rosenthal, Robert, Judith A. Hall, M. Robin DiMatteo, Peter L. Rogers, and Dane Archer. *Sensitivity to Nonverbal Communication: The PONS Test*. Baltimore: The Johns Hopkins University Press, 1979.

This report of the design and development of the PONS Test (Profile of Nonverbal Sensitivity) and of the research conducted with it contains a chapter on sex differences in decoding skills. Various research shows that overall females excel over males, but with variations depending on which and how many channels are used. Women decode negative emotions better than positive. Various statistical analyses failed to support strongly the hypothesis that female superiority in decoding nonverbal signals decreases with age.

1302. Ross, Michael, Bruce Layton, Bonnie Erickson, and John Schopler. "Affect, Facial Regard, and Reactions to

Crowding." *Journal of Personality and Social Psychology*, 28 (1973), 69-76.

Twelve males and 12 females discussed problems in groups of eight in either crowded or uncrowded conditions for either five or 20 minutes. Males rated themselves and others more positively in the uncrowded condition, females in the crowded condition. Males had more gaze in the uncrowded condition, females in the crowded.

1303. Saine, Thomas J., Madlyn A. Levine, and Gaylynn E. McHose. "Assessing the Structure of Nonverbal Interaction." *Southern Speech Communication Journal,* 40 (1975), 275-287.

Forty-two undergraduates, pretested for speech anxiety, were videotaped in dyads in a waiting room prior to their supposed delivery of a speech. Analysis of their nonverbal behavior revealed that speech anxiety affected the structure of nonverbal communication. As speech anxiety increased, nonverbal behavior became more random. Speech-anxious subjects, as opposed to exhibitionists or reticents, were relatively immobile. Sex of the members of the dyad had no effect on the findings.

1304. Schiavo, R. Steven, Barbara Sherlock, and Gail Wicklund. "Effect of Attire on Obtaining Directions." *Psychological Reports,* 34 (1974), 245-246.

Two college females, one dressed "hippie" fashion and the other conventionally, requested directions from 120 women in a shopping district. The conventionally dressed confederate received more responses and more detailed responses than the "hippie."

1305. Shuter, Robert. "A Field Study of Nonverbal Communication in Germany, Italy, and the United States." *Communication Monographs,* 44 (1977), 298-305.

In this field study, such a wide range of behaviors relating to distance, axis of body, and tactile responses in male-male, male-female, and female-female dyads was found that no gender-free cultural conclusions were possible. In general, in Germany and America, male-male pairs were less tactile and stood further apart than male-female pairs, which were less tactile and further apart than female-female pairs. The reverse was found in Italy, where the greatest contact was between male-male pairs, less between male-female pairs, and least between female-female pairs.

1306. Siegman, Aron W., and Stanley Feldstein, eds. *Nonverbal Behavior and Communication.* New York: John Wiley & Sons, 1978.

   In this comprehensive survey of theory and research on nonverbal behavior are a few references to sex differences, including in use of space, in pitch and vocal anatomy, and in extralinguistic behavior. Each chapter has a list of references.

1307. Slane, Steve, and Gary Leak. "Effects of Self-Perceived Nonverbal Immediacy Behaviors on Interpersonal Attraction." *Journal of Psychology,* 98 (1978), 241-248.

   Using 40 male and 40 female undergraduates induced to behave nonverbally either in a liking or a disliking manner toward a male or a female confederate, researchers found that subjects in the "liking" condition reported greater attraction to the confederate than subjects in the "disliking" condition. No sex of confederate differences were found; female subjects generally liked the confederate more.

   * Slevin, Kathleen F., and Jack Balswick. "Children's Perceptions of Parental Expressiveness." *Sex Roles,* 6 (1980), 293-299. See item 374.

   * Sterling, F.E. "Net Positive Social Approaches of Young Psychiatric Inpatients as Influenced by Nurses' Attire." *Journal of Consulting and Clinical Psychology,* 48 (1980), 58-62. See item 578.

1308. Sterrett, John H. "The Job Interview: Body Language and Perceptions of Potential Effectiveness." *Journal of Applied Psychology,* 63 (1978), 388-390.

   This study used 160 midlevel male and female managers responding to a videotape of a male applicant using various intensities of body language (hand gestures, eye contact length, level of dress, and length of pauses before responding). Analysis of variance revealed no significant differences by intensity of body language and judgments of applicant traits. Female managers, however, rated high-intensity body language applicants low on ambition; males rated them high.

1309. Stillman, JeriJayne W., and Wayne E. Hensley. "She Wore a Flower in Her Hair: The Effect of Ornamentation on Nonverbal Communication." *Journal of Applied Communications Research,* 8 (1980), 30-37.

This study tested the hypothesis that diners will leave a larger tip for a waitress who wears a flower in her hair than for the same waitress without a flower. Six waitresses who alternately wore or did not wear a flower in their hair collected data on responses of patrons for four nights. All waitresses received larger tips on the nights that they wore flowers.

1310. Trenholm, Sarah, and William R. Todd de Mancillas. "Student Perceptions of Sexism." *The Quarterly Journal of Speech*, 64 (1978), 267-283.

Sixty-three female and 26 male undergraduates described personal incidents of sexism (both sexes), supplied words and nonverbal descriptions of sexual behavior, and identified sexist behavior in media. A content analysis of each of the categories and a percentage by sex of number of responses to each factor revealed that women were not more sensitive to sexism than men, as had been hypothesized; however, both sexes gave more examples of sexism directed toward women than toward men. Moreover, the type of sexism differed by sex; women were viewed as sexual objects and men as inflexible in their sex roles.

* Tulkin, Steven R., and Jerome Kagan. "Mother-Child Interaction in the First Year of Life." *Child Development*, 43 (1972), 31-41. See item 378.

1311. Weitz, Shirley, ed. *Nonverbal Communication: Readings with Commentary*. New York: Oxford University Press, 1979.

This collection of 26 research articles on nonverbal behavior focuses on facial expression and visual interaction, body movement and gesture, paralanguage, proximity, and multichannel communication. Many references to female nonverbal characteristics are included. References are given at the end of each chapter.

1312. Weitz, Shirley. "Sex Differences in Nonverbal Communication." *Sex Roles*, 2 (1976), 175-184.

To determine the relationship between sex-role attitudes, affiliation, dominance, and nonverbal communication styles, 24 male and 24 female undergraduates in same- and opposite-sex dyads were videotaped as they discussed an issue. These tapes were rated for warmth and dominance, sex role, attitude, and affiliation.

Women elicited more warmth and men more anxiety from their partners. Nonverbal behaviors of women in opposite-sex interactions were significantly related to the male partner's scores of dominance and affiliation, suggesting a possible monitoring mechanism through which women adjust their nonverbal communications to fit the personality of the male in the interaction. Liberalism in sex-role attitudes was found to correlate with nonverbal warmth in men. The nonverbal presentations of men and women in the microprocesses of dyadic interaction were found to relate significantly to the macrostructure of societal sex roles.

1313. Wellens, A. Rodney, and Martin V. Faletti. "Interrelationships of Six Measures of Interpersonal Attraction." *Psychological Reports,* 42 (1978), 1022.

The verbal and nonverbal behavior of 36 males and 36 females in mixed-sex dyads were recorded and assessed, and a liking-for-other-questionnaire administered. Males who talked more to their partners tended to smile more and to sit closer. Females' behavior was the same except for sitting closer; they tended to sit first and chose the end of the couch, allowing the male to establish the distance between. Self-report measures of liking and physical attractiveness showed little relationship to the behavioral measures, though they were positively correlated.

* Whalen, Ardyce C. "The Presentation of Image in Ella T. Grasso's Campaign." *The Central States Speech Journal,* 27 (1976), 207-211. See item 498.

* Wolosin, Robert J. "Cognitive Similarity and Group Laughter." *Journal of Personality and Social Psychology,* 32 (1975), 503-509. See item 314.

1314. Woods, Donald J., and James Brooks. "Nonverbal Affective Selfdisclosure: Effects on Observers' Judgments." *The Journal of Social Psychology,* 105 (1978), 155-156.

A written description of a coed, manipulated for two levels of reasons for being upset, two levels of nonverbal behavior, and two levels of verbal selfdisclosure, was evaluated by 64 coeds. Nonverbal disclosure was significantly associated with higher ratings for emotionality, instability, and need for psychological help. A significant interaction between ratings of verbal and nonverbal disclosure and the same three characteristics also occurred.

* Woolfolk, Robert L., and Anita E. Woolfolk. "Effects of Teacher Verbal and Nonverbal Behaviors on Student Perceptions and Attitudes." *American Educational Research Journal,* 11 (1974), 297-303. See item 526.

PART FOUR
COMPREHENSIVE REFERENCES

COMPREHENSIVE REFERENCES

1315. Bernard, Jessie. *The Sex Game: Communication Between the Sexes*. New York: Atheneum, 1972. (Orig. pub. 1968 by Prentice Hall)

    In Chapter 6, "Talk, Conversation, Listening, Silence," Bernard notes that "to converse" originally meant to have sexual rather than social intercourse. She analyzes communication between men and women particularly as it relates to their sexuality, whether biological, social, or cultural in origin. The range of topics covered is extensive: communication between the sexes at home, at work, at play and in social life; conversation; barriers to communication; miscommunication and noncommunication; signs and silence as communication; deception; and listening. Notes are included along with a brief bibliography.

1316. Crane, Loren D., Richard J. Dieker, and Charles T. Brown. "The Physiological Response to the Communication Modes: Reading, Listening, Writing, Speaking, and Evaluating." *Journal of Communication*, 20 (Sept. 1970), 231-240.

    No significant differences between 30 male and female college students were found on their emotional arousal (measured by Galvanic Skin Response) to the four communication modes; all showed increasing order of arousal from reading to listening to writing to speaking to evaluating. Significant differences by individual words and heart rate occurred, however, with males responding more to the name of their major, their university, *death*, and *success*, and females responding more to their first name, *evil*, and *pain*.

1317. Deaux, Kay. *The Behavior of Women and Men*. Monterey, Cal.: Brooks/Cole Co., 1976.

    In this wide-ranging book, Deaux reviews material on stereotyping in personality and in performance, on self-evaluation and achievement, on aggression, on strategies used in interaction, and on behavior in groups. Chapter

6, "Communication Styles," is a review of research, mostly from the 1960s and early 1970s, on time in talking and conversation topic, on sending and interpreting nonverbal signals, on touch, and on personal space. There is no bibliography, but each chapter has extensive footnotes.

1318. Eakins, Barbara W., and R. Gene Eakins. *Sex Differences in Human Communication*. Boston: Houghton Mifflin Co., 1978.

This comprehensive textbook on sex differences in communication contains chapters on causes of differences, power, communication between the sexes, vocal differences, sexism in language, and nonverbal communication. No bibliography is included, but each chapter has between 39 and 84 references to both popular and scholarly sources.

1319. Frieze, Irene H., Jacquelynne E. Parsons, Paula B. Johnson, Diane N. Ruble, and Gail L. Zellman. *Women and Sex Roles: A Social Psychological Perspective*. New York: W.W. Norton and Co., 1978.

Chapter 15, "Women and Interpersonal Power," discusses power as an aspect of interaction in a social relationship. The difference in the types and uses of power by males and females is discussed, and the authors conclude that women's lack of power is tied to their lack of status. Chapter 15, "Being Feminine or Masculine--Nonverbally," focuses on nonverbal messages that communicate dominance or status (masculine) and those communicating warmth and expressiveness (feminine). Dominance and high status are seen in males' use of space, body posture, physical size, and "verbal" space (talk dominated by men). Low status and non-dominance are seen in females' eye contact, smiling, and greater encoding and decoding abilities. Included is a 42-page bibliography.

1320. Henley, Nancy, and Barrie Thorne. "Sex Differences in Language, Speech, and Nonverbal Communication: An Annotated Bibliography." In *Language and Sex: Difference and Dominance* (item 1326).

1321. Henley, Nancy, and Barrie Thorne. *She Said/He Said: An Annotated Bibliography of Sex Differences in Language, Speech, and Nonverbal Communication*. Pittsburgh, Penn.: KNOW, Inc., 1975. Rpt. from *Language and Sex: Difference and Dominance* (item 1326).

This fourth version of the bibliography contains 147 fully annotated items some of which date from the beginning of the century. It includes sex differences in vocabulary and syntax, phonology, conversation patterns, dialects and varieties, multi-lingual situations, language acquisition, verbal ability, and nonverbal aspects of communication.

1322. Maccoby, Eleanor E., and Carol N. Jacklin. *The Psychology of Sex Differences*. Stanford, California: Stanford Univ. Press, 1974.

   This massive examination of studies is divided into sections on intellect and achievement, social behavior, and the origins of sex differences. Individual chapters review material on self-concept (Chapter 4); power, including aggression and dominance (Chapter 7); and verbal abilities (Chapter 3). A 232-page annotated bibliography is included.

1323. Sherman, Julia A., and Florence L. Denmark, eds. *The Psychology of Women: Future Directions in Research*. New York: Psychological Dimensions, 1978.

   This nineteen-chapter book includes sections on female development, attitudes toward women, achievement and status, and power. Each chapter has a list of references. It is printed entirely without generic masculine pronouns, substituting *tey*, *ter*, *tem*.

1324. Shimanoff, Susan B. "Sex as a Variable in Communication Research, 1970-76: An Annotated Bibliography." *Bulletin: Women's Studies in Communication*, 1, No. 1 (1977), 8-20.

1325. Spradley, James P., and Brenda Mann. *The Cocktail Waitress: Woman's Work in a Man's World*. New York: John Wiley & Sons, 1975.

   This ethnographic examination of the world of the American cocktail bar, based on first-hand observations at a college bar, is designed to investigate the culture through the eyes of the cocktail waitresses. It includes chapters on the joking relationship between waitress and customer, on territory, and on communication ("How to Ask for a Drink"). It also includes a list of references.

1326. Thorne, Barrie, and Nancy Henley, eds. *Language and Sex: Difference and Dominance*. Rowley, Mass.: Newbury House Publishers, Inc., 1975.

This collection of twelve papers, seven published for the first time, covers topics from sexist dictionaries to interruptions in communication. Also included is the authors' selective but extensively annotated bibliography, *Sex Differences in Language, Speech, and Nonverbal Communication: An Annotated Bibliography,* pp. 204-305. See items 104, 184, 854, 902, 905, 936, 954, 998, 1021, 1224, 1246, and 1278.

1327. Walum, Laurel R. *The Dynamics of Sex and Gender: A Sociological Perspective*. Chicago: Rank McNally College Publishing Co., 1977.

Two of the thirteen chapters of this book are particularly relevant. In "Language: The Inescapable Barrier" (Chapter 2), Walum succinctly reviews research on sexist language, on use of space, on demeanor, on socialization through etiquette, and on features of speech, including sex differences in vocabulary, intonation, grammar, and sentence structures. In "The Question of Power" (Chapter 12), she reviews the lack of power for women in business, government, mass media, academia, and politics, and the emphasis on achieving power through social movements and coalitions. References, but not a bibliography, are included.

SUBJECT INDEX

References below are to numbered items, not to pages. For larger subject units, see the Table of Contents.

achievement motivation 5, 66, 69, 278
address forms 853
adult-child communication 170, 185, 321, 322, 327, 330, 335, 336, 338, 339, 341, 343, 347, 349, 351, 352, 354, 356, 362, 363, 364, 372, 373, 374, 377, 378, 379, 380, 381, 839, 845, 882, 933, 1227, 1259
aggression 11, 18, 82, 98, 116, 131, 151, 383, 430, 457, 638, 777, 908, 1032, 1155, 1240
American Indian women 419, 843
anxiety 12, 176, 193, 214, 295, 313, 630, 685, 738, 739, 1135, 1141, 1179, 1242, 1284, 1312
  speech 148, 391, 392, 393, 394, 398, 399, 404, 405, 406, 411, 412, 415, 416, 527, 735, 787, 789, 1303
apprehension of communication See anxiety, speech
articulation 852, 854, 860, 1234, 1247, 1284
assertiveness 9, 17, 38, 48, 64, 70, 82, 84, 183, 193, 241, 245, 256, 299, 308, 312, 328, 393, 448, 499, 557, 579, 632, 635, 644, 769, 782, 785, 842, 875, 911, 1108, 1200
Atkinson, Ti-Grace 475
attraction and liking 32, 83, 90, 92, 93, 94, 97, 102, 106, 107, 108, 117, 119, 120, 161, 162, 167,
173, 175, 181, 196, 208, 238, 247, 256, 298, 420, 547, 550, 600, 646, 658, 671, 675, 705, 712, 715, 723, 724, 727, 731, 733, 739, 741, 745, 755, 764, 773, 774, 781, 787, 791, 820, 1036, 1042, 1054, 1060, 1062, 1068, 1112, 1114, 1120, 1128, 1134, 1145, 1158, 1165, 1168, 1193, 1215, 1240, 1253, 1267, 1281, 1307, 1313
authoritarianism 453
authoritativeness 701, 702
bibliography See also review of literature
  gaze 1040
  language of women 1019, 1020
  masculinity/femininity 60
  nonverbal communication 1293, 1326
  psychology of sex differences 1382
  sex differences, language 850, 1320, 1321, 1326
  sex, variable in research 1324
  sex roles in task groups 270
  women in politics 491
black families 355
black women 6, 23, 65, 161, 261, 280, 335, 344, 355, 414, 435, 508, 514, 529, 535, 602, 614, 638, 815, 825, 837, 876, 877, 891, 1034, 1037, 1080, 1082, 1083, 1085, 1137, 1139, 1144, 1163, 1174, 1187, 1199, 1213, 1237

469

brain (hemispheric dominance) 804, 833, 869, 1002, 1205, 1251
brainstorming 207
Bright Eyes 419
Brown, Hallie Q. 414
Bryant, Anita 397
bust size 1112, 1132
  clothing 578, 928, 931, 1190, 1287, 1292, 1294, 1298, 1304
coalitions (small group) 217, 260, 263, 285, 303,
cohesiveness 178, 187, 202, 219, 220, 227, 248, 268, 334, 741, 744
competence 81, 83, 88, 93, 94, 162, 166, 174, 204, 208, 242, 420, 457, 541, 583, 660, 889
compliance See also conformity 140, 681, 689, 922, 1157, 1287,
conflict 43, 74, 97, 100, 113, 125, 178, 205, 319, 344, 345, 370, 371, 375, 448, 593, 796
conformity See also compliance 197, 228, 667, 668, 670, 673, 680, 690, 698, 699, 703, 1093
consciousness raising 30, 192, 195, 222, 226, 229, 231, 241
consensus 334
conservatism 28
conversation 96, 105, 106, 112, 114, 133, 136, 149, 155, 184, 225, 291, 311, 341, 633, 709, 776, 812, 813, 816, 821, 862, 875, 895, 908, 911, 935, 1046, 1064, 1177, 1242, 1252, 1259, 1272, 1278, 1312, 1315, 1321
cooperation 258, 259, 267, 305

coping 21, 67, 74, 323, 344, 718
counselor sex, effect on self disclosure 736
credibility 404, 405, 415, 530, 655, 660, 803, 809, 820, 1130, 1221
deceit/lying 649, 775 1031, 1081, 1300, 1315
decision making 118, 163, 194, 211, 222, 243, 255, 265, 273, 309, 329, 348, 382, 435, 436, 437, 583, 635
defensiveness 317
deviance 208, 273, 304, 313, 327, 349, 700
Devlin, Bernadette 486
dialect 819, 837, 873, 1321
Diller, Phyllis 863
discrimination 242
dominance 95, 136, 149, 151, 158, 163, 184, 189, 208, 223, 236, 254, 265, 316, 324, 325, 348, 353, 359, 361, 368, 520, 591, 602, 620, 707, 821, 844, 1020, 1122, 1217, 1261, 1273, 1290, 1312, 1322
domineeringness 325, 359, 368
double bind 1254
Duniway, Abigail S. 472
Elizabeth I, Queen of England 396, 402
embarrassment 3, 1052
empathy 150, 531, 546, 552, 784
Equal Rights Amendment 464, 466, 478, 652, 779
expletives 797, 831, 840, 841, 879, 898, 930
facework 3
fear of success 278, 559
femininity 1, 21, 42, 61, 63, 71, 83, 162, 226, 440, 457, 697, 708, 711, 786, 819, 1268

feminism 82, 87, 192, 229, 390, 422, 460, 461, 463, 469, 471, 488, 652, 1001, 1110
feminists 18, 33, 85, 86, 250, 348, 884, 1095, 1104, 1109, 1186, 1196, 1294
field dependence, independence 900, 1033, 1156
Field, Totie 863
fluency 907, 1084, 1248, 1249, 1264, 1284
frequencies, formant 1226, 1231, 1236
Friedan, Betty 469
German women 26
gestures 1031, 1033, 1122, 1263, 1289
Goldwater, Mrs. Barry 484
gossip 846, 908, 951
Grasso, Ella 498
Griffiths, Martha W. 473
groups
  sensitivity See sensitivity groups
  social 188, 189, 195, 196, 204, 214, 219, 237, 247, 249, 261, 281, 291, 294, 304, 311, 439
  task 186, 187, 190, 194, 197, 198, 200, 201, 203, 206, 208, 209, 210, 213, 215, 216, 217, 222, 223, 227, 228, 230, 232, 239, 244, 246, 251, 252, 253, 254, 255, 258, 259, 260, 262, 265, 268, 270, 272, 273, 275, 276, 277, 278, 282, 283, 284, 285, 287, 288, 289, 293, 296, 303, 305, 306, 307, 309, 310, 622, 1103
hesitation 835, 881, 1227, 1242
humor 42, 49, 98, 261, 269, 503, 504, 631, 844, 852, 863, 871, 908, 1006, 1026, 1028, 1132, 1262, 1325

Humphrey, Mrs. Hubert 484
image 479, 482, 483, 498, 931
influenceability See conformity and persuasion
instructional programs 38, 59, 193, 308, 331, 340, 425, 433, 458, 466, 469, 499, 500, 515, 519, 566, 641, 848, 901, 909, 1015
interruptions 82, 128, 130, 147, 148, 149, 158, 184, 311, 316, 341, 379, 382, 506, 821, 867, 911, 1290, 1295
interview 124, 126, 132, 137, 138, 139, 147, 151, 154, 162, 175, 176, 181, 540, 706, 716, 719, 740, 904, 1029, 1031, 1033, 1038, 1042, 1062, 1065, 1069, 1084, 1122, 1149, 1157, 1187, 1195, 1223, 1235, 1264, 1281, 1284,
  job 31, 153, 154, 453, 1099, 1102, 1308
  performance review 565
intonations 1224, 1228, 1238
Japanese-American women 645
Johnson, Mrs. Lyndon 484
Jordan, Barbara 487, 489, 490, 495, 496
jury decisions 210, 273, 277, 287, 300, 561, 682, 820, 1013, 1103, 1125, 1126, 1155
lateralility See brain
laughter 314, 1272
locus of control 54, 246, 263, 275, 328, 609, 681, 695, 1123, 1152
lone woman See token
Mabley, Moms 863
masculinity 2, 13, 33, 55, 61, 63, 83, 85, 162, 413, 697, 754, 786

menstruation 1188, 1249
Mexican-American women See also Spanish-American women 882, 897, 1139
monologues 637, 900
Morgan, Elizabeth 417
Mott, Lucretia 469
networking 199, 231, 235, 246, 425, 491, 516, 581, 586, 771, 824
Nixon, Mrs. Richard 484
nonverbal communication
  decoding 869, 1076, 1078, 1090, 1091, 1253, 1270, 1274, 1276, 1282, 1292, 1300, 1301, 1316
  encoding 269, 868, 869, 1078, 1083, 1091, 1300
  judgments based on 1262, 1265, 1268, 1276
obscenity 872, 884, 939, 940, 1026
O'Hair, Madalyn 403
Pankhurst, Emmeline 481
pauses 902, 1235, 1263, 1264, 1272, 1284
perception 14, 20, 80, 88, 256, 548, 825, 868, 873, 1276, 1310
personality characteristics 1, 5, 8, 17, 18, 42, 46, 51, 52, 61, 73, 80, 84, 89, 243, 301, 358, 615, 693, 782, 819, 842, 1065, 1093, 1100, 1101, 1106, 1113, 1121, 1204, 1218, 1222, 1241, 1260, 1263, 1272, 1298
Phelps, Miss 385
phonation time 643
phonology 812, 834, 849, 856, 860
pitch 852, 1031, 1238, 1243, 1306
politeness 382, 779, 802, 806, 811, 814, 815, 831, 852, 903, 1044, 1296, 1300, 1301, 1327

power See also dominance 5, 38, 149, 164, 172, 240, 246, 274, 284, 324, 326, 337, 341, 342, 355, 369, 474, 497, 564, 594, 609, 612, 761, 794, 812, 820, 821, 857, 858, 864, 866, 911, 922, 923, 935, 992, 996, 1006 1011, 1020, 1056, 1150, 1203, 1208, 1209, 1210, 1217, 1277, 1278, 1279, 1318, 1319, 1322, 1323, 1327
problem solving See also groups, task 67, 99, 123, 134, 141, 158, 160, 161, 166, 174, 186, 200, 206, 209, 233, 275, 309, 376, 435, 588, 601, 604, 867, 1295
profanity 261, 803, 809, 830, 832, 841, 852
qualifiers 799, 811, 835, 858, 860, 867, 875, 881, 902, 1012
questioning 96, 177, 325, 373, 377, 452, 501, 762, 779, 811, 839, 858, 867, 903
questions, tag 799, 811, 813, 817, 835, 858, 862, 866, 867, 875, 893
rate of speaking 701, 702, 789, 805, 852, 1222, 1250
research problems 670, 829, 831, 876, 1008, 1009, 1027
review of literature
  aggression 777
  anxiety 789
  assertiveness 785
  communication accuracy 838
  conformity 667
  decoding nonverbal communication 1274
  empathy 784
  family 327, 350, 367
  gaze 1040, 1053, 1056

Subject Index

generic noun and pronoun 989
leadership 485, 580, 595, 598, 613
listening (attention) 656
nonverbal communication 1251, 1278, 1286, 1290, 1300
persuasibility 694
persuasion 670
physical attractiveness 1092, 1097
political women 485
self confidence 34
self disclosure 722
sex differences: in achievement 34; in cognition 1005; in group communication 191; in language 1020; in leadership 580; in speech 831, 896
sex roles 7, 1319
sexist language 924
small group communication 250, 257, 266, 286
space 1144, 1153
speech anxiety 789
verbal and nonverbal communication 1278
vocal characteristics 1278
women in management 455
women in organizations 580
women's language 822
rhetorical analysis 390, 396, 397, 400, 402, 403, 408, 413, 417, 419, 459, 460, 461, 463, 464, 465, 466, 467, 468, 469, 470, 473, 476, 477, 478, 479, 481, 486, 489, 490, 492, 495, 496, 619
risk taking 197, 201, 215, 220, 251, 252, 253, 274, 275, 307
Rorschach test 536, 538, 542

Schlafly, Phyllis 478
self derogation 503, 583, 863, 1028
self esteem 10, 27, 40, 55, 58, 60, 61, 62, 63, 66, 68, 75, 634, 1322
self presentation 3, 290
self references 719, 740
sensitivity groups 279, 313
sex, requests for 133, 842
sex differences 896, 1316, 1318
achievement 34
aggression 638, 777
articulation 1234, 1247
adult-child communication 170, 185
assertiveness 9, 70, 299, 632, 644, 769, 785
attitude toward body 35
attraction and liking 39, 83, 90, 92, 93, 162, 256, 715, 724, 733, 739, 741, 745, 773, 774, 781, 791, 1042, 1054, 1068, 1112, 1120, 1128, 1134, 1145, 1158, 1165, 1193, 1281
authoritativeness 702
body movement 1030, 1086, 1122, 1261, 1279, 1286, 1297
brain 1251
clothing 1292, 1298
classroom communication 503, 524, 527
code switching 897
communication accuracy 838
comprehensibility 701
conflict 113, 125, 345, 369, 370, 371, 448, 593, 796
conformity 228, 667, 668, 673, 680, 1093
conversation 136, 155, 333, 776, 816
cooperation 143
coping 323

Subject Index

(sex differences, continued)
counseling 529, 543, 546, 547, 551
deceit 649, 775, 1301
dialect 819, 837, 873, 874, 905
dominance 95, 136, 143, 149, 151
dyads 99, 121, 129, 136, 137, 139, 142, 143, 177, 180, 760
empathy 784
emotion, expression of 48, 103, 374, 786, 1079, 1091, 1250, 1256, 1276
evaluation: ability/competence 81; audience attitudes 1255; body stereotyping 1268; credibility 1130; debate 401; emotions 1244, 1245; physical attractiveness 40, 432, 548, 1093, 1094, 1096, 1110, 1111, 1113, 1115, 1117, 1118, 1121, 1131; speaker 1262; speech course 44; speeches 386, 387, 388
eye contact/gaze 321, 1038, 1039, 1040, 1041, 1042, 1044, 1048, 1050, 1053, 1054, 1056, 1057, 1060, 1064, 1065, 1066, 1067, 1968, 1069, 1070, 1074, 1075, 1277, 1278, 1279, 1288, 1302
facial expression 103, 321, 1044, 1076, 1077, 1078, 1079, 1080, 1082, 1083, 1084, 1086, 1087, 1088, 1089, 1090, 1091, 1272, 1277
family communication 10, 318, 321, 322, 325, 332, 333, 341, 342, 345, 346, 348, 350, 351, 352, 353, 355, 356, 359, 360, 361, 362, 368, 374

humor 42, 49, 269, 503, 504, 631, 852, 863, 1026, 1028
ideal speaker 410
interruptions 82, 148, 149, 158, 184, 311, 341, 506, 867, 911, 1290
interviewing 137, 139, 151, 154, 176, 706, 716, 719, 740, 1038, 1069, 1122, 1187, 1195, 1235, 1281
intonations 1224, 1228, 1238
jury judgments 210, 277, 287, 300, 561, 682, 820, 1103, 1155
language See also speech and style of speaking 798, 801, 812, 819, 823, 824, 827, 829, 833, 834, 837, 849, 850, 851, 855, 856, 862, 865, 867, 873, 874, 875, 876, 880, 883, 887, 891, 894, 895, 896, 897, 899, 905, 922, 998, 1003, 1004, 1010, 1012, 1017, 1020, 1021, 1320, 1321, 1327
leadership 190, 236, 269, 272, 279, 294, 315, 424, 434, 450, 563, 580, 582, 588, 589, 590, 591, 592, 593, 595, 596, 600, 601, 603, 607, 609, 610, 615, 616, 621, 622, 623, 624, 644
linguistic skills 1005
listening and feedback 628, 629, 630, 631, 632, 634, 636, 639, 640, 641, 643, 648, 651, 653, 654, 656, 657, 1245
management: style 425, 426, 431, 434, 436, 440, 448, 450, 456, 582; evaluation 426, 428, 430, 431, 432, 442, 443, 445, 446, 447, 449, 450, 453, 582

Subject Index

networking 516, 586
nonverbal communication:
  encoding 269, 868, 869,
  1078, 1083, 1091, 1300;
  decoding 869, 1076,
  1078, 1090, 1091, 1253,
  1270, 1274, 1276, 1282,
  1292, 1300, 1301, 1316
pauses 902, 1235, 1272
personal adjustment 48
personality 8, 17, 18, 42,
  46, 51, 52, 61, 73, 80,
  89, 151, 243, 301, 615,
  693, 782, 819, 842, 1065,
  1093, 1100, 1101, 1106,
  1121, 1204, 1218, 1222,
  1260, 1263, 1272, 1298
persuasion and persuasibility 129, 174, 224, 547,
  610, 659, 660, 661, 662,
  664, 667, 668, 669, 670,
  673, 678, 679, 680, 681,
  682, 684, 687, 688, 689,
  690, 693, 694, 695, 697,
  698, 699, 700, 803
phonology 643, 834, 849,
  856
physical attractiveness
  40, 432, 548, 1093, 1094,
  1096, 1097, 1103, 1110,
  1111, 1113, 1115, 1117,
  1118, 1121, 1131, 1185
politeness 806, 831, 852
  903, 1296, 1300, 1301,
  1327
power 149, 164, 172, 240,
  246, 284, 324, 326, 337,
  341, 342, 355, 369, 474,
  497, 609, 820, 858, 864,
  866, 911, 922, 923, 935,
  992, 996, 1006, 1020,
  1150, 1203, 1208, 1209,
  1210, 1217, 1277, 1278,
  1279, 1318, 1319, 1322,
  1327
problem solving 99, 123,
  134, 141, 174, 186, 200,
  206, 209, 233, 275, 376,
  588

public speaking 29, 384,
  386, 387, 388, 393, 396,
  398, 399, 401, 404, 405,
  406, 407, 409, 410, 411,
  412, 415, 416, 639, 803,
  872, 1089
risk taking 197, 215, 252,
  274, 275, 307
Rorschach responses 536,
  538, 542, 870
self disclosure 110, 111,
  145, 533, 544, 545, 704,
  706, 707, 708, 709, 710,
  714, 715, 716, 717, 718,
  719, 720, 722, 725, 726,
  729, 733, 734, 735, 736,
  738, 740, 741, 742, 745,
  746, 747, 748, 750, 751,
  753, 754, 756, 757, 758,
  759, 761, 762, 763, 764,
  765, 767
silence 184, 509, 1020,
  1242, 1315
small group 141, 185, 186,
  188, 189, 190, 191, 197,
  200, 203, 204, 206, 207,
  208, 209, 210, 213, 214,
  215, 216, 218, 221, 224,
  227, 228, 230, 236, 237,
  238, 239, 240, 243, 244,
  246, 248, 249, 250, 255,
  256, 258, 259, 260, 261,
  265, 267, 268, 269, 271,
  272, 274, 275, 277, 278,
  279, 281, 282, 283, 284,
  285, 286, 287, 288, 289,
  292, 293, 299, 300, 301,
  303, 304, 305, 306, 307,
  310, 311, 314, 353, 439,
  506, 626, 680, 682, 700,
  741, 1113, 1138, 1146,
  1166
smiling 132, 269, 321, 999,
  1084, 1086, 1087, 1088,
  1089, 1258, 1272, 1313,
  1319
social skills 770

476 Subject Index

(sex differences, continued)
speech See also language
and style of speaking
189, 333, 339, 776, 800,
801, 803, 805, 806, 809,
812, 816, 821, 825, 831,
839, 840, 841, 842, 852,
853, 854, 861, 864, 872,
884, 886, 887, 893, 896,
898, 902, 903, 906, 911,
1003, 1004, 1008, 1010,
1017, 1020, 1026, 1320,
1321, 1327
space/distance 136, 237,
238, 268, 281, 763, 1038,
1133, 1135, 1138, 1139,
1140, 1141, 1142, 1143,
1144, 1145, 1146, 1148
1150, 1151, 1152, 1153,
1154, 1155, 1160, 1161,
1163, 1164, 1165, 1166,
1167, 1170, 1172, 1173,
1174, 1175, 1176, 1177,
1178, 1180, 1181, 1182,
1183, 1184, 1185, 1187,
1189, 1190, 1191, 1192,
1193, 1194, 1195, 1197,
1198, 1201, 1202, 1203,
1204, 1277, 1278, 1279,
1297, 1305
speaker ratings 1241
speech anxiety 399, 405,
411, 412, 416, 735
speech comprehension 398,
409
stereotyping 46, 80
style of speaking See also
speech 189, 269, 799,
800, 806, 811, 813, 816,
831, 834, 835, 836, 841,
850, 852, 858, 859, 860,
861, 866, 875, 881, 889,
893, 896, 902, 903, 907,
911, 922, 1011, 1016,
1020, 1021, 1023, 1169,
1170, 1321, 1327
telling stories 1233

time in talking 118, 136,
137, 158, 351, 506, 554,
704, 716, 776, 795, 902,
1272, 1290, 1317
topic of conversation 110,
145, 261, 332, 716, 734,
747, 751, 756, 829, 831
touch 58, 383, 1193, 1206,
1207, 1209, 1210, 1211,
1212, 1213, 1214, 1215,
1217, 1219, 1220, 1277,
1278, 1279, 1305
trust 101, 123, 328, 750,
1027
verbal abilities 1023,
1025, 1322
verbal vs. nonverbal decoding See also nonverbal
communication: decoding
1002, 1253, 1270
verbal vs. visual decoding
869
vocabulary: general 828,
831, 854, 855, 858, 860,
862, 883, 886, 894, 1278,
1321, 1327; maledicta 261,
803, 809, 832, 841, 852,
884, 1026
vocal characteristics 1091,
1222, 1224, 1225, 1226,
1228, 1229, 1233, 1234,
1235, 1236, 1237, 1238,
1239, 1240, 1243, 1244,
1245, 1246, 1247, 1250,
1278
sex identification
nonverbal cues 1259, 1265
vocal cues 1225, 1226,
1236, 1237
sex role orientation (masculine, feminine, androgynous)
6, 11, 13, 14, 16, 20, 24,
26, 45, 47, 48, 56, 60, 62,
77, 85, 87, 90, 92, 97, 120,
122, 180, 211, 223, 224,
241, 244, 254, 316, 456,
540, 579, 632, 660, 673,
688, 708, 711, 735, 754,

Subject Index

793, 855, 1128, 1260, 1282, 1295
sex role stereotyping 7, 11, 15, 19, 33, 43, 46, 50, 63, 66, 70, 77, 80, 84, 85, 86, 87, 92, 93, 94, 106, 110, 117, 120, 125, 134, 152, 162, 180, 181, 236, 246, 270, 283, 301, 302, 439, 443, 445, 446, 450, 451, 474, 480, 512, 513, 533, 539, 540, 549, 589, 594, 595, 606, 607, 611, 619, 637, 673, 689, 718, 762, 794, 817, 818, 823, 852, 854, 859, 862, 889, 893, 896, 922, 930, 934, 950, 959, 995, 997, 1025, 1097, 1099, 1117, 1120, 1127, 1128, 1228, 1265, 1273, 1275, 1301, 1312
sexism 49, 79, 242, 454, 482, 522, 1006, 1310
sexist language 823, 917, 919, 921, 924, 927, 928, 929, 932, 934, 935, 936, 939, 941, 944, 945, 947, 948, 949, 952, 953, 954, 955, 959, 962, 966, 982, 1010, 1012, 1020, 1318, 1327; guidelines to eliminate: 913, 914, 915, 916, 942, 943, 946, 956, 960, 964
shyness 1147
silence 147, 184, 314, 509, 789, 1020, 1223, 1242, 1286, 1291, 1315
small group communication *See* groups, sensitivity; groups, social; *and* groups, task
smiling 132, 269, 321, 631, 999, 1049, 1084, 1086, 1087, 1088, 1089, 1149, 1258, 1263, 1266, 1272, 1283, 1295, 1313, 1319
social skills 770

Spanish-surnamed women *See also* Mexican-American women 294, 677, 825, 834, 904
speaker ratings 1241
speaking vs. writing 1223
speech course, rating 44
speeches, comprehension of 398, 409
Stanton, Elizabeth C. 390, 462
status 141, 216, 232, 270, 276, 278, 302, 304, 506, 520, 540, 636, 646, 791, 830, 853, 864, 905, 1011, 1037, 1055, 1202, 1204, 1208, 1210, 1217, 1219, 1269, 1273, 1277, 1278, 1279, 1319, 1332
stereotyping *See* sex role stereotyping
storytelling 1233
Stowe, Harriet Beecher 421
stress 244, 323, 394
style of speaking 144, 189, 269, 332, 333, 345, 346, 793, 799, 800, 806, 811, 813, 820, 831, 834, 835, 836, 841, 850, 852, 858, 859, 860, 861, 866, 875, 881, 889, 893, 896, 900, 902, 903, 907, 911, 922, 1011, 1013, 1016, 1020, 1021, 1023, 1169, 1170, 1223, 1241, 1317, 1321, 1327
syntax *See also* questions, tag 800, 806, 812, 820, 822, 858, 862, 866, 867, 874, 876, 877, 878, 881, 893, 896, 900, 902, 903, 907, 1223
Taylor, Helen 494
teacher-parent communication 518
teacher-student communication 501, 502, 503, 505, 508, 510, 511, 513, 514, 517, 521, 524, 525, 526, 527, 1043, 1202, 1204, 1266

Thatcher, Margaret 483
Thomas, Helen 935
time in talking 118, 119,
  120, 124, 128, 136, 137,
  153, 158, 160, 176, 183
  218, 348, 351, 372, 506,
  554, 604, 704, 713, 716,
  776, 795, 854, 900, 902,
  903, 904, 1223, 1258,
  1272, 1290, 1313, 1317,
token woman *See also* deviance 313, 439, 584
Tomlin, Lily 863
topic of conversation 110,
  111, 124, 130, 132, 145,
  186, 189, 219, 226, 261,
  332, 333, 335, 704, 716,
  730, 734, 737, 744, 747,
  749, 751, 756, 763, 768,
  789, 816, 829, 831, 904,
  1084, 1264, 1284, 1285
trust 91, 101, 118, 123
  171, 328, 750, 1027
verbal ability 89, 1023,
  1025, 1322
verbal vs. nonverbal signals
  869, 999, 1002, 1252, 1253,
  1254, 1262, 1270
vocabulary *See also* expletives, obscenities, *and*
  profanity 822, 828, 834,
  854, 855, 858, 860, 862,
  883, 886, 894, 917, 1026,
  1278, 1321, 1327
vocal tone 1031, 1091, 1221,
  1262, 1278
volume 852, 1238, 1240,
  1243
warmth 7, 11, 507, 512, 551,
  875, 1033, 1114, 1204,
  1267, 1273, 1312
Wilson, Edith B. 493
Winnemucca, Sara 419
Women's movement *See* feminism
Wright, Frances 408